FIRSTHAND REPORT

The Story of the

FIRSTHAND REPORT

Eisenhower Administration

SHERMAN ADAMS

HARPER & BROTHERS, NEW YORK

For Rachel

I wish to acknowledge the help of Joe McCarthy in the editing of the final manuscript for publication.

S. A.

Contents

see the President?"—Invaluable Gabriel Hauge—Tom Stephens brightens his corner—"Is he wearing a brown suit?"
—"Can't a President pick his own cabinet?"—Patronage
problems: "I owe no one anything"—Stassen's hold-out
at Chicago—Homburgs versus tall silk hats

President's stag dinners—Eisenhower and Herbert Hoover—
Social life in the capital—The Soviet ambassador tries to
make friends with me—A Vermont joke comes in handy—
My favorite year with Eisenhower

Illustrations

The following, grouped as a separate section, will be found after page 300

FIRSTHAND REPORT

1 Eisenhower Takes Over

A few weeks after Dwight D. Eisenhower was elected President of the United States in 1952, he called me into his office at his headquarters in the Hotel Commodore in New York, where I was finishing up the last remaining odds and ends of the job I had held during the campaign as his personal aide and political chief of staff. He had just returned from a brief vacation at Augusta and a chilly meeting in the White House with President Truman, where the change-over in the administration had been discussed.

The last time I had seen Eisenhower, the day after Election Day, he talked with Herbert Brownell and me about the procedure of selecting his Cabinet and important agency heads, but he had said nothing to me then or previously during the campaign about what position in Washington he had in mind for me, if any. I never asked him for the slightest consideration, having made up my mind early in the game that if Eisenhower wanted me in his administration, he would tell me in his own good time. I could see that he was about to bring it up now.

"Well, I've been thinking about you," Eisenhower said to me. "I could visualize you as a member of the Cabinet, but I need somebody to be my assistant in running my office. I'd like you to continue on at my right hand, just as you've been in the campaign. You would be associated with me more closely than anybody else in the government."

Eisenhower paused and looked at me.

"I thought this might be something you would like to do, but you should have no hesitation in expressing your feelings about it," he added.

The first thing I felt was a great lift at being offered such an opportunity, and then an uneasy feeling that Eisenhower might expect me as his assistant to live in the White House as Harry Hopkins did during the Roosevelt administration. As much as I wanted to work closely with him, I could see the problems that would raise. When I asked about this, it was clear he had no such idea, for he said, "Have you ever seen the living quarters in the White House?"

I said I hadn't.

"There isn't enough room there for another family," he said.

I thanked him for wanting me on his staff and agreed to talk to my wife about it during the approaching Thanksgiving weekend, which we were planning to spend with our four children at our home in Lincoln, New Hampshire. I don't remember that I ever went through the formality of officially accepting Eisenhower's invitation to serve as The Assistant to the President. When I came back from New Hampshire, I merely walked into his office and said to him, "I'd better go down to the White House and see about planning a staff office there."

He nodded, picked up his telephone and called John R. Steelman, Truman's assistant at the White House, and made an appointment for me.

That was the beginning for me of six extraordinary years, a unique experience such as few people have lived through. I lived from day to day with momentous decisions and great events behind the scenes in the governing councils of the most powerful nation in the world at a time that was the most crucial period in the world's history. From my privileged position as Assistant to the President, I had an intimate view of Eisenhower as he made those decisions and as he reacted to those events. I saw a great military leader, under intense pressures, in sickness as well as in health, applying himself to the responsibilities of the presidency.

When I left Eisenhower's service in 1958, it occurred to me that I might perform a useful work if I wrote an account of some of my own observations during my years as Assistant to the President. I did not conceive this book as a chronological history of everything that happened in the Eisenhower administration. Nor is it an attempt necessarily to show Eisenhower's principal accomplishments. I plead no case nor seek to prove anything; I only want to describe the more important affairs of Eisenhower's terms of office, how he handled them, and to tell something of the background and circumstances surrounding his decisions. In doing so I hope I may give the reader a more vivid understanding of Eisenhower as a man; a man, I might add, who was unselfishly serving his country as President in the face of physical difficulties, with the inclinations of an old soldier who had been looking forward to a far more leisurely and carefree life in his later years. This book is simply my own personal view of Eisenhower as he appeared to me as we worked together in the White House. The opinions expressed here are mine, the result of my own observations and reflections.

The newly elected Eisenhower who asked me in 1952 to be his assistant in Washington was a bright and exuberant man, full of charm and bounce and vigor. He was going into the presidency with a heavy load on his mind, well aware of the responsibility he was shouldering in a world of turmoil, but at the same time far from being overwhelmed by it. He was tremendously buoyed up by the huge popular vote he had received in the election. He needed his great majority to give him the assurance and confidence to begin his administration with the feeling that the people were solidly behind him. He had once admitted that he would rather be licked than just squeak by in the national election. I suppose every incoming President who is swept into office as decisively as Eisenhower was enters the White House on the offensive, convinced that his plans are the best for the country and that his program has the majority of the people solidly behind it. As his years in the White House went by, Eisenhower found out, of course, that the policies and purposes which he assumed had been endorsed by voters could be blocked and frustrated by the politicians in his own party, not to mention the jolt he received when the Republicans lost the majority control of Congress to the party of the opposition. Periodically his confident offensive drive changed to impatient defensiveness. He complained occasionally about what he called the biggest problem of his presidency—the public's lack of understanding of what he was trying to do for world peace and domestic economic security. Besides, he felt that every responsible American citizen owed it to his country to take an interest in the problems of government and to express an informed opinion about them. Like all Presidents of modern times, he soon became irritated by our outmoded administrative system, which crowds the chief executive with such a staggering variety of constitutional and ceremonial duties that he is often unable to find the time for sufficient deliberation before coming to the great decisions for which he alone is responsible. When he wanted to think about the Middle East or, for another example, a new approach to the disarmament muddle, he found he had to listen to the merits of a bill concerning compensation for a woman who had been hit by an automobile on an Army post while crossing the street on her way to a laundromat. I have always thought that Eisenhower went to the roots of his biggest problem when he said with some exasperation at a staff meeting in his first year in office, "When does anybody get any time to think around here?"

During Eisenhower's first year as President, he was under constant pressure from serious problems that crowded in on him from all sides —the settlement of the Korean War, the Bricker Amendment, the struggles for domestic economic stability, tax relief, mutual security and defense spending controls, the Red-hunting hysteria of Senator McCarthy, farm program troubles, the Taft-Hartley Act, dissension among conservative Republicans, the atomic arms race with Russia and the controversy over the long-delayed Saint Lawrence Seaway, to name a few of the more prominent ones. In reaching decisions on such issues, Eisenhower followed a course of action that was new in the White House. He consulted more often with the Cabinet, the National Security Council and the legislative leaders in Congress than any President in history.

The Cabinet, as well as the Security Council, became under Eisenhower a force in the determination of government policy that it never had been in previous administrations. Abraham Lincoln and Theodore Roosevelt ignored their Cabinets on many urgent matters and Woodrow Wilson never took the trouble to talk with his Cabinet about the sinking of the *Lusitania* or America's declaration of war in 1917. Harold Ickes wrote in his diary that he wondered what use the Cabinet was during Franklin D. Roosevelt's administration. "The cold fact is that on important matters we are seldom called upon for advice," Ickes said. "We never discuss exhaustively any policy of government or question of political strategy. The President makes all his own decisions. . . . I never think of bringing up even a serious departmental issue at Cabinet meetings." Roosevelt and previous Presidents depended on individual Cabinet members for advice, of course, and delegated to them considerable authority in the running of their respective departments, but Eisenhower was probably the first President who made the meetings of the assembled Cabinet a forum for the debate of every important public question not concerned with security affairs. The questions for discussion, sharp and definite, were shaken down into calculated courses of action, with the President making the final decision. In the vast majority of cases, these questions, often under presidential prodding, found unanimous answers. The minority views were well and carefully buried.

Eisenhower never made a policy decision on an important domestic issue until after his course of action had been talked over and supported in a Cabinet meeting. Foreign policy was more immediately brought up before the National Security Council but every significant new problem in that area was also reviewed by the Cabinet. In the first Cabinet meeting at the Commodore Hotel in New York a week before his inauguration, Eisenhower said, "No one of you, whether a Cabinet member or one who functions as such, is relieved of his part of the responsibility for making government policy. No major decision will be made by the National Security Council but what will be reviewed by the Cabinet and brought back to the NSC." The Cabinet, for example, sweated through each tortuous step in the dealings with Syngman Rhee during the effort to end the Korean War and was briefed regularly by Eisenhower and Dulles on the intricacies of our relationships with various governments in Europe, the Middle East, Africa and Asia. Eisenhower made it plain that each Cabinet member was to have a voice not only in the affairs of his own department but in any other question that the government happened to be deliberating at the moment. Henry Cabot Lodge would argue stoutly with George Humphrey about such a vitally important matter as tax policy, and Oveta Culp Hobby would throw out some cautionary suggestion about backing off price and other controls. The strongest and most influential champion of the Saint Lawrence Seaway in the administration was George Humphrey. While his Treasury Department had no direct concern with the opening of the Great Lakes to ocean shipping, Humphrey repeatedly stressed the benefit he saw in the seaway for the entire Midwest.

The President encouraged outspoken opposition to his own views in Cabinet meetings. "I have given way on a number of personal opinions to this gang," he good-naturedly remarked one day. In fact, it was more or less understood that he preferred to have an objection to an Eisenhower policy or program brought up before the assembled Cabinet rather than in a private discussion in his office. He took pains to see to it that such disagreements were fully aired and ironed out and that a meeting of minds was reached before the matter was dropped so that he felt secure in the position he would take. He would put an emphatic stamp of finished business on it by ending the conversation with something like "Well, unless we hear something different, that's the way we'll handle it."

Sometimes the prevailing view of the Cabinet was either too lukewarm or too opposed to a proposal for it to gain much momentum. A few weeks after his inauguration, he had a meeting in the Cabinet room at the White House with Walter Reuther and David J. McDonald, head of the United Steelworkers. Eisenhower asked me to sit in with them. He was curious about Reuther, whom he had never really met before, and the CIO president, with his remarkably quick and dexterous mind, good manners and convincing line of talk, made quite an impression on the President. To anyone unfamiliar with his remarkable ability to capitalize on points that came up in the conversation and to turn them to his own advantage, Reuther made a lot of sense. He made a favorable first impression on anyone, including me. McDonald was the pipe-smoking, thinker type who had less to say. Eisenhower thought there might be something in Reuther's idea that labor, management and government had no real differences because their goals were the same—prosperity and security for the nation. Why, then, Reuther asked, couldn't harmony be built up by reaching agreements in what he called "great areas of common ground"? Underneath Eisenhower's disarming cordiality I detected a certain wariness. While he left the door open for further discussion, I could see that he was not going to get his neck in that noose blindfolded. On the other hand I could see that he was rather intrigued with Reuther's proposal.

When he broached the idea to the Republican leaders in Congress, they hit the ceiling. The President had not yet learned that to most of them Reuther was political anathema. Eisenhower quickly saw that, to use one of his own expressions, he was getting into a can of worms.

Not to be wholly eclipsed, Martin Durkin, Eisenhower's first Secretary of Labor, who was himself anathema to the CIO's Reuther because he had served as a union leader in the rival AFL, brought into the Cabinet practically the same proposal. Eisenhower gamely suggested that the Labor Secretary sound out business and labor people to see if they would be amenable to serving on such a peace committee. His efforts fell so flat that Eisenhower quietly forgot the whole plan.

Now and then, in his determination to reach a difficult but desirable objective, the idealistic and optimistic Eisenhower would reveal a faith in the higher motives of mankind that astonished the more cynical members of the Cabinet. For a while he was hopeful that the administration could persuade businessmen to hold the price line and stop labor leaders from demanding higher wages simply by appealing to their patriotism and sense of fair play. His Cabinet cynics argued a little vainly that in a free enterprise system something much stronger than inspirational exhortation would be needed to prevent men from trying to make more money.

Because Eisenhower knew from personal experience much more about NATO than he knew about the intricacies of the Taft-Hartley Act, he was more confident and incisive in discussions of global strategy at meetings of the National Security Council than he was in many of the detailed debates on domestic issues with the Cabinet. The Security Council, created by an act of Congress after World War II, is an advisory body on all aspects of national defense, and its top-secret proceedings range from reports on new nuclear weapons and the radar screen on the northern periphery of the hemisphere to intelligence on the political situation in the Malay Peninsula. The Council's membership consists of the President, the Vice President, the Director of Civil and Defense Mobilization and the Secretaries of State and Defense. The meetings include, in addition, anyone else whom the President wishes to invite, which, during Eisenhower's terms of office, meant the Secretary of the Treasury, the Budget Director, the Chairman of the Joint Chiefs of Staff, C. D. Jackson and later Nelson Rockefeller in their capacities as Special Assistants for Cold War Planning, the Director of the Mutual Security Program, Central Intelligence Agency Director Allen Dulles, and always Robert Cutler when he ran the Security Council's staff as Special Assistant to the President. Eisenhower asked me to attend as frequently as I could, but I found more pressing duties often prevented me from doing so. The President added the Budget Director and the Secretary of the Treasury as regular attendants at the Council meetings. Although they were not statutory members, Budget Director Joseph M. Dodge recommended their attendance because of a study he had made of the Council's operation during the Truman administration which showed it was paying little attention to costs in making its recommendations to the President. The presence of the government's fiscal watchdogs at the meetings reflected the President's belief, often voiced, that the nation could be destroyed by spending itself to death as well as by force of arms. Thereafter no major new commitment was ever undertaken without a close appraisal of the capability of the country to bear the financial burden. Without such consideration Eisenhower insisted that nobody could have much of an idea of the implications of any policy that was being put into effect. Dodge also pointed out that there had been too much delay in putting the National Security Council's suggestions into action. It was plain that the President needed a liaison officer who had the executive mandate to organize and tighten up the Council's activities from the planning stage right through to getting action on every policy decision.

Thus the office of Special Assistant to the President for National Security Affairs came into being, headed first by Robert Cutler, and then successively by Dillon Anderson, William Jackson and Gordon Gray. To ensure that the President's decisions got action instead of lingering under a pile of papers in somebody's desk drawer, the Operations Co-ordinating Board was created under a presidential assistant who worked under Cutler's watchful eye.

Eisenhower had to use a different approach in dealing with the Republican leaders from both houses of Congress, the third group with which he worked closely in making policy decisions. While Congress was in session, the leaders had weekly meetings in the White House with Eisenhower nearly as often as the Cabinet and the National Security Council did, and the President gave them the same active role of participation in all of the important problems with which they were concerned. This was a notable departure from the executive procedure of Truman, who did not tell anybody in Congress about his decision to send naval and air forces into combat in South Korea in 1950 until the day after he had given that order to General MacArthur. But Eisenhower found that there is quite a difference between working with a group of advisers that you have selected, such as the Cabinet and the Security Council, and one that is not of your own choosing. The weekly meetings with the legislative leaders became a chore that a President without Eisenhower's unfailing patience and determined optimism might have seen crossed off his calendar as not worth the effort. The influential Republicans in Congress were, for the most part, conservatives who did nothing to help Eisenhower get the nomination nor did they accept the fact that he virtually saved their party from a deepening oblivion. They gave him only intermittent support and considerable opposition and personal aggravation. The Republican majority in Congress was so small during the first two years of the Eisenhower administration that the President had to seek Democratic backing for his legislative programs and this added more strain on his relationship with the right wing of his own party.

Later, when the Democrats gained control of Congress, Eisenhower had to depend more and more on bipartisan support to get his legislative program through Congress, with the result that he felt he had to be more guarded in his criticism of the opposing party. Whenever he thought any one of us became too harsh he would remind us that we were not going to get anywhere in Congress without Democratic votes. This failure of the President to crack down more often on the opposition was one of the grounds on which the conservative Republicans complained about lack of political leadership. Another rift was grounded in the Eisenhower-Dulles policy of treating the many vital decisions in the field of foreign affairs on a strictly bipartisan basis. The President avoided even discussing the really momentous decisions with the Republicans in Congress until he and Dulles had laid out their course of action at a meeting of the leaders of both parties. Although this procedure undoubtedly kept many crucial questions out of partisan debate at the time, the President ultimately won little immunity from political criticism, for his conduct of foreign policy came under broad attack by the Democrats in the 1960 campaign.

These bipartisan conferences took the form of carefully worded statements by Dulles and the President of impending action, followed by a few questions. There was usually little free expression of either support or opposition, so that the assent of the leaders often had to be assumed by their silence. These meetings would ordinarily include Democrats like Sam Rayburn, John McCormack, Harry Byrd and Richard Russell, who usually drew back cautiously from a public endorsement of a stand that Eisenhower wanted the government to take on a controversial issue, such as support of United Nations sanctions against Israel during the Gaza Strip dispute. After an hour during which Dulles did most of the talking, Eisenhower discovered that he had few who were willing to go to bat for him. The legislators hurried back to Capitol Hill, leaving it to him and Dulles to carry the load.

It all added up to frustration for the President but he went on cheerfully as long as he was in office, never relaxing his efforts to win a better understanding and more help for his programs. Along with the weekly leadership meetings, he arranged with Jerry Persons to invite groups of members of Congress to a series of White House luncheons and breakfasts so that he was able to break bread with everybody in the Senate and in the House. "I want them to get a better understanding of what I'm driving at," he said. To the consternation of Tom Stephens, who had the difficult duty of arranging the President's appointments, Eisenhower was always telling Congressmen to drop into his office for a talk. When they took the invitation literally, there was usually some project of personal importance for which they wanted the President's support. With Senator Malone it was the tariff. With Senator Bricker it was his amendment. With Senator Daniel it was Texas' right to offshore oil. And even though the President's view differed with the Senators', he insisted on listening to their argument.

"Let him come in and get it off his chest," Eisenhower once said resignedly when Senator Malone wanted an appointment. But it turned out that the Senator had another purpose than just talking about the tariff. He had come to the White House with a photographer to have a picture taken of himself presenting to the President a new book that he had written. The book happened to be one that opposed Eisenhower's ideas on tariff and foreign trade and disagreed with the administration's views on world affairs generally.

Eisenhower made a valiant effort to get along with the legislators of both political parties. Unsparingly he used meals, meetings, messages and personal conferences to win their support for the programs he sent to Congress. Before he announced any new policy decision he was careful to go over it in detail with the appropriate legislative leaders; with the Republicans on domestic issues, with the bipartisan leadership on foreign affairs. During these discussions, I was often a participant and almost always a close observer. Many of these conferences reveal the origins of Eisenhower's policies, their shape and direction. In describing some of these discussions, I have tried to show how policy was conceived and carried out, leaving the characters to speak for themselves as the more memorable and significant events are unfolded in the pages that follow.

2 Eisenhower and the Republicans: The Nominee and the President

My association with Dwight D. Eisenhower began in a most informal setting. It was in a bathroom at the Conrad Hilton in Chicago that I was asked to serve as Eisenhower's floor manager at the 1952 Republican convention. Herbert Brownell, who was directing the drive for Eisenhower's nomination along with Senator Henry Cabot Lodge, Governor Thomas E. Dewey and General Lucius D. Clay, extended the floor managership to me during a hurried conference in the bathroom two days before the convention opened because that was the only place in the commotion-filled Republican headquarters suite where we could find quiet and privacy.

Before that time I had met Eisenhower personally only once, although I had officially launched his candidacy by placing his name in the New Hampshire primary the previous January.

In fact, one of the most significant reminders of the six momentous years that I worked with Dwight D. Eisenhower hangs on a wall of our home at Lincoln, New Hampshire, and is connected with this primary. It is a letter written in December, 1951, by Gordon Tiffany, then the Attorney General of New Hampshire, to the County Clerk of Dickinson County in Kansas, where Eisenhower's home town, Abilene, is located. I was then Governor of New Hampshire, but I held another office of which I was to become almost equally as proud. The state's Eisenhower-for-President committee had just been organized and I was its chairman. In order to enter our candidate's name

12

in the approaching presidential primary, we were required under the state law to show evidence that he was a member of the Republican party. There was little doubt of Eisenhower's Republican leanings, but, like many military men, he had never formally declared his party affiliation. Harry Truman, among others, had tried to talk him into running for President as a Democrat. Ike heading a Democratic ticket could not lose, they told him.

So I asked the Attorney General to inquire if the pollbooks at Eisenhower's county seat listed any party designation with his name. The County Clerk, C. F. Moore, wrote back promptly and economically, neatly typing his reply on the bottom of the letter he had received from New Hampshire:

Mr. Eisenhower has never voted in this county as far as I know, the Primary laws were first put into operation in the year 1928 and he has never voted since then, I have been county clerk since January 14th, 1927, Dwight has never been in the city as far as I know of until after war No. 2 at least he has never voted or I would have known it as the party filiation books are still here ever since the primary or branding law was passed in the spring of 1927 and never went into effect until the Primary Election of 1928.

Dwights father was a republican and always voted the republican ticket up until his death, however that has nothing to do with the son as many differ from their fathers of which I am sorry to see, the multitude beleives in going into debt and see how much they can spend, it has become a habit & will sink this nation into bankrupsy.

I don't think he has any politics.

Subsequently, I explained the New Hampshire primary statute to Henry Cabot Lodge, national chairman of the Eisenhower drive, who went to NATO headquarters in Paris and talked with Eisenhower about it. The General announced on January 7, 1952, that he was, indeed, a Republican. Our problem was solved, and the Democrats, then and there as it turned out, lost the election.

The lively primary campaign which I managed in my state brought Eisenhower 46,661 votes in the March preferential balloting, almost eleven thousand more than his nearest contender, Senator Taft. After that I campaigned for Ike around the country. But I never met the General until June 9 of that year, when he invited the New Hampshire delegates to visit him at the Morningside Heights residence in New York that he was then occupying as president of Columbia

University. He had just returned from his NATO assignment in Europe. He seemed ruddy, fit and relaxed and his manner with us was warm and easy.

Eisenhower talked with the delegates about his basic views on national issues, stressing his belief that more responsibility should be given to state and local government in such programs as education and labor-management matters. Then he brought Mrs. Eisenhower into the room, saying, "I want you to meet my Mamie." After the meeting with the delegates, I came back to have lunch with Eisenhower and Senator Carlson. We talked mostly about the coming convention and our delegate strength in various states. This was my first close look at Eisenhower and I told myself right away that I had not been wasting my time in working for his nomination for the past six months. He seemed on first impression a remarkably straightforward and uncomplicated man, with nothing devious or complex about him. I noticed that he had no time for trivialities. He focused his mind completely on the big and important aspects of the questions we discussed, shutting out with a strongly self-disciplined firmness the smaller and petty side issues when they crept into the conversation. I remember him saying that day, for example, about someone who aggravated him, "With a guy like that, I simply write his name on a piece of paper, put it in my lower desk drawer and shut the drawer!" When he found out after lunch that neither Carlson nor I smoked, he remarked that he had been a chain cigarette smoker himself but he had stopped smoking abruptly and completely when his doctor suggested cutting down to a more moderate rate. "I found that the easiest way was just to put it out of your mind," Eisenhower said.

I also noticed that Eisenhower did not express an opinion on something unless he knew what he was talking about. Confronted with matters outside his experience and knowledge, he asked questions and listened with attention. Although he had never held political office himself, I could see that Eisenhower's military experience had given him a considerable knowledge of government and government officials and the ways and means of getting things accomplished in Washington. He knew budgets and he had been through the mill in dealing with Congressional committees, and had attended Cabinet meetings. In his work as a commander in World War II and in NATO, he became well acquainted with our State Department and with the foreign offices of the European governments. Despite the fact that Eisenhower was running for office for the first time in his life, actually he knew more about the intricacies of high government than many professional politicians. And he had formed many firm beliefs and convictions about government and politics that were to weigh heavily on his later decisions. Thinking about Eisenhower's convictions, I often recall an observation made by Major General Wilton B. Persons, better known as Jerry Persons, Eisenhower's long-time aide and personal friend. When Robert Burroughs, a former Republican national committeeman from New Hampshire, went to Paris in the summer of 1951 to urge the NATO commander to run for President, he received a warning in Persons' Alabama idiom. "He don't take shovin'," Persons said.

I did not see Eisenhower again until after I had accepted my commission as his convention floor manager in the bathroom at the Conrad Hilton Hotel. Incidentally, I suppose that Brownell and Eisenhower's other advisers selected me as floor manager partly because I was the only prominent Republican in Ike's camp at that time who had no previous identity as either a Taft man or a Dewey man. I had been in state politics in New Hampshire since 1940, when, after twenty years in timberland management, I had been elected to the State Legislature as a Republican by the voters of my heavily Democratic town of Lincoln. I had gone on to Congress in 1945 and then to the Governor's chair, but I had played no national role in the 1948 Republican convention or campaign so I had no label of past association with either of the two opposing wings of the party.

Another factor that might have led to my selection as floor manager, and in turn to my appointment as Eisenhower's assistant during the campaign, was my activity in behalf of the so-called Houston Manifesto, drafted by the Republican governors at the conference of governors in Houston that June. The manifesto was a condemnation of questionable tactics which had been used in Texas and a few other Southern states in the selection of convention delegates. In these states the votes of precinct meetings and local caucuses favorable to Eisenhower were being disregarded by Republican state committees because of their claim that Democrats had been allowed to vote at these local meetings. The state committees had then selected delegates of their own choosing favorable to Taft. However, the precinct meet-

ings and caucuses had been legally conducted and the high-handed
action of state committees in substituting delegates of their own choosing was to constitute the crucial issue in the fight between the Eisenhower and Taft forces at the 1952 convention. Eisenhower's chances
of winning the nomination depended a great deal on whether his popularly supported delegates from Georgia, Louisiana and Texas could
be seated instead of the contesting Taft delegates from those states.
With Brownell and Lodge engineering the parliamentary moves,
Governor Arthur B. Langlie of Washington introduced the "fair play"
amendment to the convention rules based on the principle of the
Houston Manifesto. It proposed to prevent the seating of any con-
tested delegate until his status was decided by a vote of the entire
convention. The only time I formally addressed the convention was
when I made a speech in support of Langlie's amendment, which was
approved after a vigorous debate by a vote that did not even require
a roll call.

Then came another Eisenhower-Taft battle over the application of
the Langlie amendment to the specific question of the respective rights
of the contesting delegates from Georgia to be seated. Young Don
Eastvold of Washington carried the brunt of the Eisenhower argument
against Vernon W. Thompson, the able attorney general of Wisconsin,
and Senator Dirksen. Eastvold handled his assignment succinctly and
effectively and his motion passed, scoring the decisive blow that paved
the way for Eisenhower's triumph. It was in this heated debate that
Dirksen issued his ill-advised blast at Dewey, thereby talking himself
out of whatever chance he might have had to become Eisenhower's
vice-presidential running mate.

I went directly from my bathroom conference with Brownell to
see Eisenhower at the Blackstone Hotel. I explained to him that I
would have to know as floor manager if there had been any private
political commitments made in his behalf in lining up delegates for
the convention. Eisenhower's reply was quick and emphatic; he had
made no promises to anybody, and nobody, acting in his behalf,
would make any promises. He made it plain that if he was going into
the White House, he would go there under no obligation to anyone.

I saw Eisenhower once more briefly toward the end of the convention when he called me to his room at the Blackstone to thank me

for my work as floor manager. While we were talking, Nixon came in. The party leaders at the meeting I had just attended across the street at the Conrad Hilton had recommended him as Eisenhower's running mate and when I left the room he and Eisenhower were talking together in a mood of happy optimism.

When the convention came to its close, I felt as if I was on the verge of a collapse. Mrs. Adams and I agreed that we could not go back to New Hampshire until I was able to take up again my duties as Governor. We decided to get out of sight and hide someplace and we both thought of the Tetons in Wyoming. We spoke to Senator Frank A. Barrett, who was then Wyoming's Governor, and he said that Tom Oliver's Lazy 4-F Ranch at Moose was the place for us. We flew with the Governor directly from Chicago to Cheyenne and then made the journey up over the divide from the Wind River Valley into the Buffalo fork of the Snake, declaring that it was the grandest spot we had ever seen, a place where we could enjoy the rest of our lives in complete equanimity.

Just as the exhilaration of the countryside was beginning to have its effect, I received word that Denver was trying to reach me on the telephone. I had assumed that nobody knew where we were, but, as I was to learn, when Eisenhower wanted somebody, he got him. My conversation with him was brief. He asked me to be his righthand man during the campaign. I had to remind him that I was still Governor of New Hampshire and that my term of office would not be up until the following January. However, I added, I would be willing to go back home and consult with the Governor's Council and the people who had elected me to see if I could get a leave of absence. Eisenhower expressed the hope that my mission might be successful.

We returned posthaste to Concord, where I put the question of the propriety of my taking leave of absence up to the five members of my Council. One of them, C. Edward Bourassa of Manchester, was a Democrat. I remember his comment: "I wish I had an opportunity like that." My absence from the governorship for the rest of the year would not jeopardize the administration of the state's business. Since I was completing my second term of office and I was not a candidate for re-election, there was no need of my preparing a legislative program. Under the state constitution, my substitute would be the reliable and experienced president of the state senate, Blaylock Atherton, to whom I could turn over the chief executive's duties with complete confidence.

So, with the support of my Council and friends, I issued a statement in which I accepted Eisenhower's invitation to serve as his campaign chief of staff, or, as the announcement of my appointment from Denver described it, liaison man between the General and the Republican National Committee. Some newspapers referred to me as Eisenhower's "personal campaign manager" but we discouraged the use of that title because it confused the status of Arthur Summerfield, who, as newly elected national chairman, was the campaign manager ex officio. In my statement I explained that I was giving up my Governor's salary and that I would be ready to return to New Hampshire at any time if the state's business needed me. My statement said, "I am sure that this arrangement can meet the needs of the state at the same time that it provides a contribution from New Hampshire to a great cause, the election of the first Republican President in 24 years." I was, of course, blasted by the Democrats and by the state's leading pro-Taft newspaper but the criticism had more thunder than weight. One of my friends, Earl Hewitt, commented editorially in his Hanover *Gazette* that I had stepped from the Governor's role into the Eisenhower campaign the previous January "with a longer stride" than I had realized. How right he was.

The task that I faced during the next three months was at times the most frustrating experience of my life, and, at other times, the most satisfying. During the campaign, as later in the White House, Eisenhower never defined or outlined the precise duties and responsibilities that he wanted me to assume. Evidently I was supposed to know what I was supposed to do. Sometimes, in taking a line of action on my own, I may have overstepped or fallen short of what Eisenhower had in mind, but I did not hesitate nor did I ever feel confused. In general, my job in the campaign was to bring some harmony and co-ordination into the relationships of the various factions in the Eisenhower following, especially between the orthodox, old-line Republicans in the National Committee and in the state organizations and the unorthodox, progressive Citizens-for-Eisenhower and independent groups. My efforts were complicated by Eisenhower's own personal disenchantment with the traditional GOP politicians. Our experience in the convention with the exclusive little state organization cliques during the controversy over the seating of the Louisiana, Georgia and Texas delegates made Eisenhower suspicious of many of the state committee politicos, who clung jealously to their authority to the exclusion of new and younger blood. It was only natural that he came to feel that the Citizens-for-Eisenhower groups were more expressive of his liberal aspirations than the regular Republican committees. This did not make my liaison post either easy or enjoyable.

There were many times during the campaign of that election year and in the six following years, when I was in the White House as Assistant to the President, that I was reminded of the last line of County Clerk Moore's eloquent little letter. "I don't think he has any politics." As a candidate and as President of the United States, Eisenhower had a strong aversion to engaging in partisan politics. A high-minded idealist, he had assumed that the Republican politicians had nominated him mainly because they wanted a President with his wartime and NATO experience who stood the best chance of bringing permanent peace to the world. It came later as a grim disillusionment when he realized that many of the Old Guard Republican leaders were really using his prestige and popularity only to wrest political power from the Democrats.

I first noticed this on the day early in August, 1952, when Arthur Summerfield, Chairman of the Republican National Committee, and other party leaders came to the Brown Palace Hotel in Denver to present to Eisenhower and his staff their carefully prepared plan of strategy for the coming presidential campaign. Summerfield was accompanied by Sinclair Weeks and Douglas Stuart, the National Committee's finance directors, Robert Humphreys, a smart public relations director, and other political officials. Representing the Republicans in Congress, Senator Everett Dirksen and Congressman Leonard Hall attended. Murray Chotiner, Richard Nixon's campaign manager, was there as a spokesman for Nixon, who had gone over the plan and approved it. Of the original Ike men, preconvention Chairman Senator Lodge was at the presentation as Eisenhower's special adviser. So were Walter Williams and Mary Lord from the progressive "amateur" Citizens-for-Eisenhower, whose ambitious plans to attract liberal-minded independent voters from the Democrats were discounted by the conservative National Committee but warmly applauded by Eisenhower.

The National Committee's strategy plan was ably presented by Humphreys, Summerfield's principal aide. Its big objective was to concentrate on a strong consolidation of the various factions in the Republican party. For the benefit of the "independent" Citizens-for-Eisenhower, Humphreys emphasized that efforts in the Willkie and Dewey campaigns to woo the so-called "dissenting," or liberal, uncommitted vote had only ended in disaster. As it turned out on Election Day, of course, Eisenhower was swept into office, not only by the solid but minority Republican party, but also by independents and by what Eisenhower chose to call the rebellious "discerning Democrats" in such unlikely places as Texas.

When Humphreys finished with the presentation, Eisenhower said nothing. I could see that beneath his usual outward composure something had annoyed and upset him. I asked him later what had bothered him.

"All they talked about was how they would win on my popularity," he said. "Nobody said I had a brain in my head."

Eisenhower had no interest and took little part in the behind-the-scenes maneuvering of the politicians. At the start of the 1952 Republican convention, he heard the uncommitted Governor John Fine of Pennsylvania telling a national leader of the party that he planned to come out for Ike on the following Tuesday. The party leader advised Fine to be more cagey about it. Wait till Thursday, he argued, when the chips would be down. To anybody experienced in politics there was nothing unethical in this advice; it was merely an opinion on timing an endorsement for strategic advantage. But to the direct and straightforward Eisenhower it was devious tactics. "That looked like pretty slippery business," he said to me about the party leader afterward. "I made up my mind he would bear watching." The incident strengthened his mistrust of the party professionals.

As President, Eisenhower could never understand the logic of legislative leaders in his own party who opposed his vitally important foreign programs because they were afraid that such spending might hurt the Republicans in the next Congressional elections. Putting political considerations before world peace and security seemed to Eisenhower not only the height of false economy but ridiculously dangerous. This issue caused the late Senator Robert A. Taft to hit the ceiling in the Cabinet Room one morning in the most explosive emotional outburst against the President that I saw in all my six years in the White House.

Taft's violent and most embarrassing attack on Eisenhower occurred when the President, with Secretary of the Treasury George M. Humphrey and Budget Director Joseph M. Dodge, met with the Republican leaders in Congress on April 30, 1953, to break the bad news that the new administration would not be able to balance the first budget, as Taft and his cohorts had expected. That was the so-called Truman budget for the fiscal year of 1954, drawn up by the previous administration with a deficit originally projected at $9.9 billion. Despite the many untouchable commitments made by the preceding Democratic government, Eisenhower had succeeded in cutting that deficit down to $5.5 billion. The President explained that he could not go any lower at that particular time because he was then in the process of making an expensive and vitally important change in the nation's defense program, converting the old plan, which assumed a possible enemy attack upon the United States at a certain fixed future date, into a new policy of fluid readiness against attack at any time.

Taft heard the President out in grim silence and listened impatiently to further explanations from Dodge and Roger Kyes, who was then Deputy Secretary of Defense. Then Taft exploded, losing control of himself, pounding his fist on the Cabinet table and shouting at the stunned President, who was sitting opposite him.

"With a program like this, we'll never elect a Republican Congress in 1954," he shouted. "You're taking us down the same road Truman traveled. It's a repudiation of everything we promised in the campaign!"

Taft went on to declare that he had no confidence in the Joint Chiefs of Staff and that Eisenhower in maintaining a high level of defense spending was being badly taken in by these professional military men. "I talked against a tax cut in 1953," he said, "but I can't go on opposing one for 1954. You've got to go over this program again and try to eliminate this deficit completely." Humphrey cut in on him to say that further reductions were impossible and Taft shot back again with a heated charge that the Eisenhower administration wasn't moving an inch from where Truman had stood on spending.

When Taft stopped talking, a heavy and uncomfortable quiet fell upon the room. Eisenhower moved in his chair, flushed and upset, as if he were about to say something, but, before he could speak, John Taber, the veteran Republican Congressman from New York, turned to Kyes and began a quick and aimless conversation about his confidence in the Defense Department's ability to effect further economies without impairing national security. Humphrey and Senator Leverett Saltonstall joined in this small talk, trying to give Eisenhower time to calm down and compose himself before making a reply to Taft.

When Eisenhower did begin to speak, he was able to review in quiet, measured tones the reasons for the cost of our global peace strategy—the need for spending security funds to combat Soviet influence in Western Europe, the Middle East and Southeast Asia. A position of strength in those areas, he said, was as important to the military defense of North America as a retaliatory bombing threat. He went on to express his confidence in the National Security Council's judgment on the proposed change in defense strategy and politely disagreed with Taft's feeling that the unbalanced 1954 budget would hurt the Republicans in that year's elections. The tenseness in the room passed away. After some hopeful speculation about the reduction of the 1955 budget, the meeting broke up in peace, if not in harmony.

Eisenhower said later that he was about to make an angry reply to the Taft tirade when the hurried intervention of anxious small talk from the other men around the table made him pause and collect himself. "I was thinking that if there was any one thing that persuaded the American people to vote for me, it was my knowledge and understanding of defense problems," he told me after the meeting. "And here was Taft challenging my judgment in those matters. But that was not the time or place for that kind of an argument." Eisenhower had succeeded again, as he often did, in observing one of his favorite rules of conduct: "Never lose your temper, except intentionally." If he had struck back hotly at Taft and if Taft had left the meeting in a rage, the damage to the administration might have been incalculable. As it turned out, when Taft came to the White House for the next Republican legislative leaders' conference a week later, he make a joking reference to his outburst at the previous meeting, and laughed it off apologetically.

Despite the basic difference in their viewpoints, Eisenhower and Taft got along well together. To the annoyance of some of their respective supporters in the opposing wings of the party, they both leaned over backward in an effort to work together for Republican unity. Eisenhower's independent and liberal followers were deeply distressed by the General's approval of the statement issued by Taft after their famous breakfast meeting at Morningside Heights during the 1952 campaign, which was played up as a surrender to the Ohio Senator's conservative principles. Many of us original Ike backers who had fought Taft at the convention felt at that time that Adlai Stevenson scored an embarrassing touché when he remarked of the Morningside Heights peace parley, "Now we have the spectacle of the candidate who won the nomination seeking out his defeated rival and begging for a kind word. It looks as if Taft lost the nomination but won the nominee."

Actually, when you look back again now at Taft's statement of the points of policy on which he said that Eisenhower agreed with him, there seems to be small ground for the charge of surrender or compromise on Eisenhower's part. Taft did not misrepresent or change Eisenhower's previous opinions when he said in the statement that they saw eye to eye on the need to make a drastic reduction in government spending, on the evils of unlimited executive power and strongly centralized government and on "liberty against creeping socialism." Eisenhower's view did coincide with Taft's on all those domestic questions. But Taft tried to minimize their disagreements on foreign policy, which in certain aspects were very great. In the Senate, Taft had recently supported former President Herbert Hoover's "Fortress America" or "Gibraltar of Freedom" isolationist defense concept, a line of thinking that burned Eisenhower up. He could not understand the reasoning of people who clung to the outdated notion that the United States could go it alone in world affairs.

During the campaign, Taft offered me constructive and helpful advice about the position Eisenhower should take on such matters as the Taft-Hartley Act. After the Republicans gained control of Congress by a slim margin in the election, Taft asked his close friend, Senator Frank Carlson of Kansas, a loyal Eisenhower backer, to come to his office in Washington one Sunday morning. Taft said that he wanted to be the majority leader in the Senate but that he was afraid Eisenhower would not want him in that post. This came as a surprise to Carlson; it had been assumed in the party that Taft would be reluctant to serve as the Senate leader under an Eisenhower administration. Styles Bridges of New Hampshire as senior Republican Senator let it be known through friends that he might consider the leadership post although it is doubtful if at any time he had any intention of assuming his rights of seniority. Carlson told Taft that he would go to New York and talk with Eisenhower about it the next morning. Taft was still doubtful that Ike would accept him. But when the question was put to him the next day, Eisenhower told Carlson without a moment's hesitation that he would be most happy to have Taft as the Republican leader in the Senate. Taft was relieved and delighted when Carlson telephoned the news to him.

Shortly after Eisenhower took office as President, he told Taft to feel free to call him or to walk into his office at the White House at any time without making an appointment, regardless of whether the President was occupied with other business. Outside of his personal staff, this was a privilege extended to only one other government official, Secretary of State John Foster Dulles. It was typical of Taft that he never took advantage of the invitation. When he wanted to discuss something with the President, Taft always called me first, told me what was on his mind and asked me to arrange an appointment for him. When he came to the White House, Eisenhower often would reprimand him good-naturedly for going through such formality instead of just dropping in on the spur of the moment.

As majority leader in the Senate, Taft made a conscientious effort to support Eisenhower's programs even when he was not wholeheartedly in favor of them. The appointment of Martin P. Durkin, a Truman Democrat, as Eisenhower's first Secretary of Labor galled Taft. Durkin, president of the plumbers' union, was an enemy of the Taft-Hartley Law and frowned upon by Republicans generally. Taft called the nomination "incredible," but nevertheless swallowed his pride and voted for Durkin's approval. Similarly, Taft put aside his own feelings in response to an appeal from Eisenhower and fought against the conservative Republicans and Senator Joseph R. McCarthy for approval of Charles E. Bohlen as Ambassador to Moscow early in 1953.

Taft's emotional explosion at the leadership meeting came as a startling surprise to Eisenhower because of this feeling of friendship and understanding that had been growing between the two men. Only two weeks before that meeting, Eisenhower had invited Taft to Augusta for a round of golf in a foursome that included Clarence Schoo, the fiber box manufacturer from Springfield, Massachusetts, and myself. The President and Taft had a good time, neither of them realizing that it was the last game of golf Taft would ever play. Late in the afternoon he complained of a pain in his hip, which, it turned out, was the first sign of his fatal cancer infection.

Eisenhower's distaste for partisan politics reflected itself in the lack of any firm or militant command over the Republican party. He preferred to leave the operation of the political machinery to the professionals. While the relations between them were at least superficially cordial, the President constantly criticized party officials for their lack of a dynamic grass-roots organization and, more particularly, for their failure to build up the ranks through policies which would attract the young, independent voter.

When Taft resigned on June 10, 1953, as Republican leader in the Senate because of his illness, Eisenhower could have replaced him with a Senator of his own choice. Instead, the President carefully refrained from having anything to do with the selection of the new majority leader and even asked his Cabinet members and other administration officials not to express an opinion about their preference as Taft's successor. Eisenhower felt that such an intrusion in a Senate affair was inappropriate and might well be resented by the Republicans in Congress.

And so it was that Senator William F. Knowland of California became the Republican leader in the Senate. It would have been difficult to find anybody more disposed to do battle with much of the President's program in Congress. I remember an encounter I had with Knowland at the 1952 Republican convention, when I was serving as Eisenhower's floor manager. Wondering if there was any remote possibility of getting some California votes, I approached Knowland and asked if we could discuss the situation. He hardly spoke to me. He only scowled, shook his head violently and turned his back to me. Later when it became apparent that Eisenhower would be leading Taft on the first ballot, Warren Burger of the Minnesota delegation, one of Harold Stassen's managers, went to Knowland and suggested that both

Minnesota and California should switch to Ike so that the General could be nominated by a substantial vote inasmuch as he would be nominated anyway. Knowland said to Burger coldly, "We don't want any credit or any responsibility for *that* nomination."

And this, a year later, was the man who was to serve as Eisenhower's party leader in the Senate. Knowland, with the Joe Martin–Charles Halleck feud smoldering in the background, made the weekly meetings of the party Congressional leaders in the White House an ordeal for Eisenhower. Many of the President's aims and hopes actually received more sympathy from the Democratic leaders in Congress, Lyndon Johnson and Sam Rayburn. When Eisenhower complained wearily at one meeting that the Republicans never seemed to agree with each other on anything, Martin chuckled and said, "Maybe that's the result of these last twenty years that we spent out in the wilderness." The President struggled patiently, trying to win co-operation from Knowland. He had the Senator down repeatedly to breakfast at the White House. He publicly praised the Californian whenever he had an opportunity. But he would get just so far. Then Knowland would knock over the apple cart, and Eisenhower had to begin all over again. The President carefully avoided any pitched battle with the Republican leader. Even the gentle reproof was uncommon. On one occasion, during a shakedown on Red China, the President was obviously out of patience with the single-track thinking of the stubborn Senator. "There's one thing I have learned not to do," he told me later. "There are times when you must never say 'never' "—meaning that the single-minded Senator had no room in his thinking for a "maybe," an "if" or a "perhaps." The President found his relations with the Republican leaders substantially improved when Knowland left the Senate to run for the governorship in California and his post passed on to Everett Dirksen of Illinois. The change in the House leadership from Martin to Halleck gave Eisenhower added satisfaction, for the Hoosier Congressman had always given him aggressive support, whereas Martin, though always co-operative, seemed to him uninspired and lackadaisical in getting the administration's program through the House. "Under the new leadership," the President observed in a discussion we had last year, "the meetings have become a pleasure, something I actually look forward to."

Like Knowland, most of the Republican leaders in Congress were not Ike boosters before the 1952 convention. Eisenhower was well aware that they did not share his enthusiasm for many of the foreign programs which he considered essential to U.S. security. But because he had been elected by the resounding endorsement of 34 million American voters, the biggest popular backing in the history of free elections, he assumed that his own party members in Congress would put aside their own prejudices to give him some allegiance in what he was trying to do. He told them a story at one White House leadership meeting to illustrate his hopeful expectations. "A veteran from World War II went to the race track to put a bet on a horse named General Ike," Eisenhower related. "A friend told him this horse was just an old plug and didn't have a chance to win. But the veteran placed his bet just the same. 'If I followed him for two years all over Europe,' he said, 'I can follow him for one more mile.' "

Eisenhower always had firm confidence in his own powers of persuasion to bring an understanding to the leaders of his party of the undodgeable and irrefutable facts of the world situation. But he rarely carried an argument to the point of really getting tough and using a reprisal to bring the dissidents into line. His reluctance to use the whip had its effect. There being no penalties for deserting the party line, there was often little semblance of party unity. Before I worked for him, I assumed Eisenhower would be a hard taskmaster. He did have a penchant for orderly thinking and procedure and, particularly, for careful follow-through on assignments. But he seldom called anybody down when he was displeased with his work and I never knew him to punish anybody. When General Matthew B. Ridgway split with him on the question of armed forces manpower levels and when General Maxwell Taylor questioned the government's anti-missile program, the President was deeply embarrassed but did little more than provide for the early retirement of these officers. It was Eisenhower's reluctance to enforce internal discipline among the Republicans, his refusal to stoop to the ward-boss, strong-arm tactics that were Harry Truman's stock in trade, that made his political leadership appear by comparison hesitant and ineffectual. Though contrary to his nature, a tougher, more relentless line would have brought better results in getting his legislative program through Congress.

When Eisenhower divided sharply with the Republican conservatives, when it became apparent to him that many of the Democrats were more willing to accept his foreign programs than his own leaders were, he began to speculate in private talks with me about whether he really belonged in this kind of Republican party. Had the time come for a realignment of the political parties in the United States? For six of the eight years that his Republican administration was in office, Congress was controlled by a Democratic majority and, to make matters worse, the Republican minority was often against the White House, too. To Eisenhower's orderly and logical mind, such a situation made no sense and somehow should have been prevented. How is it possible, he asked me, to place responsibility for conduct of the government on one political party when the President and the Congress are working at cross purposes? Although he did not advocate the British parliamentary system for this country, he did think long and earnestly about the best means of providing under our Constitution that the political party of the President and that of the Congressional majority be the same.

Eisenhower's thoughts about a new political party—accepting a role of leadership in world affairs, liberal in its policies affecting human welfare but taking a more conservative stand than the Democrats on domestic government controls and spending—were confined to a few thinking-aloud sessions with me in the privacy of his office. He carried them no further for he was well aware of the dangerous confusion that might come from breaking up the two-party system. He recalled, too, how the third parties launched by Theodore Roosevelt and the elder Robert M. La Follette became one-man ventures rather than popular movements. Eisenhower decided to go on hoping that the Republican party could be changed by younger blood into a broader and more effective political force.

These conversations I had with Eisenhower about a new party came back to embarrass me in 1956. In fact, they brought me the closest thing to a reprimand that I ever got from the President. When Eisenhower decided to run for a second term, a few of his friends and associates suggested that I and the White House staff should cooperate with an experienced political journalist in writing a book about Eisenhower's first three years in office, something that would reveal to the public his work and the real nature of his problems as President, and display his personality and human qualities. Roscoe

Drummond, the New York *Herald Tribune*'s Washington correspondent, was first suggested as the writer of the book but he was unable to undertake the work. He suggested Robert J. Donovan, another capable *Herald Tribune* reporter in the capital, and, although the book was not solely my idea, I became Donovan's guide and main source of information. I did not consult the President about the project and he had nothing to do with it. There was no censorship of the book, outside of the usual checking for breaches of government security. It was published in that election year as *Eisenhower: The Inside Story,* a title that made me none too happy because I felt it sounded too much like a gossipy exposé, which the book wasn't. It did, however, go into delicate political situations that gave me some uncomfortable moments.

In my complicity with this journalistic effort, I am sure the end justified the means, but I suppose I made one mistake. Discussing with Donovan the uneasiness and disappointment that the President felt in encountering the reaction of Republican party leaders to his political philosophy, I mentioned, as an illustration, Eisenhower's thinking out loud about the realignment of the political parties to represent better the contrast of view on the principal issues of the age. Donovan dressed this item up in masterful fashion and made it a feature of a chapter on Republican discord and Eisenhower discouragement, which also revealed that the President in the Cabinet meeting of May 8, 1953, had remarked that he was tired of having the administration "kicked in the shins" by Congressmen who should be supporting it.

At a Republican leadership meeting in the White House shortly after Donovan's book was published, Senator Knowland pounced on that chapter and said that he hardly thought the President's suggestion of forming a new political party would be helpful to the political success of the Republicans in that presidential election year. Senator Knowland had scored a point.

After the meeting, the President beckoned to me and asked me to step into his office for a moment. He had the most delightfully painless way of taking a person to task that I have ever seen. Without saying much, he could make you feel just terrible. He was able to put his finger on me squarely in this case because, as he took pains to point out, he had only discussed his reflections about a new party with me. Donovan could not have picked up this spicy incident from anybody else, because nobody else knew about it. "We should be a little more wary about getting ourselves into that kind of a bind," Eisenhower said. Afterward I remarked to Goodpaster that one of those adventures in a lifetime was just about enough.

Long before he came to the White House, at the very beginning of his first campaign for the presidency in the summer of 1952, Eisenhower knew that many of his personal liberal beliefs would come into sharp conflict with the ultraconservatives of the Republican right wing. This was one of the grim necessities of party politics. As much as he disagreed with Senator Joe McCarthy and Senator William Jenner and wanted no identity with them, he nevertheless had to run on the same ticket with them in Wisconsin and Indiana. Eisenhower tried, without much success, to draw a line of differentiation between a general, party-line endorsement for a whole state Republican slate, which he was always willing to give, and a specific declaration of personal support for a particular candidate, which he never intended to give to the McCarthys and the Jenners. When it came to a show-down, the Old Guardsmen of the National Committee tried to look the other way and forget Eisenhower's deep feeling against becoming identified with those with whom he so violently disagreed.

Much to his chagrin, Eisenhower found himself on the same campaign platform with Republicans of the very type he so studiously tried to avoid. His remonstrances to me and others on his personal staff were unavailing since we had little to do with the rally programs and arrangements. Fearing that McCarthy would make an unwelcomed attempt to grab on to Eisenhower's coat tails, Governor Thomas E. Dewey pleaded with us in New York not to let Ike go into Wisconsin. In a meeting of Eisenhower's closest advisers, Dewey was voted down. Sure enough, when the Wisconsin-bound Eisenhower campaign train made a stop in Peoria, Illinois, Governor Walter Kohler of Wisconsin came aboard to ride into his state with us, and with him was McCarthy. The next morning the Senator smilingly entered Eisenhower's private car with Kohler preparatory to appearing on the platform with him when he made his first scheduled speech at Green Bay.

"I'm going to say that I disagree with you," Eisenhower told McCarthy.

"If you say that, you'll be booed," McCarthy said. Eisenhower shrugged his shoulders and said, "I've been booed before, and being booed doesn't bother me."

McCarthy appeared on the platform at Green Bay, standing beside Eisenhower and waving triumphantly to the crowd. In his speech Eisenhower said that, although he supported the Wisconsin Senator's efforts to rid the government of Communists, it was well known that there were differences between McCarthy and himself. There were no boos. McCarthy walked out of the candidate's car after the whistle stop looking very black indeed.

That morning on the train we showed Governor Kohler the speech that Eisenhower was to deliver in Milwaukee that night. Eisenhower at that time, as now, was smoldering with resentment at the treatment that General George C. Marshall, as Truman's Secretary of State, had received in abusive Senate speeches by Jenner and McCarthy. Jenner had openly called Marshall "a front man for traitors" and McCarthy, while not directly making the same charge, lumped Eisenhower's wartime superior among government leaders whom he described as "half loyal" or "disloyal." Many of Eisenhower's supporters, including Arthur Hays Sulzberger, publisher of the *New York Times,* were mortified that their candidate had been led into a situation which could be construed as even a tacit endorsement of any Republican who had brought into question the loyalty of a man in whom Eisenhower so enthusiastically believed. In the conferences among the speech writers preparing the Milwaukee address, a brief reference to Eisenhower's dedication to George Marshall was deliberately included to serve as an example of his differences with the Wisconsin Senator. Governor Kohler, reading the speech, suggested that the allusion to Marshall should be omitted since it was out of context and was a too obvious and clumsy way to take a slap at a Senator who, like Eisenhower, was a Republican candidate seeking the support of Wisconsin voters. Although he agreed with the principle it expressed, Kohler felt strongly that the defense of Marshall stood out sharply from the rest of the speech, a discussion of domestic Communism, as an unnecessarily abrupt rebuff to McCarthy. To him it looked as though Eisenhower was going out of his way to stir up an issue which did not call for an airing on that particular platform. I decided that Kohler was right.

I brought the Governor, with Ike's trusted aide, Jerry Persons, to Eisenhower and started a discussion of the speech. I had only begun when Eisenhower interrupted me impatiently and asked me if I was about to suggest that the reference to Marshall should be deleted. "That's what I'm going to recommend," I said. "Take it out," Eisenhower snapped. That ended the discussion.

That evening, minutes before the speech was to be delivered, I found myself in the middle of one of the many hot arguments that I had to decide then and during the next six years. Gabriel Hauge was handling the final drafting of the speech and he came to me deeply disturbed over the omission of the reference to General Marshall. Hauge was as high-minded and as zealous a stickler for principle as Eisenhower had on his staff. I brought in Arthur Summerfield to go over with Hauge the political angles involved in the decision. There was no joy for me in having to decide against Hauge's plea, but I had to agree with Kohler's opinion. After all, he was the Governor of a state where we were guests and some adjustments had to be made for party harmony.

There were immediate repercussions. The story of the planned reference in the speech to Marshall and its last-minute deletion found its way to reporters and into the newspapers. It was widely interpreted as an endorsement of McCarthy by Eisenhower and it was even erroneously reported that the defense of Marshall had been taken out of the speech at McCarthy's request. McCarthy correctly denied this. He had said nothing to us about the speech. Arthur Sulzberger sent me a telegram which read, "Do I need to tell you that I am sick at heart?" Political columnists used the Milwaukee speech incident to contend that the conservatives who had fought against Eisenhower's nomination were now growing in influence around him. One of the commentators pointed out that I was the only remaining Ike booster in the candidate's camp on whom the liberals could pin their hopes. This observer would have been sorely tried if he had known that I was the one who recommended to Eisenhower that the reference to Marshall be deleted.

A week later, when our campaign train completed its westward tour in Los Angeles, Paul Hoffman came to me complaining about the Milwaukee episode and asked me if I would talk about it with Sam Goldwyn, another Eisenhower enthusiast, who, Hoffman said, was greatly disheartened by it, too. I invited them both to have dinner with Mrs. Adams and myself in our room at the Ambassador Hotel, where Hoffman and Goldwyn spent an hour telling us that independents were blowing away from Eisenhower like dry leaves in an October breeze. Patiently I then went over all of the problems of the Wisconsin adventure with them. I arranged for them to ride with us in the gay red convertible that had been assigned to me when the Eisenhower party paraded to the Auditorium for that evening's gala rally and I found them seats on the stage, placing Goldwyn in my own chair and putting Hoffman in one that I wangled from the security police. When the fireworks of the night were over, Hoffman took me aside and said, "That was good work you did with Sam tonight. Confidentially, I was afraid we were going to lose him." Then Goldwyn came to me and whispered with great seriousness, "You were fine with Paul tonight. I really thought we were going to lose him."

Outwardly, Eisenhower took McCarthy's invasion of the campaign train calmly. In Indianapolis, when Ike found himself being introduced by Jenner before a huge audience at a rally in the Butler University field house, I knew that although he was inwardly in turmoil he would make the best of the extremely uncomfortable situation. I also knew I would hear about it afterward. Summerfield was well aware that Eisenhower was not going to give Jenner any unqualified endorsement and wanted someone else to make the introduction that night. But there was Jenner on the platform presenting Eisenhower to the crowd. Even though he was upset, Eisenhower managed to give a speech that was a rip-snorter and the ovation that followed it was tumultuous. Then came the crusher. With a big theatrical display, Jenner jumped forward, grasped Eisenhower's wrist and held his arm high in the air for all the nation to see.

While Eisenhower maintained his customary self-control I had the uneasy feeling that he thought I should have insisted upon different arrangements. Later I had it out with Summerfield over his lack of control of the situation. I was probably too rough and unsympathetic to the political predicament that Summerfield had on his hands in Indiana, a state with a Democratic governor, where Jenner, the Republican candidate for the United States Senate, urgently needed a prominent role at the Eisenhower rally. On the other hand it seemed to me at the time that Summerfield was too ready to sacrifice Eisenhower's personal wishes and feelings for the sake of party politics.

Summerfield became national chairman in that first campaign for the same reason that Knowland became majority leader in the Senate. Striving to maintain a neutral and disinterested position, Eisenhower kept away from behind-the-scenes party maneuvering, and refused after he was nominated to have anything to say about the selection of a national chairman. At that time the Republican leaders were logically seeking to piece the party together and consolidate the warring Taft and Eisenhower forces. Summerfield was regarded as a Taft man, but he was acceptable to the Eisenhower followers for a number of reasons. For one thing he had agreed not to swing his Michigan delegation to Taft before the convention.

But Eisenhower did have a great deal to say about the selection of Richard M. Nixon as his vice-presidential running mate in 1952. "I had a list of names," he said to me when we talked about Nixon some time later, "and Nixon headed it." Eisenhower added that he did not realize until afterward that Nixon was only thirty-nine years old at the time. Realizing that in the campaign he was going to face the McCarthy issue of Communists in the federal government, Eisenhower wanted above all a vice-presidential nominee with a demonstrable record of anti-Communism. Nixon, the investigator of Alger Hiss, was eminently qualified in that respect. He was also strongly recommended by Herbert Brownell, on whom Eisenhower had depended heavily for advice and guidance. Eisenhower and Brownell had dinner alone one evening in Chicago during the convention and talked about Nixon.

I well remember the meeting of Republican leaders who gathered in a rather small parlor at the Conrad Hilton Hotel the afternoon after Eisenhower was nominated to go through the procedure of agreeing upon a vice-presidential candidate. They were packed in tightly, talking among themselves happily about the Eisenhower victory. The group included Brownell, who presided, Lodge, Dewey and six other Republican governors beside myself, Senators Duff, Carlson, Seaton and Smith of New Jersey, Sinclair Weeks, General Lucius Clay, Paul Hoffman, Christian Herter, Summerfield, Harry Darby, Ralph Cake and a handful of other Republican National Committee officials. Brownell called the meeting to order in his quiet, prosy monotone. It reminded me of a ward committee in Philadelphia discussing the selection of a candidate for alderman. It was by no means obvious that the decision on Nixon had already been made by Eisenhower, on the recommendation of his principal advisers, Brownell, Lodge, Dewey and Duff.

Senator Smith spoke up first, proposing consideration of Taft as a move toward party harmony, and there was talk about it. Brownell and Lodge made no move to oppose it. Summerfield said he thought it was a fine idea. Weeks remarked that if nominating Taft as the vice-presidential candidate was the only way the Republicans could promote party harmony he was all for it. But, he added, Taft was more needed by the party on the floor of the Senate than in the presiding officer's chair. Russel Sprague ventured the opinion that if Taft was Eisenhower's running mate the Republicans would not carry New York.

A number of other names were then mentioned, but the choice soon narrowed down to Nixon and Governor Driscoll of New Jersey. Senator Carlson was called from the room to the telephone. He returned, explaining that the call had been from Taft. The Ohio Senator had a message that he wanted Carlson to deliver to the meeting: he had promised to suggest to the group for consideration as a vice-presidential candidate the name of Everett Dirksen.

That caused a stir in the room. On the convention floor a few nights before, Dirksen, who was to become in later years the Republican leader in the Senate and a valued convert to Eisenhower's theories, had argued loudly against the Ike forces about the qualifications of the Georgia delegation. Approaching the climax of his remarks, he had paused dramatically to glare at Dewey and the New York delegation, pointed his finger in their direction and shouted, "Re-examine your hearts before you take this action. We followed you before and you took us down the path to defeat." Then, pointing at Dewey, he cried out, "And don't take us down that road again!"

Dirksen's unjustified attempt to link the Eisenhower cause of 1952 with the Dewey defeats of 1944 and 1948 turned the Ike supporters bitterly against him. And here was Carlson relaying Taft's suggestion of Dirksen as a vice-presidential candidate.

The deep voice of Governor Beardsley of Iowa was heard as he spoke in calm, measured tones. "Mr. Chairman, all I have to say is that after what Dirksen said the other night, the people of Iowa wouldn't use him to wipe their feet on."

That was the end of Dirksen. Brownell called quickly for a show of hands on Nixon, who had been suggested by Wes Roberts. Every hand in the room went up and there was a bustle and scraping of chairs as we immediately adjourned and hurried back to the convention hall.

3 Campaign Highlights

Two months later, many of the people who voted for Nixon at that meeting wanted to have him dropped from the Republican ticket. The New York *Post* came out with its so-called exposé of the "Nixon Fund," which had been raised by California admirers of the vice-presidential candidate in 1950 to help defray his political expenses. Eisenhower knew nothing of the fund's existence before the uproar about it started that September while we were campaigning in Iowa and Nebraska. Neither did I nor anybody else on Eisenhower's staff, as far as I know, but the fund was not a secret. During the previous two years Nixon had mentioned it to several people and had answered questions from newsmen about it. So the New York *Post*'s exposé of it was really not an exposé at all. As was to be expected, the Democrats seized upon the story. What was not to be expected was the alacrity with which some Republican newspapers called for Nixon's elimination from the ticket. Even the New York *Herald Tribune,* Eisenhower's favorite paper and an influential voice in the Republican party, editorially advised Nixon to make a formal offer of withdrawal.

It was a difficult predicament for Eisenhower. Many of his close personal friends and supporters, especially from the political independents and the Citizens-for-Eisenhower groups, lost no time in opposing Nixon. Summerfield and the National Committee generally came to his defense. Taft thought the whole matter was ridiculous. Eisenhower was deeply concerned with the effect upon voter opinion if Nixon were replaced on the ticket as a result of this episode. "There is one thing I believe," Eisenhower said to me privately, "if Nixon has to go, we cannot win."

Eisenhower turned for guidance to Herbert Brownell, who had gone back to his law practice in New York after the July convention. Brownell was summoned to Cincinnati, where he met the Eisenhower campaign train. He and I sat down with Eisenhower in the General's private car, with the shades on the windows carefully lowered, and discussed the Nixon situation. Brownell did most of the talking in his quiet, calm manner. He advised Eisenhower not to take any stand, one way or the other, on whether Nixon should be kept on the ticket until after Nixon had a chance to present his own case to the American people, as we arranged for him to do the following Tuesday on the NBC television and CBS and Mutual radio networks. This was sound advice, but it was a risky and unpopular tightrope for Eisenhower to straddle at that time. His silence stirred up many false and capricious reports of battles between the allegedly pro-Nixon National Committee and the reputedly anti-Nixon entourage of Eisenhower.

The next few days were hectic ones for all of us on the Eisenhower campaign train. I arranged through Paul Hoffman in California for an independent and nonpartisan analysis and audit of the Nixon fund, which was found to be legal and aboveboard. We also raised $75,000 in pledges from three Republican organizations to pay for the television and radio time for Nixon's presentation. I kept in close touch with Ralph Cake at the Eisenhower headquarters in New York, where voluminous reports on popular reaction to the Nixon issue were pouring in from all sections of the country. We were also receiving highly valuable reports from the Gerard Lambert public opinion sounding organization, which had been working for us since August. The Lambert reports from opinion seekers scattered all over the nation proved to be more reliable than any of the several private polls being conducted at the time. On that Monday, September 22, the day before Nixon's now-famous appeal to the people on television and radio, Eisenhower's friends and independent supporters were urging him more strongly than ever to remove Nixon from the ticket. But on the same day, the Lambert polls showed that less than 20 per cent of the people interviewed saw anything wrong with the Nixon fund, and only 10 per cent said that the outcry over the fund would make them less likely to vote for an Eisenhower-Nixon ticket.

On Tuesday night, when Nixon with his wife Pat at his side, appeared on television from the NBC studio at the El Capitan Theater in Hollywood, Eisenhower and his campaign group were in Cleveland. We watched Nixon on a television screen in the manager's office upstairs above the auditorium of the Convention Hall, where Eisenhower was scheduled to speak right after Nixon went off the air. The General sat on a couch with Mrs. Eisenhower in front of the television set and the rest of us, about thirty people, were crowded around the sides of the room. The Nixon telecast was also being shown to the large crowd in the auditorium downstairs who had come to hear Eisenhower speak. It was by far the most eagerly awaited political talk ever given on television up to that time. According to the Neilsen estimate, nine million television sets, half of all the TV receivers then in use in the whole country, were tuned in on Nixon.

Eisenhower was visibly moved and deeply impressed by Nixon's dramatic appeal. He turned to his wife when the broadcast ended and said that he thought Nixon was a completely honest man. We could hear that the crowd of thirteen thousand people in the auditorium downstairs was also carried away by Nixon. They were cheering and shouting their approval. Eisenhower conferred hurriedly with a few of us and decided to replace his prepared speech with a talk about Nixon's performance. Most of the people were ushered out of the room while Eisenhower sat down at the long table beside the television set and began to write out in longhand what he planned to say. As he worked thoughtfully on his talk, he could hear the crowd downstairs that awaited him stamping its feet in rhythm and roaring, "We want Nixon! We want Nixon!"

A few minutes later Eisenhower arose from the table and went into an adjoining office with Jim Hagerty, Arthur Summerfield, Jerry Persons, Robert Humphreys and me and read aloud to us what he had written. He praised Nixon's courage and honesty but he did not yet say definitely whether he had decided to keep him on the ticket. "I am not ducking any responsibility," he said. "I am not going to be swayed . . . by what will get the most votes. . . . I am going to say: do I myself believe this man is the kind of man America would like to have for its Vice President?"

Robert Humphreys suggested that a message should be sent to Nixon about his performance on television. Eisenhower quickly dictated a telegram, which Jim Hagerty wrote down, and this message was added to the speech that the General gave downstairs a few minutes later. In the telegram, Eisenhower told Nixon that his presentation had been "magnificent," adding, however, that before he could "complete the formulation of a decision I feel the need of talking to you and would be most appreciative if you could fly to see me at once. Tomorrow night I shall be at Wheeling, West Virginia."

On the Pacific Coast, Nixon was at first highly elated by the widely favorable reaction to his television and radio talk. Then he was deeply hurt and disappointed by the tone of reservation in Eisenhower's telegram and in his talk at Cleveland. Nixon felt that Eisenhower could have come out immediately with unqualified support of his running mate instead of postponing a decision until they had a face-to-face meeting. Nixon talked to his associates about resigning from the ticket. When he went over the events of that momentous evening later with his biographer, Earl Mazo, he explained that just before he went on the air with his emotional appeal to the people, he received a telephone call from Governor Dewey. Dewey told him that most of the Republican leaders wanted him to withdraw. After the broadcast, when he learned that Eisenhower was still hesitating about a decision, Nixon connected this hesitancy with the jarring telephone call from Dewey. "We were all on edge and quite high-strung at the time," Nixon recalled.

Nixon sent a cool reply to Eisenhower's request for a meeting in Wheeling the next evening. He said he was leaving Los Angeles for Missoula, Montana, to resume his interrupted campaign tour and that he would not be back in the East for the rest of that week. The only ones in our party who knew that night in Cleveland that Nixon was seriously considering pulling himself out of the ticket were Summerfield and Humphreys. They heard that disturbing news in a telephone conversation with Murray Chotiner, who was with Nixon in Los Angeles, and they kept it to themselves overnight, hoping that they could persuade Nixon to change his mind and fly to Wheeling the next day.

Summerfield and Humphreys managed to reach Nixon by phone in Missoula the next morning at six o'clock, Cleveland time, and they took turns talking to him persuasively. Finally Nixon agreed to fly to Wheeling for a reunion with Eisenhower, provided that Eisenhower would assure him, before he made the trip, that he was to remain as the vice-presidential nominee. Even though it was only six o'clock

in the morning, Humphreys discovered that, while he and Summerfield were pleading and arguing on the telephone with Nixon, a group
of Cleveland newspaper reporters were huddled against the door of
his hotel room, trying to eavesdrop on the conversation. He ran the
newsmen off, and went back to the telephone with Summerfield to
make arrangements for the meeting in Wheeling. At nine o'clock they
made contact with me when our campaign train stopped at Portsmouth, Ohio, on its way to West Virginia. I brought Eisenhower into
a phone booth at the railroad depot, where he told Summerfield to
assure Nixon that as far as he was concerned Nixon would remain on
the ticket. Eisenhower had already made that decision privately and
he was merely waiting until he and Nixon could appear together to
announce it publicly. This was relayed to Nixon in Montana and
the vice-presidential candidate began his long flight to Wheeling.
Humphreys said later that in the feverish work of pacifying Nixon
and making arrangements with him and Eisenhower and with the
people in Wheeling for that night's meeting he and Summerfield were
on the telephone constantly in their Cleveland hotel room from six
until ten o'clock, in their pajamas and with no breakfast.

By a happy coincidence, I had invited Senator Knowland, Nixon's
colleague from California in the Senate, to join our campaign train
group a few days earlier. Knowland was a valuable liaison man to
have with us while we were getting Nixon and Eisenhower together.
He was a great help in smoothing over this difficult misunderstanding
because he knew Nixon privately much better than either Eisenhower
or I did at that time. In fact, I had then seen Nixon only twice, once
in Chicago after he was nominated, when he came to Eisenhower's
room at the Blackstone Hotel to thank the General for choosing him,
and once in Denver, when he talked over campaign plans with us. I
think Eisenhower had seen him hardly more than that either.

I was with Eisenhower when he met Nixon's plane in Wheeling
that night and I rode in the same car with the two candidates when
they drove from the airport to the stadium, where they appeared together at the outdoor rally. Eisenhower never said a word in his
conversation with Nixon about the strain that had been put on their
relationship by the Nixon fund controversy or about the pressure
that had been exerted on him to drop Nixon from the ticket. Nor did
he mention Nixon's refusal the night before of the request for a meet-

ing in Wheeling. As a matter of fact, Eisenhower did not say a word of criticism of any kind about the whole episode. That may be rather hard to believe, but that is the way Eisenhower is. He only sympathized with Nixon about what Nixon had gone through in the past week. Nixon talked about the favorable reaction to his radio and television appeal and said he believed that the tide of critical opinion had turned, as, indeed, it had. After his dramatic talk on the air, opposition to him within the Republican ranks virtually disappeared, thus ending the most dramatic episode of the campaign.

There were many memorable highlights in the hectic 1952 campaign, but one that I remember especially was the preparation of Eisenhower's famous "I shall go to Korea" speech, which gave his closing drive in the week before the election the big, dramatic push that routed the Democrats in defeat. A key figure in Eisenhower's creative idea department was C. D. Jackson, now the publisher of *Life* magazine. Jackson brought into our speech-writing team an able colleague, Emmet Hughes, then *Life*'s text editor and formerly a foreign correspondent for *Time*. Eisenhower was scheduled to speak at the Masonic Temple in Detroit on October 24, and all of us agreed that an extra-spectacular message would be needed that night to bring the campaign to an exciting climax. One of our strongest weapons was the unsettled Korean War, which some Republican orators had been calling "Truman's War." Hughes was assigned to work on a speech for Detroit that would be a hard-hitting attack on the Democratic administration's inability to bring the conflict in Korea to a peaceful close. While he was drafting the speech, Hughes was struck by the dramatic possibilities in having Eisenhower promise that he would make a personal trip to Korea. He built up a discussion of foreign policy centered on the Korean situation that came to a stirring finish with Eisenhower declaring, "That job requires a personal trip to Korea. I shall make that trip. I shall go to Korea!"

When a political speech writer comes up with a good speech, his big problem is, ironically enough, to keep it away from the candidate's campaign managers, friends and various advisers and assorted hangers-on. Everybody wants to get in on the act. It has been said that Lincoln's Gettysburg Address was effective because nobody was around to suggest changes after Lincoln jotted it down on the train that day. Hughes tried out the Korean War speech first on Brownell,

Arthur Vandenberg and Harold Stassen at our New York headquarters in the Hotel Commodore while Eisenhower was campaigning in New England. They liked it. Then Hughes showed the speech to C. D. Jackson, who was all for it too. Hughes and Jackson plotted ways and means of keeping Eisenhower's staff advisers and the politicians on the campaign train from tampering with it. They agreed that even if the rest of the speech was revised, chopped up or scuttled they would fight to the end to keep in Eisenhower's pledge to make a personal trip to Korea.

Jackson and Stassen brought the speech to Buffalo, where Eisenhower was to appear the night before he arrived in Detroit. Before Jackson sprang the grand idea of a promise to go to Korea on Eisenhower, he drew me aside and sounded me out on it. I did not hesitate to endorse it, but I warned Jackson that Eisenhower would have to be convinced clearly in his own mind that he would be able later to point to something in the way of accomplishment from such a trip to Korea. Otherwise the whole plan would be bound to backfire, I said.

Jackson read the speech aloud to Eisenhower that evening in Buffalo while the General was stretched out on the bed in his hotel room, his head propped up on pillows, resting after the day of touring in New York State. A small audience consisting of Robert Cutler, Gabriel Hauge, Fred Seaton, Stassen and myself listened to every word intently. Jackson staged a masterly performance. When he reached the climactic "I shall go to Korea!" it sounded fine and there was no opposition from any of us. Later that night, however, Jackson had a bad moment. At the dinner where he was appearing in Buffalo, Eisenhower sat next to Governor Dewey. He turned to Jackson during the dinnner and asked him to show the speech to Dewey. Jackson turned pale. He could imagine what Dewey might do to the "I shall go to Korea" idea if he could lay his hands on it. Jackson hesitated, thought fast, and stammered something about the dinner table being the wrong place to edit an important campaign speech. The crisis was temporarily averted.

Jackson faced a worse ordeal the next day on the train when we went through the Gethsemane that Eisenhower always suffered during the final drafting of every major speech. At each whistle stop on that journey to Detroit, politicians flocked aboard with suggestions about what the candidate ought to say that night. Among them was Knowland, with a speech of his own in his pocket that he wanted to substitute for Hughes's speech. "After all, General," Knowland said at one point, "I come from California, a part of the country considerably closer to Korea than where Jackson comes from!" But Eisenhower never gave in to the self-appointed editors and the speech remained pretty much as Hughes had written it. We knew it was right long before Eisenhower delivered it. When mimeographed copies of it were distributed to reporters on the train, they said to us excitedly, as soon as they saw the "I shall go to Korea" line, "That does it— Ike is in." The speech had the same immediate effect on the audience in Detroit and on the television and radio audiences across the country. As Jack Bell, the Associated Press political reporter, wrote of the Detroit speech later, "For all practical purposes, the contest ended that night." It was said later that Adlai Stevenson's advisers also had the idea of having their candidate promise the voters that he would make a trip to Korea if he was elected. But Stevenson turned down the suggestion.

Mrs. Adams and I spent Election Day quietly in New York, having voted by absentee ballots. We invited Bobby Cutler to join us that afternoon for a trip to the Bronx Zoo. When we returned to the Commodore, where we were to await the returns with Eisenhower that night, Sinclair Weeks asked us where we had been. My wife explained that we had been at the zoo, watching the wild animals.

"Quite a change from a political campaign," Weeks remarked.

"No, not much," Rachel said quietly.

My greatest satisfaction on that Election Night was making a telephone call, after we went to our room around midnight, to Gerard Lambert in Princeton, New Jersey. In August this eminent surveyor of public opinion, whose soundings of voters' views were of great value to us during the campaign, warned us that we would be wasting time trying to win support in the South. I argued that Eisenhower had a good chance of taking Texas inasmuch as he had been born in that state. Lambert offered me odds of one thousand to one against such an upset, and he was so positive that Eisenhower could not win more than 36.8 per cent of the Texas vote that he asked me to acknowledge his prediction in writing so that he could preserve a record of my disagreement in his files. When I called him at his home on Election Night I could tell from his disgruntled tone of voice that I had roused him from his bed.

"I suppose you're calling me to say that Ike has carried Texas," Lambert said. "Well, I had that figured out yesterday."

The day after Eisenhower was elected, he invited Brownell to come to his home at Morningside Heights to talk with him about the selection of a Cabinet and he asked me to sit in on their meeting. He wanted to explain to Brownell the procedure that he planned to use in picking his Cabinet members and other principal officers in the executive branch of the government. Brownell and General Lucius Clay were to serve as a two-man nominating committee that would suggest to Eisenhower a choice of several available and well-recommended candidates for each vacancy. I think Eisenhower at that time had more confidence in Brownell's political advice than he had in anyone else's and in General Clay he had a close friend and counselor, a tough-fibered and keen observer who had taken hold of many a difficult situation for the President-elect. Eisenhower told Brownell that he and General Clay could consult, on a limited basis, with whomever they pleased in drawing up the lists of suggested candidates and he mentioned certain people—Taft and Dewey among them— who might be helpful in recommending likely prospects for some of the Cabinet posts. Eisenhower made it plain, however, that he himself would make the final choice and that he wanted to be given a selection of several names for each position so that he could be free to pick the man for the job on his own responsibility.

At the time of his election, Eisenhower probably had made up his mind definitely about only two of the men that he hoped to appoint, John Foster Dulles for Secretary of State and Joseph M. Dodge as Budget Director, a post of Cabinet rank. If Brownell and General Clay had any other candidates to suggest for those two posts, Eisenhower would have been ready to consider them, but I do not recall that anyone else was seriously mentioned for either the State or Budget chairs at the Cabinet table. As Eisenhower had said often, he made no promises to anybody during, or before, the campaign, but if he had avoided a definite commitment to Dulles or Dodge, I am sure that they were not exactly caught unawares when he asked them to join his administration. Eisenhower had several long talks about foreign policy with Dulles in Europe during the spring of 1952 and also sought his advice during the campaign. Of Dulles' capability and training for his forthcoming duties, Eisenhower often would say to some of us, "You know, Foster seems to sense the intricacies of what those people are driving at better than anybody I have listened to." But Brownell and I are both quite sure that Eisenhower did not formally invite Dulles to be his Secretary of State until several days after he was elected President. He wanted to be free to look over the field carefully.

Eisenhower became an admirer of the remarkably talented and modest Joe Dodge shortly after World War II when Dodge reorganized the German banking system and developed an economic program for Japan. Dodge and his wife were invited to New York on Election Day to spend that evening with the Eisenhowers as they listened to the voting returns and I knew Dodge was scheduled for the budget directorship as soon as Eisenhower was elected.

George Humphrey and Charles E. Wilson were Eisenhower's next choices. They were approached by General Clay when they were at Sea Island, Georgia, attending a meeting of the Business Advisory Council with Clay during the first week of December, a month after the election. When they expressed to Clay their willingness to serve as the Secretaries of the Treasury and Defense, Eisenhower invited them to his office at the Hotel Commodore and gave them those posts. Eisenhower did not actually ask anybody to join his Cabinet until after Brownell or Clay had settled all questions of the candidate's availability and readiness to accept the position. Henry Cabot Lodge, who had been surprisingly defeated for re-election to the Senate in Massachusetts by John F. Kennedy that November, was invited by Brownell and Clay to state his preference for any position he wanted in the administration. Lodge could have had the place in the White House that Eisenhower later offered to me, but he was more interested in foreign affairs. Being well aware that Dulles would be Eisenhower's choice as Secretary of State, Lodge traveled with Brownell and Clay to Augusta, where Eisenhower was resting up after the campaign and the election and asked for and promptly received his first choice—the ambassadorship to the United Nations.

While the other Cabinet members were being selected and screened by his nominating committee, Eisenhower returned from Augusta to New York to prepare for his promised trip to Korea. On his way north, he stopped in Washington for a discussion with President Truman about routine matters connected with the change-over of the government administration. Eisenhower went to the White House with cool reluctance and had little to say to Truman during his visit; he could never forget the personal attacks that Truman had made on him during the campaign. Because Eisenhower was never trained as a politician and had no personal experience with the give-and-take that the professional politicians regard as part of their occupation, he did not so easily shrug off campaign oratory after the election was over. Eisenhower had been particularly hurt by Truman's approval of the Democratic charge that Eisenhower had been politically involved in the Yalta and Potsdam deals that gave East Germany, Poland and China to the Communists. Truman had also said that Eisenhower shared the same platform during the campaign with Senator Jenner when Jenner called General Marshall a traitor. This, of course, was not true. Nobody ever abused General Marshall in Eisenhower's presence; Jenner had made his attack on Marshall in the Senate long before Eisenhower started to campaign. In all of the six years I was with Eisenhower in the White House he made it a point to have nothing whatever to do with Truman, except for one casual nod of recognition when he encountered his predecessor at the funeral of Chief Justice Fred Vinson in 1953. One of the few times I saw Eisenhower angry was when Eric Johnston and Nixon came to him in 1957 with a plan for a big rally in support of mutual security at which he would appear side by side with Truman. Although mutual security is a cause close to Eisenhower's heart, he put his foot down hard on appearing on the same program with his predecessor. There was something more fundamental behind this than simply campaign disaffection. The truth was, as I learned from my own careful observation, that Eisenhower had little respect for Truman the President.

It was Truman who hit the ceiling three weeks after his session with Eisenhower when he read in the newspapers that the President-elect had accepted an invitation from General Douglas MacArthur to listen to a solution to the Korean War that MacArthur offered to give him. Eisenhower was then on his trip to Korea that he had promised in Detroit at the close of the campaign. While he was aboard the cruiser *Helena* in the Pacific he heard that back in New York, at a meeting of the National Association of Manufacturers, MacArthur said he had a "clear and definite" formula for ending the war in Korea without "increased danger of provoking universal conflict." MacArthur would not say to the public what his plan was but he offered to give it to Eisenhower in private.

Eisenhower immediately sent word to MacArthur that he would be glad to meet with him when he returned to the United States. MacArthur's reply of thanks to Eisenhower included a back-handed slap at Truman, the President who had relieved him of his command in the Far East. "This is the first time that the slightest official interest in my counsel has been evidenced since my return," MacArthur said.

Truman read this exchange on his way back to Washington from his mother-in-law's funeral in Missouri. He lost no time issuing a heated statement suggesting that if MacArthur had a plan for ending the Korean War it should be submitted at once to the proper authorities in the government. The next day at a press conference he lit into both MacArthur and Eisenhower, doubting that MacArthur had any kind of a workable plan and charging that Eisenhower's trip to Korea was political demagoguery.

Soon after Eisenhower returned to New York he met with MacArthur but they never disclosed the plan. I was curious about it, along with everybody else, but I never asked Eisenhower what it was until I visited him in Newport last summer a few months before he went out of office.

The solution was a precisely stated intention to drop an atom bomb after full notification to the North Koreans of our purposes. MacArthur was sure that there was not the remotest chance we would actually have to carry out our threat; the Communists would simply throw up their hands and the war would be over. Although not as blunt and specific as MacArthur had suggested, it was indeed the threat of atomic attack that eventually did bring the Korean War to an end on July 26, 1953.

That spring we moved atomic missiles to Okinawa. In May, during talks with Nehru in India, Dulles said that the United States could not be held responsible for failing to use atomic weapons if a truce could not be arranged. This message was planted deliberately in India so that it would get to the Chinese Communists, as it did. Long afterward, talking one day with Eisenhower about the events that led up finally to the truce in Korea, I asked him what it was that brought the Communists into line. "Danger of an atomic war," he said without hesitation. "We told them we could not hold it to a limited war any longer if the Communists welched on a treaty of truce. They didn't want a full-scale war or an atomic attack. That kept them under some control."

4 The White House Staff and Cabinet

I did not go to Korea with Eisenhower that December because his appointment of me as his assistant, a few days before he left for the Far East, gave me all I could do in New York during every minute of the crowded hours until Inauguration Day. I was literally buried with the work of planning and organizing a White House staff and getting myself familiar with the dimensions of my coming responsibilities. As I have said, when Eisenhower asked me to be the Assistant to the President he never specifically defined my responsibilities or outlined their limits. He never gave me, nor did I ever seek, a delegation of presidential power and authority, as so many capital correspondents and politicians have assumed. I realized that the columnists referred to me as "The Assistant President" and "the second most powerful executive in the government" because my duties in the White House were too broad and general to be described precisely. Eisenhower simply expected me to manage a staff that would boil down, simplify and expedite the urgent business that had to be brought to his personal attention and to keep as much work of secondary importance as possible off his desk. Any power or authority that I exercised while carrying out this appointed task was solely on a *de facto* basis and, except when I was acting on an explicit directive from the President, my duties and responsibilities were implied rather than stated.

Some of the work that I handled as routine in the President's office—and which made me a subject of much lively discussion and

50

criticism in Washington—was the settlement of occasional conflicts between Cabinet Secretaries and among agency heads. I always tried to resolve specific differences on a variety of problems before the issue had to be submitted to the President. Sometimes several meetings were necessary before an agreement was reached. But with a few exceptions I was successful. The exceptions, more often than not, occurred when a Cabinet Secretary and the politicians reached an impasse, and caused the biggest rumpus. When the Iowa delegation and other farm-belt Congressmen became incensed at Benson's refusal to support the price of hogs in 1955, it was all Jerry Persons and I could do to keep many of the Republicans from actually stumping against the administration's farm program.

Generally I found it easy to get people to make their own decisions. If you can keep both sides quiet so that they will listen to a calm and careful outline of the facts in the case, the argument usually finds its own solution. Another effective method was to point out, with emphasis, that a resourceful department head should be able to find an answer himself without expecting the President to find it for him. One day when I was arguing this point with a Cabinet member he snapped at me, "Are you telling me I cannot see the President?"

"No, sir," I said to him. "But if I had a matter of this kind to settle, I'd settle it myself without involving the President."

He settled it himself.

Although there have been claims to the contrary, every responsible top government official in the Eisenhower administration knew that he had access to the President whenever he wanted it. Any allegations that I or any other member of the White House staff used presumptuous or arbitrary tactics to keep high-ranking executives or legislators from seeing Eisenhower are completely false. As often as I took the initiative in getting problems settled in the lower echelons, I was occupied in arranging meetings and conferences between the President and Cabinet people, and often with legislators, on plans and programs that needed topside judgment. Whenever members of Congress requested appointments, Persons and I arranged them unless we knew of good reasons not to do so. We knew, of course, the people with whom Eisenhower saw little purpose in trying to reason. He had only a wry face whenever Senator McCarthy's name was mentioned. Nevertheless, Persons would often ask Eisenhower to see some of the irreconcilables. In such instances Persons never went over my head. We always worked in complete understanding and agreement.

This is not to say that Eisenhower was at all squeamish about seeing anybody who had a chip on his shoulder. While I was in the White House the President was continually facing up to arguments and knocking many chips from many shoulders. Most of his Cabinet members, notably Dulles, Humphrey and Benson, and most of the members of Congress whom he dealt with constantly could hardly be classified as yes-men.

In planning a staff operation for the White House, I took into careful consideration the helpful recommendations of the Hoover Commission as well as the results of a private study sponsored by Temple University, which had examined closely the working procedures of the President's office and its relationships with executive departments and agencies. Eisenhower himself had been taking a keen personal interest before he went into office in suggestions for streamlining federal government organization and had often discussed that complex task with his brother Milton. These talks led to the formation of an advisory council consisting of Nelson Rockefeller, Milton, and Dr. Arthur S. Flemming, an expert on government personnel management. At that time Flemming was on leave as president of Ohio Wesleyan University, and later became Director of Defense Mobilization and Secretary of Health, Education and Welfare. It would have been difficult to find three men who worked together as diligently and accomplished as much as this Advisory Committee on Government Organization, which started its research informally but was given official status by an executive order after Eisenhower took office. The Rockefeller Committee, as it became nicknamed after its chairman, worked with a small, knowledgeable staff and came up with suggestions that rapidly crystallized into specific recommendations that Eisenhower put into action. I spent considerable time with the Rockefeller Committee at its early meetings and with the consultants who had conducted the Temple University studies of the White House. Our original plan for the organization of the President's personal staff followed closely the chart prepared by the Temple University group, with revisions based on Rockefeller Committee recommendations. Its line of command stemmed from the Assistant to the President, who was responsible directly to the President, to the various staff components—the secretaries to the President, the special counsel, the administrative assistants and the special assistants—all nominally under my supervision. This setup was what Eisenhower wanted. We modified and changed it somewhat in later years but basically it stood up well under the heavy pressure of work that never quite snowed us under. "The organization plan must make it plain to everybody that I am looking to you to co-ordinate this office," Eisenhower said to me.

Several key men on the White House staff were picked by Eisenhower himself—James C. Hagerty, the press secretary who had done so well in that capacity during the campaign; General Wilton B. Persons, a long-time associate of Eisenhower, who handled Congressional relations; Emmet Hughes, the chief speech writer; and Thomas E. Stephens, who was Secretary to the President. Before Eisenhower's inauguration, Stephens was slated for the position of Special Counsel and Arthur Vandenberg, Jr., who had been Eisenhower's secretary in Denver and later manager of his New York headquarters, was to fill the post of Appointment Secretary. But for personal reasons Vandenberg was unable to continue with the White House assignment. I suggested Bernard Shanley as Counsel and asked Eisenhower what he thought about Stephens' taking Vandenberg's position. Eisenhower agreed to both changes. It was also Eisenhower who selected the late Brigadier General Paul T. Carroll as his liaison man with the Defense Department. General Carroll held also the new post of staff secretary that we created to control and co-ordinate the daily flood of work into and out of our office. When General Carroll died and I was looking for someone to suggest as his successor, Jerry Persons and Robert Cutler told me about a young colonel named Andrew J. Goodpaster. Persons had watched Goodpaster when they were both at SHAPE and Cutler had worked closely with him at the Pentagon during the war. Their glowing account of Colonel (now Brigadier General) Goodpaster's qualifications prompted me to ask the President about him. No man ever received a higher compliment. "I would ask nothing more than for my son to grow up to be as good a man as he is," Eisenhower said. That settled it. The post is one of the most sensitive in government, requiring the ability to get along with busy executives working under high tension and the judgment to know when gently to apply the needle.

Another innovation, the Cabinet Secretariat, was given the responsibility for arranging the agenda for each Cabinet meeting. For the first time in history there was now an organized staff unit with the explicit duty not only of preparing for the meetings but also of following up to insure that every decision was carried into action. The post of Secretary to the Cabinet went to Maxwell Rabb. A Boston lawyer, he had come to us at the suggestion of Henry Cabot Lodge to serve originally as my assistant, specializing in minority group problems, such as civil rights, immigration and antidiscrimination matters. My other principal assistant, Charles F. Willis, Jr., was assigned to the colossal work of personnel problems, the endless chore of trying to fill government jobs with people who were both competent and acceptable, as well as available. In the early years of the administration, this was by far the most worrisome headache of the President's office.

Eisenhower and I both felt that the complex and wide-ranged variety of work in the White House could be handled most efficiently by a small group of versatile trouble shooters, who could move with knowledge and assurance into any problem that happened to be pressing the President at the moment, whether it involved economics, agriculture, civil rights, party politics, foreign affairs, labor unions, defense, atomic energy or water power. Eisenhower was well aware of the objection to this idea, especially in Congress, as smacking too much of the militaristic Prussian general staff concept. Although Eisenhower never seriously considered trying to put a general staff system into effect in the White House, he and I knew that the varied work of his office could not be neatly compartmentalized and divided among specialists who closed their eyes to everything outside their respective narrow areas of responsibility. I have often thought that if a President could organize a general staff of assistants capable of dealing with anything confronting the White House he would have to have more men like Gabriel Hauge.

Hauge, who is now chairman of the finance committee of the Manufacturers Trust Company in New York, threw a bright beam of light across the whole White House staff operation during the years that he worked for Eisenhower. Like Tom Stephens, another rock of good sense and sound judgment, he was a much more important and valuable figure behind the scenes in the administration than most people in Washington realized. Eisenhower said to me once, "If I had Hauge, Hagerty and Tom Stephens in a room and they agreed on a

course of action, I could feel pretty sure it was the right thing to do."
I found Hauge at the Eisenhower headquarters at Denver when I
arrived in August, 1952, to take over my staff duties. He came to
Eisenhower on the recommendation of the Dewey organization, where
he had worked under Elliot Bell of the McGraw-Hill publishing company. Hauge was one of the ablest men Dewey had. Previously he had
taught economics at Harvard and Princeton and had directed sta-
tistical research for the New York State Banking Department. On the
Eisenhower campaign train in 1952, Hauge labored with Robert
Cutler in what we called a little facetiously "the speech-rescue squad,"
preparing notes for Eisenhower's whistle stop talks and revising the
final drafts of major speeches. I learned then that Hauge's outstanding
quality was versatility; along with his fine grasp of economics as it
applied to public affairs—he understands, for example, the Federal
Reserve System, something that not too many people comprehend—
he could write about and discuss almost anything in the wide field of
federal government responsibilities with an unusual command of the
language. Eisenhower was impressed by Hauge, too, but after the
election I had some difficulty persuading him to add Hauge to our
staff. Eisenhower thought of Hauge primarily as an economist and he
was not sure that he needed a personal economic adviser in the White
House. It was the old question that we had gone over for many an
hour with the Rockefeller Committee and other experts: should the
President's staff be composed of specialists in the field of banking and
finance, for example, or should it be selected for well-rounded versatility, depending on Treasury officials, the Council of Economic Advisers and such for economic advice? Fortunately, Eisenhower was
won over in favor of Hauge because he decided that this particular
economist could also be useful as a writer and a general adviser, which
indeed he was.

Incidentally, Eisenhower was to learn, too, as his years in the
White House went on, that the President does need opinions on fiscal
problems constantly from a staff economist like Hauge who has a
comprehensive understanding of the effect of the policies of the federal government upon private business. The need of a composite
judgment in these decisions can hardly be overestimated. In the early
days of his administration, Eisenhower had another sound analyst in
Joe Dodge, who possessed a rare insight into the whole field of the

relationship between government and business. For a banker, Dodge had a mature sense of public responsibility in shaping federal policy. With Humphrey's great knowledge of business and finance, Eisenhower had the advantage of breadth of view in keeping to the middle of the road. While he had great respect for Humphrey's judgment, it seemed to him that Humphrey was sometimes too quick to think of government economic problems in the terms of private industry and occasionally too impatient for fast action.

Eisenhower came to have a high regard for Hauge's calm way of sticking firmly to his convictions under the stress of an argument, respecting the opposition's objections without being upset or shaken by them and never backing away from a showdown. Hauge felt the same way about Eisenhower; one of the few ornaments on the President's uncluttered desk was a small block of dark wood, given to him by Hauge, inscribed with a line in Latin that said, "Gentle in manner, strong in deed."

Tom Stephens was something else again. "There's a fellow who never says much, but somehow he seems to grow on you," Eisenhower once said of him. Born in Ireland, Stephens studied law after working as a real estate title searcher and insurance fraud investigator, became skilled in Republican politics in Dewey's 1948 campaign and served as John Foster Dulles' administrative assistant when Dulles was appointed to fill an interim term in the Senate in 1949. As an agent for Dewey and Brownell, Stephens had bird-dogged around the country lining up Eisenhower delegates before the 1952 convention. He was Eisenhower's appointment secretary during the campaign, hustling the visiting firemen and campfire girls in and out of our special train and hotel suites without a casualty. Shrewd and humorous, he was a penetrating judge of people and an entertaining character who saw to it that the atmosphere in the White House never became oppressively dull. One time when he was in Denver with the President, Stephens became solemnly involved in a business partnership with a grizzled silver prospector. On the occasion of Jerry Persons' fifty-eighth birthday, he arranged for a Chinese-American Secret Service man named Alfred Wong to impersonate an administrative assistant to Chiang Kai-shek who purported to do the same sort of legislative liaison work for Chiang as Persons did for Eisenhower. Persons was clearly impressed with this demonstration of staff devotion.

It was Stephens who developed the theory that when Eisenhower came to his office in the morning wearing a brown suit the President's staff was in for a tense and trying day. He would stand watch at the glass door to the oval office in the West Wing that the President entered every morning at the end of the short walk through the portico from his residence. If it was a brown suit Eisenhower had on, Stephens would relay an alert signal to the office staff.

During that last hectic month in the Commodore before we moved to Washington, when I was organizing the White House staff, we were deluged, from the President on down, with the work of filling the countless and various jobs in the government that were to be vacated by the change from the Democratic to the Republican administration. Finding the right people was hard enough in itself. Harold Talbott, who was to serve later as Secretary of the Air Force until he became involved in a conflict-of-interests situation, established an office in the Commodore with a small staff that worked on compiling a long list of names, drawn from all walks of life, of desirable candidates. From this list we drew many good prospects whom we would not have known about otherwise, such as the late Roger Steffan, my assistant in charge of the management of the White House in the early days of the administration. But finding a likely appointee was only part of the battle. He still had to be persuaded to pull up stakes in his home town and private business or profession and to move his family to Washington, usually at a substantial financial sacrifice. This was not all. He had to be cleared for security with the Federal Bureau of Investigation and for political acceptability with the senior Republican Senator of his state or, where there was no such Senator, with the Republican state organization. When Martin Durkin, a Truman Democrat, was Secretary of Labor, the filling of administrative positions in his department was an ordeal. It seemed as though almost every man that Durkin suggested for Eisenhower's approval was a prominent New Deal Democrat, the very type of federal official that the Republican party was trying to clear out of Washington.

The whole process of political patronage and the pressure put upon the White House to provide federal jobs for Republican politicians to hand out as favors was a constant annoyance to Eisenhower while he was President. He wanted no part of it, and still he could not turn away from one of the most important duties of the presidency. He properly insisted on making the final decision on his own appointees and carefully avoided giving the Republican National Committee any responsibility in the selection of government officials, a duty the committee would have been happy to assume. Eisenhower insisted that the members of the Cabinet and his own staff have the final recommendations on the capability and the qualifications of the executive heads of the government whose appointment was his sole responsibility.

Eisenhower selected and appointed his Cabinet before consulting any of the powers in the Republican side of the Congress. This created quite a stir in Washington. A delegation of Republican Senators, Taft, Bridges, Millikin and Saltonstall, came to Eisenhower in New York and pointed out to him that they had certain traditional prerogatives that they wanted observed. It was customary, they explained to him, to clear each presidential appointee with the Republican Senators of the appointee's home state. They recognized, they said, the right of the President to have whom he wanted in his Cabinet, but it was implicit that they hoped there would be no more appointments like Martin Durkin. As to the rest, they wanted to be consulted. Eisenhower was in something of a quandary. He wanted to get along with the legislative leadership, but the Senators' admonition made him a little indignant. He was aware of the tradition of "senatorial courtesy," which gives a Senator the privilege of barring a suggested nominee from a federal appointment if the nominee is "personally obnoxious" to the Senator. But Eisenhower did not believe that for purely personal reasons this privilege should be exercised as a veto over Cabinet appointments. He did not agree that the Senators from New York, for example, should have the privilege of sidetracking the appointment of John Foster Dulles simply because he might be "personally obnoxious." Picking the Cabinet was his personal business, Eisenhower felt. Years later, when the Senate refused to confirm his nomination of Lewis Strauss as Secretary of Commerce, Eisenhower was astonished and incensed.

When it came to obtaining political approval of appointees in those states having no Republican Senators, the delegation had no pat formula. Nobody had an answer that would fit every case. "In some states, the governor is the one to deal with," Eisenhower said, while describing the delegation's visit later at a Cabinet meeting. "In another state, the Senator is everything. In the South, it may be a Democrat-for-Eisenhower. Anyway, no matter whom you ask me to appoint, the Senate has to approve of him."

Eisenhower gave each Cabinet member and agency director complete responsibility for his department and almost never intervened in the selection of their assistants and other key personnel. He told me on one occasion that one of the rare instances in which he departed from this hands-off policy was when he suggested that Dulles appoint Lieutenant General Walter Bedell Smith as Under Secretary of State. That appointment caused some grumbling among the Republicans because Smith, Eisenhower's chief of staff in Europe during World War II, had been in the Truman administration as Ambassador to Moscow and Director of the Central Intelligence Agency. A number of the Secretaries in the Eisenhower Cabinet, especially Dulles, Benson, Brownell and his successor, William P. Rogers, drew back sharply from making politically inspired job appointments. Eisenhower himself received suggestions for appointments from members of Congress with polite appreciation, but if a Senator or a Congressman made the mistake of trying to apply pressure to get somebody a job, the President would turn cold immediately. More than once, when a Republican leader sought a favor for somebody who had been helpful to the Eisenhower cause during the 1952 campaign, the President said with vehemence, "I owe no one anything for putting me into this position. I didn't seek this honor, and those who sought it for me did so, not for me, but because they believed it was for the best interests of their country." Now and then, of course, Eisenhower did make an appointment strongly endorsed by the Republicans in Congress but curiously enough the people who were appointed under those circumstances never seemed to work out as well in their assignments. In every such case that came to his attention, Eisenhower took pains to inquire into the sources of the recommendation, and then let it be known through his staff that he was always wary of political endorsements that did not have the benefit of the careful investigations he insisted upon for every one of his own appointments.

Then, too, the Republicans who expected a luscious windfall of federal jobs to fall their way as soon as Eisenhower was elected did not understand that it was impossible after twenty years of uninterrupted Democratic rule to dislodge instantly the firmly entrenched Roosevelt- and Truman-appointed job holders without seriously disrupting the government. At a Cabinet meeting in December, 1953, Eisenhower cited the case of a staunch Democrat who had been appointed director of the Kansas City office of a federal government agency during the Truman administration and was still in his job. The continued presence of this well-known Trumanite in such a prominent position, Eisenhower said, seemed to imply that the Republicans were unable to find one of their party members to replace him. The President urged that the matter be looked into at once. Two of our White House staff men looked into it that same afternoon and found out that the Democrat was being kept in his job for three good reasons:

1. The local Republican state and county committee chairman wanted his employment by the Eisenhower administration continued so that he would not campaign for the Democrats in the next election.

2. The Washington director of the federal agency that employed him reported that he was one of the most efficient district chiefs in the whole country.

3. His daughter was engaged to the son of one of the most important Republican politicians in the Kansas City area.

While he was President, Eisenhower took pains to see to it that nobody received special consideration for a federal job because he claimed a personal friendship with him or with the Eisenhower family. His fear that such an applicant might be hired seemed almost to be an obsession. He delivered a strong warning against such favor seekers at his first meeting with the Cabinet in 1953 and brought up the rule again emphatically from time to time in later years. "If anybody says he wants a job because he's a friend of mine, throw him out of your office," he said. At a Cabinet meeting on July 29, 1955, he issued another reminder. "To my knowledge, this principle has never been violated," he said, "but this week I heard that somebody in one of our departments was going easy on a particular subordinate because that person was supposed to be a friend of mine. May I remind you once again if anybody seeks a favor out of alleged friendship with me, let his plea fall on stony ears." Still worrying about it in 1957, he sent me a note saying that there were many new faces in the government, some of whom might not know of his strict order that any job seeker who claimed special favor because of his personal friendship with the President should have no consideration whatever. Would I see to it that the head of every department and agency was explicitly apprised of his order? I would and did, calling each one of them on the telephone personally to reissue the President's warning against name-dropping job seekers.

The patronage pickings were so lean under Eisenhower that they became a subject of grim humor among the Republican politicians in Washington. At a meeting of legislative leaders not long after Eisenhower went into office, Senator Saltonstall asked Joe Martin, the House's GOP leader, if he had been able to get any new jobs for his constituents from the new administration. "New jobs?" Martin said. "I lost two that I got when Truman was in office."

The first meeting of Eisenhower's Cabinet, on January 12, 1953, was an extraordinary event in the history of the presidency. First of all, it took place not in Washington but at the Commodore in New York. Furthermore, it was held before Eisenhower became President, a week before his inauguration. Aside from its timing, the two-day session was unusual because, in addition to his Secretaries, the group included presidential assistants and directors of important government agencies to whom Eisenhower planned to give Cabinet rank and status. Among these were Henry Cabot Lodge, Ambassador to the United Nations, Director of Defense Mobilization Arthur Flemming, Budget Director Dodge, Director of Mutual Security Harold Stassen, Special Assistant C. D. Jackson, in charge of cold war psychology planning, Robert Cutler, assistant to the President for national security affairs, and myself. As Eisenhower explained it, these officials held positions in the government equal, in his opinion, to those of Cabinet Secretaries in responsibility and importance, but in previous administrations their lack of rank forced them to deal with Cabinet departments at almost a clerical level. Eisenhower aimed to raise their posts to the same rank as Secretaries so that they could work among the top-level officers of the government, where they properly belonged.

Many of the faces at that first Cabinet meeting had been familiar ones during the campaign—Summerfield, who would have to give up the Republican national chairmanship to be Postmaster General, Cutler, Lodge, Brownell, Nixon, Stassen and Weeks. Governor Arthur Langlie of Washington could have had the Interior post but he felt obliged to serve the four-year term as head of his home state, to which he had just been re-elected. Douglas McKay, who was completing his term as Governor of Oregon, was named instead of Langlie. Ezra Taft Benson, who was to have a hard row to hoe for eight years as Secretary of Agriculture, had been recommended by Senator Taft, no relation. When Eisenhower asked Brownell and General Clay to select and screen candidates for the Cabinet, he told them that he would like to have one woman in the group but he said that he had no one particular in mind. Nor did he have any specific Cabinet position reserved for a woman Secretary. Oveta Culp Hobby, Houston newspaper publisher, wartime commanding colonel of the Wacs and Democrats-for-Eisenhower, was an obvious choice because her independent Texas background would add a Southern and bipartisan flavor to the Cabinet. When General Clay talked with her, he asked her if she would accept the directorship of the Federal Security Agency, explaining that Eisenhower was planning to convert the agency into a Cabinet-grade department that would cover the areas of health and education as well as security. With that understanding Mrs. Hobby agreed to take the Security Agency position and in a few months she became the Cabinet's first Secretary of Health, Education and Welfare.

One face in the Cabinet that was brand-new to me was that of Martin P. Durkin, president of the plumbers and steamfitters union and an avowed Truman Democrat, whom Eisenhower had named as his first Secretary of Labor, principally on the recommendation of Stassen. This was a hard appointment for Taft and practically everybody else among the Republican partisans to swallow. Moreover, it was an experiment doomed from the start to failure. In appointing a labor union man to head the Department of Labor, Eisenhower was trying to put into practice a highly commendable theory. He felt that organized labor had had too much access to the White House during the Truman administration and that the President's office had interfered too much in the negotiation of labor-management contracts. He placed one of labor's own men at the command of the Labor Department in the hope that the union leaders would go there with their problems instead of to the White House. But there was too much basic conflict between the strongly prolabor Democratic views of Durkin and the conservative domestic policies of the Eisenhower administration. Durkin lasted only eight months in the Cabinet.

When Durkin's sponsor, Harold Stassen, was appointed Mutual Security Director with a Cabinet member's rank, it was widely and erroneously assumed by politicians that Eisenhower was recognizing a debt that he owed Stassen for the switch of the Stassen-pledged Minnesota delegation, which gave Eisenhower the presidential nomination on the first ballot at the 1952 Republican convention. The fact is that Eisenhower knew he owed Stassen nothing for his nomination at Chicago. Until halfway through the balloting, when it became apparent that Eisenhower was only a few votes away from the nomination, Stassen was still trying to hold on to his delegates, still hoping desperately that there might be an Eisenhower-Taft deadlock and that he might win the nomination as a compromise candidate.

Stassen's performance at the 1952 convention was a strange and curiously unrealistic one for a supposedly professional politician, almost as strange and unrealistic as his attempt to remove Richard Nixon from the Republican ticket in 1956. Back in 1951, when Stassen was president of the University of Pennsylvania, he came to see me in New Hampshire, anxious to find out, among other things, whether I would support him for President if Eisenhower did not become a candidate, or if Eisenhower and Taft became deadlocked in a fight for the nomination. He said he had seen Eisenhower in Paris and had advised him to run for President and he assured me that he would support Ike if the General became a candidate. Meanwhile, he said, he was preparing a campaign of his own in case Eisenhower was not available. During the primaries in 1952, when the Ike bandwagon was beginning to roll, Stassen was urged by his advisers to throw in his lot with Eisenhower, but he refused to do it. Even Eisenhower's powerful showing as a write-in choice of the primary voters in his own home state of Minnesota failed to convince Stassen that his cause was lost. He apparently looked on Eisenhower's rising strength only as something that could stop Taft and turn the convention toward himself.

When the convention opened in Chicago, several of the Minnesota delegates who were pledged to give their first vote to Stassen as a favorite son candidate wanted to change to Eisenhower because of the strong indication that Ike would get the nomination on the first ballot. The chairman of the delegation, Senator Edward J. Thye, felt the same way when he conducted a private survey of Eisenhower's strength and found out that Ike might get as many as 595 votes on the first roll call, as, indeed, he did. He needed only 609 votes to win.

On the morning of the day that the balloting was to begin, the Minnesota delegation caucused in the large hotel suite of Mrs. Elizabeth Heffelfinger, a national committee member from the state, who told Stassen that she and a few other delegates wanted to cast their first vote for Eisenhower. Stassen argued that Eisenhower would not get the nomination on the first ballot and that he himself would win 125 to 150 votes on a second ballot if there was a recess between the two roll calls to enable him to gain time in which to round up more delegates. Stassen disagreed with Thye's estimate of Eisenhower's strength and there was a heated argument, which ended with Thye's announcing that the delegation would keep a close check on Eisenhower's votes during the first roll call and, if he was as strong as Thye expected him to be, the delegation would switch to Eisenhower at the end of the roll call to assure Ike's winning on the first ballot. Stassen was against this, of course, but since Thye was the delegation's chairman there was not much he could do about it.

Halfway into the first ballot, it became clear that Eisenhower was moving strongly. Dan Gainey, Stassen's floor manager, asked Bernard Shanley to call Stassen on the telephone for permission to release the delegation at the end of the roll call. Gainey and Warren Burger, who was also managing Stassen's campaign, had no desire to be left alone on the station platform while the Eisenhower train pulled out without them. The reply that Shanley brought back from Stassen was a baffling one. Stassen said he "hoped" that the delegation would stay with him "until after the convention has recessed and we have a chance to regroup before the second ballot." Knowing that there would be no second ballot, the Minnesotans went for Eisenhower, giving Ike more than he needed for the nomination.

Stassen nevertheless campaigned for Eisenhower after the convention, wrote speeches and statements with considerable ability and worked hard to bring leaders of organized labor into the Republican camp. Besides, he tried with some success to stir up crusades among religious and ethnic groups. By the time of his election, Eisenhower had developed a high regard for Stassen's abilities, which he showed by appointing him Director for Mutual Security and later head of the foreign operations projects. These were jobs of the utmost importance, Eisenhower continually reminded the Cabinet, in maintaining peace and holding together the free world. There is no denying that Stassen was always a forceful and energetic operator but his unpredictable independence of action rubbed people the wrong way, blew up stormy scenes and left him few friends among the more conservative people in the administration. One outspoken Cabinet member asked Eisenhower one day what he saw in Stassen. The President said that he believed Stassen was a broad-visioned Republican liberal with a large following of young progressives who would give the party a new vitality. The Cabinet member shook his head and said, "You could put all of Stassen's followers into a small closet and you wouldn't have any trouble shutting the door."

The first Cabinet meeting opened with a prayer by Ezra Taft Benson, who is one of the Council of Twelve Apostles of the Mormon Church. Eisenhower had asked me to inquire if the Cabinet members felt a prayer appropriate at their meetings. Later, in the White House, the prayer was usually a silent one, after which the President would lift his bowed head and say, "Thank you." The main reason the meeting took place a week before the inauguration was to give the Cabinet an opportunity to hear Eisenhower's inaugural address and to let the members discuss it and criticize it, and also to explain to them the Inauguration Day program. Eisenhower announced that all of them and their families were invited to attend a special service in the morning of that day for the President-elect and his family at the National Presbyterian Church in Washington. He added hastily as an afterthought that, of course, no Cabinet member should feel under any pressure to go to the Presbyterian services; anybody could go instead to a church of his own choice. Eisenhower's religious faith, I learned in the years I worked with him, was a dominant and living force in his life and in his purposes. Always steadfast in his loyalty to his own church, he still had respect for the faith of others and their ways of expressing it. "Each of us has his own problem and none is the same as the others," he once said to me. He was always apprehensive when he was approached by church people to use his position as President to promote or publicize a religious cause.

When Eisenhower finished with his reading of the proposed inaugural address, the Cabinet gave him a warm round of applause. He deserved it. Eisenhower, working long hours with Emmet Hughes, had gone through many drafts of what he wanted to say and it was now close to its final stage.

"I read it far more for your blue pencils than I did for your applause," Eisenhower said. "One reason I wanted to read it to you now is so you can think it over and tear it to pieces."

Charles E. Wilson, whose nomination as Secretary of Defense was already in controversy because of his General Motors stock, was the first to speak up, as he was usually ready to do at every Cabinet meeting. He commended the President-elect for "flying the flag pretty high." Eisenhower remarked that along with waving the flag the inaugural address had to talk about the basic terms of Americanism as they applied to everyday modern living. "This talk is going out to probably one of the greatest audiences that ever heard a speech," he said. "You want every person who hears it to carry home with him a conviction that he can do something."

An inaugural speech, Eisenhower went on, could not sound too much like a lecture from a schoolteacher but it did require a level of dignity that would make it read well at the Quai d'Orsay and at 10 Downing Street.

"Lincoln didn't say, 'Eighty-seven years ago,'" Eisenhower said. "He said, 'Fourscore and seven years ago.' Instantly, on the opening of that speech, that established a certain stateliness."

Dulles wondered if the speech emphasized economics too strongly as a cure for Communism abroad.

"Unless we put things in the hands of the people who are starving to death, we can never lick Communism," Eisenhower said.

"In India today, the great peril of Communism comes from intellectual centers," Dulles said.

Henry Cabot Lodge questioned a description of Moscow in the speech as a place that had changed from a center of autocracy to a center of revolution. This might sound as if the Soviet Union were no longer autocratic, he pointed out, and to many persecuted people in the world the mention of revolution has a dramatic appeal. "You are right," Eisenhower said. There was talk of changing "autocracy" to "despotism," but the whole reference to Moscow was later dropped out of the final draft of the speech.

When Joseph G. McGarraghy, chairman of the Inaugural Committee, and J. Mark Trice, executive secretary of the Joint Congressional Inaugural Committee, outlined the plans for the inauguration ceremonies, Eisenhower questioned them sharply about how long the parade would last. For weeks he had been warning me to see to it that the procession would be over before dark. He wanted the luncheon at the Capitol after the inaugural formalities to be cut short so that the parade could begin and end as early as possible.

"Speaking as one who has marched in one of the blankety-blank things and waited an hour on Pennsylvania Avenue while someone went to lunch in the Treasury, I would like to help out several thousand people who have to wait in the cold," Eisenhower said. "You put those people there all day long and finally they march past the reviewing stand when darkness has hit us. They see all their preparation and work gone and you have made some enemies. To my mind it's a little too bad we can't start this thing at eleven instead of twelve. If that Congressional committee can seat us quickly, I don't see why we can't have a bite to eat in fifteen minutes because the poor devils who march in that parade are going to have nothing to eat at all."

"You have to wait until the stroke of twelve to get the ceremony started because the President's oath goes up to twelve noon on January twentieth," Trice said.

Eisenhower said that in the past on such occasions some people had been guilty of setting the clock forward or backward.

The President-elect broke away from the custom of wearing a tall silk hat on Inauguration Day and prescribed dark Homburgs, dark overcoats, striped trousers and a choice of either cutaways or short dark gray formal jackets, or club coats, as Dodge called them, as the regalia for himself and his staff. The coat and trousers I wore were an inheritance and their labels bore the insignia of A. Shuman and Company, a Boston firm that went out of business around 1920, but I was never properly cited for this signal contribution to antiquarianism. Silk hats had been worn at inaugurations for the previous hundred years and some of the Democrats in Congress objected to this departure from what they called an old tradition. Eisenhower observed that if he was obliged to stick to tradition all of us would have to wear tricornered hats and knee britches. That gave Bobby Cutler an opportunity for a quip:

"If Mrs. Hobby comes in knee britches, I want to be in the front row," Cutler said.

Many other things were discussed in those two days of the first Cabinet meeting—price controls, the projected deficit of nearly ten billion dollars in the coming fiscal year and the gloomy prospects for the tax cut that was a Republican goal, patronage, reorganization of the executive branch of the government, compulsory military training, cold war psychology, and East-West trade. When Sinclair Weeks asked a question about export licenses for trading behind the Iron Curtain, Eisenhower remarked again that in his opinion there was no instrument in diplomacy quite so powerful as trade.

"I am a little old-fashioned," Wilson said. "I don't like to sell firearms to the Indians."

Eisenhower turned on Wilson quickly and said, "You should say first what trade is, and what it is doing. Suppose you couldn't make a single firearm without raw material out of the enemy's country. The last thing you can do is to force all these peripheral countries—the Baltic states, Poland, Czechoslovakia and the rest of them—to depend on Moscow for the rest of their lives. If you trade with them, Charlie, you've got something pulling their interest your way. You immediately jump to guns and ammunition. I am not talking in those terms. It must be selective. You are not going to keep them looking toward us and trying to get out from under that umbrella unless you give them something in the way of inducement to come out. You just can't preach abstraction to a man who has to turn for his daily living in some other direction."

"I am going to be on the tough side of this one," Wilson said.

"Charlie, I am talking common sense," the President-elect said.

The preinaugural Cabinet meeting in the Commodore gave the participants a sense of the direction in which the new administration would be heading and it gave Eisenhower a feeling of the way his team members would work together as a group. It was evident that Dulles would keep close to his own field of foreign affairs, that Wilson would be heard from on almost every subject that came up before the Cabinet, that the persuasive and forceful arguments of Humphrey would be influential in the government and that Dodge would be relied upon in reaching the organizational and fiscal decisions. I felt as the meeting ended that the Cabinet was one of unusual competence that would operate smoothly as a unit.

My only contribution to the Inauguration Day program was to seek the indulgence of James M. Petrillo so that the musicians who were scheduled to perform at the parade, the two inaugural balls and various other events would be free for the day from union restrictions. Petrillo could not have been more co-operative if he had been an Eisenhower Republican. On the morning of the big day, when I was attending to a variety of details in the Eisenhower suite at the Hotel Statler, Tom Stephens asked me if I knew anything about writing prayers. He explained that the President-elect had decided after returning from the services at the National Presbyterian Church to begin his inaugural address with a prayer and he was then in the process of writing it on a sofa in his room. "All I could do about it was to hand him a Bible," Tom said. I said that a prayer was a very personal thing and that I thought it would be better, unless Eisenhower asked us for help, to leave him alone and let him work it out for himself, which he did.

President Truman invited the Eisenhowers to have breakfast at the White House that morning but the invitation was politely declined. When Eisenhower arrived at the executive mansion to pick up the President for the ride that they would take together along Pennsylvania Avenue to the Capitol, he waited outside, assuming that Truman intended to join him there and go on to the Capitol. Truman made a point of mentioning that later in his memoirs, implying that Eisenhower had declined an invitation to come in. Eisenhower was not aware of such an invitation and certainly intended no discourtesy to the President. I never knew Eisenhower to be discourteous to anybody. Truman also said that he and Eisenhower had sat side by side all the way from the White House to the Capitol without speaking to each other. Then, according to Truman, Eisenhower turned to him for the first time and asked him who had ordered Major John Eisenhower home from Korea for the inauguration. Truman replied rather sharply that he had put through the order himself. The ride in silence is easily explained by the tension of the few minutes they were together when Eisenhower's mind turned to the ceremony and the responsibilities ahead. So far as I know, Eisenhower never spoke of this incident; it was the kind of thing he never would talk about to anybody.

Eisenhower was understandably curious about the source of the order returning his son from duty in Korea to the inauguration because John had been concerned about it. The order to return temporarily to Washington for the celebration came to John in Korea about January 8 just after he received a new duty assignment as G-2 of the Third Infantry Division, a coveted post that he had wanted. John felt that it was more important to him to hold on to the G-2 position than to attend his father's inauguration as President, and he wrote to his father about his concern. When he received a rather sharp reply from his father, he realized his protest had been to no avail. Evidently, the order had been issued by someone in Washington out of courtesy to the Eisenhowers and should be politely observed. Later John found out at his divisional headquarters in Korea to his great relief that the trip to the inauguration would not interfere with his G-2 assignment, so he was able to leave happily and enjoy his trip to Washington.

In the meantime, the President-elect naturally wondered who in the Army or in the government had taken it upon himself to bring John home for the inauguration and he asked General Omar N. Bradley, the Chairman of the Joint Chiefs of Staff, about it. Bradley said he knew nothing about the order. This led Eisenhower to put the same question to Truman on their way to the inaugural ceremony. Since the order had evidently by-passed the chain of command, Truman might have felt that Eisenhower was questioning the way that the order had been handled. If so, Truman was mistaken. The President-elect was simply interested to know who had brought back his son from Korea. Although the episode resulted in some ill will, there is no doubt that it was done with the kindest of intentions.

I made a discreet attempt to get out of taking part in the Inauguration Day parade, but I was told that this would be an unthinkable affront to the committee in charge of the event, which had laboriously made a place for me in the procession. Eisenhower's determined effort to get the parade over with in the daylight was to no avail. The last marching units did not pass the reviewing stand until long after dark and it was seven o'clock that evening before the new President could enter his new home. By that time, I had already been at work in the White House for a few hours, showing the staff members where each of them was going to work and lining up their duties for the next day, the next week, getting ready for the next few busy and eventful years.

5 At Work in the White House

Eisenhower always wanted his weekly meetings with the Cabinet, the National Security Council and the legislative leaders, and, on other days, his most important business appointments, to be scheduled for the earliest possible hour of the morning, eight o'clock if at breakfast, eight-thirty, or nine o'clock at the office. This required some members of his official family to make a drastic change in their habits of living. Noting one day that Herbert Brownell had some difficulty in getting to an early Cabinet meeting on time, Eisenhower jocularly held up his Attorney General as an example of "one of those big city boys who need their sleep in the morning." One reason why I worked well with Eisenhower was that I shared his eagerness to be on the job early. I found that among people in high places in Washington this was regarded as odd behavior but it was a habit that I could not break because I had been doing it all of my life. I found it a useful habit because Eisenhower's staff was no place for anybody who had trouble getting to work at seven-thirty.

At that hour I usually met with Tom Stephens to go over some items on the President's work schedule for the day. A check with Ann Whitman, the President's personal secretary, another early riser, often revealed the Eisenhower mood, which was of great help in smoothing out the arrangements for the day's activities. Mrs. Whitman could catch the scent of trouble when the rest of the staff was oblivious to an impending crisis. "The President isn't very happy with the remarks for the Chamber of Commerce meeting this morning," she would confide. That was a signal for me to find out why the President wasn't happy with the remarks and to see to it that something more solid was provided.

If it was a Wednesday, the day that Eisenhower had his weekly press conference, I called the key members of the staff together for breakfast with Jim Hagerty in the basement mess hall of the White House that was operated by the Navy staff from the U.S.S. *Williamsburg,* the presidential yacht that Eisenhower placed in mothballs after he took office because he felt it was a needless expense. Hagerty had the questions lined up that were likely to be asked by the correspondents and he and I and the rest of the staff would figure out how they could best be answered. It was easy enough to anticipate from the recent developments in world news what questions we could count upon and, if the reporters were planning to bring up something special, Hagerty usually heard about it in advance through his private pipelines.

We were back upstairs at our desks soon after eight o'clock and Eisenhower was usually already in his office unless he had a breakfast appointment with a member of Congress or another government official, which would keep him a little later. Ready for him when he arrived were the latest State Department, CIA and military intelligence reports and the staff secretary, at first General Carroll and later General Goodpaster, would be on hand to give him the essentials in all the various intelligence information. Once a week the White House staff was briefed by the CIA and at the weekly National Security Council meetings the President listened to another summary of top-secret world developments by Allen Dulles, the CIA head. Eisenhower glanced at several newspapers every morning but the one more often at the top of the pile was the New York *Herald Tribune.* He paid little attention to the newspapers that continually belabored him, such as the St. Louis *Post-Dispatch,* and seldom read the Washington papers. He once said to me, "If you want to find out how the people feel about things, read the papers, but not the New York or Washington papers."

Although he was interested in histories of the Civil War and occasionally relaxed in the evening with a paperbound Western story, Eisenhower was not much of a reader. He was impatient with the endless paperwork of the presidency and always tried to get his staff to digest long documents into one-page summaries, which was sometimes next to impossible to do. He seldom exchanged written memoranda with me or with the Cabinet members or his staff. He preferred to get his information from talking with people who knew the issues involved in the matter he was considering. He listened intently, keeping the conversation brief and to the point with no wandering digressions, and he interrupted now and then with a quick and penetrating question that brought the whole discussion into clearer focus.

Eisenhower disliked using the telephone. The only person in the government who spoke to him frequently on the telephone was Dulles, who consulted the President constantly on foreign policy matters that required an immediate decision. It was understood that other Cabinet officers and agency directors with questions for the President would come to his office rather than call him on the telephone. Now and then, when Eisenhower was at his farm in Gettysburg or on a golfing vacation in Augusta, I would telephone him to let him know of a vote by Congress on a bill that was of anxious concern to him or to schedule an appointment that had to be attended to, such as a decision on the defense budget which Humphrey and Dodge had requested. If I had to telephone him on government business, it was always something that he could answer with a brief "Yes" or "No." One of the very few times that I ever received a phone call from Eisenhower that had nothing to do with affairs of state was one summer day when he was at Newport. I picked up my telephone in Washington and, after he had disposed of a small item of business, I was astonished to hear him ask, "Are your eyes blue?" He was painting a portrait of me from a colored photograph in which the color of my eyes was indistinct.

On rare occasions I was called on the telephone by an official abroad who sought presidential guidance. Early one morning just as I arrived at the office the White House operator called me to say that a call was waiting from far away in the South Pacific. It was the most distant telephone call I had ever received. Picking up the phone, I heard the voice of the American ambassador at that overseas post in a state of excitement, yelling at me, "They've taken down the American flag! What'll I do?"

I was able to decipher after some patient questions that a group of natives, as a prank no doubt, had raised their national flag over our own at the embassy. I suggested he present the native flag to the local foreign minister without taking any offense, explaining the circumstances.

"That's a good idea," the ambassador said. "I'll do that. Good-by."

Eisenhower's preference for getting to work early in the morning was based on a conviction that people think better at that time of day. He was always hopeful, too, that if he could get his work cleared away early in the day, he might find time late in the afternoon to get out of doors on the golf course or with a Number 8 iron on the back lawn of the White House for the fresh air and exercise that he so vitally needed. In arranging his work, he had to allow for unexpected crises that were always interrupting his schedule. One morning in the midst of negotiating an arrangement for the truce in the Korean War, he had to turn aside, once to confer with the Cabinet about new Civil Service regulations, and again to make a decision that could not be postponed on the wheat surplus problem. Then, after returning briefly to a study of more messages from Korea, he had to meet with Senator Taft, Senator Smith of New Jersey, Congressman Samuel Mc-Connell of Pennsylvania and Under Secretary of Labor Mashburn for a hurried last-minute check on amendments to the Taft-Hartley Act.

On Wednesday morning, the President would go over to the Indian Treaty Room in the old Executive Office Building for his press conference at ten-thirty. At ten o'clock sharp, after he had finished with two hours of appointments and pressing business, Hagerty and I, accompanied by key staff people, would go into his office to go over with a fine-tooth comb the subjects that were likely to come up in the press conference. If we expected the correspondents to discuss scientific developments or atomic tests, for example, we asked Dr. James R. Killian or Lewis Strauss to attend the prepress conference meeting. Hagerty would state a probable question and the one in the group most qualified would talk about how it could best be answered. The President said to me after one such briefing session, "I don't really need prompting from you fellows on these questions, but it's well for me to listen to you because you might point out some angles that I might otherwise overlook."

When Hagerty, with his principal assistant, accompanied the President to the press conference, none of the White House staff members tagged along behind them to watch the show. Eisenhower did not approve of that. He wanted his people to be at their desks, working, when there was no real need of their presence elsewhere. But Eisenhower did ask me to sit in on all of his important meetings and, when I could, on office appointments with government officials and with visitors where important decisions were to be discussed. He did not invite me to his meetings specifically to make any comments, although I was always free to do so if I had anything to say. On many occasions I listened until I thought the meeting had lived out its usefulness, and then I arose as a broad hint that the participants do likewise. Invariably they did. Eisenhower merely wanted me to hear everything that was going on so that I would become as familiar as possible with his attitude on most of the passing problems. I was then to use this knowledge in making decisions for him in the matters that he left for me to resolve.

It took a while for some members of the Cabinet and other high-ranking government executives to accept me as a spokesman of Eisenhower's viewpoints but, after I had served a year as his assistant, the President himself, at least, felt that I had reached that position. At that time I had an opportunity to return to private industry at a much more attractive income, and that necessarily opened up the question of my leaving the White House. I talked to the President about it, reminding him that he had often urged us to speak up if an opportunity came along that we felt, for our own economic security, ought not to be turned down. "I shall have to think of someone who can take your place," he said quickly. "During the time you have been here you have established yourself in the confidence of the Cabinet. Anyone coming in to replace you would need the time to do the same—that is," he added as an afterthought, "unless we can find someone who is already in that position. I can't think of anyone right off except possibly Cabot Lodge. I'll have him in for a talk." After a day or two, Eisenhower called me in. Lodge was happy with his work at the United Nations. He told me afterward that he enjoyed his post as Ambassador to the UN more than anything he had ever done. In my own mind I was sure that Lodge, if he could help it, would have nothing to do with scrubbing the administrative and political back stairs as I was doing at the White House. "So I guess you will have to stay here," the President concluded with a grin. I forgot my economic security and stayed on as Assistant to the President for another five years.

It was impossible, of course, for me to sit in on all the meetings and office appointments that Eisenhower wanted me to attend; I had too many telephone calls, too much paperwork and too many appointments at my own office, as well as a White House staff to supervise. Somebody who made a count of such things once estimated that my outgoing and incoming telephone calls were usually 250 a day and that figure was probably not far from right. Because Eisenhower disliked talking business on the phone, Persons and I and a few other staff members would speak for him on the telephone on many matters that required his personal attention.

A considerable amount of my time on the telephone was spent on personnel problems with Cabinet members and Republican leaders, and with Eisenhower's advisers in professional and business life, gathering and listening to suggestions about filling a particular position. Then, after boiling the list down to a handful of the most attractive eligibles, I sought the President's preference. I never had the slightest hesitation in interrupting Eisenhower at his desk, or after work, for a decision that took only a brief "Yes" or "No." Whether he was at his desk or taking a swim in the White House pool or even, on occasion, in his bedroom, I was expected to come in when and if I decided it was necessary. Needless to say, the reasons for disturbing him in his private residence had to be urgent indeed. I remember that once when I needed a decision on an appointment I went out on the back lawn, where Eisenhower was practicing golf shots. Dulles was already there ahead of me on a related errand. The President saw me coming and with a simulated sigh said, "Look, Foster, here comes my conscience!" After the President had looked at the list and made his choice, I was back again on the telephone; to the Special Counsel to initiate an FBI investigation; to Charles Willis, or later Robert Gray and Robert Hampton, to follow up with clearance with the Senator concerned and the National Committee; at the proper time to the man himself to find out whether he could be persuaded to move to Washington. Eisenhower seldom if ever offered anybody a job personally. It was wrong, he felt, to put a person in the embarrassing position of being forced to say "No" to the President of the United States, and, of course, it was also embarrassing for the President to have his personal request turned down. With top-flight businessmen, the chief difficulty was getting them to work for the government at all. It was not so much the financial sacrifice and the personal upheaval in being transplanted to Washington as it was the facing up to the hazards of adjustments in public service. Government ought to be run more on business principles, they said, but the politicians always were getting in the way, and they didn't want anything to do with politics.

Despite all the telephone calls, the checks and the clearances, an occasional appointment would bounce back to haunt us. I thought I had seen to all the necessary preliminaries in the President's nomination of Tom Lyon, who had been highly recommended by Secretary of the Interior Douglas McKay and Senator Arthur Watkins of Utah for the position of Director of the Bureau of Mines. But the nomination of Lyon caused an uproar in the Senate when the examining committee heard Lyon himself say that he had no respect for the mine safety program that he would have been required to administer. That gave John L. Lewis an opportunity to shout forth in round and solemn syllables and forced the annoyed President to withdraw the nomination. I don't know yet how McKay and Watkins could possibly have overlooked this rather basic flaw in Lyon's qualifications but I had to share with them the glory of the fluff.

No matter how hard we struggled during that first year of Eisenhower's administration to put the best possible people into the places of the higher-ranking holdovers from the Roosevelt and Truman regimes, there was a steady rumble of criticism from the politicians of our own party. We weren't cleaning out the Democrats fast enough. Too many of our appointees were from New York and the Eastern seaboard and not enough of them were Taft men. I can honestly say that Eisenhower never bothered to find out whether a prospective appointee had supported him at the 1952 Republican convention. He knew which of his Cabinet members had been for Taft but beyond that small circle I doubt if he could have passed an examination on the past party loyalties of most Republican job seekers. Soon after he went into office, Lodge gave him a brief typewritten list of names of extreme right-wing Republicans who had been violently opposed to him and advised him to give them a wide berth. Lodge added that not only had they done their best to sink Eisenhower when he was a candidate, but some of them had contributed to his own defeat by John F. Kennedy in the Massachusetts Senate race in 1952. Eisenhower added one more name of his own choice to the list in longhand and handed it to me one day and forgot about it. He made no prohibition to me about the people on the list, for, as he said, he had no personal acquaintanceship with most of them and he certainly did not anticipate that those particular Republicans would have any inclination to work in his administration anyway. Actually there was no ground for the talk of the administration's alleged discrimination against Taft Republicans. Along with Ezra Taft Benson, Eisenhower appointed to his official family as presidential assistants two prominent Taft men, I. Jack Martin and Howard Pyle.

When I was being pressed to come up with a recommendation for the Veterans Administration, I decided, more or less as an experiment, to see if I could find a candidate who would satisfy the two main qualifications that we were accused of neglecting—a Taft adherent from the Midwest or the Rocky Mountains. I noticed a statement in a Washington newspaper attributed to a Republican leader in the Senate that a Taft man couldn't get over the White House threshold. There was a steady chant of such complaints, the most vocal from the National Committee, that the East or California seemed to be providing too many of our sub-Cabinet and agency appointees. With these criteria, and without departing from Eisenhower's high standards of fitness, I began my hunt. After prolonged inquiries in the middle of the country, I discovered Harvey Higley, a Wisconsin businessman who had the backing of Tom Coleman, leader of the Taft forces in that state. Higley was subsequently approved by Eisenhower and confirmed by the Senate and proved to be an able administrator. But it had taken six months to fill the job.

Behind Eisenhower's continual battle with the Republican politicians over patronage was his insistence that the Cabinet and agency heads should assume final responsibility for choosing their own subordinates. He went through well-publicized motions of transferring patronage responsibility from me to Leonard Hall in the spring of 1953, but at the same time he reassured the Cabinet that this merely meant that Hall and the National Committee would be allowed to recommend candidates for open positions. Hall's candidates, however, would get no more than equal consideration with other candidates. Dulles refused to let the Republican party have too much say on State Department job appointments because he felt that he had to depend on Democrats in Congress for support of his foreign programs. Ezra Taft Benson, always difficult with politicians, ran the Department of Agriculture with little regard to any preferred status for Republican job applicants. Charles Halleck once arranged for a group of Republicans in the House to talk with Benson about farm problems. As the men were sitting down, one of them mentioned that Truman Democrats were still controlling the Department of Agriculture's field offices in North Dakota. An argument on patronage broke out and lasted for the rest of the meeting. The farm problems were never discussed.

Eisenhower was exasperated by the time that was spent on patronage wrangles at his weekly meetings with the Republican legislative leaders. "I'll be darned if I know how the Republicans ever held a party together all these years," he said after one such session. "This business of patronage all the time—I'm ready to co-operate, but I want, and we all want, good men." At one meeting that Senator Taft attended shortly before his death, Eisenhower mentioned the difficulty he was having trying to find the right person for an important job. "He doesn't have to be a general," Taft remarked. "We have enough of them around here already." Knowland recalled that during the Truman administration Republican Congressmen were shown the courtesy of being consulted about job applications from their districts. They had been receiving no such consideration, he added darkly, since the Republicans had taken over the White House.

Philip Young, Eisenhower's Civil Service Commission chairman until 1957, was a special target of the patronage-seeking Congressmen. In 1949, Truman had given Civil Service status to hundreds of thousands of government employees who had entered the federal service without examinations during the national emergency period in 1941 and early 1942, before and after the attack on Pearl Harbor. Halleck introduced a bill that aimed to vacate all jobs held by Civil Service people who had not taken examinations, but Young opposed the measure because of the widespread confusion it would cause and because of the damage it might do to the Civil Service system. At a legislative leaders' meeting, Congressman A. L. Miller of Nebraska told Eisenhower that he should fire Young. The President, trying to keep his temper under control, said to the Congressman, "Mr. Miller, I love to have your advice, but when it comes to picking my assistants, *I* pick them." As a matter of fact, Young was one assistant who had been picked by Eisenhower personally. After the post had been turned down successively by several well-qualified candidates, not knowing where to turn next, I asked Eisenhower if there was anybody he could think of, something that I rarely had to do. The Civil Service chairmanship was a position of Cabinet rank, regarded by the Rockefeller Committee as a crucially important command post in the government. Eisenhower immediately thought of Young, an experienced young man who had worked as a government administrator during the war and then dean of the Graduate School of Business Administration at Columbia. It was an inspired choice that made me wish I could go to Eisenhower with all of my personnel problems. Young not only had an impressive background—he was the son of Owen D. Young—and the right talents, but he was ready and able to come to Washington right away and his approval by the Senate only took ten days, a near record. Few appointments went through that smoothly.

Lunch at the White House, like breakfast, was a working meal. I usually asked my secretary to invite some Republican Senator or Representative with a problem, so that I and the staff member chiefly concerned with it might help with this particular task in Congressional relations. The chief trouble with this idea was that there were not enough lunches to cover all of the members of Congress who had problems to present to the White House.

At other times I invited Cabinet or agency heads to lunch so that some item of business could be taken up and disposed of, usually with other staff members present. We also spent lunch hours going over the piles of requests for Eisenhower to speak at dinners and conventions, some of them for dates two years away. I set up what I called a calendar committee, composed of Stephens, Hagerty, Hauge and other principal staff members, who met periodically to shake down the recommendations which we would make later to the President. Stephens prepared a mimeographed list of them, which we studied and discussed, declining most of the invitations and putting some on a tentative list. When a presidential speech had been prepared by the staff writers, I called this same staff group together for a thorough study and discussion of the draft before it went to the President. This was part of my routine staff work.

In spite of all the pressures on the President to make speeches

outside of Washington, a third of those invitations that he did accept
were selections of his own choice and not the result of any outside
pushing. Of those that he was persuaded to make, the ones that made
him wince were the purely political ones. He did not mind quite so
much making speeches that were politically inspired but given before
nonpartisan audiences. They were probably the best political speeches
he made. A typical example was the address the President made to
the Future Farmers of America at Kansas City late in 1953. The invitation came to the White House through Ezra Taft Benson, whose
policies even in that first year of the administration were already
under fire, much to the distress of the Republican politicians in the
farm belt. Leonard Hall, then the Republican National Chairman,
came in to ask me to help him. "Can't we get the President out there
to make a speech?" Hall said to me. "They'll listen to him but they
are getting down on Benson."

I told Hall that I would see what I could do, and immediately
summoned the indispensable Hauge and a few experts from the Department of Agriculture to see if we could work out a plan for a
speech. In this instance we agreed to steer clear of any partisan approach and work in a world peace theme stressing the contribution of
the American farmer. A few days later we met again to study the
first draft of the writing and decided that the slant was right but it
needed better brushwork and stronger treatment. So it was agreed
that I should call a farm expert in Des Moines and ask him to come
and help.

In preparations like this, Eisenhower would not know about the
plans in progress. Indeed, until an acceptable working draft had been
prepared and tentative plans drawn up by myself and the staff, he
would not want to know. I found early in the game that Eisenhower
expected anyone who proposed a speech to him to have the reasons
for making it thoroughly thought out, a draft on paper and the trip
phased into his calendar so that it did not disturb other commitments. "What is it that needs to be said?" Eisenhower would say. "I
am not going out there just to listen to my tongue clatter!" Hall and
I and the rest of the staff learned that we had to have a finished draft
in shape and in the President's hands at least two weeks before it was
to be delivered so that he could put it into his desk drawer and brood
over it at his leisure. The preparation usually meant days, sometimes

weeks, of staff work. Since, in the meantime, anything could happen to change the picture, we learned to keep our own counsel until we had plans in apple-pie order. Then Hall and I, probably with Persons and Hauge, would tell Tom Stephens that we wanted fifteen uninterrupted minutes with the President. Before such a conference took place, Hall, Persons and I would decide who was going to carry the argument. If I was chosen to take the responsibility for the project I would start out by telling Eisenhower the purpose of our appointment and ask Hall, in the example I have cited, to sum up quickly the state of affairs in the farm belt.

"We thought you might like to go out to Kansas City for the Future Farmers convention," I would say to Eisenhower. "Benson thinks this is as good a forum as there is, and it is the younger group that we have been trying to reach. You have been intending to have a look at the plans for the Eisenhower Library at Abilene. You could leave after Cabinet that morning, go to Kansas City and speak and go on to Abilene the next morning. Perhaps Mrs. Eisenhower might want to go along from there to Denver and spend the weekend with Mrs. Doud. If she did not want to fly to Kansas City she could take the train and you could both go on from there. Here's a basic draft of a speech you could give. We thought we'd leave it with you so you can look it over."

Eisenhower would glance at the speech, read a few lines, and ask a question or two about the reasons why Hall had reported such distress with the Benson farm program. "I don't believe for a minute the farmer wants the government to be his boss," Eisenhower would say, tossing the draft into his desk drawer. I knew the discussion was over and that the President wanted to mull it over. A few days later, the President would call Hauge or myself into his office. The speech would be on his desk. "This moves along pretty well," he would say, handing back the draft, "but it seems to labor too much in trying to meet a lot of picayune criticism. After all, the farmer wants to understand his role in America and in the world today. A farmer is like any other American. When he understands his responsibilities he will meet them as well or better than any other citizen. Can't we get the feel of that more into it?"

That would mean more hours of brain-racking and writing by Hauge. Finally, Eisenhower would sit down at his desk alone and think about what he wanted to say, marking up the revised draft himself and dictating to Ann Whitman the changes he was making. Once, while he was in the laborious process of straightening out a speech, he could see that the staff was somewhat nonplused in trying to find language that would suit him. Looking the writers right in the eye he said, "I have never yet had a speech prepared for me that I did not change." In considerable degree, Eisenhower was his own speech writer. When he got through with it, and Hauge had a last look, Hagerty "wrapped it up" by sending it downstairs for mimeographing and Ann Whitman typed it on a typewriter with extra-large-sized letters so that the President could read it easily while he was delivering it.

My varied duties as Assistant to the President also included the fiscal and maintenance supervision of the White House office, one part of my job that was pleasantly free from the intrigues of party politics. I soon found out that Frank Sanderson and William Hopkins, who managed the bookkeeping and clerical end of the office, needed little help from me. Their service dated back to the administration of Herbert Hoover and it mattered little to them or to the foremen of the electrical and plumbing crews whether the occupants of the front office were Trumans or Eisenhowers. Except in an advisory capacity I had little to do with affairs within the executive mansion but when Howell Crim, the Chief Usher, and another old hand, broke the bad news about the precarious state of the electrical equipment that serviced the White House, I lost no time in taking action without any inquiry about my authority. Water seepage had made the transformers unsafe and had corroded the lead cable into the office building and there was an excellent chance for explosions in the White House and in manholes on Pennsylvania Avenue at any minute.

The problem of finding adequate office space in the White House for the President's staff was insurmountable. Truman had worked out a plan for a new office for the President but it had been rejected because it intruded too much on the symmetry of the buildings and the landscaping plan of the grounds. The staff had to be separated inefficiently, with some of their offices in the West and East Wings of the White House, making a trip through the ground floor of the President's house necessary in going from one to the other. Still others had to move into the adjacent Executive Office Building, the hideous relic that had housed the State, Navy and War departments in President Grant's administration. We helped the situation somewhat by moving the Secret Service offices and the headquarters of the White House police, a separate branch of the Washington police force, from the East Wing to a convenient place outside the building. Shuffling around the business offices of the co-operative Sanderson enabled us to get most of the principal members of the staff into the West Wing, near the offices of the President and myself.

The White House staff, Stephens and Hagerty in particular, spent considerable time working with the Secret Service on the President's personal safety. The detailed planning that surrounds every movement of the President is precise and meticulous. Eisenhower, for example, was never permitted to paint a picture on the White House lawn, but he was allowed to practice golf shots there. Sitting or standing still before an easel, he might have been too easy a target for a marksman with a long-range rifle but golf practice was less dangerous because it kept his body almost constantly in motion. If he went fishing, Secret Service men with rods and fishing togs were stationed upstream and downstream within watching distance to see to it that nobody whose identity was not known to them went near him. On a golf course, they moved along near him through the woods and thickets at the edge of the fairways.

When Eisenhower went on a trip away from Washington, we worked out a carefully detailed trip pattern with the Secret Service agents several days, sometimes even weeks, before his departure. The trip pattern mapped and timed to the minute the exact route that the President would follow and described what he would do and whom he would be with at each place where he stopped. Before Eisenhower left on the journey, a group of Secret Service men would travel over the proposed route, visiting the airports and hotels listed in the trip pattern and examining the rooms where the President would sleep and the public auditoriums or outdoor arenas or fair grounds where he was scheduled to make appearances. They would also familiarize themselves with the identity of the local people who would be near Eisenhower at the receptions, dinners and speaking engagements that he would attend, and commit to memory the faces and physical appearance of waiters, bellboys, elevator operators, doormen, hotel managers, reporters and photographers who would come into close contact with the President. If a gate-crasher or any other unauthorized stranger turned up in a group of people around Eisenhower at any time during the trip, the Secret Service men would spot him immediately. At all hours of the day and night a Secret Service man was stationed outside of the door of the President's hotel room, with access to a nearby telephone that he could instantly use to call security headquarters in Washington in the event of any kind of an emergency. If the President was planning to occupy the room for a few days, another telephone was connected with the White House on a reserved long-distance circuit.

Large crowds always made the Secret Service men uneasy. Their most harrowing ordeal with Eisenhower that I ever witnessed was during the parade that displayed him before a huge and wildly excited mob of people in Panama in 1956. The procession moved at a snail's pace through narrow streets jammed with solid masses of humanity for as far as the eye could see, and all the way from the United States Embassy residence to the Presidencia the shouting and screaming crowds of people of every race and color pressed closely against both sides of the open car in which Eisenhower was standing and waving. As I watched the frantic people leaning out of every window and balcony that almost overhung the little, winding, narrow street, it seemed as though some of them were near enough to touch him. The Secret Service men, moving along on foot beside the President's car, were being themselves so jostled and jammed that they would have been powerless to prevent an assassin from having a free hand. The fact that the President of Panama had only recently met such a fate further aggravated their predicament. They could only pray that nothing happened to the President and, happily, nothing did. Eisenhower never worried about his safety and regarded the elaborate precautions of the Secret Service as something of a waste of time and effort. He believed that if an assassin was seriously planning to kill him, it would be almost impossible to prevent it. One night in Denver when we were talking about it, he pointed to the fire escape outside of his hotel room window and said to me, "If anybody really wanted to climb up there and shoot me, it would be an easy thing to do. So why worry about it?"

At about six o'clock my working day at the White House came to an end. There were always some of my associates still at work at that hour, but we tried to wind up our day by then. To have tried to keep on working into the evening would have been neither good management nor good sense. Eisenhower wanted the staff to keep fit, as he himself tried to do. He always sought a little relaxation after five o'clock, but he often spent the hour before his dinner in the oval room office on the second floor of his residence where many of his predecessors had worked out their policies and programs in far less troubled times. Here Eisenhower often sat around informally with members of his Cabinet and staff, or with influential members of Congress such as William Knowland, Lyndon Johnson, Everett Dirksen, Sam Rayburn, Walter George or J. W. Fulbright, or with defense chiefs, or with close friends who had some advice to give. Over a drink and a canapé, at this time of the evening, Eisenhower smoothed the road for many of his goals and legislative purposes.

6 Eisenhower and Dulles

During the six important years that John Foster Dulles served as Eisenhower's Secretary of State, there was never much doubt about who was responsible for the foreign policy of the United States. In broad general outline, that policy was a reflection of the President's strong personal belief in America's obligation to assume a role of participating leadership in world affairs and his stern disapproval of the aloof "Go It Alone" philosophy of isolated independence preached by conservative Republicans and many Southern Democrats. Within that framework Eisenhower delegated to Dulles the responsibility of developing the specific policy, including the decision where the administration would stand and what course of action would be followed in each international crisis. Although, as Eisenhower often points out, the Secretary of State never made a major move without the President's knowledge and approval, I think that the hard and uncompromising line that the United States government took toward Soviet Russia and Red China between 1953 and the early months of 1959 was more a Dulles line than an Eisenhower one.

Always hopefully seeking world peace, Eisenhower was willing to listen to any well-reasoned proposal that might lead to disarmament. To Dulles, disarmament was something in the nebulous future and he had little enthusiasm for a change in policy that promised to give the Communists relief from harassment. Dulles viewed with skepticism Nelson Rockefeller's open-skies plan of aerial inspection that Eisenhower proposed to the Russians at Geneva in 1955. Dulles did not believe that disarmament could become a reality in the 1950s, any more than it had been in 1919. Dulles had been a close observer of President Wilson's failure to establish a lasting peace and his recollection of it haunted him during the 1955 meeting with the Russians. In that summit conference, the Secretary passed the word to his staff that he wanted disarmament talks "closed out quietly." Dulles, as is well known, was opposed to such summit conferences unless there was concrete evidence beforehand that the Communists were going to be willing to compromise. When Eisenhower's Paris summit conference with Khrushchev collapsed in 1960, I could hear Dulles saying, "Now do you see what I mean?"

Eisenhower, of course, was well aware that his own approach to foreign problems was far more conciliatory than Dulles'. When I mentioned this to him one day after Dulles had died, Eisenhower went back to the 1952 campaign and recalled to me a speech he had delivered at the American Legion convention that year concerning the liberation of countries that had fallen under Communist tyranny. Eisenhower had spoken of freeing such people "by peaceful instruments." Talking on the same subject in Buffalo a few days later, Dulles, attacking the Truman policy as the containment of enslaved peoples under Communist domination, called for liberation but significantly omitted to mention the use of "peaceful means" in accomplishing it. Eisenhower called Dulles to task on this difference in their words. The apparent belligerency of the Dulles speech caused some fear in Europe that the Republicans might go so far as to make war to free these peoples. Dulles readily admitted that Eisenhower was right and that his own choice of words had been wrong. The following week Eisenhower restated his attitude emphatically in another speech in Philadelphia: "To aid by every peaceful means, but only by peaceful means, the right to live in freedom."

Eisenhower deferred to the tougher stand of Dulles in foreign policy because he agreed with his Secretary of State that the United States had to be more positive in its dealings with the Communists. Dulles contended that the Truman administration had only fought rear-guard actions against moves that the Soviets initiated and Eisenhower supported his determination to stop the erosion of the free world by reversing that situation. Summing up the foreign problems of the day at an early Cabinet meeting in 1953, Dulles spoke of Eisenhower's desire to bring the Korean War to an end. "How?" he said. "By *doing* something!" At the time that the hard-line policy of Dulles was fashioned and put to work, little was said against it. The evaluation of a foreign policy is essentially a pragmatic process. If it works, it is fine. If it fails, it is bankrupt, no matter how well it may have been conceived originally. If Russia and China had weakened internally under the pressure of Dulles' antagonism, there would have been no criticism of his tactics. But while he was trying to put a hammerlock on the Communists, they continued to show economic progress.

Eisenhower gave Dulles a free hand and wide responsibility in shaping the administration's foreign policy mainly because he believed that the Secretary of State had more experience and knowledge in the field of diplomacy than any American of his time. "Foster has been in training for this job all his life," Eisenhower often said. Back in 1907, at the age of nineteen, Dulles was a secretary at the Second Hague Peace Conference. In 1917, when World War I broke out, Woodrow Wilson sent him to Central America to negotiate with those countries for the protection of the Panama Canal and after the war he was a counsel for the United States at the Versailles peace conference. He was an adviser to the United States delegation at the organization of the United Nations in San Francisco in 1945 and negotiated the peace treaty with Japan.

If Eisenhower depended heavily on Dulles, it was equally apparent that Dulles needed a President like Eisenhower. The two men formed a close and intimate working relationship, with Eisenhower giving Dulles more trust and confidence than any President in modern times had bestowed on a Cabinet member, so that the Secretary's opinions and decisions would be accepted around the world and at home as the opinions and decisions of the President and the government. In the quiet of Eisenhower's home, Dulles had talked about this relationship before they had begun their official association. "With my understanding of the intricate relationships between the peoples of the world and your sensitiveness to the political considerations involved, we will make the most successful team in history," Dulles had prophesied. Far from relieving Eisenhower of the burden of foreign problems, this unique partnership required him to spend more time in consultation with Dulles than he did with other department heads. The Secretary had to deal with the President directly on every important development in world affairs and he wanted no one to come between him and Eisenhower. Dulles had seen his uncle, Robert

Lansing, Secretary of State under Woodrow Wilson, virtually supplanted by Colonel Edward M. House, Wilson's unofficial adviser. The memory of Cordell Hull's being ignored while Franklin D. Roosevelt conferred with Sumner Welles, and Harry Hopkins' shouldering aside Edward Stettinius, was vivid in Dulles' mind. Taking no chances, Dulles saw to it that nobody but himself talked with Eisenhower about major policy decisions. He was in the White House more than any other Cabinet member and he was the only government official who frequently spoke with the President on the telephone. When a message was brought to Dulles during a Cabinet or National Security Council meeting, he would sometimes halt the proceedings and discuss it with the President in undertones at the table until they disposed of the problem.

In order to help him keep in the closest touch with the economic and military problems of foreign policy, Eisenhower appointed special assistants in those areas to work directly under the White House and side by side with the State Department. It was a delicate experiment. While they represented the President, these assistants assumed theoretically none of the prerogatives of Foster Dulles or any other Cabinet Secretary. They were expediters and co-ordinators, but they were also men capable of creating new approaches to the solution of problems which divided the world. From time to time, Dulles found in his diplomatic domain such presidential assistants as Harold Stassen in mutual security, foreign operations and disarmament, Lewis Strauss in atomic energy affairs, C. D. Jackson in cold war psychology planning, Clarence Randall and Joseph Dodge in foreign economic policy and Walter George and James Richards as special consultants in foreign affairs. The President made none of these appointments without Dulles' full approval. Still, Dulles watched these specialists intently and, at the first sign of what he suspected to be a possible threat to the tight and straight line-of-command between himself and the President, he straightened out the difficulty quickly. If he thought he couldn't straighten it out himself, he did not hesitate to take it to me and finally to Eisenhower. In every instance where Dulles decided the situation was intolerable, he insisted on a change, and the President without exception went along with his wishes. Jackson's job as a foreign policy idea man infringed delicately on Dulles' official bailiwick, but Jackson knew how to handle the Secretary and always managed to get along with him cordially. Nelson Rockefeller, who succeeded Jackson, had no such success. Nor did Stassen, whose diplomatic missions drove Dulles to such distraction that Stassen's work for the President in foreign affairs was finally brought to an end. Rockefeller's working methods, in contrast to those of Jackson, annoyed Dulles. Jackson had worked alone, with little or no staff. He formed his own ideas and put them to work in close collaboration with the Secretary. When Rockefeller, on the other hand, went to work on a dramatic peace plan that could be presented by Eisenhower at the 1955 summit conference at Geneva, he organized a large group of technical experts, researchers and idea men and moved them into seclusion at the Marine Base at Quantico, Virginia, away from Dulles and the State Department. The air of secrecy around the Rockefeller operation and the number of people involved in it made Dulles apprehensive. "He seems to be building up a big staff," Dulles said to me suspiciously one day. "He's got them down at Quantico, and nobody knows what they're doing."

Eventually the Quantico Panel, as the Rockefeller study group was called, came up with the open-skies inspection plan, which Eisenhower believed workable, not simply as a new weapon in the cold war, but as a possible breakthrough in the disarmament stalemate. Although Dulles would have been skeptical of any proposal coming from the Rockefeller operation, the lukewarm attitude that he took toward the open-skies plan was based mainly on his doubt that anything would come out of it. Dulles' caution and the military opposition to the open-skies proposal were so strong that Eisenhower was still undecided when he arrived in Geneva whether he would present it to the Soviets. Even during Dulles' last illness, when it was becoming apparent that he would never be able to return to the State Department, he was still zealously guarding his position. He made a telephone call one day from his sickbed at Hobe Sound to a State Department official raising the question of whether one of the President's principal special assistants was not getting too forward in making decisions in the foreign policy field.

Eisenhower's and Dulles' first break with the conservative Republicans in Congress, the forerunner of many such bitter disputes on foreign policy in the following years, concerned their stand on the so-called "enslaved peoples" resolution during the first two months that Eisenhower was in office. In the 1952 campaign the Republicans had exploited politically the identification of the Democrats with the widely resented secret concessions to the Russians at Yalta and Potsdam. The foreign policy plank in the GOP platform, on which Dulles had been consulted, promised that the Republicans would repudiate "secret understandings such as those of Yalta." But when the subject came up in discussions with the legislative leaders after Eisenhower was in the White House, Dulles was opposed to any such specific repudiation of the Yalta, Teheran and Potsdam agreements as the conservative Republicans proposed. He pointed out that some parts of the Yalta agreement were binding on our positions in Berlin and Vienna and a blanket disavowal of those pacts would only cause the United States government embarrassment and confusion in its Western European alliances. He urged Eisenhower, in his first State of the Union address, to refer to the secret agreements only in general terms, without mentioning Yalta by name. This caused an uproar from the Republicans, who had confidently expected that one of the first acts of the Eisenhower administration would be an official out-and-out withdrawal from any and all deals negotiated with the Stalin government by Franklin D. Roosevelt and Harry Truman.

To keep the campaign pledge, Dulles and Eisenhower wrote a carefully worded resolution for the approval of Congress which assured the people in Communist-dominated countries behind the Iron Curtain that the United States would use all "peaceful means" to obtain their freedom. The resolution denounced "any interpretations or applications" of secret agreements that "have been perverted" to place free peoples under Soviet despotism, but it did not denounce the agreements themselves directly and it still made no specific mention of Yalta, Teheran or Potsdam.

There was prolonged wrangling about the wording of the resolution at the meetings of the Republican legislative leaders for the next few weeks. Eisenhower became increasingly annoyed by the determination of the Republican Congressmen to use Yalta as a political weapon against the Democrats. To him, the Yalta issue was a dead relic of the past and he had no sympathy with the eagerness of the Republican politicians to rake it up out of the ashes. Eisenhower and Dulles were also reluctant to sponsor a resolution on the secret agreements that would offend the Democrats in Congress too deeply because they were getting as much support for their programs from the Democrats as they were from the leaders of their own party in Congress. Eisenhower said at one point that in his opinion the resolution needed bipartisan backing in order to be effective and suggested bringing Democratic legislators into the discussions. This dumfounded Senator Taft and his followers. Taft declared that the resolution written by Eisenhower and Dulles admitted that the agreements made by Roosevelt and Truman were valid and that he could never agree to such an admission. Dulles came back with the flat assertion that the agreements were valid, as everybody at the meeting really knew, and that the United States could not run out on them. If we repudiated the agreements, Dulles pointed out, Russia would then be free to repudiate certain other agreements that were an advantage to the Western Allies. That was a hard argument for Taft to answer.

To the immense relief of Eisenhower and Dulles, the controversy over the enslaved-peoples resolution was ended by an unexpected event, the death of Joseph Stalin on March 5, 1953. At the next meeting of the legislative leaders on March 9, Dulles said he felt that Stalin's death made the resolution no longer necessary or fitting. The Republicans, who saw that they were getting nowhere with Eisenhower in their effort to make the resolution a condemnation of the Roosevelt and Truman administrations, were by this time almost as satisfied as the President to drop it.

The Yalta agreements came up again in that same month to sharpen the worsening conflict between the Republican leaders and Eisenhower and Dulles. Never one to let political considerations get in the way of an appointment which he believed was of advantage in furthering policy objectives, Dulles had selected Charles E. Bohlen to be the Ambassador to the Soviet Union. Bohlen had been Roosevelt's Russian language interpreter and adviser on Russian affairs at the Yalta conference. The mere fact that Bohlen had been at Yalta with Roosevelt was enough to make him a renegade in the eyes of most Republicans. His nomination seemed to them all the more preposterous when he testified before the Senate Foreign Relations Committee that he saw nothing wrong with the agreements made at Yalta.

Senator Taft found himself in a curious situation when the Bohlen case came up for discussion at the President's meeting with the leg-

islative leaders in the White House on March 9—the same meeting
in which, a few minutes earlier, Dulles had finally disposed of his
deadlocked battle with Taft over the Yalta issue in the proposed
enslaved-peoples resolution. A dedicated enemy of the Yalta agreement and all the other foreign entanglements of the previous Democratic administrations, Taft was naturally against Bohlen. But Eisenhower asked him at the White House meeting to support Bohlen's
confirmation in the Senate. Taft's decision in this dilemma increased
his stature in the President's estimation. The Senator recognized the
responsibilities of his leadership and, laying aside his strong personal
feelings, agreed to do what Eisenhower wanted. This was one more
example of Taft's great qualities. The Senator also reasoned that if
the Republican majority in the Senate failed to support Eisenhower
on this vote it would be a serious blow to the President's prestige.

Other Republicans in the Senate, notably Senator Joseph R. Mc-
Carthy, were not restrained by such respect for the President. Bohlen
was a target that McCarthy was unable to resist. Turning away from
the Yalta issue, McCarthy joined with Senator Pat McCarran of
Nevada in questioning Bohlen's loyalty. McCarran charged that
Scott McLeod, the newly appointed State Department security officer,
had recommended that Dulles should reject Bohlen as a security
risk. When Dulles denied this, McCarthy claimed that the Secretary
of State was being untruthful and demanded that he be brought before the Foreign Relations Committee to testify under oath. McCarthy
said that he knew what was in the FBI file on Bohlen and that calling
Bohlen a security risk was "putting it too weak."

Disturbed by the uproar created by McCarthy and McCarran and
the insinuations of differences between Dulles and himself, McLeod
came to the White House and talked with Jerry Persons about resigning from the State Department. Actually McLeod had made no recommendation to Dulles about Bohlen. He had found some unsubstanti-
ated and speculative derogatory material in Bohlen's FBI file and
merely had called Dulles' attention to it. As Dulles testified later before the Senate committee, this was customary procedure in the
State Department. But the FBI investigation as a whole, Dulles
added, had raised no doubt about Bohlen's loyalty. After Persons
talked with McLeod, he came to me and we decided that if McLeod
resigned at that time the already unpleasant situation would only

seem worse. McLeod remained at his post. McCarthy went on demanding that Eisenhower should withdraw his nomination of Bohlen and accused the President of failing "to get rid of Acheson's architects of disaster."

Eisenhower answered the Wisconsin Senator by coming out stoutly for Bohlen at his March 25 press conference. He said that Bohlen was the best-qualified diplomat he could find for the Moscow assignment. A reporter asked the President who made the decisions on such appointments and who screened the past histories of the appointees. Eisenhower said that he made the decisions himself. If the appointment was suggested by a Cabinet member, the President explained, that Secretary was responsible for the screening, as Dulles was in the case of Bohlen. If the appointee was suggested by somebody outside of the government, he added, Sherman Adams did the screening. He might have added that I also rescreened the nominations sent to the White House by Cabinet members to make sure before the President acted on the appointments that the sponsoring Secretary had not overlooked any embarrassing omissions.

Taft also threw his considerable weight against McCarthy. The Ohio Senator and Senator John J. Sparkman of Alabama, the Democratic vice-presidential nominee in 1952, examined the FBI file on Bohlen, and Taft told the Senate afterward, "There was no suggestion anywhere by anyone reflecting on the loyalty of Mr. Bohlen or any association by him with Communism or support of Communism or even tolerance of Communism." Then in his capacity as majority leader, Taft pushed the confirmation of Bohlen through the Senate by a vote of seventy-four to thirteen. But the decisiveness of the vote failed to reflect the dissatisfaction that the nomination had stirred up among the Republicans. Mopping his brow when it was finally all over, Taft sent word to Eisenhower that he did not want to be asked to wheel any more Bohlens through the Senate.

The news of Stalin's death caused no great excitement in the White House. The first word of the Russian dictator's fatal stroke reached Allen Dulles through the Central Intelligence Agency's communications channels in the early hours of March 4. Undecided about whether he should awaken the President, Dulles phoned Hagerty, who took the responsibility of rousing Eisenhower and informing him of Stalin's illness. It might have been expected that Eisenhower, as a military man, would have given us precise directions about when he wanted us to awaken him in the middle of the night with important news or messages but he left such decisions to our judgment. Hagerty and I agreed that we would arouse the President from sleep only when there was a need for immediate action on his part that could not be put off until morning but I never encountered a situation where I considered that necessary. In fact, the only other time that I remember Eisenhower being awakened by government business was when Foster Dulles telephoned him excitedly at two o'clock in the morning to tell him that Syngman Rhee was upsetting the truce negotiations in Korea by releasing thousands of anti-Communist North Korean prisoners of war. Even that call could have been postponed; there was nothing that Eisenhower could do about Syngman Rhee at that hour of the morning.

On the morning that Eisenhower learned that Stalin was dying, he went to his office at twenty minutes to eight and found Dulles, Hagerty, Cutler and C. D. Jackson awaiting him. He looked at them and said, "Well, what do you think we can do about *this*?" The only thing he could do at that moment was to issue a statement that expressed the hope that Stalin's successors would keep peace in the world. Eisenhower never felt that he would be able to negotiate successfully with Stalin. He had regarded Stalin as a major road block in the attempts to settle the Korean War and he mentioned to us his hope that the death of the Soviet dictator might bring a change in the attitude of Red China toward the Korean truce efforts, which it did. Soon after Chou En-lai returned to China from Stalin's funeral in Moscow, he made a new and more reasonable truce offer, expressing a willingness to accept the American demand that no anti-Communist North Korean prisoners should be forcibly returned to the Communists. Both Truman and Eisenhower had been emphatic on this condition and their insistence had made it a major obstacle in the truce negotiations.

After Stalin's death, when the new regime of Malenkov was taking over the Soviet leadership, Eisenhower agreed with Dulles and Jackson that the psychological time had arrived for the President of the United States to deliver a major speech on this country's desire for peaceful coexistence with the Communists. The speech was directed primarily at the new Russian leaders but it was also intended to reassure the neutral nations and our own allies, such as England and France, of America's willingness to respect the Soviets. The firm line that Dulles was taking against the Communists and the controversial removal of the Seventh Fleet from the Formosa Strait had spread fear abroad that the Americans, as one newspaper in India put it, were hunting peace with a gun. In 1950, Truman had ordered the Navy's Seventh Fleet to patrol the waters between Formosa and China to prevent Chiang Kai-shek and the Red Chinese from attacking each other. Theoretically, at least, this order safeguarded China as much as Formosa because it prohibited the use of Formosa and the Pescadores Islands as bases for attacks on the mainland. Seeking to put pressure on China to end the Korean War, Dulles suggested that Eisenhower's first State of the Union address should announce a revocation of the order. Eisenhower took pains to make the announcement sound as nonbelligerent as it could sound but nevertheless it was called an "unleashing" of Chiang Kai-shek against the Red Chinese and there were rumors that it would be followed by a blockade of China and a build-up of American military strength.

We made arrangements for Eisenhower to deliver his foreign policy speech before the American Society of Newspaper Editors at the Statler Hotel in Washington on April 16, 1953, and Jackson and the State Department had it broadcasted and circulated in printed form all over the world. In India alone it was distributed in eight different languages. Emmet Hughes, who was then Eisenhower's chief speech writer, did a notable job of presenting the ideas that the President gave him, as well as elevating the President's language. It was the most effective speech of Eisenhower's public career, and certainly one of the highlights of his presidency. We heard later that people behind the Iron Curtain prayed and wept as they listened to it, and Winston Churchill sent a personal message in praise of it to Molotov. In the speech, Eisenhower urged the new Russian leaders to take positive forward steps toward the settlement of issues between the Soviet Union and the Western world and to remove the threat of a third world war. Declaring that America would welcome every honest Russian act of peace, the President called for disarmament and international control of atomic energy under United Nations supervision.

Strangely enough, it was also the most difficult speech that Eisenhower ever delivered. He interrupted a brief golfing vacation at

Augusta to return to Washington and make the address before the gathering of newspaper editors. When he arrived at the White House on the morning of April 16 he was suffering from a stomach upset so vicious that he could hardly hold up his head. When I talked with him about the program for the meeting, I did not think he could go through with the speech. He was pale and weak when he stood up to talk before the television cameras at the Statler and he grew weaker, clutching at the rostrum for support, as he talked on. He told me later that he had no recollection of what he was saying toward the end of the speech and that the print he was trying to read was dancing before his eyes. But he managed to finish it, with great acclaim, and a few days after he returned to Augusta he was out on the golf course with Senator Taft in the best of health again.

In his attempt to bring the Korean War to a close, Eisenhower had to choose between the course that Syngman Rhee wanted—an all-out, total war against China that would drive the Reds beyond the Yalu River—and the honorable compromise that Truman had tried unsuccessfully to reach, an ending of hostilities withdrawing the Reds from South Korea and giving back to Rhee all the territory that the Communists had taken from him during the three years of fighting. Eisenhower and Dulles were using the thinly veiled threat of a retaliatory atomic bomb attack to bring the Chinese into truce negotiations, but the President had no intention of aggressively bringing on a total war to give Rhee all of Korea. Aside from igniting a global nuclear war with Russia, to say nothing of the stupendous cost involved, Eisenhower was certain that an all-out offensive against China would shock world opinion and turn not only the neutral nations but many of our friends in the United Nations against the United States. To drive the Reds out of North Korea by force we would have had to go it alone, isolated from our friends in the United Nations. While such a course appealed to Senator Taft, General MacArthur and many members of Congress, Eisenhower saw little sense in it.

"If you go it alone in one place," he said at the time, "you have to go it alone everywhere. No single free nation can live alone in the world. We have to have friends. These friends have got to be tied to you, in some form or another. We have to have that unity in basic purposes that comes from a recognition of common interests."

Eisenhower also pointed out that the extremists who called for a total war against Red China seldom mentioned that such a move would mean total mobilization in the United States.

Many of the conservatives of both parties in Congress were against a negotiated peace in Korea because they felt that this was the soft solution and suspected that United States recognition of Red China would follow. To the shocked surprise of everyone sitting around the table, the blunt and uninhibited Charlie Wilson asked Eisenhower one day at a Cabinet meeting if he would consider making such an offer to the Communists. The Defense Secretary spoke as if he were trying to find a bargaining point in a business negotiation.

"Is there any possibility for a package deal?" Wilson said. "Maybe we could recognize Red China and get the Far East issues settled."

Eisenhower managed to control himself.

"I wouldn't," he explained patiently. "To make a deal saying we think you are respectable if you stop fighting just isn't possible. Another thing: as long as they serve Russian Communism, why should we let another Communist country like this one into the United Nations?"

When the threat of the atomic bomb followed by the death of Stalin brought the Chinese Reds to the bargaining table, Eisenhower and Dulles found themselves ensnarled in a prolonged dispute with Syngman Rhee that was more nerve-racking and frustrating than the haggling with the Communists. Resentment against Rhee for his stubborn refusal to participate in the truce proceedings ran so high behind the scenes in Washington that Eisenhower had to remind the Republican legislative leaders rather sharply in one discussion of the Far East predicament that our enemy in Korea was still the Reds, not Rhee. The seventy-eight-year-old Korean President flatly refused to agree to any peace pact that would leave his country divided. Rather than accept a return to the thirty-eighth parallel, the boundary that he had recognized before the Communist invasion of South Korea, he was willing to face certain defeat by continuing to fight the Reds without either American or United Nations help. The endless efforts to appeal to Rhee's sense of reason and to make him understand that the United States could not hazard a possible world war for a unified Korea left Eisenhower and Dulles limp and baffled. After the opening prayer at a Cabinet meeting during the arguments with Rhee, Eisenhower said, "I can't remember when there was ever a forty-eight hours when I felt more in need of help from someone more intelligent than I am." He talked with an air of helplessness about the South Koreans' apparent willingness to commit suicide if they had to give up the northern part of their country permanently to the Communists.

"Their ambassador was in here," Eisenhower said, "and I asked him, 'What would you do if American support was withdrawn?' He said simply, 'We would die.' "

This was the morning after Dulles had telephoned Eisenhower in the middle of the night to tell him that Rhee had upset the prisoner-of-war exchange agreement by releasing thousands of anti-Communist North Korean prisoners before he was authorized to do so. As the President and Dulles explained to the Cabinet, Rhee was in a position to throw Korea and the entire Far East into chaotic bloodshed. His South Korean troops were holding two-thirds of the United Nations front lines, where combat was suspended while the truce negotiations were being carried on. If Rhee decided to break this temporary armis-tice agreement, as he had broken the prisoner exchange contract, and ordered his soldiers to attack the Communists, a Red counterattack would be likely to wipe out Rhee's forces and along with them the adjoining American and United Nations units in the remaining third of the front line sector. There would be no telling then where the Communists would stop. While the discussion was going on in the Cabinet room, a message came to Dulles from General Mark Clark, the United States spokesman then trying to reason with Rhee in Korea. The Cabinet members watched Eisenhower silently while Dulles showed him the message and, with his usual deliberate solemnity, offered a few whispered comments. "Clark is alarmed," the President said, turning to the Cabinet. "We took a firm line with Rhee. Now he says he's willing to see us walk out." He shook his head and added, "We must not walk out of Korea."

The firm line that Eisenhower had taken with Rhee was plainly stated in a letter the President had written to the South Korean leader, making clear that the United States could not become embroiled in a general war to reunite Korea. "We do not intend to employ war as an instrument to accomplish the worldwide political settlements which we believe to be just," Eisenhower wrote, adding as a final warning that the thought of a separation between him and Rhee "at this critical hour would be a tragedy." But now Clark was reporting that Rhee, in his defiant mood, was willing to stand such a separation. Eisenhower told the Cabinet again, as he had told them often during the truce negotiations, that he wished the South Koreans would overthrow Rhee and replace him with a more moderate and reasonable leader. Henry Cabot Lodge mentioned that he had talked with General MacArthur on an airliner a few days previously and the General had predicted that Rhee would be killed within a few weeks.

"On what basis?" Eisenhower asked.

"The General thinks that when this emotion dies down and the South Koreans have a chance for more reflection, certain elements will act," Lodge said.

Humphrey said he thought the only thing for us to do was to find some way of saving face in Korea. The President laughed at him scornfully and said, "Westerners saving face?"

A few minutes later there was another message from Clark, saying that Rhee was threatening to withdraw his front line troops from the United Nations command.

"We're coming to a point where it's completely impossible," Eisenhower said. "There's one thing I learned in the five years I served in the Army out there—we can never figure out the workings of the Oriental mind. You just can't tell how they will react." Then he looked around the table at the Cabinet members and said to them, "If anyone has any ideas, for God's sake, don't hold them back." But nobody in the room had anything to say.

The apparently hopeless deadlock with Rhee was finally broken by Walter S. Robertson, the State Department's quiet and soft-spoken Assistant Secretary for Far Eastern Affairs. The President, flatly refusing to surrender to what he called Rhee's blackmail, and Dulles, in despair of comprehending the workings of Rhee's mind, decided to send Robertson to Korea to try to talk some sense into Rhee's head. Neither Eisenhower nor Dulles gave any indication that they expected Robertson to accomplish a miracle. But Robertson brought the fanatic South Korean President down to earth by sitting with him in a room for several days and listening patiently and sympathetically while Rhee talked steadily about his grievances. Then Robertson began shrewdly and firmly to make Rhee understand the United States position, assuring him, among other things, that the Americans would not go to war to unite his country but, on the other hand, would not leave South

Korea without economic aid and military support after the truce. After two weeks with Robertson, Rhee agreed to leave his troops under the United Nations command and wrote to Eisenhower that he would not interfere with the peace negotiations. It was still necessary for Eisenhower and Dulles to hold Rhee's hand but the worst was over. As the negotiations with the Communists proceeded, Eisenhower made ready to launch a counterattack on the Chinese, this time with atomic weapons, if they started to fight again. Dulles also secured a promise from the British at the NATO foreign ministers' meeting that they would come back into a broadened war with us in Korea if the truce broke down.

Happily, there was no breakdown in the cease-fire agreement and even though the arrangements surrounding the armistice were at best unsatisfactory, Eisenhower had made good on the principal pledge in his campaign for the presidency: The war in Korea had been stopped. As I watched Eisenhower and Dulles weather this first trying crisis they faced together, it seemed to me that the President was shouldering a heavier responsibility in their close partnership than most of the people around them realized. Although Eisenhower depended on Dulles to make the invariably decisive recommendation on what should be done in a critical situation, I noticed that Dulles, in turn, placed great reliance upon Eisenhower to sense what the effect of doing it would be.

Eisenhower told me one day that he had become completely convinced that every important decision of the government, no matter what field it was in, had a direct effect upon our relations with other nations. The President talked with Dulles about the need of some patient explaining of their foreign policy aims for the particular benefit of those in the Cabinet who had neither an understanding nor real appreciation of the reasons behind the courses of action they intended to follow. One morning in June, 1953, at the height of the Korean truce crisis, when he was being pressed by many other urgent problems connected with such matters as the Bricker Amendment, the Taft-Hartley Act, personnel appointments and the wheat surplus, the President took the time at a Cabinet meeting for Dulles to give the Secretaries and the agency directors and presidential assistants a long talk on his conception of the basic facts of America's responsibilities as a world leader and the international predicament in general.

For all of us who were there it was a memorable experience. Dulles spoke without interruption for over an hour, talking slowly, sometimes hesitantly, pausing now and then while he collected his thoughts, weighing his words with care. Eisenhower listened to him intently and although it was a full meeting there was not a sound or a restless movement in the room. The Secretary of State began with the fundamentals of our foreign policy, explaining why the security of our defenses at home required us to spend great sums of money abroad.

Our deterrent against the Russians, Dulles pointed out, was a retaliatory striking force that could be launched quickly from bases near the enemy and this meant that the United States must maintain such bases on foreign soil in various distant parts of the world—England, Iceland, the European Continent, North Africa, Turkey, Suez and Arabia. "We must promote good will in the countries where our bases are located because we do not use coercive ideological power as the Communists do," Dulles said. "Besides this, the location of our bases makes these countries a target, an additional consideration in giving them economic aid."

Another deterrent was NATO, Dulles went on to add, and because this involved the protection of Western Europe and its industry, so vital to our own security, we financed one-third of the expense of its operation. The main point that Eisenhower was anxious to get across to his Cabinet and department heads was the relation of these gigantically expensive foreign programs to the defense of the United States. "If we lose our position in Europe," Dulles said emphatically, "we will have a much greater risk of war, which, in turn, will force us here at home into total mobilization. Then the costs will be infinitely greater than what we bear now. The 'Fortress America' concept is silly. If you just consider dollars and cents alone, it is reckless to talk of withdrawal from foreign alliances."

Turning to the Far East, the Secretary of State discussed the situation in Japan, where there were then plans to revive slowly an anti-Communist military force, and in Indo-China and Burma, where a reduction of our financial commitments would bring an internal collapse that would throw that area's rubber, tin and other strategic resources into Communist hands. India's economic plan must not fail, Dulles emphasized. Though a neutral, we must prevent her falling under Communist influence, just as we saved Italy through Mutual

Security and Defense Department offshore procurement spending.

"We can't make further cuts in Mutual Security and Defense expenditures," Dulles said, as he concluded his talk. "The world situation is not good. Everywhere we are saying, 'What are we in danger of losing?' Not 'What are we gaining?' The Communists are thinking in terms of what they can win next. We haven't been able to reverse that yet. If you are thinking of costs, consider for a moment the cost of obtaining bases in Turkey if we had to get them by a military invasion instead of by Mutual Security and Defense funds. We must all realize that we cannot cut foreign aid beyond certain limits for the sake of economy. If we do, everything collapses."

When Dulles was finished, Eisenhower looked around the table at the Cabinet members for a moment and then spoke to them with the measured tread of cold conviction in his voice.

"The basic contention of the Communists is that man long ago proved himself incapable of ruling himself," the President said. "So they establish dictatorships to make man do what he himself has failed to do. Well, we don't believe that. But, nevertheless, that is the real question confronting us. Can man govern himself? It's just that simple. Can man operate by co-operation? We have got to get our struggle understood by the whole world—what we are fighting for—for this is the struggle of man to rule himself. We talk about France and her political troubles and then our own people want to pass a Bricker Amendment. Then we see that we rule by shibboleths, by prejudice and by slogans." Eisenhower paused and shook his head, trying to control his feelings. "Well," he said, "we better get along to something else before I get worked up."

Eisenhower felt deeply that the heart of the real issue that divided him from the conservative Republicans in the endless disputes on foreign spending, on the wording and phrasing of the various amendments to the Bricker resolution and all the other superficial arguments on international affairs, was not understood in Washington, especially among some of his own people. For him the big question was whether or not the United States was willing to accept the leadership of world democracy that had inevitably been thrust upon it after World War II. Under its guise of protecting people's rights, the Bricker Amendment, in Eisenhower's opinion, was just one more expression of reluctance to assume a responsibility that we could not avoid. He wrote to Senator

Knowland on January 25, 1954, after a year of battle over the measure:

> Adoption of the Bricker amendment in its present form by the Senate would be notice to our friends as well as our enemies abroad that our country intends to withdraw from its leadership in world affairs. The inevitable reaction would be of major proportion. It would impair our hopes and plans for peace and for the successful achievement of the important international matters now under discussion. . . .

The amendment proposed by Senator John Bricker of Ohio was intended to limit the power of the President in making treaties and to increase the authority of Congress in the foreign relations field. It did not arise from any foreign agreements initiated by Eisenhower and there was no personal conflict between Bricker and the President behind it; the Ohio Senator introduced his resolution on January 7, 1953, before Eisenhower was in office. A few days before that, when we were still working at the Commodore in New York, I received a note from Dulles asking us to slow down any attempt to push the Bricker Amendment quickly through the Senate. "In my opinion," Dulles wrote,

> while a case can be made for *some* amendment to meet the theoretical possibility that the Executive might negotiate, the Senate might ratify and the Supreme Court might sustain a treaty to deprive the American citizens of their Constitutional rights, the actual amendment, as drawn, would go far beyond this and might seriously impair the treaty making power and the ability of the President to deal with current matters, notably U.S. troops abroad, etc., through administrative agreements. I think this whole matter needs to be carefully studied before there is action.

After consulting Eisenhower, I wired Jerry Persons in Washington, "Will you convey to Senator Bricker the personal wish of General Eisenhower to consult with him on his proposal to amend the treaty making power of the President before he submits his resolution to the Senate." That began a series of delaying actions on the amendment that continued with interminable discussions and disagreements for the rest of the year.

Like the enslaved-peoples resolution, the Bricker Amendment stemmed from Republican determination to prevent a repetition of the agreements made by the previous Democratic administrations at

Teheran, Yalta and Potsdam, as well as from the Old Guard's suspicion that the United States might be forced into going along with a United Nations action that might not coincide with what they believed to be in the best interests of the American people. There was a considerable sentiment for the amendment in the Senate and among conservatives generally, and the Republican leaders kept drumming in the ears of Eisenhower and Brownell that an uncompromising White House stand against it might cause a serious split in the Republican party. Persons and I were getting fatherly advice almost continuously about persuading Brownell and the President to accept some language that would be agreeable to Bricker. For some months, Eisenhower thought that might be possible. At first, he felt that the difference between himself and Bricker on the amendment was largely in the wording of the resolution. Always ready to try to mollify a dissenting Senator or Congressman on such a matter, the President invited Bricker to his office on several occasions and gave him friendly hearings. The warm and sympathetic tone of the talks gave Bricker the impression of more willingness to compromise than Eisenhower intended to give him. Bricker got enough encouragement to urge the Senate Republican leaders, Knowland and Millikin, to press the President to work out a compromise or to support a substitute amendment that would be acceptable to Bricker and his followers. But they gave up on Dulles and his legal adviser, Herman Phleger, who would not budge.

Eisenhower thus found himself caught in a crossfire between the Republican conservatives and the State Department. Dulles and Herman Phleger, both experts on constitutional law, became well entrenched in their opposition to anything resembling the Bricker Amendment, no matter how harmless or well intentioned such a proposal might appear. Dulles contended that any move against the President's authority to make foreign policy decisions was a serious weakening of the constitutional powers of the executive branch of the government and would be especially dangerous in view of the delicate negotiations with our allies in which Eisenhower would later be engaged. No changes in the wording of a resolution or its clauses and provisions would lessen this basic threat to the President's rightful authority, Dulles insisted.

But the hassle over the Bricker Amendment went on that spring, with Bricker producing on June 15 another version that was just as objectionable to Dulles as the first draft because it contained a controversial provision that Dulles contended had the effect of giving individual states in the United States the right to repudiate treaties with foreign powers. In the debate that followed, this provision became known as the "which clause." Authorship of the "which clause" was generally ascribed to Frank E. Holman, a former president of the American Bar Association, who worked closely with Bricker on the amendment and later wrote a book about his role in the fight to put a constitutional limitation on the President's treaty-making authority.

The next day Bricker came to see Eisenhower, claiming that this interpretation of the "which clause" was wrong. Still seeking a way out, Eisenhower told the Ohio Senator that he might accept other parts of the new amendment if the "which clause" were removed. To Senator Wiley of Wisconsin and other Senators who were backing Dulles, this seemed to put the President in an inconsistent position, because the Secretary of State had warned them against accepting any part of the amendment. Eisenhower, getting tired of the whole thing, protested that he was not being inconsistent. He said that he was only trying to quiet the fears of people who wanted no more Yalta agreements, but that he would support no amendment that disturbed the President's constitutional powers. In July, he backed a substitute amendment, introduced by Knowland, that simply provided that a foreign agreement would have no effect if it conflicted with the Constitution. This was a long way from what Bricker and Holman wanted and it died when they refused to accept it.

It was dead certain that Bricker would make a determined stand for his amendment as soon as the second session of Congress began in January. In December I set up a conference between the President, Dulles and Brownell to consider a new draft which came as close to a general agreement as the argument ever got. Brownell was more responsive to Eisenhower's wish to placate the Senate Republicans with some compromise, and was ready to suggest language providing that no treaty should become effective as internal law except through appropriate legislation, although this would not have affected the authority of the President to make treaties that were entirely valid as international law. At that time Eisenhower would have accepted this because he felt that the issue would be forever cropping up in years to come and it would be better to agree on something that Bricker could sponsor provided that absolutely no question of weakening the power of the executive was involved.

To seal an agreement, the President invited Bricker to meet him with Dulles at his residence on January 7, 1954. But the agreement with Bricker quickly backfired. Brownell had to tell the leaders on January 11 that Bricker had called from Ohio to say that he had found a philosophical difference, and he would have to offer the "which clause" and would not compromise any further. This caused the President to say in exasperation that Frank Holman seemed determined "to save the United States from Eleanor Roosevelt."

True to his promise, when Congress went into session again Bricker made his grand stand with the Chicago *Tribune,* the Daughters of the American Revolution and a group called the Vigilant Women for the Bricker Amendment marching stanchly behind him. On the other side was the League of Women Voters, the American Association for the United Nations, the Association of the Bar of the City of New York, several independent newspapers and Dean Erwin N. Griswold of the Harvard Law School, who wrote to Eisenhower that his administration would be remembered in history for selling out the Constitution if he gave in to Bricker. By this time, Eisenhower needed no such urging. Thoroughly disgusted with what he now considered a direct attempt to undermine the constitutional structure of the executive branch of the government, the President was no longer in a mood to argue with the Republican leaders over words and phrases. In order to make sure there was no doubt about where he stood, Eisenhower handed a letter to Senator Knowland on January 25, following a favorable report on the Bricker Amendment by the Senate Judiciary Committee. "I am unalterably opposed to the Bricker Amendment as reported," he told Knowland. "Adoption . . . would be notice to our friends as well as our enemies abroad that our country intends to withdraw from its leadership in world affairs. . . . It would impair our hopes and plans for peace."

Eisenhower's firmer stand resulted in the defeat of the amendment, but by a narrow margin. A substitute offered by Senator Walter George was also opposed by Eisenhower, although the "which clause" had disappeared. Senator Knowland, by then Taft's successor as the Republican administration's majority leader in the Senate, went against Eisenhower and voted for the George Amendment, further widening the rift between him and the President. The George Amendment missed by only one vote the two-thirds majority that it needed to pass the Senate.

As Eisenhower had predicted, the fight never quite died down. As late as 1956 the State Department was taking count of the probable Senate votes on another substitute offered by Senator Dirksen. The new version never presented any serious threat, but the division of opinion in the Senate spoke eloquently of the reason why Eisenhower and Dulles had to look to the other party for the support of their policies. The tally taken by actual inquiry of each Senator's position showed that every one of the thirteen Senators "implacably opposed to all amendments as unnecessary" were Democrats, and of nineteen Senators who "favor any amendment which could be passed" thirteen were Republicans. Whenever Bricker renewed his campaign and came to talk with the President, the atmosphere of compromise and understanding sympathy was gone.

The news of the explosion of Russia's first hydrogen bomb on August 12, 1953, reached Eisenhower at the summer White House in Denver, where the problem of the growing nuclear arms race already deeply weighed on his mind. Since the previous April, he had been considering with C. D. Jackson a speech that would warn the world of the destructive power of the H-bomb in the hope that the warning would bring about positive measures to prevent the use of thermonuclear weapons. The speech had been suggested by Jackson and Robert Cutler as a result of recommendations from scientific advisers who felt a need for more public understanding of the H-bomb menace.

Jackson had been unable to get Operation Candor, as the speech-writing project was called, off the ground. Turning out draft after draft, he could find no way to escape from a grim recital of the horrors of nuclear destruction with nothing much for Eisenhower to point to as a solution for the dilemma that mankind was facing. The President saw no benefit to be gained by talking about gory details that only underscored the crying need of finding better answers for dealing with the Communist menace. A bomb shelter program, the cost of which

neither the American citizen nor the federal government was willing
to accept, added no appeal to the gloomy picture. Obviously the
world's danger of destruction from its new thermonuclear power called
for the United States to produce an international program to lessen
that danger, a program based on an idea with dramatic appeal.

Granted that Dulles was a man of great moral force and conviction,
he was not endowed with the creative genius that produces bold, new
ideas to gain hitherto unattainable policy goals. Giving Dulles the
responsibility for initiating foreign policy brought positive results in
our taking firm stands for certain alliances, for certain treaties and
understandings and for new attitudes toward heads of various governments and plans of strategy. But just as often his point of view
was strongly negative—against certain old favoritisms, against relaxing his intransigence toward the Communists and against experi-
mental innovations by outsiders in the traditional procedure of the
State Department. Well aware of the need for ideas to fire up positive
moves in the cold war, Eisenhower had brought Jackson into the
government to work with Dulles. The Secretary and Jackson, contrary
to what might have been expected, got along well together, but Jackson found his service in Washington a frustrating experience generally.
Our government, Jackson learned, is resourceful in its ways and means
of shelving new ideas. He was reminded often of the old definition of a
government committee: a group of people who join in long discussions
to decide that nothing can be done. Even though our democratic
system is based on trial and error, it sometimes takes a heroic shaking
up to get somebody to make a trial. A detailed account of Jackson's
lonely attempts to follow through in various departments and agencies
on several ideas that he had for capitalizing overseas on the death
of Stalin would make a graphic study of the strong aversion among
foreign service career men to anything imaginative and original.

After the announcement of the Soviet hydrogen bomb explosions
was substantiated by our detection devices, Eisenhower himself began
to think about a positive idea for Operation Candor. When he came
to Washington on September 10 for Chief Justice Vinson's funeral, he
summoned Cutler and gave him a brief outline of a plan that had
occurred to him a few days before in Denver. The President asked
Cutler to pass it on to Jackson and Lewis Strauss, then the Chairman
of the Atomic Energy Commission. Cutler's message began:

In a discussion with the President this morning . . . he suggested
that you might consider the following proposal which he did not think
anyone had yet thought of:

Suppose the United States and the Soviets were each to turn over to
the United Nations for peaceful uses X kilograms of fissionable material. . . .

That was the beginning of Eisenhower's Atoms-for-Peace proposal
which he presented before the United Nations in New York on December 8, 1953, in a speech that brought universal acclaim. In Moscow, Ambassador Bohlen had given Molotov advance notice that
Eisenhower would submit an important plan for the Russians to
consider, without telling him what the President would say. After
some hesitation, the Soviet government agreed to give the Atoms-for-
Peace proposal serious consideration. Even V. K. Krishna Menon,
India's inscrutable delegate to the United Nations, admitted to me later
that the speech was "very important," which meant that Menon, no
admirer of the United States, must have been deeply stirred by it.

Eisenhower's idea was the first plan for international co-operation
in nuclear development and research to be placed before the world
powers since the failure of Bernard Baruch's inspection proposal seven
years earlier. The President began his speech with the frank admission
that the tremendous destructive power of the American and Soviet
thermonuclear weapons left little hope for survival in a future war.
Turning from the "awful arithmetic" of the atom to a note of hope
for peace, he asked for the establishment of an international stockpile
of fissionable material under United Nations supervision for the study
and exchange of peaceful uses of atomic energy. The United States,
Eisenhower promised, would diminish its own nuclear supplies to
contribute to the project and would be willing to share its nuclear
knowledge with other nations for such a purpose. He expressed a
conviction that co-operative research between nuclear-power-equipped
nations would "open new channels for peaceful discussions and initiate at least a new approach to the many difficult problems that must
be solved in both public and private conversations, if the world is to
shake off the inertia imposed by fear and is to make positive progress
toward peace." The unmistakable implication behind Eisenhower's
proposal, of course, was that a move like this one to break down
secrecy and suspicion would also be a step toward disarmament.

Although the Atoms-for-Peace plan, unlike most important proposals from heads of states, was actually Eisenhower's own idea, the difficult, and often discouraging, ordeal of carrying it through to its final completion and getting it accepted and approved had been left to Jackson. The President's Special Assistant threw himself into the assignment with the same enthusiasm and determination that he had brought into the hotel room in Buffalo on the night in the 1952 campaign when he presented Emmet Hughes's "I shall go to Korea" speech to Eisenhower. But within a few weeks Jackson was almost ready to give up the Atoms-for-Peace proposal as a failure. He had to work alone in pushing the plan through the Atomic Energy Commission, the State Department, the Pentagon and various other government offices, where he met with indifference, evasion and objections from department heads and technical experts. He came to the White House and complained to me about the lack of "command decisions." There was little I could do for him except to give him consolation and encouragement. Eisenhower was busy with other things and Dulles was preoccupied with his October meeting in London with the British and Soviet foreign ministers and the coming Bermuda conference between Eisenhower and Winston Churchill, which had been set for December 4. An idealistic venture like the Atoms-for-Peace plan was hardly the sort of thing that would fire the imagination of a man like Dulles anyway. He gave it his tacit approval, but he had some doubts about it. Lewis Strauss eventually came to Jackson's aid with technical assistance and the full support of the Atomic Energy Commission. In addition, Jackson had to consult with a few Congressional leaders. Everybody had ideas about how the speech should be worded. Between the day of Chief Justice Vinson's funeral in September, when Eisenhower first mentioned the Atoms-for-Peace idea, and December 8, when he delivered his address to the United Nations, Jackson wrote and rewrote thirty-three versions of that speech.

Until twenty-four hours before the Atoms-for-Peace proposal was presented, Eisenhower was uncertain whether he would go ahead with it. The December 8 date was selected tentatively because the President wanted to hold informal discussions with Churchill and Anthony Eden anyway, and that would give him the opportunity to show the address to his British confidants. After thinking it over, he resolved to see what Laniel and Bidault thought of it too. Henry

Cabot Lodge arranged with Dag Hammarskjöld, the United Nations Secretary General, for a possible appearance of Eisenhower before the General Assembly with the understanding that the engagement could be canceled at the last minute. If the President decided to deliver the speech, he would fly directly to New York from Bermuda a few hours before he was scheduled to talk. Eisenhower and Dulles took precautions to keep the contents of the speech strictly under wraps, with none of the advance distribution of the text in various languages that is usual with important presidential addresses. There were two good reasons for this: his indecision about making the speech at all, and if he did, the hope of providing the maximum impact upon the Russians. When word was sent to Ambassador Bohlen in Moscow to let Molotov know that the President might say something before the United Nations that would interest the Soviets, Bohlen sent a wire back to the State Department asking what Eisenhower would talk about. Playing it safe, Dulles and the President declined to let even Bohlen in on the subject of the speech.

The meeting in Bermuda between Eisenhower, Churchill, Dulles and Eden was an informal affair, with no agenda, mostly devoted to an exploration by Churchill into the possibilities of arranging talks between the Western leaders and Malenkov. As Jackson remarked at the time, Churchill was so intent on leading a peace pilgrimage to Moscow during those months immediately after Stalin's death that he would have made the crusade alone. Eisenhower and Dulles were firmly of the opinion, however, that such overtures should come from the Russians. When Eisenhower showed his Atoms-for-Peace speech to Churchill and Eden, they both liked it. Sir Winston wrote a note of praise to the President, expressing the hope that the Atoms-for-Peace proposal would calm world tensions. He objected to two minor points in the speech, one of them a reference to the atomic weapons that were being held in readiness by American forces in Europe. Churchill felt that such a note of aggressiveness did not belong in a plea for peaceful co-operation. Eisenhower and Jackson agreed with him and the paragraph was taken out. Eisenhower and Dulles then decided, after discussing Churchill's favorable reaction, to send word to Lodge in New York that the speech would be delivered.

The text of the address was still being changed and polished by Eisenhower, Dulles, Strauss and Jackson while the presidential plane, the *Columbine,* was in the air between Bermuda and New York. As the four men finished with each paragraph, it was handed to Marie McCrum, Jackson's secretary, who then read it aloud to Ann Whitman, the President's secretary, and Mary Caffrey, Jim Hagerty's secretary, as they worked side by side on two typewriters. Mrs. Whitman was typing the script in oversized jumbo type that the President would read at the General Assembly meeting and Miss Caffrey was cutting a mimeograph stencil of each page. The stencils were rushed to the rear of the plane as they were completed and inserted in a hand-operated mimeographing machine by an Army sergeant who was grinding out copies of the new speech for distribution to the press and overseas news agencies. When the plane reached New York, the typing and mimeographing were still unfinished. The pilot circled over the city for fifteen minutes while Dulles and the other high-ranking officials aboard helped the secretaries with the work of assembling the pages of text and stapling them together before the landing at La Guardia Airport.

The press and radio and television coverage that the Atoms-for-Peace speech received all over the world was amazing, considering that there was no time for advance distribution of the President's proposal. The flame of hope for peace that the speech ignited continued to burn brightly for a few months afterward. Then it flickered and died down. The plan depended on Soviet willingness to co-operate and participate but, after a stealthy look and a few cautious questions, the Russians backed away from it. Eisenhower was forced to announce nine months after the speech that the Western powers would join together in research on the peaceful uses of nuclear energy without the Soviets. But even that program ran into resistance from a complication at home that had nothing to do with its international aspects. Jackson resigned from his government position in March, 1954. His successor, Nelson Rockefeller, found that the Atoms-for-Peace program was lagging because certain key officials in the administration whose enthusiasm it needed, such as Lewis Strauss himself, were wary of government development of atomic energy for nonmilitary purposes for fear that it would be one more irretraceable step toward a limitation of private enterprise in the power business. But Eisenhower's idea still took deep root and has grown steadily, if not dramatically, in recent years. Out of his proposal came the agreement between twelve nations, including the United States and the Soviet Union, for the International Atomic Energy Agency, which is making forward strides under United Nations sponsorship in the exchange of nuclear information. In September, 1960, the same month that Khrushchev was staging his turbulent demonstration against Dag Hammarskjöld and the Western democracies at the General Assembly session in New York, American and Russian delegates were conducting friendly talks at an International Atomic Energy Agency conference in Geneva. Heading the Soviet representatives and conducting himself with unfamiliarly polite decorum was Molotov, the kaleidoscopic foreign minister of the Stalin and Malenkov regimes, who had been sent to Geneva by Khrushchev after serving a lengthy exile from Moscow doing penance in an obscure post in Outer Mongolia.

When Jackson gave up the struggle in Washington after the agreed term of his enlistment had more than come to an end, he left with Eisenhower and Dulles a recommendation for a bold foreign program. While the central point of view of Jackson's proposal was becoming more widely shared by the best-informed foreign observers, it suffered from the competition of other more pressing programs and the realities of the federal budget. Jackson pointed out that the Soviets were making significant headway in the cold war because they were concentrating on economic and trade offensives. Recalling the tremendously successful effect of the Marshall Plan in winning friends overseas, he said that the United States, to stay abreast in the race, needed to launch a down-to-earth world economic plan that could be made to work. With the hard lessons learned during his experience as the administration's cold war idea promoter vivid in his mind, Jackson went on to warn that such a plan could win support only in the hands of people who understood the nature of the Communist competition and would keep it from the watering-down process which the compromisers would put it through to make it politically acceptable to Congress. This, said Jackson, would so dilute it that it would be quite useless.

Jackson's plan never reached even that stage. The problems of applying such thinking to the policies already in operation, together with the necessity of keeping some control over the ceilings of public expense, staggered the imagination of those who nevertheless believed in Jackson's approach. In that spring of 1954 those ideas became submerged in the more immediate urgencies of the Indo-China crisis and the supreme effort of Eisenhower and Dulles to persuade France to accept the proposed European Defense Community program.

7 Trouble in the Far East

Two years later Dulles said that the Indo-China situation of 1954, along with the Korean War truce crisis of 1953 and Red China's threatened invasion of Formosa in late 1954 and early 1955, had forced the United States to the brink of total war. The Secretary of State cited these three instances as crucial tests of his so-called policy of "deterrence" in an interview with James Shepley, chief of the Washington bureau of *Time* and *Life* magazines. The statement stirred up one of the major controversial storms of the whole Eisenhower administration. The Dulles policy of deterrence, as Shepley explained it in his article, was based on the Secretary's conviction that no national leader would start a war unless he thought he could get away with it. The Korean War, for example, would not have been started by the Communists, in Dulles' opinion, if Moscow had known that the United States would be willing to fight for the protection of South Korea. Dulles believed that the Reds invaded that area because his predecessor, Dean Acheson, had suggested six months earlier that South Korea was outside of the "vital perimeter" of the United States defenses. If you are ready to stand up against a potential aggressor with an impressive deterrent of "massive retaliatory power," the Dulles theory contended, the aggression was not likely to occur. This was indeed an accurate summation of the basic theory of the Dulles strategy as it opposed the containment defense policy of the Truman-Acheson regime. But whether the Dulles policy was actually put to three crucial tests, as the Secretary believed it was, is a matter that is open to question.

"You have to take chances for peace, just as you must take chances in war," Dulles was quoted as saying in Shepley's article.

Some say that we were brought to the verge of war. Of course, we were brought to the verge of war. The ability to get to the verge without getting into the war is the necessary art. If you cannot master it, you inevitably get into war. If you try to run away from it, if you are scared to go to the brink, you are lost. We've had to look it square in the face—on the question of enlarging the Korean War, on the question of getting into the Indo-China war, on the question of Formosa. We walked to the brink and we looked it in the face. We took strong action. It took a lot more courage for the President than for me. His was the ultimate decision. I did not have to make the decision myself, only to recommend it. The President never flinched for a minute on any of these situations. He came up taut.

I doubt that Eisenhower was as close to the brink of war in any of those three crises as Dulles made him out to be. Although the President revealed that a threat of an atomic bombing and total war was made to the Chinese Communists in order to persuade them into the Korean truce negotiations, he has never suggested that the threat was as specific and as near to being carried out as Dulles intimated it was in his interview with Shepley. Moreover, there is no clear evidence that we were teetering on the brink at Geneva in the bold front that Dulles contended saved half of Indo-China from the Communists. The President knew that the American people had no appetite for another prolonged war in Southeast Asia. He was determined not to become involved without the approval of Congress and without the participation of the British, and neither Congress nor the British wanted to fight in Indo-China.

The issue at stake in the Formosa crisis of the late fall of 1954 was the same one that developed into a hot argument between Nixon and Kennedy in the presidential campaign of 1960, the question of whether the United States should defend the islands of Quemoy and Matsu from a threatened invasion by the Chinese Reds. A strong body of opinion, headed by Admiral Radford and Senator Knowland, held that these islands close to the shore of the Chinese mainland, occupied by Chiang Kai-shek's Nationalist forces, should be protected by the United States from any kind of attack. Eisenhower had no desire to provoke a war with China unless Formosa itself was in jeopardy. The ultimatum from Eisenhower to the Chinese Communists, that

Dulles subsequently referred to as a step to the brink of war, was an unprecedented resolution passed by Congress in January, 1955, giving the President his requested authority to use United States armed forces to safeguard Formosa and the Pescadores Islands. But Eisenhower carefully worded the resolution so that it did not specifically guarantee a defense of Quemoy and Matsu along with protection of Formosa and the Pescadores. He inserted a wait-and-see clause that gave him the privilege of deciding in the event of an attack on Quemoy and Matsu whether the safety of Formosa and the Pescadores was actually threatened before committing himself to a fight over the smaller islands near the Chinese mainland. The Formosa Resolution was not quite the belligerent challenge that Dulles said it was in his interview with Shepley. Eisenhower did not draw a definite line across the Strait of Formosa and warn the Communists that if they crossed it there would be war.

During the furor that followed the publication of Shepley's article there was naturally some speculation and concern among us on his staff about how Eisenhower would handle the inevitable questions that would be put to him about it. Eisenhower never wasted any time talking to me about newspaper stories and articles. Had he not been asked about it in his press conference he would not have taken any public notice of the Shepley article. In the briefing session with the President before the press conference, Hagerty began a discussion about how the expected questions from the reporters on the Shepley article could be handled. Eisenhower told us abruptly and with a little irritation that he had already decided how he would reply to such questions and quickly changed the subject. Sometimes when Eisenhower disagreed with a public statement made by somebody in the administration his displeasure crept into his replies to questions at a press conference. In this case, Eisenhower was very careful about what he said. He observed that Dulles was the best Secretary of State he ever knew and he reminded the reporters that the tactics used in stopping Communist aggression in the Far East involved decisions of the National Security Council that a President could not discuss with propriety in public. But he did make one remark that revealed what he felt under the surface. He did not know, he said, whether unfortunate expressions had been used by Mr. Dulles or by the author of the article. But Eisenhower was saying they had been used by someone, and in his carefully guarded way of speaking he was taking exception to the wisdom of what Dulles had been credited with saying. Incidentally, after the President's press conference, Dulles took full responsibility for the interview by confirming the substance of what Shepley had reported.

It is true, however, that in the Indo-China crisis of 1954 Eisenhower and Dulles were ready to go closer to the brink of a hot war with China than our English-speaking allies wanted them to go. If the Communists had pushed on with an aggressive offensive after the fall of Dienbienphu, instead of stopping and agreeing to stay out of Southern Vietnam, Laos and Cambodia, there was a strong possibility that the United States would have moved against them. A complete Communist conquest of Indo-China would have had far graver consequence for the West than a Red victory in Korea.

In a press conference on April 7, 1954, Eisenhower used an illustration in his answer to a question in order to bring out the ultimate strategic importance of Indo-China's position in Southeast Asia. Applying what might be called the falling domino principle, he compared Indo-China to the first of a row of dominoes which is knocked over, making the fall of the last one a certainty. The fall of Indo-China would lead to the fall of Burma, Thailand, Malaya and Indonesia. India would then be hemmed in by Communism and Australia, New Zealand, the Philippines, Formosa and Japan would all be gravely threatened. Eisenhower had been more than willing in 1953 to support the Navarre plan, named after the French commander in Indo-China, which called for the United States to contribute $400 million to the French defense effort. But that was only a beginning.

Torn by political strife in Paris and by troubles in North Africa, the French soon used up the resources and desire to fight alone in Indo-China and turned to Eisenhower for more help. He was drawn to their cause, not only because the situation in Southeast Asia was threatening the United States defenses in the Pacific but also because he and Dulles were anxious to win the French over to the proposed European Defense Community treaty. This was a plan for a unified defense alliance of the Western European nations, with West Germany as one of its members, that would have relieved the United States of the need to maintain large armed forces in that area of the

Continent. The unification of the free states of Western Europe had been for several years a personal crusade of Eisenhower's. Whenever someone in the White House mentioned the union of the states of Europe as indispensable to their stability and security, Eisenhower's face would light up. "That goes back to the best speech I ever made," he told us once. "Get a copy of the speech I made about it to the English Speaking Union in 1951 and read it." The French were opposed to the European Defense Community because they could not put aside their national aversion to building up once more the military power of Germany, the country that had brought so much abject misery to France in two terrible invasions. With the support of the National Security Council, Eisenhower increased the American share of the cost of the Indo-China war from $400 million to $785 million, or virtually the whole expense of the French military operation. Behind this decision was the hope that picking up the check in Indo-China would help to win approval of the European Defense Community treaty in Paris. The money that the United States would save from such a military merger of the European countries would repay the investment in Southeast Asia many times over.

But the French wanted more than money and technical aid when their forces were pinned down by the Communist Vietminh native troops at Dienbienphu. They asked Eisenhower for an air strike by United States planes from aircraft carriers. Admiral Radford, who was then the Chairman of the Joint Chiefs of Staff, was in favor of the move. Eisenhower was against it. Having avoided one total war with Red China the year before in Korea when he had United Nations support, he was in no mood to provoke another one in Indo-China by going it alone in a military action without the British and other Western Allies. He was also determined not to become involved militarily in any foreign conflict without the approval of Congress. He had had trouble enough convincing some Senators that it was even necessary to send small groups of noncombatant Air Force technicians to Indo-China.

Yet it became apparent in that uncomfortable April of 1954 that the United States had to make some kind of threat of armed intervention in Indo-China, whether the American people wanted it or not. The Defense Department was alarmed by the danger of the Southeast Asia situation and there was worried speculation in the Cabinet and

National Security Council meetings about what the Communists would do if the French surrendered or pulled out of Indo-China, as they might if their weakening government in Paris collapsed. In a supposedly off-the-record question period at the American Society of Newspaper Editors meeting in Washington on April 16, Vice President Nixon said that it would be necessary to send American troops against the Communists in Indo-China if the French withdrew. That sent out stories on the news wires that the United States was about to fight in the Far East again and Nixon was damned in Congress for "whooping it up for war." Dulles quickly issued a statement that the use of American soldiers in Southeast Asia was "unlikely." Nixon was mortified by the confusion he had caused, but Eisenhower, who was in Augusta at the time, called the Vice President on the telephone and told him not to be upset. Trying to cheer up Nixon, the President reassured him that the uproar over his comment had been all to the good because it awakened the country to the seriousness of the situation in Indo-China.

As a matter of fact, two weeks earlier at a Sunday night meeting in the upstairs study at the White House Eisenhower had agreed with Dulles and Radford on a plan to send American forces to Indo-China under certain strict conditions. It was to be, first and most important, a joint action with the British, including Australian and New Zealand troops, and, if possible, participating units from such Far Eastern countries as the Philippines and Thailand so that the forces would have Asiatic representation. Secondly, the French would have to continue to fight in Indo-China and bear a full share of responsibility until the war was over. Eisenhower was also concerned that American intervention in Indo-China might be interpreted as protection of French colonialism. He added a condition that would guarantee future independence to the Indo-Chinese states of Vietnam, Laos and Cambodia.

A few days later Dulles went to London and Paris to lay this proposal before Churchill and Eden and the French Foreign Minister, Bidault. Dulles had trouble with Bidault, for the Laniel government was on the verge of falling. The Minister wanted fast military action in Indo-China from the United States alone, without waiting for the British to make up their minds about the Eisenhower-Dulles allied invasion plan, but he finally gave Dulles his reluctant agreement.

Churchill and Eden seemed well disposed to joining the Americans in an effort to stop the Communist aggression. Dulles returned to Washington in a confident mood.

Then the plan fell apart. The British changed their minds and decided to avoid decisive action on the Indo-China crisis until after they had a chance to discuss it with the Russians and the Red Chinese at the conference on Asiatic problems between the world powers that was to open in Geneva the following week. Dulles was glum and disheartened. As Eisenhower sadly explained the situation to the legislative leaders in the White House on April 26, the failure to get the British and French to agree to a unified program of action meant that Dienbienphu would fall within a few days. Eisenhower admitted quite frankly that he did not know what was going to happen next. Bidault had been very despondent. There was even danger that the French might give up the Indo-China war rather than accept the U.S. approach suggested by Eisenhower and Dulles. Eisenhower repeated that we were not going to "carry the rest of the world on our back" and that he had no intention of sending in American ground forces independently, but warned once more that there might be tremendous consequences ahead and that the leaders should keep in mind the possibility that some U.S. units might become involved. But the free world must understand that our most effective role did not lie in furnishing ground troops, he added. He remarked later that the one bright light in the whole discouraging effort to form an alliance of the democracies in this desperate attempt to save Dienbienphu was Magsaysay, the President of the Philippines. Magsaysay sent word to Eisenhower that he would do anything the United States wanted him to do—even though his own foreign minister took the opposite view.

"The French have asked us to send planes to Dienbienphu," Eisenhower told the Congressional leaders, "but we are not going to be involved alone in a power move against the Russians."

"If we don't offer to do something, they'll say we're not facing up to the situation," Senator Knowland said.

"Well, they've said that before," Eisenhower said. "They said it about the Democrats during the Chinese situation in the forties. And they said it about Stimson when the Japanese invaded Manchuria in the early thirties."

"Eventually, there has to be a showdown on this question of

whether or not the United States government intends to oppose aggression overseas," Senator Millikin said. "If our allies are not going to stand together with us then we had better review our position. If that review comes to the conclusion that we are not going to stand alone against aggression, then the sooner we bail out the better."

"What if we go it alone and our allies back out on us?" Eisenhower said. "We can no longer fight just a defensive war."

"The Fortress America idea is a damned foolish one," Millikin returned, "but the day may come when we shall have to resort to it."

"If we ever have to go back to that," Eisenhower rejoined, "there will be a tremendous explosion in the world."

The talks at Geneva dragged on through May and June, while Dulles struggled with the almost nonexistent French government to keep Indo-China from falling completely into the hands of the Communist Vietminh forces after the collapse of Dienbienphu. Sinclair Weeks asked Dulles at a Cabinet meeting in May if the nibbling of the Communists at the territory of the free world did not resemble the expansion of the Nazis and the Japanese before World War II.

"The nibbling has already reached the point where we can't see much more territory go to the Communists without real danger to ourselves," Dulles said. "The problem, of course, is where to draw the line. This is more difficult in Asia than in Europe. In Asia, you can draw a line and the Communists can burrow under it with subversive activities in apparently non-Communist areas that you can't see on the surface. It's not difficult to marshal world opinion against aggression, but it is quite another matter to fight against internal changes in one country. If we take a position against a Communist faction within a foreign country, we have to act alone. We are confronted by an unfortunate fact—most of the countries of the world do not share our view that Communist control of any government anywhere is in itself a danger and a threat."

After Mendès-France succeeded Laniel as Premier in June, the French government worked out a compromise truce agreement with the Communists in Indo-China, similar to the one that we negotiated in Korea, with the Reds taking the northern section of Vietnam, including the Red River Delta and Hanoi, and giving up the southern half of the peninsula, which they could have conquered after the fall of Dienbienphu. The willingness of Eisenhower and Dulles to unite with the British and French in a joint military action to save the rest of Southeast Asia did serve eventually as a deterrent that stopped further Red aggression, even though it was never carried out. The British and the French were satisfied with this truce, but it caused no satisfaction in Washington. Like most of us in the government, Eisenhower felt that the Communist aggression in Indo-China had paid off in victory, even though a partial one. Furthermore, the weakness of the Southeast Asia states was pathetically evident.

Then in August came another bitter blow to Eisenhower and Dulles: the French deputies defeated the European Defense Community treaty, 319 to 264. I well remember Eisenhower's reaction. With Herbert Hoover, Jr., we left Washington on the *Columbine* during the afternoon of August 30, headed for a Denver vacation. The news of the peremptory vote in the French Chamber had shocked Eisenhower. At a brief stopover at the Iowa State Fair I sat directly behind the President as he rose to speak to a predominantly farm audience, which crowded every nook and cranny of the grandstand. Instead of talking about some problem of the American farmer as everyone anticipated, the President turned to the world situation, and specifically to the defeat of EDC. "A major setback for the U.S.," the President called it, and in Washington Dulles described it as a tragedy that endangered the whole of Europe. As I listened to the President that afternoon in Des Moines, I wondered what interest such an audience would have in the failure of a defense alliance four thousand miles away. But when Eisenhower finished he received an ovation.

Eisenhower quickly reaffirmed his earlier promise to pave the way for West Germany's sovereignty and its admission to NATO if the European Defense Community plan failed. But it was Anthony Eden who played the major role in organizing a Western European alliance as a substitute for the European Defense Community and brought membership status in NATO to West Germany. Eden called a conference in London in October of the powers who had participated in the Brussels Pact of 1948—the United States, Great Britain, France, Canada, Belgium and the Netherlands—and invited them to join with Italy and West Germany in forming the Western European Union to replace the EDC. The dramatic clincher that made the proposal acceptable to all of the countries at the conference was Eden's offer to maintain four British infantry divisions and a tactical air force on the Continent, a commitment that did not make Churchill too happy because posting United Kingdom occupation troops on the Continent was a radical departure from past British policy, and besides, he wanted the United States to make a similar proposal, which Dulles refused to have anything to do with. Without bona fide European unity, Dulles stated, they would have to do without us. Nevertheless, the Eden gesture, Dulles solemnly told the Cabinet later, was a historic event, and might have won approval for the European Defense Community treaty had it been made earlier.

The loss of North Vietnam to the Communists was not without one redeeming blessing. In September of 1954 at Manila, SEATO, the Southeast Asia Treaty Organization, came into being as an alliance of powers—Britain, France, Australia, New Zealand, the Philippines and Thailand—for the protection of Southeast Asia and the Southwest Pacific. Eisenhower and Dulles conceived it as one more defensive link in the shield against further Communist encroachment, but most of the nations of Southeast Asia were concerned simply with the defense of their borders rather than with the broader threat of Communist aggression. It was this cross-purpose that had delayed the realization of the SEATO project, which Eisenhower had hopefully referred to in his address to the newspaper editors on April 16, 1953. Dulles explained to the Cabinet that we had always wanted primarily to direct the treaty against Communist aggression, but most of the others did not see it our way. In addition, the urgent desire of the French to close out the war in Indo-China sidetracked the consideration of SEATO during the long negotiations at Geneva.

In the light of the fierce debate in 1960 between Nixon and Kennedy about the status of United States prestige abroad, and the intervening events of history, in Suez, in the Near East and in the diplomatic reverses of 1960, a remark that Dulles made to the Cabinet in that October of 1954 is worth recalling. SEATO was a reality. All open warfare had stopped. Dulles felt the recent London Conference of the Brussels Pact powers had accomplished more than any other conference in which he had ever participated. The Western European Union was developing well. There had been finally a settlement of the extremely knotty Trieste question. The Secretary, with great deliberation, said to the Cabinet, "The United States has never been so respected nor had such good relations as now."

Another factor in the attitude of other SEATO powers toward concerted action against Communist aggression was the difference of opinion between Britain and the United States on the Red China issue. At the time Dulles was signing the SEATO treaty in Manila, the Chinese Reds were shelling the Nationalist-held offshore island of Quemoy. Once again the simmering controversy over Red China policy and her admission to the United Nations came to a boil. Eisenhower's position differed substantially from that of his own party leaders in Congress and of a few of the military chiefs who wanted an all-out showdown with the Peiping regime. For the most part these were the same protagonists who had contended that Korea in 1953 was "the right place and the right time" for a naval blockade of China and a full-scale American attack aimed to return Chiang Kai-shek's Nationalist government to power on the Chinese mainland. The Communist bombardment of the offshore islands in that fall of 1954 and the threat of an invasion of Formosa that it implied seemed to them to call for a hardening of our policy to the extent of supporting Chiang in rugged retaliation. Among them were those who even advocated a full-scale attack with atomic weapons.

The President rejected a hot-headed plunge into atomic war as a solution to the Chinese problem. On the other hand he disagreed with Churchill and the British, who took the view that since the Red regime in China was a reality and the Nationalist government of Chiang Kai-shek did not have a ghost of a chance of retaking the mainland, diplomatic recognition of China would only be looking facts in the face. Furthermore, the British argued, admitting China to United Nations membership would reduce tension and the danger of war. Eisenhower assured the Cabinet and the Republican leaders that he had no intention whatever of giving in to the British on the Chinese question. "How can we agree to admit to membership a country which the United Nations has branded an aggressor?" he asked the leaders. "What sense does it make to talk about recognizing the Reds in view of their refusal to release Korean War prisoners and their attacks on American planes over the China Sea and illegal imprisonment of U.S. airmen?" But Eisenhower fought against being hamstrung by any inflexible policy which would fail to recognize that there might come a time when a break between Russia and China or some other unexpected development might make recognition of China a desirable strategic move in the best interests of the United States. So when Senator Jenner sought to have the United States issue a statement that it would never, under any circumstances, recognize the Peiping government, Eisenhower vehemently opposed it. He also acted against a rider to a United Nations appropriation bill in 1953 that would have cut off American financial support of the United Nations if Red China was admitted to its membership. It was another of those times when you must never say "never." Such repudiation of treaty obligations, he argued, would force the United States to stand alone and friendless in the world.

As much as Eisenhower disagreed with the British position on the Red China issue, he still gave no serious consideration to encouraging Chiang to undertake a full-scale war in retaliation for the bombardment of Quemoy and Matsu in 1954. As soon as Dulles heard about the Red attack, he hurried home from the SEATO conference in Manila and asked the President to call an unprecedented meeting of the National Security Council at Denver, where Eisenhower was trying to compress a few days of limited work, relaxation and rest between the late adjournment of Congress and the next emergency he knew he would soon have to face in Washington. It had been a hard year for him, with the Indo-China crisis and the collapse of the European Defense Community plan piled on top of such domestic troubles as the economic recession and the turmoil of the Army-McCarthy hearings. Eisenhower had spells of depression that summer and the reasons for them were not difficult to understand. Ann Whitman and I agreed that he was being faced with too many vexing problems that either had no solution or that required great personal concentration before making decisions for which he alone was responsible.

It was an open secret that the Joint Chiefs did not entirely agree among themselves nor with the National Security Council about the course of action to be taken should the Reds actually begin an invasion of the offshore islands. They would have been happier with a more precise statement of intentions than Eisenhower thought it wise to give. While the President was willing to use force against the Communists if Formosa itself was threatened, he was not going to be rushed into a mobilization for a hot war over some small islands near the China coast unless it was clear that the Reds were moving to attack Chiang's Nationalists, to whose defense we were firmly committed. In any case, he was determined again, as he was in the Indo-China crisis, not to resort to any kind of military action without the approval of Congress. The tension between the United States and China continued to grow tighter that fall and then, late in November, the demands in Washington for action reached fever pitch when the Peiping government announced that eleven American airmen, prisoners from the Korean War, and two civilians, had been sentenced by a Chinese Communist tribunal to prison terms of four years to life for "espionage inside China." Senator Knowland came to the White House and asked Eisenhower to blockade the Chinese coast until the prisoners were released. The President firmly disagreed with Knowland. Eisenhower suspected that the United States was being deliberately goaded by the Communists in the hope that they could provoke us into an impulsive action that would drive a wedge between us and our allies. He pointed out that because the captured airmen were prisoners from the Korean War, the United Nations was responsible for negotiating for their release. "We have to act in this the hard way, and the hard way is to have the courage to be patient," Eisenhower said.

The Communists made another challenging jab at Eisenhower on January 18, 1955, by occupying the small island of Yikiang in the offshore Tachens, two hundred miles north of Formosa. Peiping's radio broadcasters made much of this seizure of Nationalist territory, claiming that if the United States ignored this attack it would mark the first strategic move in a drive against Formosa that would violate and destroy the mutual security treaty that Chiang Kai-shek and the United States had signed in December. Again Eisenhower turned the other cheek, explaining that the Tachens were of little or no military importance. But he agreed with Dulles that some kind of bold and decisive warning had to be issued to China and a few days after the Tachens incident the President sent his Formosa Resolution to Congress.

This unusual request by Eisenhower for authorization from Congress to use the armed forces to protect Formosa and the Pescadores Islands against a Chinese Communist invasion had no precedent in United States history. Eisenhower was well aware that as President he already had the power to go to war against the Reds without consulting Congress. I remember his making a careful change in the message that he sent to the Capitol with the intention of making this point very clear. In the original draft of the message prepared by the State Department there was a sentence that said, "The authority I request may be in part already inherent in the authority of the Commander-in-Chief." Eisenhower crossed this out and wrote in its place, "Authority for some of the actions which might be required would be inherent in the authority of the Commander-in-Chief."

In other words, in turning to Congress for support of his warning against the Communists, Eisenhower did not want Congress to assume that he was signing over to the legislators the constitutional right of the President to use the armed forces on his own responsibility. He had two reasons for asking Congressional endorsement of the "No Trespassing" notice that he was serving upon the Chinese government: the declaration of his readiness to fight for Formosa would have more impact on Peiping with the backing of Congress behind it and, secondly, Eisenhower did not want to repeat the mistake he believed that Truman had made in 1950 in sending air and naval forces to South Korea without consulting Congress. Truman had said afterward that he had not had time for such consultation but Eisenhower was of the opinion that such an excuse could never have been used in the long and drawn-out antagonism of the Formosa crisis, where the storm signals had been up for many months.

In the Formosa Resolution, Eisenhower left the defense of Quemoy and Matsu purposely in doubt. When and if the Reds began an actual assault in the area, he would then decide what to do. As for using our own armed forces, he told Congress that this would be limited to "situations which are recognizable as parts of, or definite preliminaries to, an attack against the main positions of Formosa and the Pescadores." Senator Hubert Humphrey, the Democrat from Minnesota, tried to put through an amendment specifically limiting the use of military force to a defense of Formosa and the Pescadores, but it was defeated. The resolution passed through the House by a vote of 410 to 3 and through the Senate by 85 to 3. The champion of the Eisenhower proposal in Congress was seventy-seven-year-old Senator Walter George of Georgia, who had become Chairman of the Senate's Foreign Relations Committee to Eisenhower's warm satisfaction after the Republicans lost control of Congress in the 1954 elections.

One of the incongruities of political life was George's prestige and leadership in the Senate at a time when his strong support of Eisenhower's foreign policy was contributing to his decline in popularity among his conservative Democrat constituents back home in Georgia. Eisenhower never forgot George's personal sacrifices in behalf of the administration's programs. When the Senator finally had to bow to the inevitable consequences of his support of the President, Eisenhower appointed him after his retirement from the Senate as an adviser to the State Department with the rank of a presidential special assistant.

More than two months went by with increasing tension in the Formosa Strait before the President's threat seemed to take any effect upon the Chinese leaders. The Communists turned away from attempts by the United States, Britain and New Zealand to arrange through the United Nations a cease-fire agreement that would halt the artillery bombardments of Quemoy from the mainland. Dag Hammarskjöld's United Nations mission to Peiping to seek the release of the American airmen who were being held as prisoners was apparently getting nowhere. The U.S. Seventh Fleet evacuated some fourteen thousand Nationalist regular and guerrilla troops from the Tachen Islands without incident but Dulles remarked at a Cabinet meeting that a move to evacuate Chiang Kai-shek's forces from Quemoy would be a different matter.

Dulles was readier to fight for Quemoy and Matsu than Eisenhower was. The Secretary of State spoke often of the grave psychological impact that the loss of the offshore islands would have on the Nationalists and he complained of the inability of the British and of our other allies to understand the tremendous shock that a retreat from Quemoy and Matsu would be to the free people of East Asia. Criticism of Eisenhower's reluctance to announce a clear-cut determination to defend the offshore islands as well as Formosa mounted in Congress. The President explained his stand to Sam Rayburn at a two-day luncheon discussion of foreign problems with House and Senate leaders at the White House late in March. Rayburn said that he assumed that the United States would become involved unavoidably in any kind of a Communist attack on Quemoy and Matsu. Eisenhower disagreed with the necessity for such an assumption. He told Rayburn that in the event of such an attack he would wait until he had definite information on the strength and deployment of the invading force before committing American armed force against it. If there was a reasonable chance of the Nationalists' stopping the attack by themselves, Eisenhower said, he would hold back from going to their assistance. A successful defense of the islands without United States aid would be a crucial blow to Communist prestige and a tremendous boost to the morale of anti-Communist governments in that part of the world.

"Foster and I are living twenty-four hours a day with the question of what to do if something happens in Quemoy and Matsu," Eisenhower said to Rayburn. "That is the most difficult problem I have had to face since I took office."

Rayburn remarked that our allies seemed to be giving us no support in the Formosa crisis.

"The question that bothers the British and the French is the possibility of a general war starting over Quemoy and Matsu," the President said. "They will support us in defending Formosa and they won't be lukewarm about it either."

But on the second day of the meeting, when the Senate leaders replaced the legislators from the House at the conference table, Lyndon Johnson asked Dulles the same question and the Secretary of State made it plain that he did not wholly share Eisenhower's confidence in our allies. Dulles said emphatically that the British and the French were giving us no military support in Asia and were opposed to our use of atomic weapons in a defense of Formosa. But we could not allow our policies in Asia to be dictated by our European allies, he insisted. Eisenhower quickly interrupted Dulles to point out that Turkey, Pakistan, the Philippines, Australia, New Zealand and South Korea were all in favor of our support of Chiang Kai-shek. It was difficult to make the world understand our position in Formosa and our concern for Quemoy and Matsu, the President added.

Dulles seemed to imply strongly during the discussion of the Far Eastern situation, although he worded it discreetly, that he was deeply annoyed by the hesitancy of the British and the French to join with the Americans in making a bold and unified stand against the Red Chinese. Determined not to be persuaded by our European allies into an appeasement of the Peiping regime, he showed then some of the willingness to pull away from the traditional partnership with the British and the French that he later displayed in the Suez crisis. Dulles suspected that the Russians might be encouraging a Chinese Communist attack on Formosa in the hope that an American retaliation with atomic weapons would drive a rift between the Western Allies and help Communist propaganda all over the world. That suspicion did not soften his determination to take a belligerent stand on the Formosa issue, even if he had to do it alone.

At the height of the tension, Admiral Robert B. Carney, the chief of naval operations, did not help matters by telling a group of Washington reporters in a supposedly off-the-record discussion that the Chinese Reds were expected to invade Matsu momentarily and Quemoy within a month. This prediction, of course, found its way into the newspapers, along with reports that the President's military advisers were urging him to destroy Red China's industrial capability in order to prevent such invasions. With irritation bordering on despair, Eisenhower remarked that he could not recall any country receiving such detailed news of an enemy's invasion plans before the invasion took place. "They have information I do not have," Eisenhower said.

How far Admiral Carney was off the track became apparent the following month at the Asian-African Conference in Bandung, where Chou En-lai announced that the Chinese government was ready to discuss the question of relaxing tension in the Formosa Strait area. This led to several months of talks in Geneva, which did not really get anywhere but which caused the threat of a war between the United States and China to simmer down. It was evident that the Formosa Resolution had accomplished its purpose. At the end of May, V. K. Krishna Menon returned to India from Peiping, where he had been sent by Nehru to intercede in the Formosa trouble, with the news that four of the imprisoned American fliers were to be freed by the Chinese. Nehru wrote to Eisenhower in June that the other prisoners would be released later. The President felt great appreciation for Nehru's efforts, at the same time noting that Hammarskjöld had done a great deal in obtaining the releases of the imprisoned Air Force personnel.

Eisenhower came out of the Indo-China and Formosa crises well aware that the intentions of the Communists in the Far East were still as uncertain and dangerous as ever, but deeply thankful that he had avoided war for the time being, at least. He and Dulles had managed to obtain a remarkable bipartisan support in Congress for their hard decisions; during the six-months period before the SEATO conference in 1954 Dulles held more than ninety meetings with Congressional leaders of both parties. I don't know of any human being in the service of his country who took the beating that Dulles took in his years as Secretary of State and still accomplished so much. Like the farmer's wife, his work was never done and much of it still remains to be done. Nevertheless, his tremendous activities will fill many pages of history.

8 McCarthy and the Army

If Eisenhower could have had his own way in dealing with Joseph R. McCarthy, he would have ignored the Senator completely. During all of McCarthy's overpublicized Red hunting, his irresponsible attacks on the administration and the embarrassing spectacle of the televised Army-McCarthy hearings, Eisenhower would have preferred to look steadily at a point at least two feet over McCarthy's head. I was away from Washington on government business on December 2, 1953, when C. D. Jackson, supported less articulately by a few other advisers, urged the President to put McCarthy in his place by attacking the Senator for his violent extremism, drawing attention particularly to the disruption which all this was causing in our foreign relations. In this Jackson was acting entirely within the role Eisenhower had given him. I was not surprised when I heard later what Eisenhower said in refusing to follow Jackson's recommendation. It sums up what he felt about McCarthy. He said, "I will not get into the gutter with that guy."

Jackson became aroused at that time by a speech McCarthy made on November 24, which was supposed to have been a reply to Harry Truman's defensive radio and television talk on the Harry Dexter White case a few days earlier. Because Truman had accused the Eisenhower administration of "McCarthyism," the Wisconsin Senator demanded equal time from the netwoks to answer Truman. Most of his speech, however, turned out to be a tirade against the White House and the State Department. McCarthy was mad at the President because at his press conference the week before Eisenhower had belittled McCarthy's cherished Communists-in-the-government issue and predicted that it would play no part in the 1954 Congressional elections. The Senator attacked the State Department for retaining John Paton Davies, Jr., a career diplomat whom McCarthy accused of pro-Chinese Communist leanings, in the counselor's post at the embassy in Peru. He attacked the Eisenhower administration for giving Mutual Security aid to Britain when the British were trading with Red China.

The next day Jackson wrote me an angry letter, pleading for Eisenhower and a few Republican Senators to take up the McCarthy cudgel.

I hope this flagrant performance will open the eyes of some of the President's advisers who seem to think that the Senator is really a good fellow at heart [Jackson wrote]. They remind me of the people who kept saying for so many months that Mao Tse-tung was just an agrarian reformer. If every egg head in the country can rise to a fever pitch when Brownell talks about Truman, can't a single Republican work up some temperature when McCarthy refers to Eisenhower as he did?

Jackson proposed some language that Eisenhower might use, denouncing McCarthy by name, but the President put it impatiently aside, declaring once again, as he had done on many previous occasions when the McCarthy issue came up, that for him to engage in a name-calling contest would be to descend to the Senator's level. Instead, Eisenhower explained calmly at his press conference that the United States did not intervene in trade policies of its allies and reasserted his determination to keep subversives out of the government. He made no direct reference to McCarthy. Neither did Dulles in the official State Department reply made to McCarthy's charges two days earlier.

If Eisenhower had been able to follow his own instincts, he would not have given McCarthy's charges even the restrained acknowledgment that he did. But because he was following a policy of "playing it straight" at press conferences, he could not ignore questions from reporters on issues raised by McCarthy as long as those questions did not require a discussion of personalities. During the first two years that Eisenhower was in office, McCarthy was riding high and the controversy over McCarthyism was much too hot a news topic to be kept out of the White House press conference discussions. So Eisenhower was forced repeatedly to make a public recognition of

McCarthy's existence, and his annoyance steadily mounted at his having to do so. His only alternative was to refuse point-blank to entertain further questions about McCarthy or his operations, and this Eisenhower did not like to do.

Apart from his personal distaste for McCarthy, of which he left no doubt in private conversations, Eisenhower had an almost obsessive hatred for the reputation-smearing raking over of the Truman and Roosevelt administrations for the mistakes and scandals of the past, something on which McCarthy thrived. This had accounted for his refusal to make political capital out of the Yalta agreements and it made him uncomfortable about Herbert Brownell's charge of laxity against Truman in the Harry Dexter White case, to which Jackson had referred in his letter to me about McCarthy.

The White case, which is all but forgotten now, caused a major political eruption in 1953 when Brownell brought it out in an address to the Executives Club in Chicago. While reviewing White's history, Brownell came upon the startling fact that at the very time that Truman had sent White's nomination as executive director of the International Monetary Fund to the Senate for confirmation in January, 1946, he had been in possession of a detailed FBI report showing that White had been engaged in spying activity for the Soviet government. Brownell felt strongly that this should be made public. He discussed it with me and with Jim Hagerty before mentioning it to Eisenhower. He gave Eisenhower his judgment that the disclosure was justified political criticism and that it would take away some of the glamour of the McCarthy stage play. Unless the President had objection, he intended to use it in his address at Chicago. Eisenhower did not go into the details of the story with Brownell; he said later that he was even vague about who White was. He relied upon the judgment of his Attorney General as to the propriety and the political repercussions involved in the releasing of the facts of the case.

When Brownell told the astonishing circumstances of White's appointment at the Chicago luncheon, Truman quickly came to his own defense. He said he knew nothing of the FBI report when he sent White's name to the Senate and that after he did find out about it, he fired White. In such cases as this one, where government officials are basing a charge on material in an FBI report, they are always at a disadvantage. In order to safeguard the means by which the FBI obtains its intelligence, the sources of its information cannot be revealed and the facts themselves often must not be completely unwrapped. Here is a modification of the fundamental right of the accused to face his accuser, made necessary in the protection of the government and the people. Eisenhower found himself in the awkward position of trying to defend Brownell in a dispute that he wished had never been started. The press conference questions were particularly difficult for him to answer. He said that he was not at all sure that Brownell actually meant to question the loyalty of a President and that it was inconceivable, and he did not believe, that Truman knowingly damaged the United States. Did he think it was proper to subpoena Truman, as the House Un-American Activities Committee had done in its investigation of the White case? There were better means of handling such a situation, Eisenhower said. Was the FBI justified in calling White a spy after a grand jury had refused to indict White on the FBI's evidence? Eisenhower said he knew nothing about that. Was putting a traitor's label on a former President likely to harm our foreign relations? Eisenhower rejected the premise and refused to answer the question. Then he said, "Just as earnestly as I believe we must fight all Communism to the utmost, I believe we must also fight any truly unjust, un-American way of uprooting it, because in the long run I think we will destroy ourselves if we use that kind of a defense."

James F. Byrnes, who had been Truman's Secretary of State at the time of the White appointment, came forward to substantiate Brownell's charges. Contradicting Truman's claim that he knew nothing of the FBI report on White, Byrnes said he had discussed the report with Truman and had urged him to withdraw White's nomination from the Senate. Truman had then ordered one of his staff aides to call the Secretary of the Senate, Byrnes said, only to find out that the Senate had already approved the nomination. Despite Byrnes's testimony, the press defended Truman and, taking note of Eisenhower's unhappiness with the whole affair, jumped to the conclusion that, at the very least, there had been a lack of understanding between the President and Brownell on the way the case was to be handled. Actually, Eisenhower did not criticize Brownell's action in the White House, despite his own reluctance to unearth the past errors of a previous President for public rebuke. He went out of his way at the Cabinet meeting of November 12 to restate his willingness to support the individual authority of any Cabinet member in a course of action such as Brownell had chosen to follow in this instance. He remarked that the real point which Brownell's action had brought out was that White was not the kind of a man who merited a high position in government, and that seemed to have gotten lost in the headlines about the squabble between Truman and the Republicans.

When the Republican party leaders tried to make political capital out of the White case, Eisenhower bluntly turned his back on the whole Communist-in-government issue. Leonard Hall, who was then the national chairman, predicted that the Communist infiltration of the Truman administration would again be the dominant issue in the 1954 elections. When the reporters asked him about Hall's prediction, the President quickly deflated the issue, saying pointedly, "I hope that this whole thing will be a matter of history and of memory by the time the next election comes around." Such an unpolitical attitude infuriated Senator McCarthy. Six days after Eisenhower made his statement McCarthy was on the air disagreeing with it and charging the administration with failure to liquidate the "bloodstained blunder" of the Truman regime because Britain had not been forced to stop its trade with Red China. One commentator described the McCarthy speech as an open declaration of war against Eisenhower.

The reference in Jackson's letter of complaint to presidential advisers "who seem to think that the Senator is really a good fellow at heart" was a barbed criticism of the attitude of a few members of the President's official household who maintained friendly relations with McCarthy in an earnest effort to avoid a complete blow-up between the Senator and the White House. The principal protagonist in this behind-the-scenes drama was Richard Nixon. With his own creditable record of ferreting out Communist conspirators, it was to be expected that Nixon should have taken a personal interest in McCarthy's investigations. Indeed, he tried as best he could to keep the Senator within bounds. At the time the hearings were at their peak Nixon intervened with the White House staff and the Justice Department in an effort to suggest some way to get the Senator sufficiently pacified so that he would stop his unreasonable attacks on the President and the executive department. Closely allied with Nixon in this effort were Jerry Persons and Deputy Attorney General William P. Rogers who, with Nixon, tried to preserve peace between the Senator and the President, not because of deep affection for McCarthy, but simply because they felt rightly that the administration would gain nothing from an open battle with him. Eisenhower and Dulles were ready to go along with this attempt at coexistence, provided that McCarthy would keep his investigations and his accusations within reasonable bounds.

For almost a month after Eisenhower took office in 1953, McCarthy had stayed in bounds. Then, starting with his fight against the appointment of Charles Bohlen as Ambassador to Russia, he began a harassment of the State Department, delving into the Voice of America and the overseas information services and even attempting to negotiate an impromptu international agreement of his own with the Greek owners of 242 merchant ships, whom he persuaded forcefully to break off trading with Red Chinese and Soviet ports in the Far East. Egged on by Stuart Symington and John McClellan, Democratic members of his Senate investigating committee, McCarthy naïvely sent Eisenhower a letter complaining about British trade with Red China and demanding a statement of the administration's policy on commerce between the Western democracies and Communist countries. Stories about the letter, obviously planted by McCarthy, appeared in the newspapers and these reports contained wildly erroneous statements about trading with the Reds that could have affected the United States government's relations with its allies.

An official correction of McCarthy's misstatements in the news stories about his letter to the White House was impossible, however, because such a correction would have required the disclosure of highly classified secret information. Trying to decide what to do about the letter itself was another sore problem; if Eisenhower answered it with a statement of policy on trade with the Communists, as McCarthy was demanding, he could avoid neither antagonizing the British nor stirring up criticism from anti-Communist groups at home. At a White House staff meeting on May 22, Robert Cutler and Jackson, the strong enemies of McCarthy on our team, wanted to put out a public statement on the letter that would expose the Senator's misuse of information and his effort to embarrass the President. I argued against them because I felt that an attempt to correct McCarthy on the Communist trade issue would only cause confusion; the background of the argument was too complicated to be explained briefly and lucidly and public opinion was strongly against Red China trade, no matter what Eisenhower said about it. Like most of the calamities built up by McCarthy, whatever was done about it seemed likely only to worsen the situation.

It was Nixon who finally got us out of it. He called McCarthy and pointed out to him that his Democratic fellow Senators, Symington and McClellan, had gotten him to embarrass the Republican administration and that if he insisted on a reply from Eisenhower only the Democrats would benefit from it. McCarthy agreed with Nixon and asked him to retrieve the letter from the White House before it was "officially received" by Eisenhower so that no answer would be necessary.

But as time went on both Eisenhower and McCarthy became less guarded about each other. At the Dartmouth College commencement that June, Eisenhower spoke extemporaneously against "the book burners," obviously hitting at McCarthy's efforts to ban certain books from the libraries of the State Department's overseas information centers. One day he brought into a Cabinet meeting and passed around the table a European cartoon showing two American investigators, unmistakably McCarthy's young assistants, Roy Cohn and G. David Schine, asking a Czechoslovakian official if he knows of anything in his country detrimental to the United States. "Nothing except your presence here," the official replies. When McCarthy appointed J. B. Matthews, former researcher for the first House Un-American Activities Committee, as the director of investigations for his Senate investigating committee, an article entitled "Reds and Our Churches" written by Matthews appeared in the *American Mercury*. It began with the shocking announcement, "The largest single group supporting the Communist apparatus in the United States today is composed of Protestant clergymen." Eisenhower received a telegram from the national co-chairmen of the Conference of Christians and Jews, Monsignor John A. O'Brien, Rabbi Maurice N. Eisendrath and the Reverend Dr. John Sutherland Bonnell, calling Matthews' attack on the loyalty of Protestant clergymen unjustified and deplorable. Three Democrats and one Republican on the McCarthy committee tried to make Matthews resign from his director's post and, when McCarthy opposed them, the Democrats walked out of the committee.

When I saw the telegram from the Conference of Christians and Jews, I called Hagerty, Persons and Emmet Hughes into my office to draft a reply to it. There was some discussion among us about the wording of the message but none of us had any reservations about whether the President should come out immediately with a denunciation of Matthews' charges. Eisenhower quickly agreed with us. His telegram, addressed to the Catholic, Jewish and Protestant chairmen of the Conference, called the Matthews statement "irresponsible" and "alien to America," showing "contempt for the principles of freedom and decency."

Eisenhower's reply caused something of a news sensation and McCarthy obtained Matthews' resignation within an hour after it was announced. The Senator then seemed to be in some straits. Rebuffed in an attempt to uncover secret affairs of the Central Intelligence Agency, he next turned his attention from the State Department to the Army, a move that ultimately led to his undoing.

The chief cause of the trouble between McCarthy and the Army, that ended up in the countercharges of the prolonged televised Senate subcommittee hearings, was the Senator's insistence on being granted the privilege of questioning members of the Army's loyalty-security boards, who had screened certain civilian employees under investigation by the McCarthy committee. McCarthy also wanted the right to interrogate individual members of review boards who re-examined appealed cases of employees whose loyalty had been questioned. Furthermore, he wanted access to individual security files. This the Army was doggedly determined to prevent, for if loyalty review and appeal board members and secret case history files were exposed to the light of Congressional investigation its whole security program would be undermined and disrupted. The board members were Army employees themselves, and their judgments on the loyalty of fellow employees had to be protected by privacy. The Army's right to privacy in security matters was, in fact, protected by an Executive Order, which McCarthy was trying to have rescinded, largely because it was a Truman directive. The Truman order had a number of defects which the Justice Department wanted corrected, lending additional pressure for a new Eisenhower directive, which was finally forthcoming. To this McCarthy gave lip service, but continued his violent attacks on the administration.

Early in December, 1953, at the same time that his harsh speech against the Eisenhower-Dulles leadership was causing sharp repercussions abroad, McCarthy informed Secretary of the Army Robert T. Stevens and the Army's counsel, John Adams, that he intended to subpoena seven or eight loyalty-security board members the next morning in order to force them to appear at hearings he was then conducting in his attempt to uncover Communist employees at Fort Monmouth, New Jersey. Stevens and Adams managed to stall off McCarthy and came to Brownell and his assistant, Rogers, for help. But during the following month, McCarthy became more threatening in his demand for the appearance of loyalty-security board members and in his disregard for the Executive Order protecting them and the loyalty files from outside scrutiny. His challenge of the prerogatives of the executive branch became unmistakable and serious. One effect was to widen the breach within the Republican party. Henry Cabot Lodge suggested that it was high time for the administration to take a more thoughtful look at the situation. He and I arranged to meet with Brownell and John Adams on January 21 in the Attorney General's office for a talk about McCarthy.

During the discussion, John Adams brought out that at the same time that McCarthy was investigating the Army, he and his young committee counsel, Roy Cohn, had been putting pressure on Stevens and Adams in an attempt to obtain preferential treatment for their friend and former associate on the McCarthy staff, David Schine, who had been drafted into the Army as a private on November 3. The story that Adams told us was strange and incredible, and it dated back to the previous July, when Schine was called by his draft board and McCarthy tried without success to get him a commission successively in the Army, the Navy and the Air Force.

Then Cohn went to General Bedell Smith, complaining that the Army had failed to keep "a promise" to give Schine a direct commission, and asked Smith to place Schine in the Central Intelligence Agency, which the McCarthy committee was then investigating. Smith pointed out calmly to Cohn that it was hardly proper for McCarthy to seek such a favor from an agency that he was investigating.

This reminder from Smith of the impropriety of mixing favor-seeking with investigation seemed, however, to go over the heads of McCarthy and Cohn. A few months later, while they were investigating security risks among the Army's employees at Fort Monmouth, they besieged Stevens and Adams with requests for special favors and easy assignments for Schine, who was then supposed to be going through basic training as a private at Fort Dix. Cohn openly intimated that the McCarthy committee's probe of the Army would become tougher if Schine were not given elite treatment. On one occasion, when Adams mentioned the possibility of Schine being sent overseas, Cohn said that if that happened Stevens would no longer be Secretary of the Army.

Stevens was asked to make Schine his special assistant in charge of uncovering subversives in the Army. When that proposal failed, Cohn suggested that Schine be assigned to West Point to watch out for Communist propaganda in Army textbooks. One night when Adams was giving a lecture in Amherst, Massachusetts, Cohn called him on the telephone asking him to get Schine excused from kitchen duty the next day. McCarthy and Cohn made a long and strenuous effort to get Schine a civilian-clothes assignment in New York City. One day during a heated discussion about the Army's refusal to give Schine such a privileged type of duty, Cohn ordered Adams out of his car in the middle of three lanes of traffic at Park Avenue and Forty-sixth Street in New York. An odd twist in these goings-on was that McCarthy, behind Cohn's back, confided to Stevens that he really wished the Army would send Schine far away "to get him out of my hair."

In most of its details Adams' story was brought out later by testimony in the hearing before the Senate subcommittee. Some incidents in the Army testimony were disputed by Cohn but this was imbedded in such a maze of counter charges by McCarthy and his associates that the subcommittee sometimes found itself in a welter of confusion.

It seemed only logical to me that the facts of McCarthy's and Cohn's efforts to high-pressure the Army into giving Schine special treatment should be made known to the other Senators on the McCarthy investigating subcommittee. I suggested at the meeting in the Attorney General's office that John Adams should draw up a detailed chronological account of the whole affair and confront the subcommittee with it. Not entirely by accident, the Army's report on its troubles with Schine fell into the hands of a few newspaper correspondents before it was seen by the subcommittee, and their stories built up a backfire against McCarthy, as intended. He protested loudly that the disclosures about Schine were an attempt to blackmail him into giving up the Fort Monmouth investigation.

But just when it seemed as though the Army had McCarthy on the ropes, he came up with the damaging case of Major Irving Peress. A dentist who had been in the Army for a year, Peress had been inducted as a captain under the Doctors' Draft Law. After receiving his commission, he refused before a loyalty-security board to answer questions about alleged Communist activities and associations. But even though he was marked as a security risk, Peress was promoted to the rank of major according to the routine procedure of correlating civilian earnings with military pay. The Army had already decided to discharge Peress when McCarthy discovered him at Camp Kilmer, New Jersey, and called him for questioning on January 30. He invoked the Fifth Amendment at the McCarthy subcommittee hearing. McCarthy then sent Stevens a demand that Peress be court-martialed. Instead, three days later, the Major was given an honorable discharge.

When the Peress case became known at the White House, we asked questions promptly but received sorry answers from the Army. Persons, an Army officer himself, found the blunders were caused by red tape and inefficiency; the promotion and the honorable discharge had simply gone through channels faster than the security information could catch up with the record. McCarthy questioned Brigadier General Ralph Zwicker, the commanding officer at Camp Kilmer, to find out why and how Peress had been discharged, subjecting Zwicker, an officer with an admirable combat record, to humiliation, and calling him ignorant and unfit to wear a uniform. Incensed when his counsel, Adams, was evicted by McCarthy from the hearing when he tried to protect General Zwicker, Stevens resolved to prevent McCarthy from subjecting the Army's officers in the future to such treatment. Significantly, Stevens turned for help in this chaotic situation to Senator Symington and the Democrats on the McCarthy subcommittee, rather than to his fellow Republicans in the administration and in Congress. Symington supported Stevens and called in for advice Clark Clifford, who had been Truman's counsel. Clifford told Stevens that under no circumstances should the Army allow McCarthy to upbraid its officers.

Behind the scenes Persons sought to have the Republican members of the McCarthy subcommittee, Dirksen, Mundt and Potter, try to make some kind of peace between Stevens and McCarthy. They hastily invited the Secretary to meet with McCarthy and themselves at the famous fried chicken luncheon in Dirksen's office, next door to Nixon's suite in the Senate Office Building. Nixon himself was not involved in the luncheon but he knew and encouraged the effort to bring about some kind of a peaceful compromise out of the ruction that McCarthy had raised with the administration. Directly after the meeting Stevens returned to the Pentagon to tell the Army Chief of Staff, General Ridgway, and his other associates that he had gotten what he wanted, namely a guarantee from McCarthy that Army officers would no longer be harassed by the subcommittee. At the very same time Mundt was giving to the press a "memorandum of understanding," which he said had been agreed to at the luncheon, and it included a so-called promise from Stevens to turn over to McCarthy the names of all the Army people responsible for the promotion and discharge of Peress. That blew the lid off the teakettle.

When Fred Seaton, then an Assistant Secretary of Defense, confronted Stevens with Mundt's memorandum and with copies of the afternoon newspapers shouting that Stevens had showed "the white feather," the Secretary of the Army complained of "timid souls" at the White House who he felt had pressed him to seek an agreement with McCarthy. Actually, Stevens had gone to the luncheon in Dirksen's office on his own, although he was well aware that Nixon and Persons had made strong recommendations that the Republicans on the McCarthy committee get hold of the situation. At this point Stevens was in great turmoil and there was some talk in the Pentagon that he would resign. At no time, however, did the White House ask for or encourage his resignation. We called him to the White House immediately and Nixon, Persons and I sat down with him to draft a counterstatement that would give his side of what went on in Dirksen's office. After long, grueling discussion and arguments, I remember walking outside to the south lawn, where the President was limbering up with a golf club after a hard day's work. I told him that we had reached an agreement on a statement and would like to have him check it over. Whenever I interrupted his exercise in the late afternoon like this, Eisenhower never showed any sign of impatience or displeasure but I could tell that he wished that I might occasionally bring him some good news instead of having to confront him so often with something that had gone wrong. He listened to what I said about the agreement we had reached with Stevens, took a few more shots with his Number 8 iron, and asked me to have Stevens, the Vice President and Persons meet him in the second-floor study. Eisenhower had no material changes to suggest except that he thought Stevens should make the statement himself. He and the leaders would then support Stevens' position and the air should begin to clear.

The important words in the Stevens statement, which the Secretary read afterward to the White House reporters in Hagerty's office, referred to assurances given to him at the luncheon by McCarthy—which were omitted in Mundt's version of the discussion the previous day—that the brow-beating of General Zwicker would not be repeated in future hearings. "If it had not been for those assurances, I would never have entered into any agreement whatsoever," Stevens said.

Eisenhower came stanchly to the defense of the Army Secretary at his meeting with the Republican leaders the following Monday. Stevens, he said, was an honest man who had made a sincere attempt to co-operate with McCarthy and the Republicans on the committee, only to be talked into an agreement at the luncheon with the Senators that provoked a terrible public reaction. Stevens had gone to the luncheon, the President pointed out, on the assurance that it would be a secret affair, but he had found a crowd of a hundred reporters milling around the corridor in front of Dirksen's office waiting for him. When the Peress case first broke, Eisenhower continued, I had told the Army "to admit its mistake and then stand its ground." As a career Army officer, Eisenhower was quick to recognize and admit the blunder in the Pentagon's handling of the Peress case. But the President bluntly told the leaders there was no justification for what had followed. Deploring the personal humiliation to which McCarthy had subjected General Zwicker, the President told the leaders he was planning to issue that week a memorandum to the members of his Cabinet ordering them to insist upon fair treatment for all officials and employees of the executive branch of the government in appearances at investigation hearings.

"I don't challenge the right of Congress to investigate," Eisenhower said, "but we simply cannot defeat Communism by destroying the standards of decency and fair play in which we believe."

In a carefully prepared public statement made at his press conference two days later, Eisenhower expressed stern disapproval of the conduct of Zwicker's cross examination and put the responsibility for fairness and propriety in its investigations squarely upon the Republicans in Congress. "They are the majority party," he noted, "and therefore control the committees." That was as close as he would go toward singling out McCarthy by name. In private conversations, he was not so reticent. A few weeks later at a Cabinet meeting, while he was discussing internal security legislation he remarked that McCarthy's headlined Red hunting was actually impeding the work of removing subversives from government agencies. He added grimly that the Kremlin ought to put McCarthy on its payroll.

The Army's formal chronological complaint on the efforts by McCarthy and Cohn to obtain preferential treatment for Schine was filed with the members of the Senate Permanent Investigations Subcommittee on March 11. Along with the furor resulting from Stevens' statement and the stiffening resistance to McCarthy's intrusions on the executive department, this document was the immediate cause of the public hearings which began late in April, with the Senator now on the defensive. We tried to get the hearings transferred to the Senate Armed Forces Committee but the chairman of that committee, Senator Leverett Saltonstall, wanted no part of it. Saltonstall was facing a re-election campaign in Massachusetts, where McCarthy had a large following, and he had no desire to preside over an investigation of the Wisconsin Senator. So the hearings were conducted by McCarthy's own Permanent Investigations Subcommittee, with McCarthy handing over the chairmanship temporarily to Senator Mundt. They dragged on before an avid national television audience for thirty-six days, much to Eisenhower's disgust. The President was deeply conscious of the injury that the hearings were doing to American prestige abroad. "Our only hope now," he said at a press conference in May, "is that America may derive from this incident advantages that are at least comparable to what we have suffered in the loss of international prestige and . . . national self-respect."

As the Army-McCarthy circus became increasingly embarrassing, more and more people looked toward Eisenhower, wondering why he did not step in and put a stop to it. When he continued to remain aloof from the argument, he seemed to some of his followers weak and vacillating. The Washington *Post,* which had forecast in 1952 that McCarthyism would fade away if Eisenhower was elected, declared impatiently at the height of the Army-McCarthy controversy that it "had waited some 400 nights for the President to exert the kind of leadership that would bring that happy result." In a Cabinet discussion a few years later, the President recalled that during the hearings he received letters from private citizens asking "why I did not fire McCarthy." Aside from the fact that the President could do nothing to remove a United States Senator, and entirely apart from his firmly ingrained distaste for the personal fight that engaging McCarthy at his own level would provoke, Eisenhower felt that he had no constitutional right or responsibility to interfere in a Senate investigation, and no amount of persuasion from such respected friends as Paul Hoffman and C. D. Jackson could convince him otherwise. The closest that the President came to being involved in the hearings was in a dispute over his determination to use the constitutional separation of the legislative and executive branches of the government to keep himself out of it.

As we expected, McCarthy tried to claim at the hearings that the Army's charges against him were inspired by the White House. He based his claim on the January 21 meeting in Brownell's office, where I had suggested to John Adams that the Army should draw up a chronology of McCarthy's and Cohn's attempts to obtain preferential treatment for Schine. John Adams admitted in testimony at one of the hearings that the suggestion for the chronology had come from me, and McCarthy wanted to call me as a witness for questioning about the conversations at the January 21 meeting. He also wanted to see records of monitored telephone calls in the White House and in the Department of Defense. In no uncertain terms, Eisenhower told the Republican Congressional leaders in a meeting with them on May 17 that White House staff people, like me, were under no obligation to the legislative branch of the government and that he would permit no testimony before a Senate subcommittee concerning private meetings and telephone calls in which executive branch officials were involved. In a letter to Secretary of Defense Wilson, dated that same day, and citing constitutional rights and historical precedents, the President stopped any further testimony at the hearings on the January 21 meeting. In addition, he instructed Wilson not to permit his department's employees to disclose any conversations or communications between them and officials in other executive departments. Senator Dirksen tried to talk the President into modifying his order but Eisenhower stood firm, taking the stand that the case against McCarthy had been prepared on the Army's sole authority and responsibility, without regard to the suggestions or advice it might have received elsewhere. This argument satisfied everybody except McCarthy.

The hearings finally petered out to an inconclusive ending, contributing nothing of discernible value to the United States government except a discrediting of McCarthy, whose influence declined after his performance in the travesty. As Eisenhower often pointed out, the theatricals of McCarthy only impeded the solid, if unspectacular, progress that the administration's own security program was making in purging the government and the nation at large of Communist subversives. In an effort to give some tangible evidence of this progress, Eisenhower issued a statement early in June announcing the conviction of forty-one Communist party leaders, two other party members for espionage and one for treason, the deportation of eighty-four alien subversives and the addition of sixty-two new organizations to the Attorney General's list of subversive groups; all this during the first sixteen months of his administration, and the outlawing of the Communist party as well. Meanwhile the White House had established strict security surveillance of federal employees. In his 1954 message on the State of the Union, Eisenhower mentioned that 2,200 security risks had been weeded out of government jobs. The Washington newspapers, with their government-employed readers confused about just what a security risk was, naturally clamored for detailed information about these dismissals. Unlike McCarthy, who was always ready to name names, Eisenhower firmly refused to identify any of the dismissed employees or to divulge the reasons for their dismissals. There was sharp criticism of this policy for it caused some discharged Civil Service personnel, who had been let go for entirely different reasons, to be tagged as disloyal. Nevertheless, the members of the loyalty-security boards and the sources of information had to be protected, and the reputations of people who were suspected, but not proven, security risks could not be recklessly blackened. "I'm perfectly indifferent to the shouting of some newspapers," Eisenhower said one day at a Cabinet meeting while explaining his policy of keeping security dismissals confidential. "We know we've been just in this matter."

The numbers of government employees dismissed for security reasons continued to be announced from time to time, together with a breakdown in the various categories of risk, but no names were ever divulged.

After the Army-McCarthy hearings, Senator Ralph Flanders of Vermont, a man of conscience and courage, introduced a motion in the Senate to censure McCarthy. Eisenhower again kept his distance, but he did send Senator Arthur Watkins of Utah a message of encouragement and support when Watkins accepted the chairmanship of the censure committee which was to weigh the charges against McCarthy. When the Watkins committee recommended a censure vote, the President warmly congratulated him at a meeting in the White House for "living up to everything I expected of you." The Senate condemned McCarthy for behavior unbecoming a United States Senator by a vote of sixty-seven to twenty-two. The vote disclosed the wide gap of disagreement between the President and the leaders of his party in the Senate. Saltonstall was the only Republican leader who voted against McCarthy; Knowland, the GOP minority leader, Dirksen, Bridges and Millikin all voted for the Wisconsin Senator, who had just issued a public apology for supporting Eisenhower in 1952. It could be readily understood why Jerry Persons, Eisenhower's liaison officer charged with dealing with Congress, constantly urged the President not to interfere with the Senate's handling of the Army-McCarthy dispute. As for my own role in the McCarthy episode, I had to maintain a moderate position for the staff was divided in its opinion and some degree of equilibrium had to be kept. Those of C. D. Jackson's frame of mind would have had Eisenhower demolish McCarthy, whereas those like Persons who had to try to get along with everybody urged the President to keep entirely clear of the controversy. Although I tried to stay away from either extreme, McCarthy in a later statement named me along with the President, Dr. Milton Eisenhower, Stassen, Dewey and Paul Hoffman as a leader of "the left wing of the Republican party."

Six months after the censuring of McCarthy, there was a discussion at Eisenhower's weekly meeting with the Republican Congressional leaders about a resolution that McCarthy had introduced in the Senate, calling for consideration of the predicament of the captive states under Communist domination at the coming meeting of the United Nations in San Francisco. Nixon remarked that it was a matter that the President did not need to take very seriously. I thought to myself how times had changed. It was then, as he turned to another subject, that Eisenhower paused to ask us if we had heard the one going around Washington about McCarthyism now becoming McCarthywasm.

9 The Great Change in the Economy

After Eisenhower was elected President in 1952, he found that the government was in a far worse financial mess than he and his economic advisers had expected. Along with the rest of the people in the country who paid any attention to the situation, Eisenhower and his newly appointed officials knew that the outgoing Truman administration was leaving a heavy load of unpaid bills, together with staggering expenses which were increasing at a rate far greater than the income to meet them. But none of us, not even the Republican Congressmen who sat on the standing fiscal committees of the House and Senate and who were trained to keep a sharp eye on government spending, realized how bad the situation really was. When Joseph M. Dodge, Eisenhower's first Budget Director, revealed in detail the facts and figures of the government's financial predicament at the first Cabinet meeting in the Hotel Commodore in New York before the inauguration, most of us were stunned and dismayed.

Dodge later likened the financial plight of the departing Democratic administration to that of a family with an accumulated debt four times bigger than its annual income, with never more money in the bank than it needed to cover one month's living expenses, facing a 10 per cent reduction in income and with current bills for C.O.D. purchases hanging over its head larger than a year's total income. And these bills would have to be met with cash on the line as soon as the goods were delivered.

Shortly after the election, Eisenhower had sent Dodge to Washington at the invitation of Truman to sit in with Truman's Budget Director, Frederick J. Lawton, during a review of the budget then

153

being prepared for the fiscal year of 1954. That last Truman budget showed a projected deficit of $9.9 billion, which Eisenhower and Dodge had more or less expected. What they did not expect, and what Dodge discovered to his amazement, was that this $9.9 billion represented only a fraction of the real gap between the government's anticipated income and its current expenses. In the face of a budget deficit of $13.4 billion during the two previous fiscal years, Congress had authorized huge additional expenditures, mostly for the Korean War, without providing any income whatever to cover them. These IOUs, as Secretary of the Treasury George Humphrey called them, were what Dodge had in mind when he referred in his illustrative example to the C.O.D. purchases made by the extravagant family that would cost an entire year's income. They mounted up to a whopping eighty billion dollars. The economy-minded businessmen in the Cabinet, Humphrey, Wilson and Weeks, who, like Eisenhower himself, had dedicated themselves to balancing the budget and cutting taxes, were naturally stunned by the state of affairs. To make matters more complicated and embarrassing, the Republicans in Congress, led by Senator Taft, Speaker Joe Martin and Dan Reed, the tenacious Chairman of the House Ways and Means Committee, were pushing for reductions in income and excess profits taxes that the new administration, in the light of the financial plight it unexpectedly found itself in, could not now afford. It was hardly an inviting picture.

Despite this gloomy inheritance from the Truman administration and despite steadily rising costs of government in meeting the needs of national defense in a missile and space age, Eisenhower managed to balance the budget. This feat, surely one of his greatest as President, irked many Republicans because it took about as long as Eisenhower said it would during his 1952 campaign. But he did it in four years with a series of courageous and skillfully planned economic moves that freed private enterprise from government restriction and stimulated during his administration the greatest prosperity this country has ever enjoyed.

Eisenhower was more deeply concerned with economics than most people realized. He once told the Cabinet that if he was able to do nothing as President except balance the budget he would feel that his time in the White House had been well spent. As a professional soldier serving as President during cold war tension, he might have been expected to devote all of the nation's resources to a build-up of military strength, but Eisenhower was firmly convinced that the country's economic prosperity was as important to its security as planes and weapons. He was always fearful that excessive military spending might weaken the nation internally and continually warned the Defense Department against pushing the country into a financial crisis. One day in a Cabinet meeting he reminisced about the old days in the Army when only the chief of staff was allowed to have an automobile and other officers were handed street car tokens when they had to travel across Washington to appear at a Congressional committee hearing. Long before he became President, Eisenhower had decided that national security depended pre-eminently upon a sound economy and that the first way to promote prosperity was to rid the economy of government controls. "The initiative, the ambition and the earnings and savings of the American people are the important things in our economy," he said, during the 1952 campaign, while promising to take the shackles off free enterprise, "and not some bureaucrat in Washington telling us what to do." As much as any one single factor, it was Eisenhower's steadfast adherence to this point of view that persuaded him to join the Republicans when it came time to make a choice between the two political parties.

As devoutly as he believed in a free economy, Eisenhower as President watched and studied the trends in the nation's business constantly, always ready to modify his hands-off policy whenever he felt that the public good demanded it. He met regularly with his White House staff economist, Gabriel Hauge, and Arthur Burns, Chairman of the President's Council of Economic Advisers, and listened to them and questioned them about the stock and commodity market, the significance of business and trade statistics, credit figures, the trend in farm prices and merchant's inventories. Among the Republican leaders in Congress the Council of Economic Advisers had fallen into disrepute as a guide for executive action. The unpalatable theories of Leon Keyserling were too fresh in their recollection to stimulate any enthusiasm for restaffing the agency. Indeed, some of them would have been happy to have the Council abolished altogether. Having the President's office budget in mind, I was inclined at first toward cutting the Council down to one man, whereupon I listened to a stern lecture from Gabriel Hauge on the reasons why he felt that Eisenhower's decisions in the field of economics might well spell the success or failure of his whole administration. After talking it over with Eisenhower, we asked for funds for a three-man council, headed by Burns, professor of economics at Columbia University and an expert on business cycles, whom Hauge recommended.

When I took my first look at Burns, on the day he came to my office before I was to take him in to meet the President, I had a sinking sensation. If somebody had asked me to describe the mental image I had of the type of New Deal official we were in the process of moving out of Washington, this was it—a glassy stare through thick lenses, peering out from under a canopy of unruly hair parted in the middle, a large pipe with a curved stem: the very incarnation of all the externals that were such anathema to Republican business-men and politicians. I wondered if we would both be thrown out of Eisenhower's office. But I swallowed hard and invited the professor to follow me in.

If Eisenhower had any misgivings, he kept them to himself. To me, Arthur Burns turned out to be a pleasant surprise. He and Eisenhower got along fine. They shared the same outlook and philos-ophy. Far from being the abstract and impractical professor, Burns had his feet planted solidly on the ground and had no difficulty in more than holding his own in arguments at the Cabinet table with such hard-headed protagonists as Humphrey and Dodge. As soon as the 1954 downturn began to appear, Eisenhower set aside ample time at Cabinet meetings so that Burns could discuss the economics of the situation. These periods lasted often as long as thirty minutes and Eisenhower listened to him with fascination. The President was particularly impressed by the importance that Burns placed on the time factor in his analyses of business conditions. Going back, as he often did, to his Army experiences, in one such exchange on the role of time in the economy, Eisenhower remarked that a commanding officer in combat could recover lost men and lost weapons, or a strategic position on high ground, but he could never recover lost time. One morning, after Burns finished a detailed outline of con-tributions that various government departments could make toward strengthening the economy, Eisenhower said to him admiringly, "Arthur, my boy, you would have made a fine chief of staff overseas during the war."

The first big economic decision that Eisenhower had to face was the removal of the price and wage controls that had been hanging over the American economy since the Korean War began. Eisenhower and his associates were agreed that lifting the controls would give a healthy spurt to the economy, indirectly increasing government revenues and helping to cut down the alarming budget deficit. But there was disagreement about how soon the controls should be lifted. Humphrey and Wilson wanted the economy loosened up as soon as Eisenhower took office, reasoning that removing controls would give a much needed shot in the arm to production, which was then lagging well behind market demand. Lodge and Stassen, as well as many Democrats and labor union officials, were afraid that a quick removal of price controls would cause runaway inflation. They wanted Eisenhower to wait a few months, and back off gradually.

Eisenhower put the problem of working out a plan in the lap of Arthur Flemming, recently staff director of the Office of Defense Mobilization under John Steelman. In the period of transition, Eisenhower moved Flemming up to the position of acting director and then transferred the control mechanism to his agency. Working with Hauge, Flemming decided that controls should not all be abolished in a single stroke; rather they should be lifted gradually but soon. Michael DiSalle, Truman's erstwhile price administrator, paid me an unexpected call to say that he was worried about the effect of a sudden abandonment of controls and skeptical about the effectiveness of indirect controls, which, he assumed, the administration would substitute. DiSalle recommended the establishment of an economic stabilization commission to keep a check on prices. I turned his opinions over to Dodge and Hauge, who advised against such a commission on the grounds that our reconstructed Office of Defense Mobilization and Council of Economic Advisers would stand guard on the same area. Hauge also disagreed with DiSalle's worry about the lifting of controls.

Eisenhower liked Flemming's idea of a fairly fast but progressive freeing of the economy but he wanted the concurrence of the Cabinet before approving it. At the Cabinet meeting on February 6, there was full approval of the President's proposal to abolish all wage and some price controls immediately and the rest of the price controls during the next few weeks. The President was inclined to hold on to rent controls until the following year but the Republican leadership in Congress disagreed, with action on a bill finally doing away entirely with them on July 31.

Looking back on Eisenhower's price and wage controls decision a few years later, *Fortune* magazine expressed some surprise that the President had made up his mind with such quick decisiveness on so complicated an economic question at the time when the Korean War was not yet settled. Flemming made an interesting comment when the writer of the *Fortune* article, Charles J. V. Murphy, asked him what he thought about Eisenhower's move.

"The key to the President's approach to the whole question of controls was his conviction that the most effective mobilization base is one resting on a strong economy," Flemming said. "Those people who accuse us of putting a balanced budget before defense fail to understand this. What they haven't grasped is that the country is today in a strong position because the released civilian economy has created such a terrific demand that suppliers, conspicuously in aluminum, are already producing more than enough for any conceivable mobilization base."

In any case, the lifting of controls worked well. There was no inflation worth worrying about and business boomed. The dire predictions of those who envisioned runaway prices came to naught. But controlling federal expenditures to cut down the budget deficit and the soaring public debt was not so easy. The country was crying out for tax reductions. During the campaign, in a speech at Peoria, Illinois, that he remembered only too well, Eisenhower had stated plainly that his "goal" was to cut the annual spending of the federal government to sixty billion dollars to eliminate the deficit and to make substantial tax reductions—but he had promised to do this "within four years." Senator Taft, Representative Dan Reed and other Republican leaders in Congress had decided long ago that this was not going to be anywhere near fast enough. At the widely publicized Morningside Heights meeting before the election, Senator Taft had done his best to commit Eisenhower to a sharply accelerated program of reductions when he announced, "General Eisenhower emphatically agrees with me in the proposal to reduce drastically over-all expenses. Our goal is about seventy billion in fiscal year 1954 and sixty billion in fiscal year 1955."

With the Korean War still unsettled, it was impossible to pare down the defense expenditures, which comprised two-thirds of the expenses in the 1954 budget. With the basic changes that Eisenhower had already begun in the comprehensive plan of national defense, the requested funds essential to support the defense, atomic energy and related mutual security programs simply had to be provided. The other principal portion of the budget comprised such irreducible obligations as farm price supports, veterans' pensions, debt service and grants-in-aid to states. These expenditures were all fixed under laws enacted by the Congress. The remaining items in the budget provided for running the federal government, some $9.5 billion, which happened to be just about the size of the deficit in the budget recommended by Truman as he was about to leave office. Yet by scratching and scraping, Eisenhower and Dodge pared it down so that the estimated deficit was reduced from $9.9 billion to $5.5 billion. In the strait jacket they were in, it was a remarkable achievement. But when Eisenhower presented this revised budget to the Republican leaders from Congress at the end of April, Senator Taft showed how disappointed he was by completely losing his patience in the memorable incident described earlier.

We also had difficulty trying to convince Dan Reed that the promised day of the balanced budget had not yet dawned. In his capacity as Chairman of the House Ways and Means Committee Reed stubbornly insisted on filing a bill to reduce income taxes on individuals and gave notice of his intention to allow the excess profits tax to expire on June 30. Waving aside protests from the administration that it could not afford any such loss of revenue, Reed clarioned that he was carrying out a Republican "promise" in cutting the taxes and warned that his program would be held up "over my dead body." These two measures would have cost the Treasury some $3.5 billion. At a meeting of the Republican legislative leaders, Eisenhower emphasized that he had made no promises of tax cuts for the year, or for the next two years, for that matter, and that there would be no tax reductions until the budget could be brought into balance and there was something left to apply on the national debt. Such conservatives as Taft, Millikin and Speaker Joe Martin, who had been hungry for tax reduction, agreed with the President that the excess profits tax should be extended. Martin told Eisenhower that the Reed bill would make no progress. In other words, he would see to it that it didn't.

Efforts were made to persuade Reed to listen to reason. Eisenhower had him down to the White House for a talk and various influential Republicans made it their business to drop in to see him at the Capitol. But Reed would not budge. His bill was finally blocked by parliamentary maneuvering; friends of Eisenhower on the House Rules Committee refused to report it out. Reed retaliated by refusing to call a meeting of his Ways and Means Committee, the starting point for revenue bills, for the consideration of the extension of the excess profits tax that the President and Humphrey had urgently requested. He figured that the tax would expire on its termination date, June 30, before the administration could get it extended. But Reed was finally outmaneuvered by a House vote that discharged his committee from further consideration of the bill and took it directly to the Rules Committee, where it soon found its way to the floor. As Martin observed facetiously at a White House meeting, Reed seemed to be able to get Democratic support when he didn't need it but he could not get it when he did need it. Such goings-on began to give the nonpolitical Eisenhower an education on the important role played by practical political strategy and infighting at the highest level of government.

There were interesting arguments in these battles over the budget and tax reductions. Reed contended that the loss of revenue from the tax cuts he was proposing would force the administration to cut down its spending whether it wanted to or not, and therefore the budget would be balanced sooner. In further support of his position, he pointed to the rather well-accepted theory that tax cuts would stimulate business activity and prevent a depression. Under different economic circumstances that would have been a more telling argument, as even George Humphrey found reason to remember in later years. But Humphrey was more interested at that particular time in putting a damper on spiraling inflation, and told Reed that any outpouring of money in the form of tax reductions would only further complicate his problems. The present stage of the economy, with the pressure of demand against an insufficient supply, was no time for starting an additional spurt with tax cuts.

In our time, the health of the economy as a whole has become a more definitive factor than either expenditures or taxes in government budget decisions. Budget-balancing is no longer simply an internal problem of the government, isolated from business and industry, and the economic condition of the American people as a whole. The big plus factor that made it possible for the budget to be balanced during Eisenhower's first term was the thriving and rapidly expanding business activity and industrial production that had been stirred up by the release of price and wage controls a month after he took office. The President's economic philosophy—his confidence in a free market place, unhampered by government restriction, as the basis of national prosperity and security—was put to a test in the summer and fall of 1953 and the winter of 1954, when the clouds of recession appeared in the economic sky to bring uneasiness about the future once more.

Various reasons were advanced for the downturn of 1953-54, with its swelling industrial unemployment, heavy and sluggish inventories and falling farm prices. The public finger was pointed at George Humphrey's attempt to tighten credit in April of 1953 after the lifting of price controls. Apprehensive about inflation, the Secretary of the Treasury brought out an attractive issue of thirty-year 3.25 per cent bonds that mopped up enough money that would otherwise have gone into corporate stocks and mortgages to cause a mild panic. As the President's Economic Report noted later, this sufficiently dried up the money supply to slow down normal growth and even embarrass some businesses in locating their current cash requirements. Humphrey admitted himself that he had tightened credit a little too much. Instead of fighting inflation he found himself with deflation on his hands. Coming to the rescue, William McC. Martin, Chairman of the Federal Reserve Board, took prompt steps to ease the situation, lower interest rates and loosen up the money supply. The crisis passed, but it left its mark as an error in Humphrey's fiscal calculation and raised some questions about the stability of the administration's money policies.

More responsible for the recession was the decline in the economy that came with the settlement of the Korean War and the slow-up in full-scale emergency military production. Whatever caused it, signs of distress and discontent appeared everywhere that summer. A delegation of sixty cattlemen crowded into the President's office one day in June to ask for a federal beef-buying program as a relief for ruinously low prices. I arranged the meeting as I had done the previous summer at Denver, when they had come in to plead with Eisenhower, if he became President, to keep the government out of their affairs and let them alone. Eisenhower's recollection of their argument, and some of their faces, was as clear as my own. He pointed at one rancher and said to him, "I clearly recall something you said out there. You said, 'Listen, General, I don't care what plan you come up with as long as you take the government out of the cattle business.' That right, Bill?" Bill nodded and admitted that it was right. Whereupon Eisenhower listened sympathetically to their predicament, but the federal government still did not get into the cattle business.

In discussions at the White House, the expression "countercyclical" became a familiar term. In the language of Arthur Burns, upswings and downswings in the economy were cycles, and measures to counteract them were countercyclical. As anxious as he was to keep enterprise free from government, the President was ready to take extraordinary steps to keep the country out of a depression, had that actually threatened. Among many such measures, he was ready to launch a public works program to ease unemployment if the emergency became dangerous. He had long talks about such a project with Hauge and Burns, who suggested that federal spending could be applied to several low-priority Defense Department supply and construction needs that were then being held back because of the budget deficit. But Eisenhower and his advisers agreed that the government would not get into emergency construction work of its own except as a last resort. Furthermore, it would not resort to large-scale spending until after it had exhausted its efforts to revive employment by liberalizing the monetary and loan policies, easing credit and reducing taxes. Back in March, when the country was at the top of the Korean War boom and Humphrey's only worry was uncontrollable inflation, Hauge had said to the Secretary of the Treasury during a discussion about the ability of the economy to carry the defense load without dislocation, "We are going to have to shift our mental gears on this preoccupation with inflation sometime before too long. Saying this, believe me, is not meant as an argument for a military WPA to keep the economy fully employed. If we can't keep the economy humming without that, we had better turn in our suits right now."

Eisenhower stood fast in his faith in a free economy throughout the recession, calmly resisting the pressures for federal intervention that came from lobby groups, labor unions, business leaders and jittery Republican politicians who were worrying about the 1954 elections. He was unmoved by a call from Walter Reuther for a national conference on unemployment and by a demand for government action from a group of Democrats led by Senator Paul H. Douglas of Illinois. On the morning of September 25, 1953, when Burns gave the Cabinet a long and detailed report on the Council's view of the economic situation, together with specific recommendations to combat further recession, Eisenhower observed that he was ready, if it became necessary, to use the full resources of the government to prevent "another 1929," as the Republicans had pledged during the 1952 campaign. But he made it plain that he was not wavering in his economic creed. The best way to combat a depression, in his view, was to spur the individual on to greater, and freer, economic activity.

Burns said that morning that the recession was not critical and pointed out that the strength of the economy had been shown in its recent survival of the deflating credit squeeze. He strongly recommended, however, that the administration should allow the tax cuts that it had resisted in the spring in an effort to reduce the next budget's deficit. Eisenhower and Humphrey followed this advice from the economists, allowing the excess profits tax and the Korean War emergency increase in the personal income tax to expire at the end of the year. These reductions, with cuts in the excise taxes, would add $7.4 billion to the nation's spending money, and, of course, a corresponding cut in federal revenues. But, as Eisenhower was to report later, expenditures were also in the process of going down to the tune of eleven billion dollars annually, an ace in the hole that not even the President knew he had at that time. Burns also advised a continuance of easy credit policies by the Treasury and the Federal Reserve to make money more available. Humphrey came around to agree with Burns's ideas, but pointed out the complexities of trying to maintain fiscal stability in the government while bolstering domestic prosperity with one hand and meeting the requirements of a strong national defense with the other. Humphrey had come into the Cabinet strongly determined to cut both government spending and taxes and to balance the budget, and he had been ready at first to swing his ax on anything that stood in his way. But after listening to Dulles talk

about the international situation and the importance of Mutual Security and foreign aid, he had not been so sure about the sanctity of
his clear-cut convictions. At one meeting in the White House, when
conservative Senator Millikin was pressing him for a commitment
on tax reductions, Humphrey indignantly reminded the Senator of
"the atomic Pearl Harbor that is hanging over our heads."

As the autumn turned into winter, unemployment rose higher and
the talk at Cabinet meetings about balancing the budget waned. Instead, Eisenhower and Humphrey turned their attention to Burns's
proposal for planning a public works program. But there were no
signs of panic around the Cabinet table. The President said at a press
conference in March, when a group of Democrats in the Senate were
asking for higher income tax exemptions, that the time had not yet
come for any "slam-bang" emergency program. Obviously, David
McDonald, the leader of the United Steelworkers, did not agree with
him. Two weeks later McDonald came to the White House to urge
the President to start a five-billion-dollar works program, a five-
billion-dollar home-building and slum clearance program, a three-
billion-dollar increase in unemployment compensation and pensions
and a four-billion-dollar cut in income taxes. Contrary to what his
critics charged, Eisenhower was not sitting on his hands and doing
nothing. In the White House and in all departments of the executive
branch, everybody was working hard on plans for remedial action or,
as the President himself described it, "a massive inventory of worth-
while public works" that could be put "on the shelf" until needed.

Fortunately, they were never needed. The recession clouds blew
away that summer without ever causing a serious storm. The tax reductions and the liberalizing of credit and money, but most of all
the basic and fundamental strength of the economy itself, brought
back prosperity with no WPA type of pump priming from the government, just as Eisenhower, Humphrey and Burns had predicted.

In fact, 1954 turned out to be the most prosperous year that the
United States ever had under a peacetime economy up to that time.
As one observer said later, in showing that free enterprise could hold
its own under pressure with no government intervention other than
indirect money control to discourage deflation and inflation, Eisenhower had successfully reversed a twenty-one-year trend toward a
socialized economy.

There were still distressing concentrations of unemployment that
fall during the off-year Congressional elections—in the coal fields,
Tennessee, Pennsylvania, and in certain cities like Flint, Michigan,
where 22 per cent of the labor force was idle. At a press conference
in Detroit, Charlie Wilson was asked why the Defense Department
did not favor areas of unemployment in awarding military contracts.
Reaching for a graphic illustration that would suggest that workers
in depressed sectors could move elsewhere in search of employment,
Wilson came out with his famous bird dog blooper: "I've always
liked bird dogs better than kennel dogs myself. You know, one who
will get out and hunt for food rather than sit on his fanny and yell."
Wilson's quips sometimes sounded better at a private board meeting
of an industrial corporation than they did in a political setting. That
day I was flying back to Washington from Spokane, where I had
made a campaign speech in the hope of keeping the Congress Republican. Changing planes in Minneapolis, I was met by a battery of
newsmen and photographers and ushered into a room that had been
provided, much to my surprise, for a press conference. When I dis-
claimed any intention of holding a press conference, I learned that
the newspapers had arranged the interview expecting me to say something about Wilson and his dogs. Remembering the President's advice,
I did not miss that opportunity to keep my mouth shut. The reporters
thought I was carrying this to excess and their ranks thinned percepti-
bly when they found I had nothing to say. One of them lingered
behind to ask if I could not at least say something nice to the people
of Minneapolis. This I found difficult to refuse.

In that 1954 election, the Democrats won back control of Congress
but by such a slim margin that Nixon, who served as the administration's spokesman and standard bearer during the campaign, called it
a dead heat. The Democrats won the Senate by two seats and the
House by twenty-nine seats. Eisenhower was surprised but the professional politicians of both parties knew that in every off-year election, except the one in 1934, the party in power lost seats in Congress.
The Republicans had such a small majority during the first two years
of the Eisenhower administration that any loss of seats meant a loss
of control. To the chagrin of the many Republican candidates who
had hoped to capitalize once more on Eisenhower's popular appeal
as they did in 1952, the President stayed out of local Congressional

contests. Along with his natural distaste for political campaigning ("By golly, sometimes you sure get tired of all this clackety-clack," he remarked to Jim Hagerty on election eve), Eisenhower felt that as President of all the people he should not become personally involved in state and Congressional district issues. When he agreed to interrupt his summer vacation in Denver to make speeches on the Pacific Coast and in the corn belt, as well as in Washington and New York, he kept strictly out of partisan squabbles and devoted his talks to the progress of the administration and its plans and hopes.

As time ran out that October, however, the inevitable happened: the Republican leaders who had worked with us in 1952 came with increasing frequency to my office in the White House with statistics from the pollsters showing that a Democratic victory was looming and the only way it could be prevented was by the President himself. Eisenhower had been explicit with me in insisting that he was not going to get into it. So it was with considerable misgivings that I finally settled with Leonard Hall, the national chairman, for a swing by the President through four states, Ohio, Michigan, Kentucky and Delaware, where the Republican Senatorial candidates were being hard pressed. While the President agreed to do it, Hall and I had no easy time persuading him to change his mind. Only one of the Republicans won, but it was agreed afterward that Eisenhower's last-minute efforts prevented a much more decisive Democratic triumph.

There were other factors that made it difficult for Eisenhower to work up much enthusiasm for many of the Republican candidates who were up for re-election to Congress. He had rarely received the unified and solid backing of his own party in the Senate and the House when he needed it most in 1953 and 1954. In spite of all Leonard Hall could do, a good many of the members of the National Committee were either lukewarm or openly hostile to the President. "They talk to me about party regularity and patronage but they don't show any regularity on a thing like this," Eisenhower said with disgust after the Republicans in the Senate turned against him in a vote on the Bricker Amendment. Although Eisenhower's withdrawal of government controls from the national economy was undoubtedly as drastic and as basic a change from the Truman and Roosevelt system as could be imagined, there were many Republican Congressmen, like Clarence Brown of Ohio, who blamed the 1954 defeat on the administration for not giving the people the change from the policies of the New Deal that they voted for in 1952.

Carrying the brunt of the campaign, as Eisenhower wanted him to do, Nixon had worked well and tirelessly, earning for himself among the Democrats an undeserved reputation for hitting below the belt. An examination of his speeches does not disclose low blows, yet Adlai Stevenson called the Vice President's references to the Communists-in-government issue "McCarthyism in a white collar." Eisenhower had set a plain example for Nixon in keeping away from extremes himself, particularly when he refused to have anything to do with those who charged the Democrats with treason in the McCarthy and Jenner manner. But this did not mean, as some Republicans seemed to think, that Eisenhower wanted his spokesmen to be kind to Democrats in their campaign oratory. He told Nixon and others, including myself, that he was well aware that somebody had to do the hard-hitting infighting, and he had no objections to it as long as no one expected him to do it. Far from being displeased with Nixon's performance in the 1954 campaign, Eisenhower wrote him a warm letter of praise for it, throwing in a kind word for Pat Nixon's efforts, too.

In the 1954 election, Leonard Hall learned the self-evident truth that was confirmed again in 1956 and 1960: no one else in the Republican party could give it the lift that Eisenhower gave it. But Hall and I both realized that it was futile to expect Eisenhower as the head of the party to make a "give 'em hell" tour of the countryside as Harry Truman liked to do when he was President. And neither of us was foolish enough to try to change Eisenhower's campaign methods; indeed, the results proved that we did not have to. Besides, the President would not get into that kind of competition. Some of the Republicans in Congress, Richard Simpson of Pennsylvania for example, complained that I shielded Eisenhower from the political facts of life and discouraged him from assuming militant command of his party. The people who made those complaints were not aware of the countless hours that I and other members of the White House staff spent with Hall and his associates trying to work out a closer relationship between the President and the Republican National Committee.

The post-mortem discussion at the Cabinet meeting after the 1954 election could have been entitled "Politics of Economics or Economics of Politics." There was certainly no Democratic mandate visible in the result. On the contrary, the closest observers saw a green light for continuing the Eisenhower middle-of-the-road program. Nixon said that he felt the losses to the Democrats were due to such factors as unemployment in the coal fields, Republican failure to organize effectively and go to work and many personality obstacles. "There were just too many turkeys running on the Republican ticket," he told the Cabinet. Eisenhower observed that with the Democrats in control of Congress the split between the conservative and liberal wings of their party would become wider and more obvious. Ezra Taft Benson remarked that with Democrats presiding over the House and Senate agriculture committees his program would be running into difficulty, a prediction that turned out to be accurate indeed. Humphrey was gloomy about the prospects of maintaining prosperity with the Democrats demanding more federal spending and more tax cuts, for, he said, the resulting inflation would be certain to cause a contraction in the economy and dry up new job opportunities. Then, to sum it up, Nixon staged a graphic portrayal of a point he wanted to emphasize, a scene unique in the annals of the Eisenhower Cabinet. He pulled out of his pocket a toy figure of a drummer, released its mechanism and placed it on the Cabinet table. While the President and the Secretaries stared at it in surprise and amusement, the toy drummer marched briskly across the table, banging on its drum.

"We've got to keep beating the drum about our achievements," Nixon said.

With the recession fading away, Eisenhower was able to redouble his efforts to balance the budget. Standing off Dan Reed's attempts to cut income and excess profits taxes until the end of 1953, the budget deficit for the fiscal year ending in June, 1954, cut down from Truman's estimate of $9.9 billion to $5.5 billion by Eisenhower and Dodge, proved to be lower than Dodge and Humphrey had estimated, actually around $3 billion. But the budget for the next fiscal year ending June 30, 1955, the first budget for which Eisenhower would be completely responsible, still appeared to be considerably out of balance, due principally to tax cuts and added expenditures during the recession in 1953 and 1954. Eisenhower made up his mind to do everything he could to wipe out the deficit for the following fiscal year that would end in June, 1956. The statement he had made at Peoria, although only one that expressed his intentions, he took as seriously as any political promise he ever made.

There was a serious political complication in his way. With a presidential election coming up in 1956, the Republicans were eager for more tax cuts in 1955. Eisenhower told them sternly that he would cut no more taxes until the budget was balanced. Humphrey, who was as anxious for tax reductions as the President was for a balanced budget, argued that tax cuts would not necessarily stand in the way of a balanced budget. The Secretary of the Treasury contended that a balanced budget would only come from increased economic activity and that further tax cuts would stimulate such activity. On the other hand, Rowland Hughes, the New York banker who succeeded Dodge as Budget Director in 1954, felt that balancing the budget would depend on how much government spending could be held down. Hughes thought the Humphrey hope for both a surplus *and* reduced taxes was possible if, and only if, expenditures were tightened. Eisenhower was skeptical about the chances of keeping expenses under such tight control and remarked rather tartly that Humphrey was too quick to recommend tax reductions on the basis of anticipated savings in expenditures that might not necessarily materialize.

Considerable pressure was put on the President to issue a public statement as Republican political propaganda which would express "hope" for a tax cut, regardless of whether it worked out or not. Eisenhower did not want to be charged with any more political "promises" about future actions that would be based on conditions beyond his control, and in this case Senator Knowland backed him up. If there was a tax reduction, Knowland said, the administration would get enough credit for it when it happened, whereas a premature statement of optimistic hope would be pounced upon and derided by Democrats if the tax cut was not made. Charlie Halleck wanted the statement issued. He claimed that the administration would have to make a tax cut for political reasons in 1956 regardless of what happened to the budget. Knowland disagreed with him. In the end, the President reluctantly agreed to make the statement in his 1955 State of the Union message, but he warned us that Humphrey would have to take the responsibility for it. He said in that address:

Last year we had a large tax cut and, for the first time in seventy-five years, a basic revision of Federal tax laws. It is now clear that defense and other essential government costs must remain at a level precluding further tax reductions this year. Although excise and corporation income taxes must, therefore, be continued at their present rates, further tax cuts will be possible when justified by lower expenditures and by revenue increases arising from the nation's economic growth. I am hopeful that such reductions can be made next year.

One of the major obstacles in the way of the President's efforts to get control of expenditures was an increase in the pay of the Civil Service. Traditionally government pay scales lagged behind private employment, and this held true for the postal service as well as for salaries of Congressional, judicial and executive personnel. With this lag and inflated living costs, government workers were in difficult straits. A special Cabinet committee that had been studying the government pay problem found that the disparity in salaries for the higher-ranking jobs was causing a serious shortage in the federal service. Congress had been more generous in raising the less-skilled, lower-grade employees but the lid had been held on the pay of the higher-skilled personnel for whose services private industry was outbidding the government. Arthur Burns was wary of a government pay raise. Fearing inflation with the upsurge in prosperity, Burns expected economic trouble in 1955 from a demand by labor unions for higher wages and he did not want to see the government take the lead in giving higher pay. But Humphrey assured the President that the increase in national productivity would permit wage and salary increases without inflation. And Congress, with so many federal employees among its constitutents, was in no mood to be stingy. The government pay raise went through, though Eisenhower kept it within reasonable bounds.

Eisenhower fought off, however, another threat to balancing the budget, a demand from the Democrats in Congress for a flat twenty-dollar reduction in the individual income tax. At first glance, the proposal seemed to be good for the little fellow, Eisenhower said, but the inflation that would be certain to follow would really hurt people with fixed incomes, especially retired persons who had saved for their old age. The measure narrowly passed in the House but it was beaten in the Senate. When the President was asked for his reaction, he said to the reporters, "Would it be allowable just to say hurrah?"

At the budget review on May 13, Eisenhower again emphasized that he would agree to no tax reduction in 1956 until he saw a surplus in black and white. Humphrey once more argued that a balanced budget and a tax cut could both be possible at the same time if expenditures were lowered.

"How much room is there for lowering expenditures after you provide forty billion dollars for defense?" the President asked.

Humphrey came back with a flat assertion that another two and a half billion could be taken out of the budget if each government department would make a determined effort to economize. That started an outburst of arguments around the Cabinet table.

Benson said that he thought every department could make further reductions in personnel. Philip Young, the Chairman of the Civil Service Commission and Eisenhower's personnel adviser, told Benson that a 10 per cent cut had just been made, but Benson insisted that another 5 per cent could be let go without causing much trouble. Young reminded the Secretary of Agriculture that 80 per cent of the government's employees were in the Defense and Post Office departments and the Veterans Administration and further personnel reduction would be certain to run into conflict with Veterans' Preference laws.

"Make a move in that direction," Eisenhower said, "and you'll bring down the wrath of every demagogue in the country on your head."

But a few months later it was just such a step as Humphrey suggested—a direct order forcing each government department to make a reduction in its budget—that finally gave Eisenhower in fiscal 1956 the balanced budget he had looked forward to at Peoria in 1952. Just after he returned from the summit conference of the Big Four powers at Geneva, the President met with the Cabinet on August 5 and unexpectedly brought up a subject that was not even on the agenda—the budget situation. He picked up a memorandum which he had carefully prepared and read it to his associates seated around the table. The memorandum was a rare command decision from Eisenhower, and he made it plain that it was to be obeyed.

Reading from the paper before him, the President pointed out that despite the unparalleled prosperity a deficit of between $1.5 billion and $1.7 billion seemed likely for the current fiscal year.

"This amounts to only 3 per cent of the federal spending planned for this year," Eisenhower said. "That 3 per cent stands as a challenge to every one of us. Surely in this giant government there are still programs, administrative costs or wasteful practices of one sort or another that we can root out without damage to anything essential.

"I think we can find at least that 3 per cent and balance the budget this year. To this end, I am directing the Budget Director to deduct 3 per cent of the expenditures planned for this year. I am confident that with determined effort throughout our government we will save at least this amount.

"If anyone finds, after earnest application, that a cut of this size is an impossibility, he is to come to me as soon as such impossibility becomes apparent. I shall talk it over with him and with the Director of the Bureau of the Budget."

Eisenhower took care to explain that he was directing the 3 per cent cut against wasteful and nonessential expenses, not against any expenditure that was really necessary.

Wilson was the only Cabinet member to raise a cry of protest. The Defense Department was already $1.75 billion over its estimated expenditures, he told the President, and he was already trying to reduce the over-all cost of his department by 5 per cent. Now the President was asking him to raise that 5 per cent to 8 per cent and he did not know how he could do it. He listed some of his staggering costs—steel, salaries, aircraft, the distant early warning line program, Air Force demands. He mentioned how he had been criticized for not spending certain sums of money that had been allotted to the Marine Corps. Brownell interrupted him to explain that although such appropriations are usually regarded by the administration as authorizations for spending that amount, Congress does not always agree with that viewpoint. Jerry Persons reminded Wilson that Truman had once refused to spend money appropriated by Congress against his wishes for the Air Force. His troubles over money with Congress, Wilson went on to say, were not only concerned with economy, they also involved force levels. "The Marines not only want the $46 million we are withholding from them," he said. "They also want the full strength authorized for them by Congress."

Eisenhower was not at all impressed by Wilson's plea. He said

Floor huddle at the 1952 Republican Convention. (l. to r.) Sinclair Weeks, National Committeeman from Mass., Sen. Leverett Saltonstall, Tom Pappas of Mass., Financial Chairman, and Gov. Sherman Adams of N. H., Eisenhower floor leader.

(WIDE WORLD)

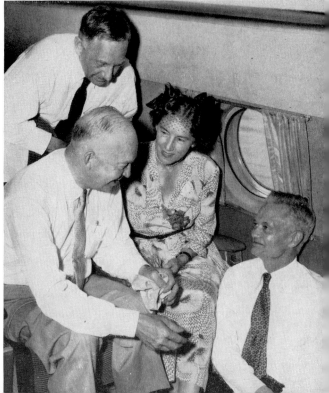

The campaign plane, Sept., 1952. Eisenhower confers with Mrs. Katherine Howard, Sec. of the National Committee, Sen. Frank Carlson of Kansas and Sherman Adams during flight from Tampa to Birmingham.

(WIDE WORLD)

Sherman Adams, Gen. Eisenhower and Sen. Fred Seaton of Nebr., talking over a campaign decision during train trip from N. Y. to Phila.　(UPI)

Sherman Adams talks with Rep. Leslie Arends of Ill. during whistlestop of the campaign train. Woman about to board train is Katherine Howard.

Gen. Eisenhower and Sen. Taft during the much publicized breakfast meeting at the General's Morningside Heights home in New York City. (WIDE WORLD)

Gen. Eisenhower with Sherman Adams leaving telephone in Portsmouth, O., railroad station after call to Arthur Summerfield, GOP National Chairman. The purpose of the call was to arrange a meeting with Sen. Richard Nixon after his famous "Checkers" speech. The man in the other phone booth is Sen. Hugh Scott of Pa. (WIDE WORLD)

Paul G. Hoffman, E.C.A. Administrator, with Gen. Eisenhower, en route to Los Angeles during the 1952 campaign tour.
(UPI)

A very tired Hagerty, snapped in an unguarded moment on the campaign train by Rachel Adams.

The author during a brief vacation in the Grand Tetons, following the 1952 Republican Convention.

Campaigning in Mass., Gen. Eisenhower conferred with Sen. Leverett Saltonstall, Gov. Christian Herter and Sen. Henry Cabot Lodge.
(RACHEL ADAMS)

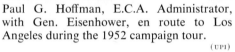

Taft's last golf game, at Augusta, Ga. (l. to r.) Clarence Schoo of Springfield, Mass., Pres. Eisenhower, Clifford Roberts, Pres. of the Augusta National Golf Club, Bobby Jones, Sen. Taft, Sherman Adams. (UPI)

Returning from his Korea trip, Eisenhower conferred with members of his future Cabinet. (l. to r.) Gov. Douglas McKay, Herbert Brownell, Charles E. Wilson, Gen. Eisenhower, John Foster Dulles, George Humphrey. (UPI)

The first Eisenhower Cabinet, assembled at the Commodore Hotel headquarters before the inauguration. Seated (l. to r.), Herbert Brownell, Attorney-General; George P. Humphrey, Sec. of the Treasury; Richard Nixon, Vice-Pres.; Gen. Eisenhower; John Foster Dulles, Sec. of State; Charles E. Wilson, Sec. of Defense. Standing (l. to r.), Joseph Dodge, Budget Director; Oveta Culp Hobby, FSA Administrator (later Sec. of Health, Education and Welfare); Sherman Adams, Assistant to the President; Sinclair Weeks, Sec. of Commerce; Douglas McKay, Sec. of the Interior; Arthur Summerfield, Postmaster General; Ezra Taft Benson, Sec. of Agriculture; Martin Durkin, Sec. of Labor; Henry Cabot Lodge, Ambassador to the UN; Harold Stassen, FOA Administrator.

At dedication of the Eisenhower Museum, Abilene, Kans. (l. to r.) Mrs. Doud (Mrs. Eisenhower's mother) partly concealed by the flag, Mrs. Eisenhower, the President and his brothers, Milton, Earl and Arthur.

In Feb., 1953, C. D. Jackson, New York publisher, joined the White House staff, as special assistant in charge of cold war planning. (WIDE WORLD)

At the Big Three meeting in Bermuda, Dec., 1953. (l. to r.) Joseph Laniel of France, Pres. Eisenhower, Sir Winston Churchill. (UPI)

Senate leaders at the White House, Feb., 1953. (l. to r.) Frank Carlson, William Langer, Vice-Pres. Nixon, Eugene D. Millikin (top of head), Robert Taft, Styles Bridges (front), H. Alexander Smith, William E. Jenner, Edward Martin (rear), William F. Knowland (back of Pres.), Alexander Wiley, George D. Aiken (back of Wiley), Charles W. Tobey, Joseph R. McCarthy (back of Tobey), Leverett Saltonstall, Hugh Butler, Francis Case, Maj. Gen. Wilton B. Persons, Homer E. Capehart. (UPI)

House leaders at the White House, Feb., 1953. (l. to r.) Jesse P. Wolcott, Edward H. Rees, Clifford R. Hope, Charles A. Wolverton, Maj. Gen. Wilton B. Persons, Samuel K. McConnell, Jr., Sid Simpson, Vice-Pres. Nixon, Leslie C. Arends, Dewey Short, Joseph W. Martin, Jr., Leo E. Allen, Pres. Eisenhower, Robert E. Chiperfield, John Taber, Daniel A. Reed, Karl M. LcCompte, Edith Nourse Rogers, Clare E. Hoffman, Chauncey W. Reed, Sherman Adams, A. L. Miller, Alvin F. Weichel.

Picnic at Camp David, Aug., 1954. Above, the President, Gen. Walter Bedell Smith, Mrs. Eisenhower and Mrs. Rowland Hughes with Sherman Adams and Mrs. Philip Young in background (ABBIE ROWE, NATIONAL PARK SERVICE); right, the author with the President and Attorney-General. (UPI)

On his swing through New England in 1955, Pres. Eisenhower was guest of Laurence Whittemore of N. H. at Parmachenee Lake, Me., above, and (below) he relaxed on the golf course of the Mountain View Hotel in N. H. with (l. to r.) Richard F. Cooper, Republican National Committeeman; Sherman Adams; a secret service man and Perkins Bass, N. H. Congressman. (PHOTO BY DON SIEBURG)

Pres. Eisenhower and Republican Congressional leaders posed in the White House cabinet room during a conference on his 1954 legislative program. (l. to r. around the table) Pres. Eisenhower, House Speaker Joseph Martin, Mass.; Rep. Dewey Short, Mo.; Maj. Gen. Wilton B. Persons, White House staff; Sherman Adams; Rep. Samuel K. McConnell, Jr., Pa.; Sen. Homer Capehart, Ind.; Sen. Styles Bridges, N. H.; Vice-Pres. Nixon; Sen. Leverett Saltonstall, Mass. Standing at left are Jack Martin, White House staff; Homer Gruenther, staff assistant; and James Hagerty, presidential press secretary. (WIDE WORLD)

A special meeting of the Security Council at the summer White House, at the time of the Quemoy crisis. (l. to r.) Arthur Flemming, Adm. Arthur W. Radford, George Humphrey, J. Edgar Hoover, the President, Lewis Strauss, the Vice-President, Charles Wilson, John Foster Dulles, Harold Stassen and Rowland Hughes. (UPI)

Cabinet meeting, July, 1955. (l. to r. around the table) Maj. Gen. Wilton B. Persons, Henry Cabot Lodge, Douglas McKay, George P. Humphrey, Vice-Pres. Nixon, Herbert Brownell, Sinclair Weeks, Oveta Culp Hobby, Philip Young, Civil Service Commission, Rowland Hughes, Arthur Flemming, Max Rabb, secretary to the Cabinet, James P. Mitchell, Arthur Summerfield, John Foster Dulles, Pres. Eisenhower, Charles E. Wilson, Ezra T. Benson, Harold Stassen, Special Assistant on Disarmament, and Sherman Adams.

Sherman Adams, Gen. Alfred A. Gruenther, George Allen and Pres. Eisenhower attend a ball game.

(WASHINGTON POST PHOTO)

James Hagerty, press secretary, with the author during the 1952 campaign.

Fishing Frenchman's Creek, S. D. Secret service man on right.

Cartoon by Gib Crockett in the Washington *Evening Star*.

that he knew from long experience that there were plenty of luxuries and nonessentials that could be given up by the military services. Humphrey mentioned that the President's midyear budget message would be released in two weeks and suggested that the 3 per cent reduction should be shown so that, with the further reduction of $100 million in expenditures, a black ink balance might appear once more.

"No," Eisenhower said. "This reduction is not yet a reality. It's still only an objective. We can't claim it now as an accomplished fact."

"Better to do that," Humphrey argued, "than to have to admit another expected deficit."

Eisenhower was unmoved. He did not propose to be trapped into making a proposal for brightening up the budget outlook that he felt he might not be able to make a reality. But some Cabinet members thought Eisenhower was either too scrupulous or too timid and they said so. Benson was one of them. With the world at peace, this was a time to cut defense expenditures if we were ever going to, he argued.

The fact was that the Cabinet economizers were convinced that if they could get Eisenhower to commit himself publicly to his command decision, the departments and agencies would be forced to find the savings. Otherwise they might find ways to circumvent it.

Benson's sunny remark about the peace of the world stirred up Dulles. Despite the smiles that we had exchanged with the Russians at Geneva, the Secretary of State told the Secretary of Agriculture, we cannot take peace for granted and we cannot allow ourselves to be lured by a few friendly words from the Communists into making an across-the-board cut in our defense expenditures.

"If we let our defenses in Western Europe and Japan fall down because the atmosphere seemed peaceful at Geneva," Dulles said, "then Geneva will turn out to be a greater tragedy for us than Yalta. Remember that the Russians are still going on with atomic tests and holding on to their satellites and working on their missiles."

Nixon came to Eisenhower's defense on the inadvisability of announcing the planned 3 per cent reduction in spending until it was accomplished. "If we announce a 3 per cent cut now, it won't be hard for the newspapermen to figure out that this means a cut of one billion in defense spending," Nixon said. Eisenhower nodded and mentioned a letter he had just received from Senator Anderson and Senator Jackson as an example of the argument on alleged defense inadequacy that the Democrats were trying to build up against the administration. The President said that he was not worried about people finding out he had directed a reduction in spending. As for anyone being misled into thinking this was a result of the apparently friendly atmosphere at Geneva, the budget message in January would be too far away from the July summit meeting to be connected with it in any way, he said.

As the discussion drew to a close, Wilson wanted to have the last word. Although he could not make any definite promise to reduce his expenses by 8 per cent, as the President wanted him to do, he promised that he would do his best.

"That's good enough for us, Charlie," Eisenhower said.

Wilson shook his head plaintively and said sadly, "I have so many people in my department who keep putting off decisions until the only thing left to do is the wrong thing."

Humphrey managed to get in a postscript of his own. When the President's budget review was published on August 25, it pointed out that the budget deficit besides being the lowest in Eisenhower's term would be less than 3 per cent of budget expenditures. Instead of announcing an arbitrary reduction, the report stated the belief that "a balanced budget will be brought into sight as the year unfolds." It remained for Humphrey to add a statement of his own at the same time calling attention to the fact that the deficit could be eliminated by only a 3 per cent reduction in expenditures.

That August when the President left Washington for his vacation in Denver, where he had his serious heart attack a month later, he was in high spirits and happy about the state of the union. The previous summer he had sometimes been depressed and moody, worried about the recession and Communist China's threats against Formosa and bothered by complaints from Republican party politicians about the progress of the 1954 political campaign. All of that was behind him now. The country was at the height of prosperity. A balanced budget was in view and there were no hard decisions immediately facing him. The prospects for world peace seemed brighter. He was elated by the favorable world reaction to his open-skies nuclear inspection proposal at Geneva that July and he was greatly encouraged by the change in the Russian attitude, though just what it meant he did not profess to know. Dulles remained suspicious of the Russians, a more realistic attitude in the light of the complete collapse of the President's hopes for some tangible accomplishments in the wake of the conference. Eisenhower was temperamentally more hopeful than the Secretary, and he chose to find more grounds for optimism that summer.

I did not go to Geneva with the President but I was a close observer of all that went on in the White House concerning the Big Four summit meeting. Dulles had been against the idea of a conference between the President and the Russian leaders when it was first proposed in the winter but Churchill persuaded him to agree to it. In the Cabinet meeting on February 18, there was a discussion about what was behind the apparently friendly attitude of the new Soviet regime, which then had the mild-mannered, white-bearded Bulganin as Premier and the tougher and rougher Khrushchev, the leader of the Russian Communist party, as the power behind the government. All of us wondered what significance, if any, could be attached to the appointment of Marshal Zhukov, Eisenhower's wartime friend, as Defense Minister. Dulles said he thought that the Soviets had been unable to run a real dictatorship since Stalin's death. The view Dulles took then of Khrushchev is interesting in view of Khrushchev's later climb to power. Dulles did not look upon Khrushchev as a real dictator and he had some doubt that Khrushchev would survive as a leader for many years; he felt that Khrushchev had more power than anybody else in Russia but that he was not all-powerful as Stalin was. Eisenhower felt, too, during the Camp David talks in 1959 that Khrushchev lacked Stalin's prestige and power at home.

Dulles was quite certain that the fear of the NATO alliance, especially since West Germany had been brought in as a member, was a major factor behind the Russian eagerness for a summit meeting. He was sure that the Soviets intended to drive a wedge between the Western Allies if they could. The treaty with Austria that the Russians had recently made, with the West looking on, was regarded by Dulles as a blandishment in a move for a united Red Germany. "See how nice and lenient we are to deal with," the Russians were saying. The Secretary of State was determined that at Geneva he and Eisenhower were simply going to look for new approaches to the old and vexing problems and steer away from getting into any important agreements.

When plans for the Geneva meeting were settled, Eisenhower and Dulles called a bipartisan meeting of the key members of Congress on July 12, mainly to assure the legislators that Geneva was not going to be another Yalta. Eisenhower promised them that no decisions would be made without their approval and there would be no appeasement. Dulles said he expected the Soviets to offer some kind of a dramatic proposal for world peace in order to win sympathy.

Our own purposes in going to the meeting, Dulles said, were to make sure that West Germany did not become an orphan country, for she had to play her part in preserving European security under the Paris accord. At the same time we had to attempt to win for the satellites behind the Iron Curtain some sovereignty and self-government (to which the Soviets might agree, he thought, if they could be convinced that they could have no peaceful relations with us otherwise), to stop the subversion of international Communism and to get the President's stalled proposal for the exchange of peaceful nuclear information off the ground. The Secretary now agreed with Eisenhower that there had been apparently a change in the Russian attitude. He felt that they were seeking a change of pace as a means of getting out of the trouble they were having with their economy and with their leadership.

Eisenhower mentioned that the Russians seemed to be making significant progress in convincing other members of the Western Alliance that they might do well to remain neutral in the struggle between America and the Soviet Union. Even the British and the French, the President remarked, were beginning to accept the Soviet argument that the cold war was merely a competition between two great powers and to disregard the deep differences in moral values that separated them.

That prompted Senator Knowland to ask Dulles what he thought of a report then recently published that the British Prime Minister, Anthony Eden, was in favor of an agreement that would leave the satellite countries of Eastern Europe under Soviet domination for the next fifty years. Dulles said he had no specific information on the report, but he pointed out that the independence of the satellites seemed to mean less to Europeans than it did to Americans.

Unlike Dulles, who entertained no such high hopes, Eisenhower went to Geneva seeking to make the meeting a solid beginning of a move toward world disarmament. The President felt then, as he still feels, that there could be no peace without disarmament. In March, when the Geneva meeting became a certainty, Eisenhower made Harold Stassen his special assistant on disarmament studies. Although he was well aware of Stassen's personal unpopularity with many members of the Cabinet, Eisenhower felt that his dogged perseverance would be valuable in this field where little had been accomplished up to that time.

After Stassen's appointment was announced, a reporter asked Eisenhower what "his thinking" was on the newly created position. "What is our thinking?" the President said. "There was nobody in the government, up until I appointed Governor Stassen to this post, that was responsible for getting together all of the different ideas affecting disarmament and putting them together so the administration can say, 'This is our program, and this is what we are trying to do in this field.' State approaches this from one way, Defense approaches it from another, your economic people approach it from still another. You have all sorts of viewpoints, and some think this will work, that will work. Let us have somebody with a small staff who cannot only do something to bring together, draw together, these views, but to devise a short, easily expressed program, maybe that all of us here could adopt and say, 'Yes, that is good.' "

As a positive and specific disarmament proposal, the President took with him to Geneva the open-skies inspection plan that had been worked out by Nelson Rockefeller and his Quantico Panel. Up to that time the idea of a mutually agreed plan of aerial surveys between two nations had never been thoroughly explored but military experts were certain that an armament build-up of any significant size could be detected from the air with modern photographic equipment. Rockefeller's researchers went into the details of such photo-reconnaissance and presented to the President a dramatic estimate of the accuracy and range of information that could be made available by such an inspection project. Eisenhower liked the idea, but he did not make a quick decision on whether or not he would offer it to the Russians. He went over the pros and cons of the plan carefully with the military leaders and with Dulles, who was skeptical of its chances of acceptance by the Soviets. When the Geneva meeting opened, the

President still had not made up his mind about when, how or if he would make the proposal.

On the first day of the talks, Bulganin resurrected an old and threadbare Soviet disarmament proposal. He asked for a ban on nuclear weapons and a limitation of United States, Russian and Chinese forces to one and a half million men, with a maximum for the British and the French of 650,000. It became apparent that Eisenhower would have to make some kind of a counterproposal if the Soviets were not going to steal the propaganda spotlight. Two days later the President called a private meeting in Geneva of the advisers who had been discussing the open-skies inspection idea—Dulles, Stassen, Admiral Radford, Robert Anderson, who was then Wilson's Deputy Secretary of Defense, Dillon Anderson, the President's National Security Affairs assistant, General Gruenther and Rockefeller. He went over the plan again with this group and then decided to propose it the next day. He had also revealed the idea to Eden, who was warmly in favor of it.

When he presented the open-skies plan, Eisenhower's own unquestionable sincerity of purpose made as deep an impression as the freshness and plausibility of the idea that he was putting before the conference. The French Premier, Edgar Faure, said afterward, "I wish the people of the world could have been in this conference room to hear the voice of a man speaking from great military experience. Had this been possible, they would have believed that something had changed in the world in the handling of this question of disarmament."

Unlike the Bulganin proposal, with the same tired talk about the banning of weapons and the limitation of armed forces that had been heard for generations, the Eisenhower plan had an arresting newness to it. The offer by the American President to open his country to aerial photo reconnaissance if the Russians did likewise ("and by this step convince the world that we are providing as between ourselves against the possibility of great surprise attack") caused hope and excitement everywhere and caught the Soviets by surprise, leaving them too stunned to make much of a reply. When we turned out in a drenching rain to welcome the President back to Washington, he spoke to us with a feeling that he had accomplished some real good. The next day, telling the Congressional leaders what had happened at Geneva, Eisenhower said that it seemed as though Russia were changing her tactics toward us. He mentioned that Bulganin had come to him at the end of the conference, saying, "Don't worry—this will come out all right." He also noted, however, that Khrushchev, not Bulganin, was calling the signals. Dulles felt that the only real accomplishment of the Geneva meeting was the progress that had been made in discussing our differences with the Russians with no rancor or name-calling.

But the new spirit of friendliness dissolved in the subsequent talks between Dulles and the Russians at the foreign ministers' meetings in October and November. The Soviets then completely rejected the Eisenhower open-skies proposal, even though we offered to accept the Bulganin plan if they participated in the aerial inspection exchange. They turned down every proposal we made for the reunification of Germany and would have nothing to do with giving up their hold on East Germany. Dulles said later in Washington that it seemed as though the Soviets had a congenital fear of anything proposed by the Western powers; they rejected seventeen different suggestions because, as Dulles expressed it, each suggestion was aimed at getting a little fresh air behind the Iron Curtain.

That was later in the fall of 1955, however. In August, when the President went to Colorado for his vacation, the hopeful atmosphere of the Geneva meeting was still undisturbed and all was well and quiet at home and abroad. As I often thought later, if Eisenhower had to have a heart attack, that was an ideal time for him to have it. When the President was incapacitated, the United States, by a stroke of rare good fortune, was facing no big and serious decisions.

10 Heart Attack

Early in August, 1955, the President summoned me into his office shortly before he went to Denver for his vacation and suggested that it was time I had a look at some of the NATO installations in Europe. "I understand you've never been to Europe, and anyone who has as much to do with the routine of handling NATO problems as you do ought to have a closer view of them," he said. "Take one of the staff with you. You can go over on Gruenther's plane, which will be going back there around the middle of the month."

This was the kind of an invitation that you did not refuse. Ever since the Republican convention in 1952, I had kept my nose close to the grindstone, except for a few days off for skiing in the winter and for black salmon fishing down east in the early spring, but I had no premonition of this combined vacation and tour of inspection that summer. In fact, I had planned to stay in Washington after Eisenhower went to Denver because Jerry Persons had planned a trip to Paris after Congress adjourned. I made my peace with Persons, who generously insisted on staying at the White House so that I could go to Europe. Jerry said he could go later, little knowing how much later that would be. I asked Andy Goodpaster, the White House staff secretary who had been stationed at SHAPE and knew the ropes at NATO, to go with me and Mrs. Adams.

The month that I spent abroad was a memorable and meaningful experience for me. At the NATO headquarters outside of Paris, in the country that had given us the helping hand in our own struggle for independence, I saw a gathering of the uniforms of the countries whose own freedom, if not survival, depended on us and I realized that these

180

military professionals of many allegiances were being held together in common purpose by the spirit and the ideals of the American President and the people whom he represented. I was struck by the extent of the role that Eisenhower's own personality played as a persuasive force in binding together these diverse languages, traditions and nationalisms. It was heartening to feel the confidence and trust that these Western European nations had in an American, and I gained a new appreciation of the nature and magnitude of the responsibility for the identity and freedom of these nations that had fallen upon the United States.

Similar thoughts occurred to me all over Europe. At five o'clock one morning I watched a review of Turkish troops in training to repel Communist aggression and I saw something that was often difficult to understand back in Washington—the justification for Mutual Security funds being spent for the military and economic strengthening of these small countries. Most of all, I was moved by the faces of the people waiting in line in front of a meat counter in East Germany and by the implacable expressions of the Red officers who kept us carefully in their sight and the armed soldiers posted behind barbed wire near the Stalinallee. Here the contrast between being a citizen and being a serf got into your bones.

On the afternoon of September 25, Goodpaster and I arrived at the air base in Prestwick, Scotland, where we were to join General Gruenther for the return flight to Washington that night. As we were checking in at the base headquarters, the commanding officer told us that he had just received word that the President had suffered a heart attack in Denver and had been taken to the hospital. There were no details available.

On the plane during that drizzly and gusty night, I began to think of how the President would expect his staff and the Cabinet to act while he was disabled. He had never given me directives for such an emergency, but then he had never given me many directives of any kind and we had gotten along all right. By that time, after working with Eisenhower for three years, I was able to rely upon a good deal more than instinct in deciding what he wanted done. It was then that the thought first occurred to me that the President had picked a good time to be ill; Congress was in recess, the urgencies of his office were at a minimum, he had no immediate obligations as head of state, the

program for the coming year was in the early stages of preparation
and did not demand immediate decisions or attention. I remember
thinking that it was probably fortunate that he was in Denver, away
from Washington and isolated from his office, but then I wondered
if Denver's elevation of five thousand feet would be good for a con-
valescing heart.

I slid back the ruffled curtain at my window and looked out at the
blinker lights on the runway as the plane landed at Goose Bay in Lab-
rador for a refueling stop. The rain was coming down harder and
wisps of fog danced along among the blinkers. I thought how lucky we
were, in the absence of the President, to have a Cabinet that was able
to work together in harmony. Apart from the parochial differences between Weeks and Mitchell, the inability of Stassen to blend into the
picture and a minor and hardly perceptible abrasion now and then,
there was no strife at the Cabinet table. I was sure that in this
emergency every Secretary and department head would be able to
handle his own business and keep to the course that the President
had set for him.

Obviously, some temporary direction had to be arranged for co-
ordination. Who was going to be boss? If I knew Nixon, he would
be wary of appearing to assume presidential prerogatives before he
became constitutionally eligible for them. Any undue eagerness to
take over the function of the chief executive prematurely would be
resented and he would be sensitively aware of this. Dulles, as the
ranking Cabinet member, had enough good judgment to run the
government but Dulles had enough problems in the foreign field
without taking on domestic ones, too. I thought that perhaps the
necessary actions of importance could be made by the Cabinet acting
as a body, with matters of secondary concern being handled, as had
been the habitual practice, by the White House staff. I hoped that no
emergency would arise during the President's early convalescence
that would require his personal action. As I lay on my berth in the
plane, looking at the tank trucks pulling away after completing their
transfusions and listening to the motors turning over and catching,
one by one, I had no thought but that the President was going to
get well, and how all of us could best help him.

When we arrived in Washington, I learned some of the details of
how Eisenhower had been stricken. He had been enjoying his vaca-

tion, apparently in the best of health, working for an hour or so at his office in the Lowry Air Force Base in the morning and spending the rest of the day playing golf, fishing, painting or playing bridge. On the day before his heart attack, he played twenty-seven holes of golf, complaining only of slight indigestion from raw onions he had eaten for lunch. After he returned from the Cherry Hills Country Club to the home of his mother-in-law, Mrs. John S. Doud, at 750 Lafayette Street, where he and Mrs. Eisenhower stayed when they were in Denver, he spent an hour in the basement working on a painting of a *Life* photograph by Hank Walker, showing the face of an Argentine woman praying at a shrine that had been desecrated by Perónist vandals. Then the President and Mrs. Eisenhower and Mrs. Doud entertained their friends, Mr. and Mrs. George Allen, at dinner. The Allens left early and the President went to bed around ten o'clock, feeling well apparently.

But around two-thirty the next morning, Mrs. Eisenhower heard her husband tossing and turning uncomfortably in his bedroom on the second floor of the Doud house, across the hall from the room where she was sleeping. She went to him and asked what was bothering him. He assured her that he was all right and she went back to her bed. A few minutes later the President came into Mrs. Eisenhower's room, suffering from intense pain and pointing at his chest. Remembering that he had complained of indigestion on the golf course the day before, she gave him milk of magnesia and put him back to bed. Then she telephoned General Howard Snyder, the Eisenhowers' physician, who was staying at the Lowry Air Force Base, and General Snyder came to the Doud house immediately.

The President was still in pain when General Snyder arrived. After examining his chest with a stethoscope and taking his pulse and blood pressure, the doctor quickly decided that he had suffered a coronary thrombosis. "I gave him by hypodermic one grain of papaverine, and, immediately thereafter, one-fourth grain of morphine sulphate, following that the usual initial dose of heparin," General Snyder wrote later in a letter to Jerry Persons that he asked Persons to show to the White House staff. Forty-five minutes later he gave the President another shot of morphine. The morphine, of course, was to ease the pain and shock. The papaverine dilates the heart arteries and the heparin guards against blood clotting. The President slept peacefully for seven hours after the medication was given to him, with General Snyder staying at his bedside, checking his pulse and blood pressure from time to time and noting with satisfaction that the pulse beat was slowing and the pressure coming down.

General Snyder decided to tell nobody about the President's heart attack until he was able to confirm his diagnosis by an electrocardiograph examination and make arrangements to transfer his patient to the nearby Fitzsimons General Hospital. The doctor was careful in breaking the news to Mrs. Eisenhower, because she has a valvular heart condition herself, and to avoid shocking her he did not tell her until the next day that her husband had been stricken with anything more serious than indigestion. He phoned Ann Whitman, the President's secretary, at the Lowry air base office when it opened in the morning and told her that the President had a digestive disorder, and this report was given to the press. "It was difficult for me to assume the responsibility of refraining from making public immediately the diagnosis of coronary thrombosis," General Snyder wrote in his letter to Persons.

I postponed public announcement because I wished the President to benefit from the rest and quiet induced by the sedation incident to combating the initial manifestations. This decision also spared him, his wife, and mother-in-law emotional upset upon too precipitate announcement of such serious import. . . . This action, I believe, limited the heart damage to a minimum and enabled us to confirm the diagnosis by cardiogram and make an unhurried transference from home to hospital.

Later in the morning, General Snyder told Mrs. Eisenhower about her husband's condition and had electrocardiograph equipment brought to the house from Fitzsimons Hospital. The examination located a lesion on the anterior wall of the heart that the doctors described as moderate in size. To keep down outside excitement, General Snyder did not ask for an ambulance to take the President to the hospital. Eisenhower made the trip quietly in his own car, walking from the house in his bathrobe with the assistance of General Snyder and two other Army doctors from Fitzsimons who had made the cardiograms. After he was put to bed in the hospital and placed under an oxygen tent, the doctor released the news of the heart attack. Murray Snyder, Hagerty's assistant press secretary—and no relation to the General—telephoned Hagerty in Washington, where Jim was vacationing, before the story was given to the reporters. Hagerty agreed with his assistant that the news should be played straight, with no details held back, and Hagerty flew immediately to Denver to take charge of the situation.

As soon as I arrived in Washington from Europe, I met with Nixon and William P. Rogers, then the Deputy Attorney General who was filling in while Brownell returned from a vacation in Spain. Because there was no immediate government business that required a presidential decision or signature, we decided that there was no need for the time being to arrange for a delegation of the President's constitutional duties. We also received word from Denver that Dr. Paul Dudley White, the eminent Boston heart specialist, who had just examined Eisenhower, was of the opinion that the President would be able to take part in conferences within two weeks. That removed any fear that we were in a drastic crisis as far as the management of the government was concerned. I asked Andy Goodpaster, in his capacity as White House staff secretary, to find out what papers, if any, the President might be required to sign during the next two weeks. Goodpaster reported that by delaying action on some measures and by proceeding with others "by the direction of the President" without his actual signature, the total number of such papers could perhaps be "reduced to zero."

The next day, when Brownell returned from Spain, he agreed with us that there was no legal necessity for a delegation of the President's powers, in view of the encouraging news from Denver, and the whole question was dropped. During the following two months, until Eisenhower was able to resume active duty, the government was managed by a committee consisting of Nixon, Dulles, Brownell, Humphrey, Persons and myself, although this group was never recognized as a formal governing council. There was never a move on the part of any of us to "seize power" or to take an unwarranted action that Eisenhower would have disapproved. As I expected, Nixon, in particular, leaned over backward to avoid any appearance of assuming presidential authority. But all of us were well aware that a national or international emergency could have arisen during the President's illness to make this unofficial government by "community of understanding" entirely inadequate. The Constitution is clear enough on successorship if the President dies or is forced to give up his office because of inability but it makes no provision whereby the President may vacate the office and again assume it at the conclusion of a temporary disability. The question continued to bother us in later years and Eisenhower made an effort with Brownell to clear it up through legislation.

We made sure that the normal activities of the government went on as usual and there was a regular Cabinet meeting on Friday, September 30, six days after the President was stricken, with the Vice President presiding from his own chair, across the table from the President's empty seat. The atmosphere was so alert and business-like that Nixon's opening remarks about the need for no interruptions and delays in work while the President was ill sounded somewhat unnecessary. There was a routine discussion by Dulles on what was going on in current foreign affairs and then we got down to what was on everyone's mind, the program for the running of the government during the President's absence. Brownell read a statement that he had drawn up at the request of the National Security Council, which was to be approved by the Cabinet before it was released to the press later that day. The statement said, among other things, that "Governor Sherman Adams, the Assistant to the President, will leave for Denver today and will be available there, in consultation with the President's physicians, whenever it may later become appropriate to present any matters to the President." Nixon questioned this arrangement; he had assumed that I would remain in charge at the White House during Eisenhower's absence. But Dulles came out firmly and emphatically for stationing me with Eisenhower in Denver as the liaison officer who would handle all matters concerning government business coming to and from the President.

Mentioning no names, Dulles told the Cabinet that while Eisenhower was absent from Washington there might be certain people outside the government who would try to set themselves up as authoritative spokesmen for the President on various public issues. He said that the best way to prevent such intruders from giving out alleged presidential views would be to reinforce my position as the sole official channel of information between Eisenhower and the world outside of his hospital room. Besides, Dulles pointed out, my place was in Denver because I had become recognized nationally as a public figure closely identified with the President. Nixon quickly seconded Dulles' remarks and said that with me in Denver the senior officer in the White House would be Persons and that all business with the President's office would be routed through him. In insisting upon having me with Eisenhower, Dulles was once again vigilantly protecting his own position as the maker of foreign policy. He wanted to make sure that nobody would get between the President and himself with suggestions for changing the foreign program or with some troublesome public statement that the President would be unable to disavow. I had worked with Dulles long enough so that he felt that with me in Denver he had less to worry about on that score.

Incidentally, any fears that may have prevailed at the time about Milton Eisenhower's becoming an unofficial force of influence during his brother's illness were groundless. As soon as the President's heart attack was announced, there was naturally widespread speculation about the selection of another Republican as candidate for President in 1956. A doctor in Washington started and publicized a Milton Eisenhower-for-President movement, much to Milton's annoyance and embarrassment and entirely without his approval. For the first five weeks that the President was in the hospital he saw no newspapers, but Milton was worried that some one of his brother's visitors might call the President's attention to these baseless rumors and upset him. He asked me to pass along to the President, as soon as General Snyder and I felt it wise, a message that said he was sorry about the political gossip involving his name but that he had nothing whatever to do with any announcements and, as far as he was concerned, they were completely unauthorized. Milton became so sensitive to the suspicions that he was trying to replace his brother or become an influential adviser that he stayed away from Denver during the early weeks of the illness, as anxious as he was to visit the President in the hospital. Finally the President, wondering about his absence, asked me to make arrangements for Milton to come out to Denver. But Milton's visit did not take place until after Dulles had paid his first call on the President.

I went to Denver with my mind made up that for the next few weeks, at least, the real key figure in the government would be Dr. Paul Dudley White, a physician who was endowed with much more than the knowledge and skill that had brought him to the top of his profession. Bound together within the confines of a frail physical fortress were a doctor, philosopher, prophet, publicist of the first order, homely countryman and avid bicyclist. Add to all this Dr. White's New England heritage, nurtured in traditions and whimsies that Americans from other parts of the country are incapable of understanding, and there emerges one of the rarest characters in all of my experience. I made up my mind that affairs involving the President would orbit, temporarily at least, around Paul Dudley White and his medical associates. Whatever action I took with Eisenhower would take their judgment into consideration, and I made this intention known to the Cabinet before I set out for Colorado. Jim Hagerty and I held a conference every morning with Dr. White and the other physicians at the hospital, carefully measuring with them the amount of work that could be put before the President that day. I remember that the first official paper I brought to him on September 30, six days after his heart attack, was a list of recess appointments for foreign service officers that required only his initials, but he wanted to sign it with his full name.

Hagerty was glad to see me when I came to Denver. He had been bearing the brunt alone. Mrs. Eisenhower had been taken ill and was in the hospital, too. He was glad to have somebody to share his troubles. The first time I went to the hospital to see the President I stayed with him for only a moment, just long enough to reassure him that everything in Washington was going along fine and there was nothing for him to worry about. He seemed weak, but cheerful and relaxed, and he said to me, "Funny thing, if the doctors here didn't tell me differently, I would think this heart attack belonged to some other guy."

After a slow and gradual start, we began under Dr. White's suggestion to increase Eisenhower's daily work steadily and he began to spend most of his time in bed thinking about government problems and discussing them with me. Dr. White felt that it was important psychologically for the President to be given as much official work as possible in order to build in him an incentive to get well and to make him feel useful and less of an invalid. I traveled from Denver to Washington every week for the Friday morning Cabinet meeting, reporting on the President's progress, keeping abreast of government affairs for him and bringing back to him résumés of the Cabinet proceedings that he studied carefully. On my second trip to Washington, on October 14, I brought with me a message from Eisenhower asking the Cabinet to consider a cut of 100,000 employees from the federal civilian payroll, which he thought could be made without lessening the quality of the government's services. At that time, only three weeks after he was stricken, he was already deeply involved in a study of the budget again. The same day was the President's sixty-fifth birthday and the newspaper reporters sent him a suit of bright red pajamas with five gold stars on each collar tab and "Much Better, Thanks" embroidered over the breast pocket. We were deluged by messages from all over the country to the President and his wife. He asked us to prepare an engraved card of acknowledgment, but there were many replies that he wanted to write personally and Mrs. Whitman with her dictation pad began to spend as much time at the hospital as I did.

The visitors from Washington, after a carefully restricted trickle in the first few weeks, began to come in a steady stream and the intervals between their visits shortened. We arranged the early visits according to Cabinet rank, first Nixon and then Dulles and Humphrey, and then other important department heads according to the urgency of the business that they wanted to discuss. Dr. White warned the callers not to talk to Eisenhower as if he were a helpless invalid and the President himself urged some effusive well-wishers to cut short their expressions of good cheer and to get down to facts and figures. Dulles talked about the foreign ministers' meeting of the Big Four, where the Russians and the Western powers discussed again the issues on Germany and disarmament that had been brought up at the summit meeting in July. Wilson and Admiral Radford talked about their $34.5 billion defense budget. Brownell talked about plans to break judicial log jams. Burns and Hauge talked about a proposal to bring economic relief to depressed areas. Persons and Kevin McCann talked about the first draft of the January State of the Union message. Benson talked about farm troubles and Summerfield talked about increasing the postal rates.

The President began to make plans for his departure from the hospital in November. The doctors assured him that he would be ready to attend Cabinet and National Security Council meetings by January. He planned to go from Denver to Washington, where he would stop briefly, and then he would stay at his farm in Gettysburg until he was strong enough to resume the routine at the White House. The doctors would have preferred him to recuperate in a warm climate, in Florida or Arizona, but Eisenhower ruled out those locations because they were too far from Washington. He was thinking only of getting back into the working harness and he wanted to establish a temporary office within commuting distance of the capital so that his staff and Cabinet members and other government officials could consult with him.

At the Cabinet meeting of November 4, I outlined the plan for the President's return to Washington that we had worked out in Denver, subject to the approval of the physicians. Hagerty and I had decided reluctantly that the usual public welcome that Eisenhower always received from crowds in Washington on his way from the airport to the White House after an absence from the capital could hardly be avoided this time. We knew that the President would insist on exchanging greetings with well-wishers along the way to Pennsylvania Avenue. We hoped to hold down the "official welcome" at the airport to one handshake by the Vice President. Weeks, Humphrey and Summerfield wanted to cut out the welcoming program entirely, but I told them that the President had already said that he did not want to disappoint the people who would be turning out to see him. We left it for Nixon to agree with the President on a final version of the reception plan in Denver on Sunday.

The following Monday, after a fluoroscopic examination, the doctors told Eisenhower that he could make his escape from the hospital on the following Friday, as he had planned. Friday brought a dismal morning, but the President left Fitzsimons in good spirits. He was given a touching farewell by the hospital staff and as he boarded his plane at the airport, he spoke a few words of thanks to the people who had come to say good-by to him. "Misfortune, and particularly the misfortune of illness, brings to all of us an understanding of how good people are," he said. With Nixon at the airport in Washington was former President Herbert Hoover, and, as we had expected, big crowds lined the route to the White House across Memorial Bridge and around the Ellipse. The President reached his official home feeling tired but with no ill effects from his long journey and every one of us took a long breath of relief. The prospects for his full recovery

were now bright. He had taken climbing exercises without any noticeable difficulty and his heart responded to the physical exertion without
stress or enlargement. During that first weekend when he was back
in the White House, he was allowed to go out on the south lawn and
swing a golf club.

Eisenhower decided after he went to Gettysburg that he would
hold a Cabinet meeting at Camp David, the presidential retreat in
the Catoctin Mountains of Maryland, on November 22, a full month
ahead of the time that he was scheduled to begin such activity. He
talked over plans for the meeting with me while I was in Gettysburg
setting up another temporary presidential office there similar to the one
that we had at the Lowry Air Force Base in Denver. I told the Cabinet
of his plan at their meeting at the White House on November 15,
explaining that the President wanted to get together with the Cabinet
at Camp David, an easy drive from his farm, because there was no
suitable place for such a meeting in Gettysburg. We arranged an
agenda for the Camp David meeting. The water resources paper was
ready; Benson wanted to discuss the agriculture program; Herbert
Hoover, Jr., would report on the foreign ministers' meeting in Geneva.
At the end of that session, Nixon had some kind words about my
service at Denver.

The return of the President to the assembled Cabinet that November morning at Camp David was a moving event for all of us. I
noticed that everybody in the room was studying Eisenhower intently, looking for a change in his appearance and in his actions. He
was a little thinner, ruddy though not so tanned as usual, but his eye
and his glance were sharp and he showed, perhaps a bit consciously
and deliberately, an added force and energy in his comments and
expressions of opinion. He was quick, decisive and keen. I could see
that the Cabinet liked what they saw. Some of them were openly
astonished by the President's fast recovery and all of them were
agreeably surprised.

As the meeting ended and some of the members were beginning to
rise from their chairs, the President asked them to remain for a moment. He said that he wanted to thank the Cabinet and his staff for
the way they had carried on in his absence.

For five weeks after his heart attack, Eisenhower said, he had
not seen a newspaper but somebody had recently shown him an

editorial which expressed surprise that the Cabinet had been able to work so well together while he was not with them. There had even been a few hints, he added with a smile, that the Cabinet worked better without him than it did with him.

"The only thing that surprised me," the President said, "was that this editorial writer should have been surprised that this Cabinet could continue to work harmoniously and successfully in pursuing a practicable middle course between too little and too much government. I knew you could do it because all of you are dedicated to this policy at home and abroad."

Nevertheless, it made him proud, the President continued, of the people he had selected for his Cabinet and grateful for the way they had conducted themselves. This Cabinet was unique, he said, because ever since Washington's administration, when there was strife between Hamilton and Jefferson, there had never been a Cabinet so unanimous in its unified dedication to a set of principles as this one. The President said that he was glad to have given the Cabinet this chance to prove itself, although he did not particularly care for the circumstances that provided the grounds of proof.

And so this interlude of sickness and uncertainty came to an end. But it left us uncomfortably aware of the Constitution's failure to provide for the direction of the government by an acting President when the President is temporarily disabled and unable to perform his functions.

It was only good fortune that carried the government without crisis through that last week of September in 1955, when the President was lying under an oxygen tent in Denver. Luckily, ill as he was, Eisenhower never lost his power of speech or his ability to make a brief order for Nixon to replace him, if that had been necessary. But if the President had been unable to talk or to think clearly, what would have happened if a massive air attack had been directed against the United States at that time? Who would have had the undisputed authority to assume leadership in the absence of the President? Eisenhower told us later in a Cabinet meeting that he had asked himself these same questions right after his heart attack. But when his physicians assured him that he would be able to talk with his staff members by the end of that same week, he stopped worrying about the situation.

The vacancy in the President's chair did not confront us as urgently during Eisenhower's two later illnesses, the operation for ileitis in June, 1956, and the slight cerebral occlusion, or, as General Snyder preferred to call it, "the vascular spasm," that temporarily impaired his power of speech on November 25, 1957. But both of those setbacks gave us some uncertain moments and raised again the same questions about the direction of the government that we had asked ourselves in 1955. However, the problem of what to do should Eisenhower be incapable of performing his duties never had to be considered seriously during either of those subsequent illnesses. In each case, he was able to resume his constitutional functions only a day or two after he was taken ill.

The President's difficulty with the ileum, or lower part of the small intestine, was nothing new. It had probably caused the vicious attack of indigestion that he had fought during his notable speech on world peace in April, 1953, and General Snyder told me that he had suffered similar upsets before that while he was stationed at SHAPE. During the spring of 1956, the President was coming back strongly after his heart attack and, with his doctors' approval, he began to increase his social activities. On the night of June 7, he attended the White House news photographers' dinner, something that he had been looking forward to because he enjoyed being with the cameramen. He seemed in the best of health and spirits and ate his dinner with relish, observing the diet that the physicians had prescribed for him.

The next morning I learned that Mrs. Eisenhower had called General Snyder to the White House during the night because the President was in considerable distress. The doctor told me that the trouble seemed to be ileitis but that it would probably pass away. Early in the afternoon, there being no improvement, the President was taken to Walter Reed Hospital. Shortly after midnight, Andy Goodpaster called me from his home and told me that the President was about to undergo surgery.

"I am leaving right now to go to Walter Reed," Goodpaster said to me.

"For what purpose?" I asked.

"To observe his competency should any military decisions become urgent," he said.

Goodpaster was our staff secretary but he was also an Army officer, a brigadier general who had served under Eisenhower at SHAPE and acted as a liaison officer between the White House and the Pentagon, and to him the President was always the Commander in Chief. When I hung up the telephone, I thought for a moment of the deep personal concern that each member of the staff felt for Eisenhower. Goodpaster was already at the hospital when I reached there a half-hour later. Hagerty joined us and the three of us stood in the corridor at the door of the operating room and watched the surgeons as they worked on the body of the President of the United States. It was an eerie and striking experience. Hagerty and I exchanged comments without paying much attention to what we were saying. Goodpaster said something about how we would have to change the office routine again. Nothing really mattered to us except how The Old Man, as we called him, was going to get out of this one. With two major physical misfortunes within a year, how could he be expected to go through the coming 1956 presidential election campaign and four more years of the hardest strain to which a human being can be subjected?

Now and then, General Snyder came outside of the operating room to tell us how it was going. The group of surgeons and assisting doctors around the President were headed by General Leonard Heaton, the commanding officer at Walter Reed Hospital, and Dr. Isador Ravdin of the University of Pennsylvania Medical School. General Snyder told us that there was no sign of malignancy, that the operation would provide a by-pass around the obstructed area and that the President's heart, pulse and respiration were all very satisfactory.

I was told later by a surgeon that the chances are six or eight to one against a man of Eisenhower's age recovering from an ileitis operation. The President not only recovered quickly, but, as he said in July to a group of Congressional leaders, he gained from the operation a great improvement in his general health. The day after he was operated on, he was out of bed and walking in his room and a few days later he had a long talk, through an interpreter, with Chancelor Adenauer. He never considered withdrawing from the approaching election campaign and he refused to cancel a planned trip to Panama, which was rescheduled for July 21 with his doctor's full approval. But Eisenhower did say to me while he was at Walter Reed Hospital that this was the last time he would go through such a period of uncertainty and crisis; the next time, he warned, if he had any doubt about his physical ability to do the job as President, he was through. Just how serious Eisenhower was in his determination to resign from the presidency if he again had cause to doubt his own competence became clear to me when I saw him fighting off the slight cerebral stroke that affected his power of speech on November 25, 1957.

On that Monday afternoon, Ann Whitman came into my office on the verge of tears. "The President has gone back to the house," she said. "He tried to tell me something but he couldn't express himself. Something seemed to have happened to him all of a sudden." When she had called Dr. Snyder the President refused to leave his desk. "Go away from me," he tried to say. But Goodpaster had been able to persuade him to leave the office and had walked back to the living quarters with him. Mrs. Whitman said that Eisenhower had felt cold that morning when he came back from the airport where he had gone to meet the King of Morocco, Mohammed V, who was arriving in Washington on a state visit. After lunch, the President still felt chilly and then he began to have trouble with his speech when he tried to talk to Mrs. Whitman.

"And just now he gave up and went home," she said. "I can't imagine what's wrong with him."

This was almost a year and a half after Eisenhower's ileitis operation and he had been in good physical condition since that time. Still, in the back of our minds, there was always the unmentionable dread of the next attack. With a woman's instincts, Mrs. Whitman was sensitive to the changing moods of the President. If he was upset or overconcerned about something, I often heard of it first from Mrs. Whitman, even when the cause of his discontent could not be seen on the surface.

I found out that when Eisenhower left his office and went to the upstairs living quarters in the White House, General Snyder ordered him to bed. Later in the afternoon, after sleeping, he still had a noticeable speech impediment even though it was improving. There were obvious signs of a cerebral occlusion but the extent of the damage was unknown. Something would have to be done about the state dinner that the Eisenhowers were to give in the White House that evening for the King of Morocco. After the physicians that General Snyder called in for consultation examined the President, they were unable to say how long he might be incapacitated but there was no doubt in their minds that he could not attend the dinner.

I called Nixon on the telephone and explained the situation to him and alerted him for possible duty as the President's replacement that night. Then I asked Goodpaster to accompany me while I had a talk with Mrs. Eisenhower. We found her resting in her high-ceiling upstairs bedroom, deeply disturbed by the condition of the President. General Snyder joined us in our discussion of what we should do about the reception and dinner for the African King. Should Mrs. Eisenhower go alone, should the Nixons take over for the Eisenhowers or should the dinner be canceled altogether? While we were talking, the President walked casually into the room. He was wearing a long robe over his pajamas and his feet were in bedroom slippers. He smiled at us, as if to let us know that nothing was wrong with him.

He started to say something, "I suppose you are dis—" but he stammered, hesitated and then struggled on with the rest of the sentence: ". . . talking about the dinner tonight."

We saw that he was trying to talk about the plans for the evening but he was frustrated and getting angry at his inability to form words.

"There's nothing the matter with me!" he said finally with effort. "I am perfectly all right!"

But it was plain to see what there was something the matter with him and he knew it. He became more upset and impatient with his difficulty in seizing the word that he wanted to say, sometimes coming out with a word or a syllable that had no relation to the word that he had in his mind. Mrs. Eisenhower turned to me in dismay. "We can't let him go down there in this condition," she said.

General Snyder and I tried to convince the President that if he appeared in public that night his speech impediment would certainly be exaggerated beyond its real importance. I told him that the King would understand his absence, that the Nixons would be happy to fill in and the dinner could go on as planned. But Eisenhower was in no mood to agree with us. Flushed and upset, he shook his head abruptly and said, "If I cannot attend to my duties, I am simply going to give up this job. Now that is all there is to it."

Then he turned away from us and walked out of the room.

I called the Vice President and asked him to take the President's place at the dinner. As upset as she was, Mrs. Eisenhower dressed and went downstairs to carry out her responsibilities as the hostess with grace and poise, and the elaborate social event went off smoothly.

The next morning Eisenhower got out of bed early, shaved himself and ate his normal hearty breakfast. This was his way of observing the law that he had laid down for himself at Walter Reed the year before; if he was to stay in the White House, he was not going to be a bedridden patient. If illness was to get him down again, if he could not go on with his work disregarding the unexplained stroke that he had suffered, he could no longer continue to be President. The doctors examined him again that morning and were relieved to find no heart involvement and apparently no other serious effects. The President was persuaded, with some difficulty, to stay away from his office at least for the rest of that Thanksgiving week. He spent most of the rest of the day busily painting in the small room near the second-floor elevator that he used as a studio. At his request the King of Morocco came in for a friendly chat and the President was plainly pleased that he was able to visit with his guest without much difficulty.

It was difficult for me and the other members of the White House staff to accept the President's illness with his calm detachment. Unlike the heart attack and the ileitis operation, this sudden and disturbing physical setback came at a time when Eisenhower was hardpressed by many urgent problems. He was scheduled to attend a NATO meeting in Paris on December 16, where his presence was sorely needed. Dulles had told the President that some of the Western European powers were losing sight of the paramount importance of NATO. Eisenhower was the greatest single force holding the alliance together. Important Congressional meetings concerning programs for the coming year were due in the next two weeks. On that Tuesday morning, the doctors could not tell us how seriously the shock of the previous day had affected the President's nervous system or whether it might be only the first in a series of more damaging strokes. We only knew that we had to lighten the President's work schedule for the time being and that was not easy to arrange.

I told Goodpaster to summon Hagerty home from Paris, where he was arranging Eisenhower's scheduled visit to the NATO conference. At that time, the chances of the President going to Paris seemed remote indeed. The reporters, having heard that the President was not feeling well, were baying at the blinds for a statement, and Anne Wheaton, who had succeeded Murray Snyder as Hagerty's assistant press secretary, was trying to pacify them without a definitive medical report to give them. I asked Nixon and Brownell to meet with Persons and myself to consider the question of the President's competency. We decided to wait and see for a day or two.

Eisenhower gave us our answer sooner than that. That same day, the morning following his stroke, when Nixon and I went upstairs in the White House to talk with him about his schedule and found him painting in his small studio, there was nothing to indicate that he had ever been ill. The following day, Wednesday, he worked on government business in his rooms and the day after that, Thanksgiving Day, he went out with Mrs. Eisenhower to church services. On Friday he drove to Gettysburg for the weekend. Two weeks later we saw him off to the NATO meeting in Paris, where he received a tumultuous welcome, giving himself and NATO a big lift.

If Eisenhower's brief and moderate disability in 1957 had left him incapable of carrying on the duties of his office, an arrangement he had made previously with Nixon would have met the problems of temporary successorship that we found so perplexing after his heart attack in 1955. Before the President suffered his cerebral stroke in November, he had personal talks with Nixon about the interim successorship problem. As a result of these discussions, the President placed in his file a letter that he wrote to the Vice President covering an understanding between them of the procedure that would be followed in the event of a presidential disability. The terms of this agreement were made public at a later date, March 3, 1958, after Eisenhower made an inadvertent reference to it at a press conference. At the time the letter was written I believed that I was the only person on the White House staff who knew of it, except for Mrs. Whitman, who typed it. I never saw the letter myself, but the

President told me about it one day in conversation.

The agreement between Eisenhower and Nixon provided that if the President became disabled, he would inform the Vice President, who would then serve as acting President, exercising the powers and duties of the office, until the period of disability ended. If the President's illness prevented him from communicating with the Vice President, the understanding provided that the Vice President, "after such consultation as seems to him appropriate," could decide that the President was not capable of performing his duties and could assume the office as acting President. In either event, the President would decide when his disability had ended and would then resume the powers of his office.

But this was only a personal understanding between Eisenhower and Nixon and it merely covered Eisenhower's term of office. Concerned over the lack of a federal law which would cover such a situation, Eisenhower and Brownell tried to initiate a constitutional amendment that would establish the validity of the office of acting President if one were needed in future years.

The question of how to stipulate in the proposed amendment the procedure to be followed in determining the incompetence of a disabled President was a thorny one. The simple terms of the Eisenhower-Nixon understanding were adequate for men of good will and compatability like Eisenhower and Nixon. But, as one reporter pointed out to Eisenhower in a press conference discussion of the amendment, what was there to prevent a dishonest Vice President, with the aid of conspirators in the Cabinet, from declaring a competent President incompetent? "There would be a thousand of this type of question which the Attorney General could answer better than I can," Eisenhower replied.

There was considerable difference of opinion within Eisenhower's own official family on whether the Vice President, in deciding on the President's competence, should rely on the judgment of the Cabinet, the Supreme Court or on representatives of Congress. I wrote a memorandum to Brownell early in February, 1957, when he was working on the proposed amendment, noting that one Cabinet member felt reliance should be placed on the Supreme Court if the President was unable to exercise his judgment. It seemed to me that the President's own declaration of his competence or incompetence should be given first consideration. I agreed with Brownell's view that the Cabinet, rather than the Supreme Court, should constitute the check on the Vice President's finding of inability on the part of the President to carrry out his duties.

The whole question came up for a thorough review in the Cabinet meeting of February 8, when the President was preparing to put the proposal before the leaders of Congress. Brownell said that after a thorough study of the problem the Justice Department had considerable trouble recommending a procedure to be followed in the situation where the President is unable to declare himself disabled. The Attorney General's staff had considered many alternatives without reaching a conclusion.

Eisenhower said that he thought a special committee, including the Chief Justice of the United States and a heavy medical representation, should decide on cases where the President was unable to declare his own incompetency. Recalling his own experience at Denver, Eisenhower said he was convinced that a President should be able under the Constitution to take himself temporarily out of office by his own statement of disability and resume office by a similar statement of his own competence.

The President noted that he and Brownell disagreed on the question of succession beyond the Vice President; he was against the present law that puts the Speaker of the House next in line, but Brownell did not want to change that rule. Eisenhower felt that the presidency should be handed down to members of the same political party as that of the President and he favored putting senior members of the Cabinet next to the Vice President in succession, as had been the law in past years. Brownell pointed out to the President that to add a change in the present order of succession to the proposed disability amendment would only provoke a loud political wrangle in Congress, and the important objective of providing for an acting President might be buried in the resulting controversy. Nixon agreed with the Attorney General. The Cabinet unanimously favored further efforts to get the disability amendment considered by Congress.

At a bipartisan meeting of the legislative leaders on March 29, Eisenhower tried to stir up some action in Congress on a constitutional amendment. The President got nowhere. Sam Rayburn said that the public would suspect that the amendment was a move by Eisenhower to turn the reins of government over to "somebody else." The President told Rayburn that by the time the amendment was finally ratified by a vote of the states he would not be able to turn the presidency over to anybody for he would have long since retired from office.

It became apparent that there was no unanimity whatever among the Congressmen. One obvious objection was their lack of enthusiasm for entrusting the decision on the President's competency to the Cabinet. Senator Knowland said that any committee considering the President's competency should include Congressional representation. Another criticism of the proposal was that it would allow a Vice President serving as an acting President, in collaboration with an antagonistic Cabinet, to prevent a President from resuming his office. Eisenhower pointed out that the modern system of communications could be used to take such a plot to the people.

Finally Senator Saltonstall, supported by Joe Martin and Charlie Halleck, suggested that the Attorney General, rather than the President, should bring the proposed amendment before Congress. That was the tip-off. It was patently clear that the Congressmen would much rather knock down a Brownell plan than one which the President himself would present. There being no unanimity and little enthusiasm among the Republican leaders, and strong opposition from Rayburn, it was apparent that the proposal would not get far and it didn't.

After the President's 1957 illness, he made another attempt but Rayburn was still against it. The Speaker was also opposed to a similar presidential disability amendment submitted to Congress early in March, 1958, by a bipartisan group of Senators headed by Estes Kefauver. Eisenhower warmly supported the Kefauver bill, which followed his earlier proposal except that it gave the acting President the right to appeal to Congress to keep a President whom he considered incompetent from regaining his office. The Kefauver amendment died from lack of support, too.

The question of what happens when an incapacitated President is temporarily unable to carry out the duties of his office is still unanswered by the Constitution. Here is a real defect in the law that Congress has swept under the rug.

Disregard of the public interest, the President called it.

11 The Woes of Ezra Taft Benson

As the President's doctors had predicted, Gettysburg in November and December of 1955 was not an ideal place to recover from a heart attack. The weather was dark and cold and the putting green at Eisenhower's farm had turned brown and soggy. Cooped up inside his house, the President was often restless and moody and the calm and optimism that he had felt about the world and the nation when he had gone to Denver for his vacation in the previous summer were all gone now. Efforts to reach agreements with Russia on the questions of Germany and disarmament had collapsed at the foreign ministers' meeting in Geneva in November and the Soviets, with the help of Nasser, were muscling into the Middle East. Eisenhower was annoyed by the pressure that was being put upon him to declare himself a candidate for re-election in 1956 before he was ready to make up his mind about that hard decision and, with an election year approaching, the administration was in serious trouble with its agricultural program.

During the eight years that Ezra Taft Benson served as Eisenhower's Secretary of Agriculture, he was unquestionably the most unpopular and the most harshly criticized figure in the Cabinet. Benson was under constant fire from farmers and farm-belt Congressmen and it seemed that hardly a month went by in the White House without the President receiving a demand for Benson's removal. As early as October, 1953, Representative Frank Chelf of Kentucky wired the President that if Benson "remains in your Cabinet he will do more to undermine the confidence of the farmers in your administration than anything that could happen." The opposition to Benson's

202

policies was not confined to any particular political group; it came from the conservatives and liberals of both parties. Senator Joseph R. McCarthy wrote to the President in 1955 that in supporting Benson the administration was engaged in "open war against the farm community." Two years later McCarthy's political enemy and successor, Democratic Senator William Proxmire, sent Eisenhower a telegram that said, "Respectfully but with great urgency I appeal to you to take immediate action to replace Ezra Taft Benson as Secretary of Agriculture. Secretary Benson's unwise and unsound policies have brought many American farm families close to ruin."

The so-called Benson farm policies that everybody indignantly called to Eisenhower's attention were actually Eisenhower's own farm policies. While Benson called the turn on the changes which Eisenhower recommended to Congress, the program was as much the President's own as any other part of his legislative recommendations. No Secretary of Agriculture could have sponsored the changes which so vitally affected the farm economy without bringing down on himself the wrath of the farmers and consequently the members of Congress from farm states. Eisenhower and Benson tried to apply to agriculture the same basic principles that were applied earlier to business and industry. Release the farmer from arbitrary government control, regulation and subsidy, then let the laws of supply and demand in an expanding economy work toward full parity prices, or, in other words, a price level commensurate with the costs of commodities the farmer needs to sustain himself, his family and his business. But such a program meant knocking out high, rigid price supports which the Democrats had used as incentives to the production of urgently needed farm commodities during World War II. That made the farmers howl. Had it not been for the mountainous surpluses of farm products hanging over the market, the Benson plans for restoring a free agriculture might have stood some chance of working out. As it was, they didn't.

The farmers hung on to high price supports as their only means of getting their full, fair share of the national income. Eisenhower and Benson regarded high, rigid supports as self-defeating, since they led into a vicious circle of overproduction, depressed prices and huge surpluses stored in government warehouses.

When Eisenhower took office, the first big agricultural problem was how to cut down these accumulating surpluses, which were at the root of low prices. Obviously, the immediate cause of the bulging surplus problem was the subsidy payments made under the mandatory, or fixed, price supports at 90 per cent of parity then in effect under the Agricultural Act of 1949 on the six basic farm commodities—cotton, corn, wheat, rice, tobacco and peanuts. In spite of Benson's impatience to launch the new program, Eisenhower would not move until the 1949 law expired in 1954, as he had promised the farmers during the 1952 campaign. Many farmers and farm-belt legislators, bitterly opposed to tampering with the law as it stood, pointed to Eisenhower's speech at Brookings, South Dakota, during the campaign. "The Republican party is pledged to the sustaining of the 90 per cent parity price support," he had said. They also kept bringing up his speech at Kasson, Minnesota, in which he had said that the farmer's fair share "is not merely 90 per cent of parity—it is full parity." To his opponents, these statements and the program to scale down supports did not jibe.

At the outset, Eisenhower could not be expected to know exactly the course his program would take. His views at that time were based upon the weight of advice he received from Congressmen and delegations of farmers and representatives of farm organizations, and not upon the results of his own study, as was later the case. When Eisenhower and Benson came to complete agreement on the same goals, Benson, as he admitted himself, was much more impulsive than Eisenhower, much less diplomatic in his approach to the changes he and the President sought. The Secretary got himself into some trouble with the farmers long before the reform program came out in 1954. Soon after the administration took office, he began to refer to price supports as "disaster insurance." When cattlemen were caught between falling beef prices and high feed costs and wanted a government loan and purchase program, he turned his back on them. Getting the government into the beef business or further into any other branch of the agricultural economy was the very thing he was trying to avoid. In trying to explain his reasons in a speech at St. Paul, the Secretary made the mistake of stating that low beef prices would stabilize the market. Seeing which way the prevailing wind was blowing, the farmers began to rub the rust off their muskets. Most farm-belt Congressmen decided right off that Benson was no friend of theirs. One wheat-state Senator wrote to me, "Members of Congress on both sides of the Capitol are disgusted and mad at the apparent lack of political savvy on the part of the Secretary of Agriculture and they feel that he neither wants the advice of Congress nor cares to work in harmony with Congress."

It would have been more accurate to say that, rather than lacking political savvy, Benson's complete dedication to principle seemed to give him an immunity to political considerations. It was this spiritual force of character that inspired the President to come to his defense time after time. If Benson had something of the ascetic about him, it was this quality that Eisenhower thought altogether too rare in a public servant. But it often made the going rough. In fact, it would have completely floored a less resolute character.

Benson used every plausible argument he could think of to get his new program into motion. In 1953, when George Humphrey was groaning about the heavy expenditures in the budget that we had inherited from the Truman administration, Benson suggested that a substantial saving could be made by putting the new proposals into effect immediately instead of delaying the reduction of costly price supports until the next year. Eisenhower had to explain to Benson again that a promise was a promise, and the present supports would not be disturbed until 1954.

As the years went on, feeling against Benson grew stronger. In 1957, when he was making a speech at the National Corn Picking Contest near Sioux Falls, South Dakota, eggs were thrown at him by a group of disgruntled farmers in the audience. Among those present on the platform with Benson that day was Senator Karl Mundt of South Dakota, who wrote to me later that the crowd of farmers listened to Benson's address "for sixty minutes without a single interruption for applause, a single smile or a friendly nod." Mundt added:

The egg throwing itself can be written off as the ill mannerisms of a few disgruntled farmers, but the letters of commendation that these farmers have been getting from around the country and the letters supporting their opposition to Benson in the daily press out here are significant and they indicate big trouble ahead. I don't believe there is a Chinaman's chance of winning the farm vote with him as Secretary of Agriculture.

Though I always considered that Benson and I were good friends, I never brought up in later conversations with him the events of that day in South Dakota. The Secretary made a smiling reference to the egg-throwing at the next Cabinet discussion of the farm situation. He seemed to have taken it without anger or embarrassment and with a kind and patient humility as a burden that had been placed on him by the will of God.

Since he is one of the Twelve Apostles of the Mormon Church, everything that Benson does is deeply influenced by his religious faith. When Eisenhower offered him the Agriculture post, he hesitated at first because, as he said afterward, "I told him that I had dedicated my remaining years to spiritual matters, that I had responded to the call of my church and that I was not sure that a minister of the Gospel belonged in the Cabinet." Eisenhower won him over, Benson recalled, by asking him in return if a position of responsibility in the government was not a spiritual job.

In Washington, Benson was sometimes difficult to deal with because he overlooked many of the required procedures of government work. Enveloped in a kind of celestial optimism, he was convinced that his big decisions were right and therefore bound to turn out for the best in the end. When he made up his mind on a course of action, he was unshakable. He often wanted to carry his plans into action immediately without taking the time for the discussions and clearances that would have made his course a much easier one. One time Benson prepared a bill for the Senate that should have been reviewed by the State Department, the Office of Defense Mobilization, the Foreign Operations Office and the Bureau of the Budget. As Joe Dodge complained to me later, Benson had prepared his legislation for introduction in the Congress without consulting any of those departments and without showing it to the White House either. Since it was Dodge's responsibility to make sure that all bills which had administration backing conformed to Eisenhower policy, his irritation was easily understood when he found that Benson's proposal differed substantially with the official viewpoint. When I pointed this out to Benson, he did not seem to be greatly disturbed.

Once in a while when we tried to get Benson to change something that he was doing, it was already too late to do anything about it. When he decided to take action on some particularly touchy matter which he felt strongly about, he avoided the road blocks which he feared other departments, even the White House staff, might set up. Whenever this included the members of his own party on the House and Senate agriculture committees there was usually a row. When the 1954 farm program was ready for introduction after a year and a half of preparation, Benson was invited to a meeting of the Senate Agriculture Committee so that certain modifications and supplementary ideas could be suggested to him. The Secretary listened politely and then told the Senators that there could be no more changes because the message had already been mimeographed. The Senators, especially the Republicans, hit the ceiling and assailed Benson for wasting their time. "Why did he let us sit there making suggestions for the recipe of a cake that had already been baked?" one of them asked me later.

Even John Foster Dulles, who could strike awe into the heart of almost everybody in an encounter, failed to ruffle Benson when the Secretary of Agriculture made up his mind in the summer of 1955 to sell one million bales of government-owned surplus low-grade cotton abroad during the following year at less than the world price. Besides reducing our own cotton surplus, Benson wanted to discourage foreign cotton growing. Any mention of selling surplus commodities overseas at whatever price they would bring always sent the State Department into convulsions. Most people are understandably perplexed by the tremendous stores of agricultural commodities that deteriorate in American government warehouses and storage bins while underprivileged people are hungry abroad. What is seldom understood is the severe economic repercussions that result in countries which grow wheat and cotton when we throw these commodities indiscriminately on the world market. We cannot afford to disrupt the markets of friendly countries, where military bases and alliances are so vital to our own security and that of the free world. Among these countries are some of the best friends we have, Canada and Australia, for example. Benson's proposal to sell an additional million bales of cotton abroad made Dulles and Under Secretary Herbert Hoover, Jr., uneasy. This could mean real trouble with cotton-producing Egypt and Pakistan. Dulles was already having enough trouble with Egypt over Suez and the Gaza Strip. Pakistan, in a strategic position as a dependable friend in the new SEATO organization, was already receiving substantial economic support under the Mutual Security Program.

Benson was also opposed by the Secretary of Commerce, Sinclair Weeks, who feared that foreign textile manufacturers would buy the cheap United States cotton, turn it into products made with lower-paid foreign labor which they would then export into the United States, where they would undersell the domestic product. When Eisenhower asked Humphrey for his opinion, the Secretary of the Treasury said that as much as he wanted to turn cotton into dollars he was afraid that the sale might wreck the world markets. "We're in a strange position," Humphrey said. "We have taught people all over the world how to grow more and better cotton through our technical assistance programs. We've even given them the tractors to raise it. And now our own cotton growers and textile people are trying to set up import quotas that will discourage foreign countries from growing cotton."

"We will never make any progress in getting rid of our huge cotton surplus and in discouraging the overproduction of foreign cotton," Benson said, "if we say that we are never going to affect any nation adversely."

The only alternative to his plan was a two-price system for cotton and wheat, Benson added. Such a plan, with a higher price at home and a low price abroad, would amount to a tremendously costly export subsidy that would cut squarely across administration policy. Dulles protested again that if anything caused the economies of Egypt and Pakistan to go into a tailspin at that time, when neutralism was gaining ground in the Middle East, the whole oil situation might also be jeopardized.

But despite the opposition of Dulles, the President supported Benson, as he often did when the chips were down. "We are not going to sit back and lose all our cotton markets," Eisenhower said. Later in the discussion, the President remarked that every time the United States tried to get its economy back on the track "after the mismanagement of twenty years," foreign countries always set up a cry of "This will break us," even though we had given them millions of dollars in aid. At the close of the meeting, Benson was able to get his foot in the door; he obtained Cabinet approval of getting his cotton proposal into writing so that any differences with State, Commerce and Treasury could be ironed out. Benson had won the first round.

The following week Benson came to the Cabinet meeting with his proposal all set and ready to roll. He mentioned calmly that it would have to be announced that very same afternoon, or by tomorrow at the latest. Leaning forward in their chairs, Weeks and Dulles reached out to grab his coattails and slow him down.

"The real objection is not just that we are giving foreign manufacturers a better price on cotton than our own government gives domestic customers," Weeks said. "We ought to sell cotton at world prices to domestic textile manufacturers, provided that they sell the products from it only in the foreign market."

That would require legislation, Benson told him. But he agreed with the idea, and added that it was part of a program he planned to put before Congress eventually. The plan that he was announcing today, or tomorrow at the latest, needed no authority but his own; legislative approval would not be required. He mentioned that he had received reports that cotton acreage had increased so much abroad that in some countries it was cutting down the production of food and feed to the point where diets were being seriously affected. Our role, he continued, was now to put the world on notice that we were planning to sell cotton competitively overseas. It was clear that Benson was not going to be slowed down. A more dedicated or stronger-willed character never served his country.

Dulles and Hoover had argued the week before that a sale of government surplus cotton overseas at a low figure would be certain to depress world prices. Now Dulles turned to the other side of the coin. If Benson's transaction failed to lower world prices, he said, the real objective of the plan, discouraging foreign cotton planting, would not be achieved.

"I'm not so sure of that," Eisenhower said. "These countries know we have a lot more cotton here to sell. That might make them reflect."

"We haven't sold any of this cotton for years and these countries know it," Dulles said. "If we start selling it now, we face another dilemma. The foreign textile manufacturers have been getting cotton at a lower price than the United States manufacturer has had to pay, but that was not due to any action of our government. Now, under this program, the United States manufacturer will find his own government selling cotton at a lower price to his competitors. This will increase the clamor for import quotas. And import quotas make it more difficult for us to get along with our friends and allies overseas."

But the President stayed with Benson.

"I am sure the question of quotas will hit us right in the face if the cotton market starts to break," Eisenhower said, "but we have to make a start in this direction. We had better try something and see what happens."

And what did happen? Benson was right. He sold his million bales of cotton without causing more than a ripple in the foreign market.

The cotton transaction was something exceptional; at other times when Eisenhower took Benson's side of the argument the results were often not so fortunate. The first Eisenhower-Benson farm program, the Agricultural Act of 1954, moved toward greater flexibility in support prices, giving the Secretary a wider range of discretion in reducing the incentive to overproduce those farm commodities which were in far too abundant supply. Benson fought for flexibility ranging between 75 and 90 per cent of parity but Congress would not drop the props below 82.5 per cent of parity. Even so the uproar from the farm belt was distinctly audible in Washington.

The results of the 1954 program did not show up on the scoreboard until the harvests of 1955. The fall Eisenhower was recovering from his heart attack in Denver the figures began to come in and none of them were encouraging. Farm prices were still falling and the huge surplus was growing steadily bigger. For every bushel that Benson managed to move out through the front door of the government warehouses a bushel and a half were coming in the back door. The combination of excellent weather, modern miracles of mechanization, new techniques from the science laboratories that brought spectacular increases in already productive acres, plus the incentives still offered in government price subsidies, sent production soaring to new summits. And that of course sent the cost of the government's agriculture expenditures zooming upward, too. Before the Benson program went into effect that year the annual cost of the farm subsidies was about $1.3 billion. At the end of the year, when Eisenhower was at Gettysburg, staring out through the windows at the gloomy weather and pondering over his problems, the farm program was costing a whopping $2.3 billion annually. Something had to be done.

Eisenhower refused to do one thing that nearly everybody in the farm belt and most of the members of Congress seemed to want him to do—he continued to refuse to get rid of Ezra Taft Benson. The practical politicians who were mystified by Eisenhower's willingness to risk his own popularity by sticking to Benson did not understand that, to the President, Benson was a symbol of the unselfish idealism and nonpolitical devotion to public service that Eisenhower deeply respected. In 1958, when the cries for Benson's scalp were still resounding through the farmlands, Eisenhower summed up at a press conference this feeling that he had for his Secretary of Agriculture: "Now I think this: when we find a man of this dedication, this kind of courage, this kind of intellectual and personal honesty, we should say to ourselves, 'We just don't believe that America has come to the point where it wants to dispense with the services of that kind of person.' "

The day before, in a discussion at the White House with the Republican leaders of Congress, the President had expressed the same opinion in more personal terms. "If I can't stick with Benson," he said, "I'll have to find some way of turning in my own suit or I'll just be known as a damned coward."

Although Eisenhower agreed with Grover Cleveland that the function of government was not to give financial support to the people, he favored a more gradual reduction of farm subsidies than the uncompromising Benson advocated. Like Syngman Rhee, Benson in his impetuous way might have been willing to make a complete sacrifice of his constituents on the altar of principle but Eisenhower would not let him go that far. The President was well aware that the farmer had grown so dependent on government hand-outs during Democratic administrations that this source of aid could not be cut off too abruptly. Besides, having grown up in a Kansas farming community himself, Eisenhower knew that the farmer's welfare, unlike that of the industrialist or the businessman, depended on unpredictable natural elements over which he had no control. I remember a remark he made to me in the summer of 1953 when we were making a trip of inspection through the drought-stricken farm and cattle-raising states. In the hot and dusty business section of Amarillo, Texas, there were few people around the stores, and shops had a lonesome and crestfallen look about them. The President turned to me and said, "I know just how these fellows feel. My father was a storekeeper like that and just such a drought put him under. He gave credit when nobody could pay his bills, and then couldn't collect. I know what these people are going through."

Unlike Benson, Eisenhower was also realistic enough to consider the farm vote, which the Secretary with his immunity to the urgencies of party politics could calmly ignore. In that late fall of 1955, when Benson was preparing a new farm program, the Agricultural Act of 1956, it was apparent that some kind of new and probably drastic proposal would have to be forthcoming to combat further sky-rocketing of surpluses, now that the act of 1954 had failed so dismally. Besides the economic crisis that overshadowed the whole farm community, the Republicans were looking over the brink of a political crisis that threatened once more their traditional hold on the farm states. Eisenhower was in what the people out in Kansas call a bind.

The soil bank plan that went to Congress on January 9, 1956, was not new. There had been various versions of the idea in the New Deal days. This time Eisenhower sent up a two-pronged thrust at the problem of agricultural surpluses: the acreage reserve aimed at the immediate reduction of four crops in serious surplus—wheat, cotton, corn and rice; and the conservation reserve, a plan to retire permanently from basic crop production a great acreage that had been brought into agricultural production since the beginning of World War II. Tremendously expensive, the whole program ran counter to Benson's conservative instincts, but in the absence of a feasible alternative he reluctantly had to accept it. This was better, as Eisenhower told him, than a giant giveaway. It was agreed that the acreage reserve plan was to be a temporary emergency measure. But Benson winced at the cost of the longer-range conservation plan, which Eisenhower told Congress would run up to a billion dollars during the next three years.

So the soil bank became the principal panacea of the new farm program, which was given a final review at the Cabinet meeting of December 9, 1955 at Camp David with the President driving up from Gettysburg to sit in on the discussion. The program also included a seven-point proposal aimed at increasing surplus disposal, a plan for refunding the federal tax on gasoline used on farms, and research, conservation and promotional campaigns. Howard Pyle outlined a public relations plan to let the public know what the program was all about, a difficult task because to the nonfarming citizen the agricultural jargon about parity, rigid and flexible price supports, basic and nonbasic commodities and two-price plans is no more understandable than the fine print in an insurance policy.

Eisenhower asked if any consideration had been given to one of his particular interests, the purchase from farmers of marginal lands that could be added to the government's forest reserves. Much of this land never should have been cleared for agricultural uses, he believed. Benson reflected his own thinking when he reminded the President that there was a growing feeling in the West against putting any more private land into the public domain. But Eisenhower stood his ground. A standing offer for such land might still be in the best interests of the country, he insisted.

Humphrey was blunt and cheerless about the Benson program. In his opinion it did not offer any long-term solution to the agricultural muddle, and nobody disputed him. The President told Humphrey that the program had to be looked at as insurance against financial disaster in the farm belt, which, if not checked, would spread to the rest of the economy.

"Therefore we'll have to raise the money for it," he said, looking around the table in mock seriousness, "even if we have to make a 5 per cent cut in the salaries of the Cabinet members."

As was to be expected, the Agricultural Act of 1956 ran headlong into trouble as soon as it was sent to Congress. The President threw his weight solidly behind it with a special message that began, "No problem before Congress demands more urgent attention than the paradox facing our farm families." As he had cautioned the Cabinet, it was the responsibility of everyone concerned with the new program to make clear that the troubles that harassed the farmer were of no recent origin; they all harked back to earlier days. That was as close as Eisenhower would get to saying that the New Dealers had got the farmers into trouble and it was now left to his administration to get them out. Rigid price supports of the past had demoralized the farm market, he told the Congress. Flexible price supports provided in the 1954 law had not had sufficient time to prove themselves. The old program had brought down an avalanche of surplus crops, needed in wartime, but now without a market. Despite the disposal of over four billion dollars' worth of these commodities during the first three years of his administration, the surplus was bigger than ever. Let the soil bank go into effect immediately, he asked, so that it would curtail spring planting.

Back from Capitol Hill came word that the Democrats, and many anti-Benson Republicans, might be willing to pass the soil bank and the rest of the bill if the administration would return to the old 90 per cent rigid price supports. The illogic of the proposition infuriated Eisenhower. The soil bank was a move to keep down the surplus, while high price supports were an incentive to do exactly the opposite. What was the sense of that, he asked the Congressmen. But the agricultural experts in Congress had reasoned that a return to rigid supports would tide the farmer over financially until the new soil bank payments came to his rescue. They also figured that high price supports would tide themselves over politically until after the coming elections.

"I'll tell you this—personally," Eisenhower told a gathering of Republican Congressional leaders on January 10, with angry emphasis. "I'm not going out of here and leave high rigid price supports to ruin our agriculture."

Two weeks later, at another heated session over the farm bill with the legislators, Benson interrupted the discussion to ask the Congressmen how they would feel about him appearing on one of Edward R. Murrow's *See It Now* television shows. The show was to be entirely devoted to the nation's agricultural problems, Benson explained, and he had been given to understand that he was to be the central character. Jim Hagerty, who was present, happened to know more about the plans for the TV show than the Secretary of Agriculture did. Hagerty explained to Benson that the documentary being prepared by Murrow was in reality a very fine hatchet job on the administration and Benson. The film for it had already been photographed from that angle, Hagerty explained, so it could hardly be changed to present a more favorable point of view. One of the scenes in the film that Hagerty had heard about showed a distressed farm family auctioning off a baby's crib. He had been told that the truth of the matter was the crib had last been used by a boy who was now nine years old.

Ructions over the farm bill and the battle to get it through the Senate and the House dominated every meeting that Eisenhower had with the Congressional leaders for the rest of that winter and well into the late spring. The President never let up on his pressure on the legislators to get the bill passed. On February 7, Senator George Aiken of Vermont, the ranking Republican on the Senate agriculture committee, brought bad news to the White House: his fellow party members on the committee, Young, Thye and Mundt, had voted at a committee meeting for the restoration of 90 per cent rigid supports. This vote had put the committee in favor of the fixed supports, eight to seven. The Republicans told Aiken they "regretted" that they had to oppose the President, but they had been "committed" to it. They wanted Eisenhower to be assured that they were still warmly in favor of the soil bank.

The President lost no time in making known how he felt about that. A vote for both the soil bank and high rigid supports did not make any sense to him. He arranged with Senator Aiken for an exchange of letters on the subject that would be released to the public the next day. In his letter, Eisenhower said, "I should be gravely concerned if the soil bank should be coupled with the restitution of production incentives certain to nullify the great benefits that the bank can bring." At that point, sentiment on the bill in the Senate was so evenly divided that Knowland predicted that it might end up in a forty-eight to forty-eight tie vote.

Aiken brought more pleasant news to the White House meeting on February 28. The sale of the million bales of surplus cotton that Benson had engineered overseas to the discomfort of Dulles was bringing Southern Democratic support to the farm bill. That relaxed the atmosphere and when Benson mentioned to the President that Senator Holland, a Democrat from Florida, was in favor of the program, Eisenhower said, "He ought to be a Republican."

"He is, except in name," Benson said.

The President laughed, and, referring to Edgar Eisenhower, said to Benson, "Ezra, you've arrived. I have a brother who is very conservative. He says the one good thing I've done here was to appoint you."

Aiken remarked that he hoped progress on the farm bill could be made in the Senate soon. Otherwise, he warned, Senator Hubert

Humphrey would get up on the floor "and talk and talk and talk."

Then reports from the wheat belt began to get ominous and an informal steering committee that I helped put together to push the agriculture bill reported that it was having serious trouble with Congressmen from the Midwest farm states. I was invited to have breakfast with the Iowa delegation in the Capitol and found what I had expected: there was just one Congressman at the table who was not after Benson's scalp. There were many Congressmen at that time who might have gone along with a farm program that was distasteful to them if they could have had the pleasure of seeing Benson pilloried in the public market place. But Benson did not propose to be pilloried. Neither had Eisenhower any intention of deserting his beleaguered Secretary of Agriculture.

It was often said that year, and I was well aware of it at the time, that if the White House staff had not deliberately shielded the President from the many delegations who wanted to present the other side of the argument, the President would not have stuck by Benson and his policies. Actually, we made sure that he listened to a full quota of visitors who were bitter enemies of the Secretary and his theories. I always tried to make sure that Eisenhower had the opportunity to base his political decisions on a complete knowledge of the crosscurrents of opinion. As one example, I remember Representative Karl LeCompte bringing to my office one afternoon a former governor of Iowa, Daniel Webster Turner, who later castigated Eisenhower and Benson for their opposition to high, rigid price supports. LeCompte and Turner were accompanied by Clifford Houck, head of the National Farmers' Organization, and no friend of Benson's policies. I listened to their estimate of the farm situation. Governor Turner said to me, "I suppose we won't be able to see the President."

"Come in tomorrow morning at nine-forty-five," I replied.

The next morning at the appointed time I showed them into the President's office, where they had a cordial and receptive hearing. Many others who shared their views were given the same opportunity.

When March came, the President had his dander up. Before he would approve 90 per cent rigid supports he would call a special session, he warned the leaders. He jokingly offered to toast the Republicans with champagne if they turned back the fixed price props. It looked at that time as if Benson might get the soil bank passed without tying to it the Senate Agriculture Committee's recommendation for the 90 per cent supports. But on a test vote rejecting high supports on milling wheat, it took Nixon's own vote to break a tie. It was the first time that the Vice President voted in a Senate ballot on a matter of substance rather than on a mere question of procedure. Then, to get his bill through the Senate, Benson virtually threw in the sponge. In order to keep the support of Southern Senators, he agreed to maintain 90 per cent supports for cotton in the face of a whopping 1955 cotton crop, estimated at two million bales. This made the wheat growers mad and they grew still madder when they learned that Benson had upped corn acreage by eight million acres in the soil bank proposal. The wheat men charged Benson with "buying votes," lobbying and giving them a "rotten deal."

Because he had opened the door to the cotton growers, Benson's position was now weakened. The Senate began a long debate, piling on amendment after amendment to the bill until it became obvious that the original agricultural act was becoming unrecognizable. On March 19, the Senate passed a bill that both sides of the aisle immediately found confusing and unworkable. The President tried to study it that night before going to bed and said the next day that he could not understand what the Senate was trying to do; he found the revised bill, with its mystical talk about double parity and multiple-priced wheat, completely bewildering and self-contradictory.

During the 1955 session of Congress, the House had passed a measure restoring 90 per cent supports, so the House bill and the new and monstrous Senate bill went into conference. When the Republican leaders discussed with the President the possibility of instructing the conferees, Charlie Halleck said that he had always opposed instructing members of a conference group and to reverse his position and do so now might cause him embarrassment. The President grinned at Halleck and said to him, "If somebody quotes Charlie Halleck against you, Charlie, tell him he's quoting a good man."

Eisenhower refused to accept the hodgepodge farm bill that Congress sent back to him and vetoed it on April 16. The next day George Humphrey said to him, "That's the best thing you ever did." Eisenhower told the Congressional leaders afterward that Humphrey's reaction had greatly reassured him. "George is not one who enthuses easily," Eisenhower said. The President said that he might have agreed to a compromise of 82.5 per cent price supports for one year only in order to get the soil bank, but he would have nothing to do with either dual parity or mandatory supports for feed grain.

Since Congress had failed to take prompt and reasonable action to provide the remedies that he had recommended, the President announced that he was taking action himself. To bolster farm incomes, he was setting price supports not less than 82.5 per cent of parity under the basic crops, with wheat at two dollars a bushel, corn at a dollar and a half and other adjustments in proportion. Now take this, he said to the Congress, and pass a straight soil bank bill and let's get on with it. He was also asking for advance payments up to 50 per cent to be made as soon as the farmer agreed to take his acres out of production.

Inevitably the Democrats claimed that Eisenhower was backing out of campaign promises. A reporter told the President at a press conference that Lyndon Johnson had reproduced on television some excerpts from the Kasson speech that Eisenhower had made in 1952, which were intended to indicate that Eisenhower had promised 100 per cent price supports. But, as the President had somewhat vainly tried to explain again and again, he was not referring to artificial price supports. Instead, he was talking about the natural parity between costs and prices that he felt a farmer could get in the free market place under a normal farm economy through the law of supply and demand.

The President eventually got his soil bank. But when he signed the new and once again revised farm program on May 28, he had to accept with the soil bank some things that he still found bitter to swallow. When Eisenhower was told that the soil bank was described by Claude Wickard, Henry Wallace's successor as Secretary of Agriculture in the Roosevelt administration, as "a partisan attempt to buy farm votes," he replied indignantly, "You mean I got that kind of a charge from *them?*"

The arguments and the headaches about Benson and the apparently insoluble farm problem went on for another four years. Curiously, Eisenhower did not seem to have suffered any political ill effects in the farm belt. On the day that Eisenhower vetoed the first agricultural bill in 1956, I had lunch at the White House with Samuel Lubell, the well-known political analyst, who had just made a survey of the farm states. Lubell accurately predicted on that day in May that no matter how deep water Benson was in, the farmers would vote for Eisenhower in November, as they certainly did. Lubell found the farmers divided on the question of Benson's policies, with the line of cleavage sometimes running through the middle of the family itself. The older folks were stringing along in their traditional Republicanism with Eisenhower, while the younger families, depending on government subsidies instead of savings as their stabilizers, were defecting to the Democrats and the Farmers' Union. When election came around, Lubell said, most of them would vote for Eisenhower because they regarded the President as a bulwark for peace in a time of uncertainty, whether they liked his agricultural policies or not. Besides, the boys were home and no longer at a fighting front overseas.

As they voted Republican in 1956, the farmers voted Republican in 1960, when their impatience with Benson was as strong and bitter as ever. On election night, as he watched himself with mixed surprise and chagrin losing the farm states one by one, John F. Kennedy was reported to have said, "Well, if that's what they want, maybe I can give it to them. Maybe I ought to keep Ezra Taft Benson as Secretary of Agriculture for another four years."

12   The Big Decision of 1956

Eisenhower once said to a small group of us, "You know, if it hadn't been for that heart attack, I doubt if I would have been a candidate again."

This observation may sound strange; a serious heart attack such as Eisenhower suffered in 1955 would have discouraged most men from running for re-election as President of the United States in the following year. Eisenhower, however, is not like most men. His illness was one factor that made him change his intention of retiring from office at the end of his first term, and, as he has since intimated, that intention was strong and definite, much more so than any of us on his staff realized at the time.

Eisenhower's conscientious sense of duty and his deep personal pride made it impossible for him to leave his work until he could do so with a feeling of satisfaction that he had it finished or that he had given all he had to give to it.

That time never came, as it never comes to any President. There were times, before the accident to his heart, that it seemed he could have given up the presidency with such a feeling. He had done the job well. During his administration, the United States had returned to peace, an uneasy one to be sure, but at least the shooting had stopped. The nation had never before reached such peaks of prosperity. The Korean conflict had been brought to an end and the recession, resulting from the changeover from a war economy, had been met, and safely passed. The change to a moderate government and a free economy had been skillfully made, and a balanced budget was in view. Red China had been held in check in the Far East and although

220

our relationship with Russia was still tense and strained—as it probably would be for the rest of Eisenhower's lifetime, anyway—things
had looked brighter in that summer of 1955. The President's disarmament proposal at Geneva had stirred hope in his leadership for peace.
He could have left the White House then with the respect and
affection of most of the people in the world.

The heart attack changed all that. He had always taken pride in his
health and stamina. He felt that if he gave up and went into retirement
after such an illness it would seem like accepting a personal defeat.
After he left the hospital and began the boring and dragging hours
and days of recuperation at Gettysburg, he looked forward anxiously
to resuming the thrill of life in the White House again. To let it be
said that such duties had worn him out, that the burden of leadership
had become too much for him, seemed more and more repugnant.
He reminded himself that he would have to wait and see what the
doctors had to say, but as far as he himself was concerned, he had
no intention of letting the politicians count him out until he made up
his own mind whether he could go on in the White House for another
four years.

Another factor that was an even stronger influence on the President's decision to run again was the lack at that time of another
Republican candidate with Eisenhower's popularity who had his
dedication to moderate government and a responsible and realistic
foreign policy. He thought there were several Republicans in the
administration well qualified for the position, Nixon, Lodge and
Robert Anderson among them, but none of these men in 1956 had
caught fire nationally. The scarcity of other presidential candidates in
the Republican ranks made Eisenhower unhappy; he had hoped that
the return of the party to power in 1952 would develop a stable of
newcomers capable of heading the ticket in 1956. When such potential successors failed to materialize, the President was forced reluctantly to agree with the advisers who told him that he was their
only hope of keeping a Republican in the White House. He hated
the thought of turning over his moderate and conservative policies
to a Democratic administration. For that reason alone, whether he
had had the heart attack or not, I believe he could have been persuaded to become the Republican candidate in 1956.

Whatever influence it had on the question, Eisenhower's heart attack dramatically heightened the suspense while the nation and the world anxiously waited in January and February of 1956 to see what his decision would be. This was not just a President weighing political considerations before making up his mind whether to run for office again. A bigger issue was at stake. After a close brush with death, would Eisenhower have the courage to face four more years of punishing physical strain in the White House?

Eisenhower told a group of us that there were two people who opposed his running for re-election, his brother, Milton, and his son, John. During the early weeks of his recovery in Denver, Mrs. Eisenhower was naturally against it, too. As time went on and as she listened to General Snyder and the other doctors, she began to change her mind. General Snyder, in whose wisdom and judgment the Eisenhower family placed great trust, told us all that for a man of the President's restless and energetic temperament a retirement from public service might be far more injurious than four more years in the White House. Knowing her husband's make-up so well, Mrs. Eisenhower gradually became as enthusiastic as any of us in support of the decision her husband eventually reached.

All of us in the President's official family, and, as far as I know, all of his intimate friends outside of the government, wanted him to run again. I do not think most of us bothered with political considerations so much as with our belief that the President was the greatest force for peace in the world. We felt great sympathy with Dulles' conviction that the retirement of Eisenhower at that time would have an alarming effect on the unity of the free world.

In this respect our feeling had not materially changed since 1954, when the first questions about Eisenhower's 1956 intentions began to come up. Most of us on his staff were confident then that he would run for re-election. At that time I mentioned that I thought the President's decision at the proper time would be based on three conditions, which I did not divulge. The press picked this up and I knew that at his next press conference the President would very likely be asked what I was driving at. So I told him that he might expect such questions. I also told him that the three conditions I had in mind were purely the product of my own personal convictions and that someday I would tell him what they were.

Sure enough, at the press conference the President was asked about "the contingencies" on which, according to Governor Adams, his decision to seek re-election might depend.

"I will tell you this much," Eisenhower said. "As I started over here this morning, Adams said, 'I have got three secret contingencies that I never told you about. But,' he said, 'someday I am going to tell you.' So I am just as ignorant as you are."

This excited some mirth among the reporters. The three considerations that I had in mind would have occurred to anybody familiar with Eisenhower's work and objectives. Did he believe that he could go through four more years carrying the full burdens of the presidency without losing his health? Did he believe that his policies during his first term had brought progress toward the realization of his greatest goal—a peaceful world? Had his domestic policies been such as to serve the best interests of all of the American people and was he genuinely wanted as President by the people? I am sure that Eisenhower asked himself these questions often and that he would not have made the decision to run again if he could not have answered them in the affirmative.

In Denver when I saw how fast and how strongly the President was recovering from his illness and later when I learned that General Snyder and Dr. White thought another term would be better than retiring—provided subsequent examinations showed a normal healing of his heart injury—I resolved to do all I could quietly to get Eisenhower to become a candidate again. Among those who had the same intention was General Clay, who had visited Eisenhower in Denver just before the President left the hospital. On that visit, Clay noticed that Eisenhower was showing some signs of the depression and the self-questioning lack of confidence in the future that most heart attack victims go through during their convalescence. Clay became concerned that Eisenhower might count himself out of a second term before he had sufficiently recovered from his illness to make a careful and balanced decision about his ability to run again. I shared Clay's uneasiness.

To discuss that possibility and the general prospects of Eisenhower's candidacy, Clay called a meeting in New York of the President's close associates—Nixon, Brownell, Leonard Hall, Persons, Tom Stephens and myself. We all agreed to do our best to discourage the President from trying to make any kind of a decision, one way or the other, about his future plans until well into 1956, at least not until after his physicians were able to make the final examination of his heart injury and to decide how well it had healed. That decision could not be made until the middle of February. Some men in the group were in favor of persuading the President to postpone his decision until June, but it was agreed to leave that matter in doubt. In the meantime, none of us and nobody in the Cabinet or on the White House staff would indulge in any public speculation about whether the President would run again.

As it turned out, we had little difficulty dissuading the President from making up his mind prematurely. He had decided to let the matter rest until the doctors gave him their findings in February. Senator Knowland and Representative Joe Martin, the Republican leaders in the Senate and the House, came to see him at Gettysburg and Knowland tried to draw the President farther out on the second-term matter than he was willing to go. Waiting until February for a decision from Eisenhower did not fit into Knowland's plans. The Senator made it clear that he had no intention of getting into a contest with Eisenhower but he thought that the party should have announced candidates before the first of the primaries in New Hampshire on March 13. But the President made it clear to Knowland that he was not going to be pushed.

After Christmas, Eisenhower finally gave in to his physicians' advice about getting away from the depressing weather in Gettysburg and went to Key West, Florida, for a stay in the sun. While he was away, I made a change in the White House office to give the President a small private room where he could rest before lunch and at other times when he wanted to get out of sight, as the doctors had advised. Bernard Shanley, who had temporarily succeeded Tom Stephens as appointments secretary, Goodpaster and I figured out a plan for shortening the appointments secretary's office so that the room could be added between it and the President's large oval office, a retreat big enough for a cot and a lounging chair. When Eisenhower saw it, he awarded us a verbal citation, saying that it was just the kind of a sanctuary that he needed and had not been able to find.

At Key West, the President met informally with the White House reporters for the first time since his illness. He told them that he was as ready to go back to work "as a person could be after the physical experience I have been through." Merriman Smith asked him if questions about his political future might be in order. The President said he had not yet gotten around to talking to his most trusted advisers. Did that mean he had not yet made up his mind?

"It means that as of this moment I have not made up my mind to make any announcement as of this moment," the President said.

He made it plain that he was not being coy; it was a question that could not be answered in a brief, offhand conversation. As soon as his mind was made up, he would let the reporters know.

Meanwhile, back in the White House, Dulles was telling the Cabinet that in consideration of the sacrifice that Eisenhower would be making if he was willing to run for office again, every Cabinet officer ought to assure the President of his readiness to stay in his job as long as he was wanted. This commitment covered a good deal more ground than some Cabinet members had in mind. When Eisenhower returned from Florida he remarked to the Cabinet that he had heard some of them talking about their desire to go home: "If I find myself here after next January," he said, "you will have to stay here, too."

The President did not get down to a brass-tacks discussion with his close associates and advisers about whether or not he should run again until the memorable night of January 13, 1956, when he invited to the White House for an informal dinner a group that consisted of Dulles, Lodge, Brownell, Hall, Persons, Humphrey, Summerfield, Hagerty, Stephens, Howard Pyle, Milton Eisenhower and myself. The dinner had originally been scheduled for the previous Tuesday, the tenth, but the date had been changed and kept under cover after some newspaper reporters heard of the meeting and asked questions about it. The President, not being superstitious, had no hesitation in switching the dinner to Friday the thirteenth. There were also thirteen men in the group, including the President.

After a pleasant dinner, with Mrs. Eisenhower joining us at the table, we went upstairs to the President's study on the second floor, where the conviviality stopped and the meeting became all at once a serious business. Usually when the President had guests in for the evening, he encouraged casual and free conversation with no set agenda. This time there was not only an agenda but a ritual that Eisenhower had carefully planned. He told us that he wanted to hear from each one of us in turn, only one man speaking at a time, our arguments for or against his running again for President. We were to speak freely and off the record, with no holds barred.

I don't imagine that the President expected to get a cross fire of pro-and-con arguments from a group like that one; every one of us, except Hall and Milton Eisenhower, were members of his Cabinet or his staff. Hall, the Republican national chairman, would be the last person in the room to discourage the President from seeking re-election. If Eisenhower was looking for cogent reasons for leaving his office, he would have hardly sought them from his own appointees, who were working with him in the government and who believed in him and what he was trying to do. I believe Eisenhower wanted to check his own thinking with that of his associates, especially to see if anyone had any solution other than his running again. But I am sure that he did not expect anyone would come up with one.

One after another, each of us had his say. Dulles spoke of the deterioration that would come to international relations without Eisenhower's wholesome influence and of the danger of a nuclear war. Several of us said that the President had given the United States a new sense of direction. Summerfield, a member of the Republican Old Guard and a convert to some extent to Eisenhower's political philosophy, said that the President had given the party a new identity that appealed to an increasing number of hitherto independent voters and that his presence as a candidate again would do much to solidify this new strength. Lodge talked about the country's economic prosperity and the unity it had brought to the American people.

When everybody except Milton Eisenhower had finished, the President asked his brother to sum up both the affirmative and negative sides of the question. This left us with no clear picture of exactly where Milton himself stood on the matter but it did enable us for the first time all evening to hear a few dissenting statements. The negative side, as Milton presented it, was not too convincing. In fact, one of the negative points sounded like the most convincing reason for Eisenhower running again. Arguing that even in retirement his brother could continue in an advisory capacity to work for world peace, Milton was forced to concede that with a Democrat in the White House such advice from Eisenhower might not be welcome.

The President listened intently to what each man had to say. When the discussion ended, he remarked lightly that nobody except Milton seemed to be on his side. My own impression of the evening was that everybody there, including Milton, sincerely felt that the President would not be so happy nor make so rapid a return to good health without the incentive and the satisfaction that public responsibilities gave him. When we went home, the President had given us no indication that he had yet made up his mind. He was still waiting for the doctors' report.

A few days later a telegram came to the White House from Harry E. Jackson, Deputy Secretary of State in New Hampshire, informing the President that petitions had been filed to place his name on the presidential primary ballot and that he had ten days to request its withdrawal if he wished to do so. Hagerty and I prepared a draft of a reply in which the President allowed his name to be entered in the primary but with the reservation that his candidacy was still undecided. The President looked it over and reached for his pen. By the time he had finished revising the message most of it was in his own handwriting. He wanted to make it clear to the voters of New Hampshire that he was still in doubt about whether his health would permit him to undertake another term. He thanked Jackson for his courteous telegram, interposed no objections but wrote that lack of objection could not be construed as indicating a final decision in favor of seeking re-election. "I hope that all who vote in your Republican primaries will carefully weigh all the possibilities and personalities that may be involved." He was explicit in emphasizing that the "accident of his illness" must not stand in the way of the free choice of every voter.

In that month of January, after his refreshing visit to Key West, Eisenhower returned to the White House and resumed again for the first time since his illness his regular weekly working routine—the meetings with the legislative leaders, the Cabinet, the National Security Council and the weekly press conference. At all these meetings, the question of his running again came up in the discussions. It was, of course, the big question of the hour in Washington. Eisenhower told the Congressmen with a smile on January 10 that he had received a letter from a well-wisher who said, "If you decide you can't run again, you ought to resign now." "Fine advice!" Eisenhower said. At his first full-scale press conference since the previous August, he was asked to comment on a statement by Senator Knowland, who said that an announcement from the President could be expected by the middle of February. Eisenhower said he had found it necessary to isolate himself from pressures in order to reach a logical decision.

The following week when the reporters asked him again about his decision, Eisenhower said: "The problem is what will be the effect on the presidency, not on me. . . . You can lay out all the factors of energy, the intensity with which you can attack your problems, the zip and the zest that you can take into conferences when you have to get something done for the good of the United States. Now this morning maybe I feel very zestful, but I do know I have had an attack."

At the Cabinet meeting of February 13, Eisenhower complained that he was finding himself in a position that he had hoped would never occur; people seemed to think he was the only man who could do the job as President. He recalled that he had wanted to put into his first inaugural address his intention of remaining in office for only one term. He had been dissuaded, he said, and now he regretted that he had allowed himself to be talked out of making that statement. His administration already had a good record of achievement to stand on, the President added, implying that he had done his share of work. One of the arguments being used in the press to urge him to run again was that a President loses his effectiveness when he has announced his intention of retiring. Eisenhower pointed out to the Cabinet that if he was re-elected he would be in that same situation during his entire second term because the Constitution prevented him from accepting a third term.

The next day, February 14, General Snyder and I invited to lunch the President's doctors, who had completed their all-important tests and examinations and would make their findings public at a press conference that afternoon. In the group along with Dr. Paul Dudley White and Colonel Byron E. Pollock from Fitzsimons General Hospital, who had made the first cardiograph tests on the morning of the heart attack, were Colonel Thomas W. Mattingly and General Leonard Heaton from Walter Reed Hospital, General Snyder's assistant, Major Walter Tkach, and Jim Hagerty. The doctors told Hagerty and me that the findings were good. There was no sign of heart enlargement. Dr. White told the reporters later that there was nothing to indicate that Eisenhower could not carry on "his present active life satisfactorily" for five or ten more years. But the choice of whether he would run for office again, Dr. White added, "is his, not ours."

A reporter asked Dr. White if he would vote for Eisenhower if the President decided to run again and the doctor said he would.

The next day Eisenhower went to George Humphrey's plantation in Georgia for ten days of quail hunting and golf. The President deliberately extended himself in the fields and on the golf links, for, as he quietly told Humphrey and Hagerty, he was making a final test of his physical strength. Evidently he was well satisfied ·with himself because as soon as he returned to Washington he began to write out a statement announcing his candidacy. When he was finished with the statement, he called me into his office and said, as he invariably did when he was making known an important personal decision, "Now you go over this with Jim."

Hagerty arranged appropriately for the President to make his decision known on February 29, which like the announcement of a presidential candidate comes only once in four years. Eisenhower would give out his statement that morning at his regular Wednesday press conference and would repeat it for television and radio audiences that night. I had favored making the first announcement before all the people of the nation on the air. But Hagerty disagreed, feeling that the President was really obligated to give the first break to the White House newspaper reporters.

Only a few people outside of Hagerty, Persons, Nixon, Hall and myself, and Milton Eisenhower, who had been invited by his brother to come to the television and radio broadcast, knew for sure what the President was going to say when he went to the press conference. He began to tantalize the reporters by talking about other things— a plea for support of the current Red Cross fund drive, the visit to Washington of President Giovanni Gronchi of Italy, the new farm bill and his opposition to rigid price supports, his approval of the Upper Colorado River development. Then the President said that he thought his next announcement would be of interest because he had been asked so many questions about it.

"I have promised this body," he said, "that when I reached a decision as to my own attitude toward my own personal future, I would let you know. Now I have reached a decision."

While the reporters listened on tenterhooks, without a noise or a movement in the room except the sound of the President's voice, he went on to say that in view of the "many factors and considerations involved"—his status as a recuperating heart attack victim—he was not certain that his party and the American people would want him as a candidate.

"But I will say this," he concluded. "I am asking for time on television and radio. I am going to the American people and tell them the full facts and my answer within the limits I have so sketchily observed; but which I will explain in detail tonight so as to get the story out in one continuous narrative—my answer will be positive, that is, affirmative." There was a hurried scramble for the telephones.

That night, speaking on television and radio, he reminded the Republicans and his public following that as a recovered heart patient he would be a candidate confined to limited campaign duty and a President who would be obliged to eliminate many of the ceremonial and social duties of the office.

"But let me make one thing clear," he said. "As of this moment there is not the slightest doubt that I can now perform as well as I ever have all of the important duties of the presidency." He also mentioned his real reason for deciding to run for re-election: his work that he had set out to do four years earlier had still not reached the completion that he hoped it would reach within one term of office.

The very first question that the President was asked at his press conference after he announced his candidacy was, "Would you again want Vice President Nixon as your running mate?"

All of that winter, before and after Eisenhower's announcement, there was speculation about whether he wanted to have Nixon as the vice-presidential candidate in the coming campaign. Without meaning to do so, the President himself added to the impression that he was doubtful about Nixon. When he was asked about Nixon at his press conferences in January and February, at first he was surprised by the question and hesitated in answering it. He had given no thought to replacing Nixon with somebody else but at that time he was not sure whether Nixon himself wanted to continue as Vice President, or whether another term in that office would be in the best interest of the young man's political future. Eisenhower did not want to come out with a strong statement in favor of keeping Nixon as his Vice President until he knew that Nixon had made up his mind. He said that Nixon was undecided and that he had advised the Vice President "to chart his own course." That sounded to the newspaper reporters and to Nixon, too, as if Eisenhower was the one who was undecided.

That January after Eisenhower returned from Key West he called Nixon to the White House and talked to the Vice President at length about his political future. The President told me at the time what he said to Nixon. He knew that Nixon had presidential ambitions and he had been thinking that Nixon's career might be strengthened if he was appointed to an important Cabinet post, Secretary of Defense, for example, instead of continuing on as Vice President for another term. The President explained to Nixon that history had shown the vice presidency to be somewhat of a political dead end; no Vice President in this century had gone on to the presidency except through accidental succession by the President's death. Moreover, Eisenhower pointed out, all of Nixon's experience in public service had been political. He had never held a difficult and exacting executive position, like that of the President, and taking a Cabinet position would give him a thorough grounding in executive work.

Eisenhower's proposal only caused a rift of misunderstanding between him and Nixon. The Vice President listened quietly and went away, saying that he would think about what Eisenhower had said, but he felt that the President was only trying to ease him tactfully out of the second place on the 1956 ticket. There had been many rumors in Washington, entirely without foundation, that Eisenhower wanted a vice-presidential running mate more acceptable to the liberal independent and Democratic voters. When the President seemed to answer the press conference questions about Nixon with an evasive hesitancy, Nixon's suspicions grew stronger. The persistent reporters, trying to build up stories of a falling out between the two men, did not help matters when they asked Eisenhower what he thought of Nixon referring to Chief Justice Warren as a Republican Chief Justice. Knowing Eisenhower's dislike of extreme partisanship, they were able to predict that the President would give them exactly the answer they were seeking: once a man becomes a Justice of the Supreme Court, he is an American citizen and nothing else, the President replied. So the fabric of the Nixon derogatory began to be loosely woven.

Hearing nothing from Nixon personally, the President assumed that he was still in the process of deciding whether he would prefer to accept a Cabinet appointment. The disappointed Nixon had no interest in a Cabinet position. If he could not remain as Vice President, he told friends at the time, he would give up politics and go into private law practice. Eisenhower said nice things about him during the repeated wrangles about the ticket at his weekly press conferences. "If anyone ever has the effrontery to come in and urge me to dump somebody that I respect as I do Vice President Nixon, there will be more commotion around my office than you have noticed yet." But the Vice President still had the feeling that he was not wanted.

As the controversy grew stronger in the political columns, I was marked by some commentators as a prominent figure in the "Dump Nixon" movement because I had been associated closely with the Citizens-for-Eisenhower and other liberal Republican groups that were labeled as unsympathetic to the Vice President. I was never opposed to Nixon; like most of the rest of us on the White House staff and in the Cabinet, I assumed all along that the situation would eventually straighten itself out and that Nixon would again be the vice-presidential candidate. There seemed to be no reason to change the winning combination of 1952. Whatever I did or said, publicly or privately, was strictly in support of the President's position as I understood it.

In the New Hampshire primary in March, Nixon was given a heavy write-in vote. Eisenhower was asked to comment on this by the reporters. The President spoke out as though he were fed up with the curiosity about the state of affairs between himself and Nixon and wanted to finish the subject for all time:

"Apparently there are a lot of people in New Hampshire who agree with what I have told you about Dick Nixon. . . . I am going to say one more thing about it and then, as far as I am concerned, I will never answer another question on this subject until after August. Anyone who attempts to drive a wedge between Dick Nixon and me has just as much chance as if he tried to drive it between my brother and me. I am very happy that Dick Nixon is my friend. I am very happy to have him as an associate in government. I would be very happy to be on any political ticket in which I was a candidate with him. Now if those words aren't plain, then it is merely because people can't understand the plain unvarnished truth."

"Before the door is closed on the Nixon case," a reporter said, "you said that you would ask him to chart his own course. Has he done that?"

"You spoke about five minutes too late," the President snapped. "I will say this, however, he knew what I was going to say this morning."

After that more than a month went by with no new developments and no sounds from Nixon. The President would have much preferred to let the matter rest until the Republican national convention in San Francisco in August. He felt that it was improper for a presidential candidate who had not yet been nominated, like himself, to name his vice-presidential choice before the convention opened. It was traditional that the vice-presidential nominee should not be selected until after the presidential choice had been made. Eisenhower had been satisfied with the procedure he had suggested in 1952 for picking the vice-presidential candidate. As time went on he saw no need of a large meeting of party leaders to make a decision that he would have made anyway, for Nixon was an inevitable choice. He had served as the administration's spokesman and representative during the 1954 Congressional and state election campaigns and he was a favorite of Republican leaders across the country. But as logical and proper as it seemed to Eisenhower to wait until the party assembled in San Francisco, his position appeared unrealistic and a little devious to Nixon's supporters. There was mounting pressure on the President to name Nixon without any further delay.

And so on April 27 when a Nixon question again came up that Eisenhower had previously parried, the President deliberately threw a cue that Nixon could hardly ignore. A reporter reminded the President that he had once said that he had asked the Vice President to chart his own course and to report back to him. Had that course been charted yet and had Nixon reported back to the President?

"Well, he hasn't reported back in the terms in which I used the expression that morning, no," the President said. Then he added, in reply to another question, "He hasn't given me any authority to quote him, any answer that I would consider final and definite."

That tossed the ball into Nixon's hands, where it got some quick handling. He called the White House that same morning and arranged to see the President that afternoon. He assured Eisenhower that he would be honored to continue as his Vice President and that he had waited this long to make sure that the President wanted him. Now he would be glad to see that any doubts about his availability were removed. Eisenhower said that there should be no longer any doubts about his willingness to have Nixon as a running mate. The President called in Jim Hagerty, told him that Nixon had a statement to make and suggested that Hagerty arrange a press conference in the White House for the Vice President then and there and settle the matter finally and conclusively.

As Nixon was telling the hastily assembled reporters that he would be honored to accept the vice-presidential nomination if it were offered to him, Hagerty broke in and added, "The President has asked me to tell you gentlemen that he was delighted to hear of the Vice President's decision."

It was one of those times when the President was pressured out of a previously prepared position by political clamor and harassment. Nixon's announcement did seem to clear the air in the White House and among the Republicans in Congress. At the Cabinet meeting two days later Dulles expressed to the President and Vice President the gratification of the Cabinet that the "team" would be once again "Ike and Dick." This statement was greeted by a round of applause. Despite the farm bill, which was bothering everybody on Capitol Hill, the Republican leaders from Congress seemed more relaxed and congenial. The President was moved to remark that the unreality of a Taft wing or an Eisenhower wing of the party was beginning to seem self-evident.

We began to make plans for the convention and the campaign. I asked the President to let me make Howard Pyle the liaison man between the White House and the National Committee on the preparation of the 1956 platform. As early as March, Pyle was asking the Cabinet members to submit their recommendations for the platform. Lodge, who had been instrumental in getting forward-looking and timely positions into past convention platforms, offered to help again, this time without title. Lodge saw little point in attacking Democratic personalities. Like the President, he urged the Republicans to concentrate on their own recent accomplishments and constructive programs.

Instead of waiting until September, Adlai Stevenson, who was to be the Democratic candidate again, opened up his campaign fire in the spring, at first directing most of it against Eisenhower himself. A reporter asked the President what he thought of the Democrats making him their principal target instead of aiming at the Cabinet. "Well, I think it is perfectly correct," Eisenhower said. "I am the head of the administration and I have been shot at before." A few weeks later the same reporter told the President that there had been a change in the Democrat strategy; from now on Eisenhower was to be pictured as an amiable figurehead in the clutches of the heartless men around him. "Sometimes I'd like to think of myself that way," the President said laughing. "But if you go back to the early days of the 1930's," he added, "I doubt if those who served on my staff would give you that kind of picture."

At a meeting with Leonard Hall, the national chairman, myself and a few others from the White House staff, Eisenhower reminded us that he had agreed to be a candidate only under the condition that his participation in the campaign would be limited. He said he would consider four or five formal campaign speeches, but no more. The Cabinet members, with a few gentle suggestions from Eisenhower, agreed to shoulder a large share of the campaign speaking load. In May, there was another medical examination, which showed that the President was responding favorably to his increased work schedule. As time went on, he became less and less conscious of his physical limitation and more confident of his capability to take on added activities.

That spring I had one of the most embarrassing experiences of my political career. Leonard Hall and Governor Thomas E. Dewey, like most of the rest of the Republicans, were anxious to do something to defeat Senator Wayne Morse, the ex-Republican turned Democrat who was coming up for re-election in the state of Oregon the following fall. On his own initiative, Dewey arranged to have a poll of opinion taken in Oregon by a reliable team of experts. Their figures showed conclusively that Morse could be beaten by Douglas McKay, the former Republican Governor of Oregon who was then Eisenhower's Secretary of the Interior. The poll did not predict a monumental victory for McKay but it showed that he could defeat Morse by a comfortable margin.

Knowing that McKay and I were good friends—I had joined in

recommending him to Eisenhower for the Interior post—Hall asked me to help persuade him to leave the Cabinet and return to Oregon to run against Morse. It was a big step to ask McKay to take. He was well established in the Cabinet, an able administrator who had fallen into nothing worse than the Al Serena controversy, a dispute over a patent given to a mining company that was alleged to have made an illegitimate profit from exploiting National Forest timber. McKay said later that he did not even remember signing the contract, but there were many such cases and he could not be expected to remember the details about all of them. In comparison with some of his predecessors, his service might have lacked sparkle, but it is difficult for a conservative to sparkle in these times and McKay was probably more conservative than anyone else in the considerably conservative Eisenhower Cabinet. I remember one Cabinet discussion of the farm problem in which McKay took a position even to the right of that taken by Benson, insisting that the agricultural muddle was proof that any kind of a planned economy does not work and that the country needed to be completely freed from all government meddling. He sounded like a voice crying in the wilderness.

Brownell, Hall, Summerfield and I had breakfast with McKay and put the facts and figures before him. Morse had no terrors for him but he told me that I would have to win the approval of his wife. I talked at length with Mrs. McKay, who was opposed, quite understandably, to her husband voluntarily giving up a Cabinet position to get into a hard fight for a seat in the Senate against such a rough rival as Morse. But Mabel McKay had a fine sense of public duty and reluctantly gave her consent.

McKay laid down one firm condition: he would not go into the Senatorial contest in Oregon if he was opposed by other Republicans in the primary. He had no desire to sacrifice his Cabinet post and take on Morse if Republican support in the state was to be divided with an intraparty primary struggle. When I went to Eisenhower to ask him to release McKay from the Cabinet, the President also had to be assured that there would be no primary contest. As the titular leader of the party, Eisenhower refused to take sides in any Republican state primary. He could not accept McKay's resignation from the Cabinet and send him into the fight in Oregon with a presidential blessing if other Republicans were also seeking the Senatorial nomination.

We were told that nobody would oppose McKay in the primary but I sent a special emissary from New York to the Pacific Northwest to make a careful double-check on that possibility. As I was preparing the President's acceptance of McKay's resignation, my agent telephoned me from Oregon to tell me that if McKay threw his hat into the ring the other aspirants would withdraw and he would have no opposition. But somewhere along the line, as often happens in political situations, somebody had slipped up in his research. At the very moment that McKay's resignation and his candidacy in the Senatorial campaign were being announced on the news tickers, McKay himself called me from Oregon to ask what had happened to our understanding. There was another Republican candidate in the primary and he stoutly refused as a matter of principle to give way to McKay, no matter how much the Republican National Committee or anybody else pleaded with him to do so. It was too late to recall McKay's resignation or the letter that the President had written him. Both the President and McKay were greatly embarrassed, but I was even more embarrassed than either of them.

Subsequently, Eisenhower had to withdraw his endorsement of McKay and explain apologetically to the other Republican candidate that he had been misinformed, as he had. McKay went on to win the primary but despite the prediction of Dewey's pollsters he was beaten in the election by Morse. I shuddered to think of what must have been going through Mrs. McKay's mind on that election night. Both she and her husband took their disappointment like good soldiers, but I never got over the feeling that I had been partly responsible for it. Afterward, until his death a few years later, McKay returned to the service of the administration as Chairman of the International Joint Commission that worked with Canada on the tough and knotty problem of developing the upper Columbia River. It was McKay's work that later helped make possible the signing of a treaty with Canada on this development, one of Eisenhower's last acts as President. As his successor in the Interior post, the President appointed Fred A. Seaton, the Nebraskan who had worked closely with me in the 1952 campaign.

Another task of political intercession that Hall handed to me turned out more fortunately. Hall decided that John Sherman Cooper, our Ambassador to India, was urgently needed as a candidate to run again for the Senate in Kentucky as he had done successfully in 1952. The national chairman felt that only the President himself could persuade Cooper to give up his diplomatic post and return to the warfare of a state campaign. When there was political persuading of that kind to be done in the White House I was usually the one who had to do it. Eisenhower never thought it appropriate for him to try to persuade anybody to run for political office.

When I talked with the President about it, he said he thought it a good idea for me to go to work on Cooper but reminded me again that the White House could not get into it if there was to be a primary contest. In this case nothing like that developed. Unlike McKay, Cooper was a hard and skeptical man to convince. Finally, I brought him into the President's office. Although Eisenhower avoided asking Cooper directly to run for the Senate, he was able to talk eloquently about the opportunity for service that was available in the Senate, and Cooper capitulated. In the Kentucky election that November he defeated the former Democratic Governor, Lawrence W. Wetherby, while the other Republican Senatorial candidate, Thruston Morton, was besting Senator Earle C. Clements. These were two of the four seats that the Republicans were able to take from the Democrats in the Senate that year.

In June, when Eisenhower went through his ileitis operation, there was speculation that the President might change his mind about his decision to run for re-election. But when Nixon went with me to visit the President at Walter Reed Hospital a few days after the operation it was obvious to us that such a thought had never entered Eisenhower's mind. He went over plans for the convention with us briskly, warning us that he wanted no long speeches. From the hospital he went again to Gettysburg and once more I followed him and established a temporary office there. We stayed there until it was time for him to make a trip he had planned to Panama on July 21, that he was determined not to put off any longer. On the day that we moved back to Washington, just before we went to Central America, Harold Stassen came to the White House to see the President and I learned that the question of whether Nixon was the right vice-presidential candidate was about to return to plague us again.

Before he went in to see Eisenhower, Stassen stopped at my office and told me what he was going to say to the President. Stassen had decided that Eisenhower would lose his independent and Democratic supporters in great numbers if Nixon was on the ticket with him again. Another vice-presidential candidate must replace Nixon, Stassen had decided, and I could see that Stassen had no intention of being talked out of a plan that he had already adopted—he was going to get the convention to name Governor Christian Herter of Massachusetts as the vice-presidential nominee.

Stassen did not come to the White House that day to ask Eisenhower or me what we thought of his plan. He was only telling us what he was going to do, and there was only one thing under the circumstances that I could say to him. I told him as strongly as I knew how that he must not involve the President in any way in his proposal.

Stassen's meeting with the President was brief and to the point. About to leave on his trip to Panama, the President had many other things on his mind that day and he was pressed for time. I did not sit in on the conversation but Eisenhower told me later that he had listened rather impatiently and had said little or nothing while Stassen told him of his plan to support Herter. As he had done with me a few minutes earlier, Stassen asked the President for no comment, no approval nor any advice. He explained that he was merely letting the President know what he was intending to do as a matter of courtesy.

Stassen was well aware that the President could not express publicly a disapproval of the plan to replace Nixon with Herter. Eisenhower had declared too often his firm belief that the vice-presidential nominee should be selected by a free choice of the convention with no interference from the White House. So he could not very well interfere now with Stassen's project.

I knew, and Eisenhower undoubtedly knew, too, that his reticence in objecting to Stassen's "Dump Nixon" campaign would only be interpreted as a consent to the idea. Stassen had the President in an uncomfortable spot. I went to Persons and asked him to let Nixon know as soon as possible what was going on.

I accompanied the President to Panama, where his physical stamina was again put to a severe test. The first day there, after fighting his way from the United States Embassy residence to the Presidencia through the wild and happy crowds that jammed the narrow streets, he reached the Panamanian presidential residence limp and wringing wet. But after a few minutes rest, he went on with the ceremonies. The next day he sat through several hours of speeches in Spanish and Portuguese at the Simón Bolívar Salon, somewhat the worse for wear, but demonstrating that he could carry a heavy load. When we came back to Washington, the Stassen-Herter story was in the newspapers.

We learned later that, after seeing the President, Stassen had tried with a conspicuous lack of success to make a direct appeal to Nixon to get off the ticket. Then Stassen had held a press conference, announcing his drive for Herter. Leonard Hall, the chairman of the Republican Committee, moved in fast and squelched the fire before there was much more than smoke, but it probably would have gone out anyway. Hall came to me and asked me what I would think of inviting Herter to make the nominating speech for Nixon at the convention. I told Hall that there would be no objections around our shop, though it was up to him to see if Herter would do it.

Before Herter gave Hall an answer, he called me and discussed the situation with me. Perplexed by Stassen's statement that he had talked with the President and knowing nothing firsthand of how Eisenhower felt about the choice of a vice-presidential nominee, the Governor of Massachusetts was plainly embarrassed by Stassen's project and wanted to know what the President thought of it. Herter would have appreciated the honor of the vice-presidential nomination but he would not accept it without Eisenhower's approval and he did not want to become involved in a factional fight within the Republican party. Besides, Herter was careful to explain that he thought well of Nixon and in no sense felt personally unhappy about the Nixon choice. Hall had told him that Eisenhower was happy with Nixon and that Nixon was the President's choice. (Actually, Eisenhower was happy enough with Nixon but the choice of Nixon in 1956 had really been made long ago by Hall and the Republican National Committee.) Before agreeing to make the nominating speech for Nixon, Herter wanted to get some confirmation of what Hall had told him from somebody in the White House.

Knowing Herter as I did, I knew that the work that interested him most was in foreign affairs. He had been in the State Department during World War I and had lectured on international relations at Harvard. It so happened that I had already spoken with Eisenhower and Dulles about the possibility of his coming into the State Department. So I had no hesitation in telling him when he called me about the vice-presidential nomination that, in making his future plans, he could take into account the fact that he would be given favorable consideration for a position of responsibility in the State Department. I also told him that I had discussed with Eisenhower the invitation from Hall for him to make the Nixon nomination speech and that Eisenhower had no objection to his making the speech if he wanted to do it. Finally, Herter called me back and told me that he had decided to make the speech for Nixon. That left Stassen's "Dump Nixon" campaign in the land of lost causes.

Never one to give up easily, Stassen continued to carry on his Herter-for-Vice-President movement until the opening of the convention. It did not seem appropriate for Stassen, a principal member of Eisenhower's staff, to be campaigning against Eisenhower's Vice President. It became my duty to suggest to him that it might be well for him to take a leave of absence from his position in the government until after the convention, to which he readily agreed.

If Stassen had not gone to San Francisco harping on his "Open Convention" theme, and if Terry Carpenter of Nebraska had not nominated Joe Smith for the vice presidency in symbolic support of Stassen, the Republican convocation of 1956 would have been a perfunctory and placid affair. Stassen sent a lengthy statement to each delegate at the convention, promising a vigorous effort to get Herter the vice-presidential nomination. He sent me a letter, enclosing a press statement, expressing the hope that there would be an opportunity to talk with me. There was. The only problem that Stassen brought to the convention, really, was the question of how he would be able to close up his Herter project with the least embarrassment to himself and all concerned. He told me he would be willing to do anything that the President asked him to do. I told him that I was sure the President would never ask him to do anything, but that if he was ready to throw in the sponge I was sure such a course of action would be highly acceptable to the President.

Our advance man who went from the White House to San Francisco to make arrangements for the President's visit to the convention

was the resourceful Tom Stephens. A long letter that Stephens wrote
to me from the convention scene, outlining some of the things he
had attended to, gives a graphic picture of the kind of details that a
President's staff worries over when a President goes away from the
White House. It also shows the concern for the President's health that
his staff and the party leaders felt that year. Here are some excerpts
from the Stephens letter:

As to the President's arrival in San Francisco, to avoid a cavalcade
where he has to stand up and wave, the later he arrives in this city, the
better. If the President arrived some time between 8:30 and 9:30 at
night I believe it would be most helpful to him. While it is not cold here
in the evening, it does get cool and if you will look at the weather
reports for the last couple of years, which I am enclosing, you will
find that it has never gone below 50° and seldom over 60° degrees
between 8:30 and 9:30 around the 22nd, 23rd, or 24th of August.

The Mayor's Committee, and Jim Murphy is chairman of the group
at the moment, is planning an "Informal Ball in Celebration of the
Centennial of the Republican Party" at the Civic Auditorium on the
night of "Len Day" [Leonard Hall Day], the 23rd. Jim came to see
me today and advised me that there would be between 5,000 and 6,000
people at this affair. He wanted to know if the President would stop
off on his way from the airport to the St. Francis Hotel at the Civic
Auditorium, which is on the way.

They plan to have a state flag for every state represented at this affair,
beside which would be the Chairman for the delegation for each represented state. If the President attended, his car would drive in the back
way and he would walk some 50 feet to the platform and say a few
words which might include a presentation of these flags to the State
Chairmen who would take them home to their State headquarters.

I pointed out two things to Jim. 1) That he should not give the impression under any circumstances at this moment that the President was
going to this affair. 2) That the President would have a long trip from
Washington, covering some eight hours, and if he was as tired as I was
when I arrived here, he would want to go to his hotel room and be
left alone.

I also pointed out that his appearance at this affair might make his
appearance at the Convention an anticlimax. I asked him to make sure
that no formal invitation to the event be extended to the President and
that I would see to it that those around the President knew of the affair
in the event that he might want to go.

No doubt Secret Service Agent Harold Nicholson has been in touch
with you in regard to the President's landing at the International Airport
rather than on government property at the Coast Guard station. I

might add here that I am asking Bill Draper's office [Bill Draper was the President's pilot] to bill the National Committee for the use of the President's plane as this is a political trip. This is in an agreement with Len Hall. If you have no objection, we are going to have the bill paid before the trip is made so it does not look like an afterthought, that we paid it after someone brought it up. The National Committee is paying the expenses of its staff members out here but not the expenses of their wives. It would seem such a policy should govern in connection with the wives of the White House staff.

The St. Francis Hotel people have been asking when it can be announced that the President is staying at the St. Francis Hotel. I did not know when it could be announced, I told them, but I was sure that when it was, such an announcement would come from the White House, not from the Arrangements Committee here or from the St. Francis Hotel.

Under the plans that have been discussed, the President would leave the St. Francis Hotel for the Cow Palace at 4:30 San Francisco time which would put him on the air around 8:00 in the East, which is prime television time. There is an organization known as the Sheriff's Posse of San Mateo County that will meet the President about a quarter of a mile from the Cow Palace and escort him to the convention. All of these men have been screened by the FBI. Len Hall is not encouraging the President's attendance at anything except the convention but believes the President should have all the facts about other events. There had been a suggestion made that an announcement be made at one of the sessions of the convention as to when the President would arrive, but Len vetoed this.

I am enclosing a floor plan of the sixth floor of the hotel and will have a copy of this plan in front of me here in case we should want to talk on the telephone about rooms.

My formal role at the convention was to arrange a presentation of the Cabinet members on a national television show. In the middle of the program, the President landed at the airport and all of the television facilities were turned to his plane, abruptly cutting off the Cabinet members from view of the watching audience.

Before the President held his press conference the next morning, I took Stassen in to talk with him. Stassen had prepared a statement "cheerfully and wholeheartedly" supporting Nixon and he asked for the privilege of discussing it personally with the President. As I expected, Eisenhower showed relief that Stassen had come to his inevitable conclusion. The President himself announced Stassen's capitulation at the news conference that followed.

Soon after I arrived in San Francisco, a few days before the President, Ann Whitman gave me over the telephone from the White House some "completely gratuitous advice" about the conduct of the convention that the President wanted passed on to Leonard Hall. Here is what I wrote down as Mrs. Whitman dictated to me:

No, repeat no, long and dreary speeches from anyone.
Every speech should have some intellectual content.
Change the pace. The same unchanging story gets as monotonous as Governor Frank Clement of Tennessee was as the keynoter at the Democratic Convention. Don't discard a suggestion because it has never been done before.
Get a genuine independent on your program. [This suggestion led to the enlistment of Emmet Hughes, the President's former speech writer, as a speaker at the convention.]
Don't forget to appeal to the independents and the Democrats.
Hold firm to the rules and get things done on time.
Guard against steam-rollering, no matter what the proposition is.
No long and dreary speeches.

Despite the seething activity at our headquarters in the St. Francis Hotel, I managed to get every speech examined with care in an attempt to avoid the length, dreariness and excessive partisanship that Eisenhower disliked. The staff at the National Committee's headquarters did likewise. There was one slip-up. In his keynote speech on the first day, amid cheers and applause, Arthur Langlie said that the Democrats "are now addicted to the principle that loyalty to a political party comes ahead of devotion to our beloved country."

The President turned to me in dismay and said, "Whoever let him say that?"

It seemed to us that the acclamation Eisenhower received at the convention did more good to his health than any medical treatment he had received since his operation in June. After he and Nixon were nominated, the President was given a reward, a few days of golf at Cypress Point on the Monterey Peninsula, one of his favorite courses.

The President needed a little relaxation before going back to what was facing him in Washington. When election time came that fall, Eisenhower was too deeply concerned with bigger things to pay much attention to votes and campaign speeches. The British and the French were bombing Egyptian airfields and landing their troops at the Suez Canal.

13 Showdown at Suez

Back on September 30, 1955, at the first tense and troubled business-as-usual Cabinet meeting a few days after the President's heart attack, Dulles gave a scheduled report on current world affairs. Because the thoughts of most of us that morning were in a hospital at Denver rather than on foreign problems perhaps we did not give enough serious attention to one of the things that Dulles mentioned. He said that for the first time the Russians were making a determined effort to move into the Middle East, where two-thirds of the world's known oil reserves were located.

Dulles went on to say that the Soviets could cause trouble in that part of the world by sending massive shipments of their obsolete weapons to the Arab nations, who were suspicious and uneasy about United States policy because of our friendship with Israel. The Secretary of State was sure that the Russians were trying to jeopardize any hope of a peaceful settlement between the Arabs and the Israeli. He said that he had complained to Molotov at the Geneva summit meeting about Soviet activities in the Middle East but Molotov had claimed that Russia's interest in the Arab republics was only limited to commercial trade transactions.

As soon as the doctors allowed us to bring serious government problems to Eisenhower, Dulles talked with the President in the hospital about the Middle East and his fears of a Soviet-supported arms build-up in the Arab states. These fears were borne out when Nasser, with the help of the Soviet Foreign Minister, Shepilov, arranged an exchange of Egyptian cotton for weapons from Russia's armament-producing satellite, Czechoslovakia. There were fresh outbursts of fighting between the Arabs and the Israeli along the Gaza border and both sides turned to the United States to match or better the Soviet-arranged arms shipment. On November 9, Dulles sent his assistant, Herbert Hoover, Jr., to Denver with a statement that the President announced that day, saying that the Americans would not contribute to an arms race. As Dulles explained the situation to a gathering of Congressional leaders from both parties on December 13, both Egypt and Israel had seen no need to build armed strength in 1950 when they made their peace agreement. "But now, since the Russians have intervened, they say they want to bargain from positions of strength," Dulles said. "They learned that expression from us."

The Tripartite Agreement of 1950 provided that the United States, Britain and France would co-operate in a joint action—either inside or outside of the United Nations—to use force if the borders specified in the armistice between Israel and the Arab nations that year were disturbed or threatened. With France weakened by the drain of the Indo-China war and its trouble in Algeria, the burden for keeping peace in the vital Middle East fell upon the British, whose economy, deeply imbedded in Arabian sands, was now in ominous straits.

The British were anxious for bold and direct action to keep Nasser in line and to protect the Suez Canal and Western Europe's supply of oil. But Dulles and Eisenhower preferred to work for a peaceful compromise. It was the reverse of the Indo-China situation, where Dulles had been unable to persuade the British to join the United States in direct military action to keep the Communists out of Vietnam. Now the shoe was on the other foot and it did not fit well. The British thought that the United States were exhibiting a fruitless, if not dangerous, lack of sure-footedness. They were afraid that Eisenhower himself did not grasp the gravity of their predicament.

Actually the President understood only too well what was at stake in the Middle East. He made it clear at a press conference when he was asked for his estimate of the situation: "Any outbreak of major hostilities in that region would be a catastrophe to the world. As you know, all of Western Europe has gone to oil instead of coal for its energy, and that oil comes from the Mideast. The region is of great —as a matter of fact, it is of extraordinary importance to all of the free world, so that just for material reasons alone we must regard every bit of unrest there as the most serious matter."

Anthony Eden came to Washington late in that January of 1956, on much the same kind of mission as the one that brought Dulles to London in April, 1954, when the Secretary was attempting to arrange a joint intervention in Indo-China. I had a long talk with Eden at a stag dinner on February 1 given by the British Ambassador, Sir Roger Makins. He was greatly concerned about the President's health and his recovery from the heart attack. I gave him assurances that Eisenhower was doing well. When I told him that in my opinion the President would run for re-election, Eden spoke as though he was both pleased and relieved. The British Prime Minister thought that his talks with Eisenhower and Dulles were going well and there was nothing in what he said to me that indicated the break between Britain and the United States which came only a few months later. In fact, Dulles remarked in a Cabinet meeting at that time that the trouble in the Middle East seemed to have brought Eden much closer to us because it made the Prime Minister more willing to stand up against the Russians. A few months earlier, Dulles said, Eden had been acting like an impartial mediator in disputes between the United States and the Soviets.

But Eden's visit to Washington did not resolve one serious difference between the American and British positions on the Middle East question; our firm opposition to colonialism made us sympathetic to the struggle which Egypt and the other Arab states were making to free themselves of the political and economic control that the British felt they had to maintain in the Middle East in their own self-interest.

The principal cause of the outburst in the Middle East that summer was Nasser's effort to finance Egypt's plan to construct the huge Aswan Dam with American and British funds. Eisenhower was in favor of helping Nasser to build the dam. The President and Dulles regarded such a grant-loan arrangement with Egypt as a sound Mutual Security project that would gain Arab favor for the Western powers and keep oil moving through placid water in Suez, the Persian Gulf and the eastern Mediterranean. But any attempt to give aid to the Arabs always met with opposition behind the scenes in Washington, where the members of Congress were acutely aware of the strong popular sentiment in this country for Israel. Had the members of Congress either underestimated or overlooked the strength of such feeling they would have been quickly reminded of it by the alert representatives of the many well-organized pro-Israel lobbies that were always effective and influential in the Capitol. Consideration for the great body of private opinion in the United States favoring Israel was a large factor in every government decision on the Middle East issues, especially in the crisis that arose later when the Israeli, deliberately rejecting our pleas against their use of force, moved into the Sinai Peninsula and gave the British and French their excuse for attacking the Egyptians at Suez.

When Dulles first discussed the proposed financing of the Aswan Dam at a meeting with the leaders of both parties in Congress, Lyndon Johnson questioned the need for large amounts of economic aid for Egypt. Dulles told the Democratic leader of the Senate that the grant-loan arrangement under consideration would make it unlikely that Egypt would change her affiliation with us for the next ten years. The Soviets were already trying to work out such a program with Egypt, Dulles said, and although we could not outbid the Russians on every project, they could make offers "on paper" to Nasser that could force us into huge expenditures. Eisenhower commented on the irony of the Russians', with a less developed and weaker economy, offering us competition in the very field where we were strongest. "This shows the advantage which a dictatorship possesses in being able to choose its own ground and then moving very fast," the President said.

Dulles went on to insist that, despite the arms deal with Czechoslovakia and other expressions of friendship between Nasser and the Russians, Egypt was far from becoming a tool of the Soviets but it could drift that way if we did nothing to prevent it. The Secretary of State was afraid that Israel, which had a superiority over the Egyptians in armed strength, might commit a provocative act that would drive Nasser farther into the sphere of Soviet influence. Sam Rayburn, wondering if Egypt was not already lost to the West and therefore too much of a credit risk, asked Dulles if there was not a feeling in Cairo that the United States had done much more for Israel than it had done for Egypt.

The Secretary of State told Rayburn that the Egyptians regard America as Israel's financial mainstay but that Nasser's government acknowledges that most of the support the Israelis are receiving from this country comes from private sources rather than from the United States government. Dulles said that only the day before Arab diplomats in Washington had asked him if we could not restrain our citizens from raising money for Israel. The Arabs admitted to Dulles, however, that the American government seemed much less unbalanced in favor of Israel than it had been a few years earlier.

Nasser balked when he saw the conditions that the United States attached to the Aswan Dam grant-loan proposal—no side deals between Egypt and the Soviets. He held up the negotiations for several months to think about the terms and during this interval he made a series of gestures to express a scornful independence from the influence of the West. He recognized Red China, built up with his Czech arms the Egyptian forces on the Israeli border, denounced the British and the French for their opposition to the nationalist movements in Cyprus and Algeria and tried to break up the Baghdad Pact which the British and the United States had put together for the collective security of the Middle East with four Arabian nations friendly to the West—Turkey, Iraq, Iran and Pakistan. Nasser tried the Western patience beyond its breaking point and, in the middle of July, when he finally got around to announcing that he would accept the United States proposal, he found himself facing a blank wall. By that time the tide of public opinion was running strong against Nasser and his tactics, and we wanted nothing more to do with his Aswan Dam. Britain followed suit and withdrew its offer of financial aid. Congress, under continual pressure from Israel's diplomatic and organization lobbies, was even more fed up than Eisenhower and Dulles with Nasser's behavior. It was extremely doubtful if the President could have obtained Congressional approval of the grants and loans to the Egyptians at that point had he asked for them. Anyway, the deal was off.

Nasser promptly retaliated with a course of action that would strike hardest at the heart of the nation that he wanted most to harm. On July 26, he seized the Suez Canal.

For the British, this was a bitter situation and to a large extent they could thank the prodding anticolonialism of the United States for getting them into it. Only a month before, on June 13, the British had withdrawn the last of their military forces from the Suez region under an agreement that the Americans had urged them to make.

Nasser had invited Shepilov, the Soviet Foreign Minister, to a celebration in Cairo marking that event. There was strong sentiment in
England for the use of military force to keep the canal out of Nasser's
hands but Dulles, hurrying to London for a consultation with the
British and the French officials, managed to apply the brakes and
temporarily stop such a move.

Dulles persuaded the British to postpone action until after a conference of twenty-two nations that used the Suez Canal, which he
arranged to be held in London on August 16. Actually Dulles invited
twenty-four governments to send representatives to the meeting but
two of them, Greece and, the most important one of all, Egypt,
declined to attend it. Dulles wanted the conference to work out a
proposal for the continued international use of the canal, which he
hoped the conference could get Nasser to agree to. In any case,
Eisenhower and Dulles were determined to reach some kind of a
peaceful solution of the Suez dispute in accordance with the principles
of the United Nations Charter. The President said in a Cabinet meeting the day after Nasser seized the canal that he considered the
waterway "an international public utility."

On a Sunday, August 12, four days before the start of the conference in London, Eisenhower called a bipartisan meeting of the
Congressional leaders at the White House for a full discussion of
the Suez crisis. The Democrats willingly interrupted their deliberations
at the Democratic national convention in Chicago in order to attend
it. Gathering in the Cabinet Room, talking among themselves about
party politics, which was the topic of the hour, the Senators and the
Representatives looked up as the meeting was called to order and
saw facing them a serious President and a grim Secretary of State.
That day Nasser had announced that he would not attend the conference in London. Mentioning this in his opening remarks, Eisenhower said that at the moment there was no unbounded hope for a
peaceful solution. He turned the meeting over to Dulles, who reviewed
the background of the Suez trouble, starting with the treaty of 1888,
still in effect, which Nasser had broken by seizing control of the
waterway from the Suez Canal Company. Dulles explained that two-
thirds of the oil that Western Europe depended upon for its heat
and industrial production passed through the canal by ship, the other
third transported overland to Mediterranean ports by pipeline that

could be easily destroyed by the Arabs. The British and the French under these circumstances could not allow Nasser to get a stranglehold on Suez, Dulles said.

The Secretary of State told the Congressmen that he had been forced to make his fast trip to London after the seizure of the canal because the British and the French were ready at that time to attack Egypt. It had taken considerable persuasion to get them to agree to hold a Suez Canal conference at all. Dulles said he had finally managed to hold the British and the French in check by warning them that an immediate use of force would turn world opinion and especially American opinion against them and that it would be regarded by the United States as a violation of their commitments to the United Nations. Dulles made it clear, however, that personally he shared the British and French feeling that Nasser was a dangerous threat to the West, and that his action was much more than a demonstration of nationalism. "I believe Nasser intends to unite the Arab world, and, if possible, the Moslem world, and then to use Mideast oil and the canal as weapons against the West," the Secretary said.

Sam Rayburn wanted to know how much provocation would be needed to make the British and the French take action against Egypt. Dulles stared through his glasses at Rayburn with surprise.

"They think there has been sufficient provocation already," the Secretary said. "They have only agreed to bide their time until the conference. They call Nasser a wild man brandishing an ax."

The Speaker asked if Nasser had said he would close the canal.

"Not yet," the President said, "but the British and the French don't trust him. That's the trouble."

Senator Russell asked how a fair solution could be reached at the London conference with Egypt absent. The Secretary said that India, Ceylon and Pakistan would be watching for any unfairness and would have considerable influence on the situation. Charlie Halleck asked if the United Nations could not restrain an aggressive move by the British and the French. The President said that in an emergency such as this one he did not think that the United Nations would be effective; he pointed out that the British and the French have veto power in the Security Council and if the matter was put before the General Assembly there would only be a long and inconclusive debate. When Senator Saltonstall expressed fears that the prestige of the United Nations might be endangered if it was by-passed completely in the steps taken to reach a settlement, Eisenhower assured him that the State Department would work in close conjunction with the United Nations. But there might be times in a fast-breaking crisis when we could not rely entirely on the slow United Nations machinery, Eisenhower said.

The President called upon Arthur Flemming to explain to the leaders of Congress the plans that were being made by Flemming's Office of Defense Mobilization to meet the oil shortage that would face the Western world if Nasser closed the canal. Flemming had formed an emergency Middle East Oil Committee, consisting of oil experts from the leading petroleum companies, to work with Interior Department officials in planning how world oil resources could be pooled during any emergency to fill as many needs as possible. They had worked out an over-all plan that had been approved by the Attorney General and the Federal Trade Commission at a late session the night before. It called for the United States government to set up what was in effect an oil cartel, a temporary monopoly control of all the oil in the world available to us, which could be rationed on an equitable basis.

The blueprint for this international oil pool had taken long hours of detailed study on questions of legal procedure, economics, engineering and transportation. The major oil companies had to agree, for example, to voluntary government control in the event of the emergency and had to be given immunity against federal antitrust action. Oil production in the United States and South America would have to be increased and alternative sea routes had to be mapped. Later, when the unrest in the Middle East continued to grow, the President was to order the construction of a fleet of large tankers, too big for the Suez Canal, to transport oil to the West around the Cape of Good Hope but these ships would not be completed in time to relieve any immediate fuel shortage. Flemming said that Britain and the Western European countries were then using 1.2 million of the 1.5 million barrels of oil that were passing through the Suez Canal daily. If the canal were closed, Flemming added, it might be possible to supply Western Europe with eight or nine hundred thousand barrels a day from the Gulf Coast and Caribbean ports. If both the canal and the pipelines across Asia Minor were cut off, a strict rationing program, with a 20 per cent reduction in oil consumption and stepped-up American oil production, might possibly save the situation.

Closing the meeting, Eisenhower tried to express some of his usual optimism by telling the Congressmen that he had been greatly encouraged by the stand taken in England by Hugh Gaitskell in opposing the use of military force against Nasser until all possible attempts to reach a peaceful settlement had been exhausted. "There are so many possibilities involved that I shudder to think of them," the President said. "The most important thing is that we must explore every peaceful means of getting to a settlement and the world must know that we are doing so." The Democrats thanked the President and, turning their thoughts from the explosive Middle East, hurried back to their convention in Chicago, where John F. Kennedy was defeated in a close bid for the vice-presidential nomination because he had agreed in the Senate with the Eisenhower-Benson position on farm price supports.

That week, while the Democrats were nominating Stevenson and Kefauver, Dulles was in London for the Suez Canal conference, where a committee under the chairmanship of Prime Minister Menzies of Australia produced a plan for international use of the canal that Nasser agreed to discuss. This prompted Eisenhower to issue a statement of gratitude to the committee, in which he made a reference to the canal as a waterway that had already been internationalized by treaty in 1888. Nasser took this to mean that the President was claiming that the canal was internationally owned and expressed regret that Eisenhower was laboring under such a delusion. Before he was corrected by Nasser, the President had already clarified his meaning at a press conference by emphasizing that he had used the term "internationalized" to describe the perpetual rights to the use of the canal given to many nations by the 1888 treaty. He said that he was well aware that the canal was owned by Egypt but that "Egypt cannot now nor in the future jeopardize those rights of other nations" guaranteed by the treaty.

Treaty or no treaty, Nasser flatly rejected the proposal from the London conference when Menzies presented it to him in Cairo. In the mood of anger and discouragement that followed the failure of the settlement effort, Eisenhower was accused unofficially in London and

Paris of letting election year considerations get into foreign policy making. When these charges were brought to Eisenhower's attention he rebuffed them sharply. In defense of his Suez policy he said that he was standing firmly for the respect of Egypt's sovereignty, for an efficient operation of the canal without political advantage to any nation and for an increasing share of the canal's profits to Egypt and nobody else. If the British or the French government was dissatisfied with his stand, they had not told Dulles or himself about it, he added.

In October, as his presidential re-election race turned into the home stretch, Eisenhower was too concerned with what was going on in Israel and in Britain and France to give domestic politics much more than an occasional hurried glance. Intelligence sources reported a mobilization of military forces in Israel far beyond what would be employed in border raids or commando operations. Obviously an invasion of Arab territory was being planned. The United States made an urgent appeal to Ben-Gurion to halt him from "forceful initiative" but our appeals to the Israelis carried little weight because we had recently turned down another request from them for arms, despite intercession in their behalf by the British and the French. Dulles called in the Israeli Ambassador in Washington, Abba Eban, and questioned him sharply but Eban told Dulles that his government in Tel Aviv was merely taking defensive measures against Egypt and Jordan, her old border foe to the east.

At the same time, big and exciting news from behind the Iron Curtain in Eastern Europe pushed the Middle East crisis off the front pages for a few days and gave Eisenhower even less time to think about his campaign for re-election. Communist factions in Poland and Hungary, under Wladyslaw Gomulka and Imre Nagy, two strongly nationalistic Red leaders who wanted to rid their countries of Muscovite domination, turned against Russia and in both countries there were violent clashes between the people and Soviet occupation troops. In Hungary the demonstrations grew into a widespread national revolution with anti-Communists taking command of the Hungarian Army and fighting a bloody and destructive battle against the Soviets and Hungarian Communists. The ruthless force used by Russia to put down the revolt in Hungary and to restore its puppet regime to power did more damage to the Communist cause throughout the world than any happening in recent years. Eisenhower could do little but watch the Hungarians suffer and offer them sympathy, relief and asylum. To no avail the President protested against the Soviet action to the United Nations and in a message to Bulganin, who told him coldly that this was a matter that could be settled by the Russian and Hungarian governments.

Then on Monday, October 29, Israel's armed forces moved into Egyptian territory on the Sinai Peninsula at the east side of the Suez Canal. It seemed obvious that the Israelis had been encouraged in this spectacular adventure by the British and the French. Under the terms of the Tripartite Declaration of 1950, the two Western European powers and the United States could use direct military force to intervene if Israel or Egypt broke their peace pact. The drive by the Israelis toward the canal gave the British and the French their excuse to invade Suez.

Sure enough, the morning after the Israelis made their move the British and the French governments sent an ultimatum to Tel Aviv and Cairo, calling on the Israelis and the Egyptians to withdraw ten miles from both sides of the canal and to stop "warlike" action. As Prime Minister Eden said in the House of Commons that Tuesday afternoon, "We have asked the Egyptian government to agree that Anglo-French forces should move temporarily into key positions." If the ultimatum was ignored, Eden added, British and French troops would go into Suez "in whatever strength may be necessary."

It had been hard for Eisenhower to believe that Ben-Gurion had synchronized his watch with those of Eden and Premier Mollet, but now the facts were before him. The President asked the British and the French to wait until the United Nations had time to take action and hastily drafted with Dulles a resolution urging all members of the UN to refrain from the use of force in the Middle East. The resolution was sent to Henry Cabot Lodge in New York, where Lodge presented it to the Security Council that afternoon. It was vetoed by the British and the French, and Lodge found himself, to his secret discomfort, supported by Russia. Now there was an open and sorry break between the United States and her two oldest and closest allies.

The next day, October 31, the President learned to his astonishment that British bombers from Cyprus had attacked the Egyptian airfields.

The news caught the President completely by surprise and the suddenness of it shocked him. He had received no previous warning from the British or the French and no advance information from our intelligence sources in Europe or in the Mediterranean.

Outside of his illnesses, that was the worst week that Eisenhower experienced in all of the years that I worked with him in the White House. It was the last week before the election and he was scheduled to make campaign trips to Texas, Oklahoma and Tennessee and to New England. The Soviets were about to crush the revolt in Hungary, and Poland was still in a state of tension. The Security Council of the United Nations was in session until late hours every night. The President was also being pressed by urgent domestic problems—drought in the farm states, a struggle for water among drought-ridden states which Eisenhower often called the toughest domestic problem we faced, besides dislocations and trouble spots in the economy, the worst of which was the threatened oil shortage which might paralyze the industry of most of Western Europe.

As if all this were not enough, Dulles was taken to Walter Reed Hospital that same week, severely stricken by a perforation in his intestine, and went through a long and difficult operation.

On the Monday of that week, the same day that he first heard of the Israeli military drive toward the Suez Canal, the President met in his office at eight o'clock in the morning with the ailing Dulles, Secretary of Defense Wilson, Admiral Radford, Allen Dulles, Herbert Hoover, Jr., and various staff members. There was a long discussion of the military moves that would have to be made in the Mediterranean; the President wanted no American intervention at Suez but our naval forces would be placed in a position to evacuate American citizens if that was necessary. Everybody at the meeting agreed that if Russia came openly to Nasser's assistance, a war was inevitable. The intelligence reports said that the Soviets were sending planes and equipment through Syria to Egypt but our military leaders had a low opinion of Egypt's capability to convert this assistance into an effective striking power. There was also a discussion of the oil stoppage, that now seemed more and more ominous.

At the same time, Eisenhower called off his campaign trip, explaining to the disappointed Republican leaders that the serious developments in the Middle East made it impossible for him to leave the White House. On Wednesday, when the news of the British air attack on Egypt came to the President, he quickly made arrangements for time on radio and television to explain why the United States was not going to back up the British and French aggression.

"The United States was not consulted in any way about any phase of these actions," the President said on the air. "Nor were we informed of them in advance. As it is the manifest right of any of these nations to take such decisions and actions, it is likewise our right, if our judgment so dictates, to dissent. We believe these actions to have been taken in errror. For we do not accept the use of force as a wise and proper instrument for the settlement of international disputes."

The next day Dulles, fighting the pain of his ulcer, made arrangements with Lodge to call a special emergency session of the United Nations General Assembly so that he could present a proposal for a cease-fire armistice in the Middle East. The debate before the Assembly on the Dulles plan dragged on all day on Thursday and into the night and did not reach a vote until the early hours of Friday morning, when it was approved, sixty-four to five, with only Britain, France, Israel, Australia and New Zealand voting against it. In the strain and confusion of the last days and nights of that hectic week, while Dulles and Lodge were on the side of Russia in the arguments on Suez in the General Assembly, they were at the same time bitterly opposing the Soviets in meetings of the Security Council, where Hungary was pleading for protection from an invasion by the Red Army. On Saturday, when Sir Anthony Eden rejected the United Nations cease-fire proposal and the Soviets vetoed Lodge's resolution against Russian aggression in Hungary, the weakened and discouraged Dulles turned himself in at Walter Reed Hospital and underwent two and a half hours of surgery.

The Sunday that began the following week was anything but a day of rest in the White House. The newspaper headlines that Eisenhower saw that morning told of a full-scale Soviet attack on Hungary, with thousands of dead bodies in the streets of Budapest, where Cardinal Mindszenty had been given refuge in the besieged American Embassy. The President sent off his message of protest to Bulganin. Having already drawn twenty million dollars from Mutual Security funds for food and medical supplies for the Hungarians, he asked me to start work on a plan that would bring five thousand Hungarian refugees immediately into the United States. A few weeks later, after complex negotiations with Austria, where the Hungarians were fleeing from the Russians in great numbers, and with our own immigration service and the Defense Department's air and sea transportation directors, we were able to offer asylum in the United States to 21,500 Hungarians. Then came the hardest part of that whole job, finding homes and work for the refugee families in this country. I found for this heavy responsibility an unusually gifted volunteer, Tracy S. Voorhees, who brought to the task along with the required tact and perseverance a valuable experience from service as a Defense Department food and offshore procurement administrator in Europe. Voorhees co-ordinated the efforts of the charitable and religious organizations that pitched in to make the resettlement program a remarkable success.

On that busy Sunday, word came to the White House from the Middle East that the British and French were loading troop transport ships at Cyprus for an invasion of Suez and early the next morning British paratroopers dropped on the north end of the canal. That Monday evening Bulganin sent Eden, Mollet and Ben-Gurion a warning that if they did not stop hostilities Russia would intervene with military force. At the same time, the Soviet Premier dispatched a message to Eisenhower proposing that Russia and the United States should form a military alliance to stop the British and French invasion of Egypt.

Consulting with Herbert Hoover, Jr., who was filling in for the hospitalized Dulles, the President immediately sent Bulganin a tough and indignant reply. Eisenhower called the suggested American-Soviet intervention "unthinkable" and dismissed the proposal as an attempt to divert world attention from Hungary, where, the President charged, the Russian Army "at this very moment is brutally repressing the human rights of the Hungarian people."

But the Russian threat against Britain and France brought fear and anxiety to both of those countries. As Dulles had warned Eden and Mollet, the armed attack on Suez turned opinion against the British and French governments, even in London and Paris. Eden's political opposition, the British Labour party, staged a jeering demonstration in Trafalgar Square demanding the Prime Minister's resignation. Hugh Gaitskell, the Labourite leader, called the aggression in the Middle East "an act of disastrous folly, whose tragic consequences we shall regret for years."

Winston Churchill backed Eden, however, and the government won a vote of confidence. But the British Prime Minister had no desire to push things too far. On Tuesday morning, as Eisenhower was voting at Gettysburg, French infantry landed on the east side of the Suez Canal without resistance. On the west side, at Port Said, the arriving British troops ran into heavy fire. In the afternoon, having landed their forces and made their point, Eden and Mollet agreed to the United Nations cease-fire proposal and that night Eisenhower was able to sit back and relax for the first time in almost two weeks as he watched the election returns at the Statler Hotel in Washington. Engrossed as he was in the developments in the Middle East and Hungary during the close of the campaign, he still was re-elected by a landslide, winning the biggest popular vote in history and losing only one state, Missouri, outside of the Democratic South—where he took not only Texas again, but Florida, Virginia, Tennessee and Louisiana as well.

A few days after the election Eden called Eisenhower directly on the telephone from London in an attempt to find a way of closing the breach between their two governments. I happened to be with the President when he received Eden's call in his office at the White House. The newspapers were filled that week with reports of the cold antagonism that was supposed to be prevailing between the two men, but Eisenhower greeted the Prime Minister with the warmth of one old friend getting together with another after being out of touch with each other for quite a while. "Well, Anthony, how *are* you?" he said, a question which, it seemed to me at the time, would have required a long and involved answer.

Listening to Eisenhower's end of the conversation, it was evident to me that Eden wanted to come to Washington for a personal talk with the President about the predicament of the British and the French in the Middle East and a solution for the Suez Canal situation. Eisenhower was in favor of such a discussion and told Eden that he was sure that a friendly resolution of their differences would come from it. The President said he would see if the Prime Minister's visit could be worked out.

As Eisenhower hung up the telephone, I noticed that he was pleased to have received the call. Eden's eagerness to talk with him gave him encouragement and lifted his spirits. It was always difficult for Eisenhower to take an aloof or diffident attitude and he was too anxious to restore the traditional friendship between the Americans and the British to let pride or the nursing of hurt feelings keep him from eagerly accepting Eden's offer to get together again. He was also confident that if he and Eden could sit down and talk out their troubles, everything would be put back on the track and things would move smoothly once more.

The President passed along to the State Department Eden's proposal for a personal visit to Washington, with his own view that it would be good for the world to see that even with our differences our firm friendship with the British was unaffected. The prospect of an Eden visit had a thorough shaking down at the State Department. With Dulles in the hospital, Herbert Hoover called me to say that the consensus of opinion was that the visit was premature and should be discouraged. Would I convey their thinking to the President? Eisenhower was resting at home and the reasons for disturbing him had to be very persuasive. But I knew how wrought up he was over the turn of events and I had no alternative. I asked Goodpaster to come along and gave Eisenhower the message and the reasons behind it. I did not feel happy about it at all. I had to explain that the State Department was opposed to him inviting Eden to this country until after the British government withdrew its forces from the Suez Canal. I pointed out to him that if he received Eden now the visit might be misunderstood as an approval by the United States of the stand that the British had taken in the Middle East.

Eisenhower understood the State Department's thinking and accepted its decision, but he accepted it with reluctance and impatience. He told me that turning down Eden's request for a personal talk did not seem to him the right thing to do. He felt that this was no time to be so concerned about appearance and propriety.

When the President was asked about the possibility of a United States–British reunion at a press conference a few days later, he took a calmer and more objective view, closer to that of the State Department, than the warm opinion he had given to me in his bedroom. We had differed with the British and the French, the President explained, on one specific point—the use of force in the settlement of differences, no matter with whom—and before we could resume meetings with them we had to get back to agreement on that point.

Eisenhower had to make a strong personal appeal to Ben-Gurion before Israel came around to agree with the English and French for a cease-fire truce. As the stalemate settled in, with the British, French and Israeli troops silently taking positions along the canal to await a settlement of the waterway dispute and the arrival of a United Nations international police force, the Moscow radio tried to stir up more trouble by announcing that Soviet "volunteers" would be sent to Nasser's aid. But Nasser himself assured the American Embassy in Cairo that he had no intention of permitting the entry of anybody's volunteers.

The tense deadlock in the weeks that followed placed Eisenhower in an embarrassing and worried dilemma. The Suez Canal was closed, blocked by over forty scuttled ships that could not be removed for several months. In retaliation for the Anglo-French-Israeli invasion of Egypt, the oil pipelines across Asia Minor to the Mediterranean, with the exception of "Tapline," a small line passing through Syria, had all been sabotaged by the Arabs. That last remaining pipeline could also be blown up by the Arabs any time they pleased. The almost complete stoppage of oil from the Middle East had thrown all of Western Europe, especially the British, into precarious economic straits. Along with the oil scarcity, the London government was facing a grave financial crisis, sorely aggravated by its political trouble in the Middle East. A run on the pound had begun and Britain's gold reserves were falling off sharply.

Eisenhower's instincts were to come to Britain's aid quickly. The oil pool plan that Arthur Flemming had worked out with the petroleum companies was ready to be put into effect immediately. George Humphrey was standing by with credit accommodations and other assistance that would tide the British over during their money crisis. Hoover, acting for the hospitalized Dulles and reflecting his views, was pushing hard for prompt action. Nobody in Washington wanted to see Eden's Conservative government go down in defeat, and along with his natural concern for the British, whom he always regarded as the closest friends that America had in the world, Eisenhower was deeply worried about the effect that a continued division between the

United States and Britain would have on the vital NATO defense alliance.

But the President was caught in a squeeze—with the position he had taken, he could not make a move to help the British until the Eden government, along with the French and the Israeli, backed down from the aggressive stand it had taken on the Suez issue and complied with the United Nations order to withdraw its military forces from Egyptian territory.

Eisenhower could not weaken the United Nations position against the use of force as an instrument for the settlement of an international dispute. Moreover, if he went to the assistance of the British before they agreed to remove their forces from Suez, he would have turned the Arab nations against the United States, the only Western power still commanding respect in the Middle East at that time. That would have turned the Arab countries over into the hands of the Russians.

As desperately as they needed oil and financial help from America, the British and their French and Israeli allies were understandably reluctant to admit their mistake and comply with the United Nations ultimatum. Their national pride and honor were at stake. The expedition against Suez had cost them heavily in prestige and friendship, not only in such previously co-operative Middle East countries as Saudi Arabia and Pakistan, but throughout the rest of the world. Only Australia and New Zealand supported them in the United Nations General Assembly. The British felt that if they backed down and withdrew their troops too quickly, they would lose more face and weaken their bargaining power in negotiations with Nasser for the future use of the canal. So, even though they realized that capitulation would be finally inevitable, they tried to hold out as long as possible.

While the British were holding out in the Middle East in the face of the growing fuel and money shortage at home, their plight was being discussed in many anxious meetings in Washington. The American government found itself in the strange anomaly of trying to punish publicly her best, but errant, friend while privately sitting up late at night attempting to devise means of getting that same friend out of the straits she had gotten herself into. Representing the President, I sat in on several such meetings late in November, two of them with Herbert Hoover, Jr., Admiral Radford, Humphrey, Arthur Flemming and a few of the Interior Department's oil experts, trying to decide how soon the go-ahead signal could be given to Flemming's plan for relieving Britain's oil emergency and to Humphrey's financial assistance proposals without jeopardizing the United Nations disciplinary action and without incurring the ill will of the Arab nations. It was, to put it mildly, a highly delicate problem.

We were fortunate to have President Hoover's son and namesake as the Under Secretary of State filling in for Dulles at that time. Like his father, the younger Hoover had started his career as a mining engineer and in later years he became a petroleum expert, joining the State Department in 1953 as an adviser on oil problems in the Middle East, where he was highly respected by the Arab leaders. Nobody in the government knew more than Hoover about what we were facing in the Suez crisis. Arthur Flemming in his capacity as Defense Mobilization Director was the administrator of the international oil pool plan, designed to meet the fuel emergency in Western Europe. Unlike Hoover, Flemming was out somewhat beyond his depth in coping with the complicated details of world oil distribution and the disrupted supply lines of the Middle East, but he had the good sense to rely on the opinions of experts who knew more about such things than he did. Radford, then the Chairman of the Joint Chiefs of Staff, was well grounded in the logistics of the situation, especially the water transportation problems. Humphrey, of course, was watching the fiscal crisis that was tightening around the Eden government.

Hoover opened the first meeting I attended by saying that he was in favor of dispensing with formalities and getting the oil pool plan into action within the next day or two instead of delaying it any longer for strategic purposes.

He said with emphasis that we were rapidly being made the whipping boy in the whole situation. The British and the French, who were getting low on oil and gas, simply could not understand why we were not doing something to help them. Furthermore, Hoover continued, the situation was bound to get worse. Once an industrial slowdown began in Western Europe, it would rapidly snowball, he warned. He called attention to the increasing urgency in the cables we were getting from London and Paris. "We are going to have to put this oil plan into action very soon in any case," Hoover said, "and it is much better for us to do it within the next day or two instead of waiting until we are forced into it." He pointed to other factors, both political and economic, that were really worse than those directly related to oil.

Flemming asked what the reaction would be in the United Nations and among the Arab states when it became known that the United States government was relieving the oil shortage in Britain and France. Hoover said there would be no objections to the oil pool if it went into effect after the British and the French withdrew their forces from the Suez Canal zone.

Humphrey did not think that Hammarskjöld would be agreeable unless the British and the French were in compliance with the United Nations' resolution. But Hoover felt that compliance was a matter to be determined. Since they had already indicated their willingness to withdraw their troops, Hoover felt that should be enough for us to go on. Humphrey was hesitant about moving too fast. He insisted that Hammarskjöld or someone else at the UN should first decide the question of compliance before we made any move.

Radford reminded the others that if the United States gave oil to Britain before the British and French troops were removed from the Canal zone, the pro-Nasser Syrians would be likely to blow up Tapline, the last source of Arabian oil in the Mediterranean. With the canal closed and all the pipelines blown up, the only access to Middle Eastern oil would be the Persian Gulf, using the long sea route around the Cape of Good Hope to Europe. Until large-capacity tankers could be built, this supply would afford only limited relief. Radford emphasized that if the Arabs closed our access to the Persian Gulf we would then be in real hot water.

Humphrey pointed out that there was much more to consider than simply the situation we were in with the British. Hoover agreed, and reported that some of the countries in the Middle East had begun to talk about pulling out of treaties with us. Although the situation was that bad, he did not think the Persian Gulf would be closed to us since he saw no problem with Iran or Iraq. He did not think the Sauds would be upset if we went ahead with our pool plan, provided the oil was moved in United States tankers.

I asked if Flemming's oil emergency committee, the group of oil company officials who were to work with the government experts in planning the oil pool operation, could not be called into session and put to work on the distribution plan even though the British and the French had not yet technically and officially complied with the

United Nations resolution. I said that getting the oil plan ready for use could not in itself be regarded as a specific commitment on the part of the American government to aid the British.

Flemming reported that he had already told the oil committee to get its facts and plans up to date and he thought the plan would be ready for operation within a few days, possibly within forty-eight hours. It would not take over two hours to get things moving, he said, since all he had to do was to get a letter to the Interior people and they in turn would get approval from the Attorney General on the anti-trust aspects of the oil pool. "Then we are ready to go," he said.

In answer to Flemming's question about the exact status of British and French compliance, Hoover stated that the decision was entirely in the hands of the United Nations. He went on to say that Hammar-skjöld had the power to work out the details and to decide himself whether or not the British and French were in compliance. "The British have already told Hammarskjöld in strict privacy that they will agree to the UN demands," Hoover said, "but they do not want to say so publicly until Nasser makes a similar statement." Hoover was sure the French would follow the British. In addition he had received assurances from the Israelis that they would do likewise. Since the whole plan was now so close to being finalized, Hoover recommended that it should be put into action at once so that we might "get ourselves off the hook with the British."

When Humphrey asked when Hammarskjöld was going to make his decision, Hoover reported that Herman Phleger, the State Department's legal advisor, was in New York at that moment conferring with Hammarskjöld on the subject.

"I think we have to take a calculated risk and go ahead with getting help to the British instead of waiting for UN approval," Hoover said. "Our reputation in London is already endangered. The economic situation in Western Europe is on the edge of disaster. We can't wait."

But Humphrey felt that such a course might get us into trouble with Saudi Arabia. He did not think we could walk out on the Sauds, who had supported us on the Middle East issue in the United Nations. Humphrey pointed out that three-quarters of the relief given by the oil plan went to the British. If we were to stiffen up their economy we might at the same time stiffen up their determination to persist in their occupation of Suez, he continued. Humphrey pointed out that the British had not said anything constructive since the previous Saturday and he was not so sure what they would do. He emphasized that Hammarskjöld should first say something that we could stand on.

Hoover than asked an unexpected question. What could stop the oil companies from going ahead with the plan on their own initiative? Humphrey replied quickly that of course everybody knew the government could stop them any time it wanted to. And Radford added that Nasser could stop the oil and that no one should forget what he could do to the last pipeline that was left. When I said that we ought to be able to find out promptly what Hammarskjöld had in mind, Radford asked whether the Secretary General had the information in our possession about Nasser's efforts to keep the whole situation as hot as he could. Hoover replied that Hammarskjöld had been kept fully informed.

Hoover then presented for discussion a proposed statement by the State Department announcing the plan to increase Western Europe's oil supply. Humphrey questioned what he said was a presumption in the statement that the oil provided by the pool and ration plan would bring a complete solution to the fuel shortage. Hoover agreed with him.

Europe had come to believe that we were forcing Britain and France to withdraw from Suez by withholding oil from them, Hoover stated. "The oil we are going to give them under this plan won't be enough to save anybody," he said flatly. As a matter of fact, it was expected to increase their present supply by only 25 to 35 per cent.

"No one is more anxious than I am to get back to close and friendly relations with our friends in Europe," Humphrey said. "If we don't do that pretty soon the world is going to hell in a hand basket." But Humphrey insisted we should stand on certain principles and that we did not run out on our word.

Radford agreed that we should do everything we could to get back to normal. He was naturally concerned with the situation in the NATO alliance, but he thought we ought to avoid letting it appear that the British were forcing our hand. It was Radford's opinion that once the Arabs understood how important the oil plan was to the British and the French, they would deny us the oil. Radford thought Flemming's statement placed too much emphasis on the transportation problem when the real difficulty was political. If the British will help us by getting out of Suez, we will be much more secure," Radford said.

The British were complaining about Nasser's attitude, Humphrey noted, but he thought there was some merit in Nasser's stand. If the British would get out or announce their intention to do so, or if Hammarskjöld would say that he had been assured that the British would comply with the United Nations resolution, that would satisfy Nasser, Humphrey said. We could hardly expect Nasser to wait two weeks for some indication of what the British were going to do. Humphrey thought Nasser should be told at once.

Flemming asked if everybody agreed that the oil plan should be put into effect as soon as Hammarskjöld made a statement indicating Anglo-French compliance. There was no objection. I asked Radford and Hoover if the Russians might move into the Middle East when the British and the French withdrew and if armed forces were likely to be needed there. They agreed that a serious situation could develop; the United Nations forces that were scheduled to replace the British, French and Israeli units at Suez would not be big enough really to stabilize the unsettled Middle East.

After that meeting two days went by with still no word of compliance from the British and the French. Then the situation so worsened in London that Eisenhower and Hoover determined to overlook any further considerations of world politics and come to Britain's help immediately without waiting any longer for the formalities of United Nations approval. Sir Anthony Eden's health broke under the strain of the intense pressure that had been put upon him. The Prime Minister was forced to go to Jamaica for a rest, turning over his responsibilities to Selwyn Lloyd. Faced with the run on the pound and a financial panic, Lloyd was preparing to announce to the House of Commons a reversal of Eden's stand against the United Nations and a withdrawal of the British and French forces from Suez. Such a declaration of defeat could cause the collapse of the Conservative government. Eisenhower and the State Department wanted to soften the blow of Lloyd's announcement and strengthen the position of the Conservatives by coming out with the news of the United States oil shipments to Britain a few days before Lloyd faced the House of Commons. Even though this meant jumping the gun by going to

Britain's aid ahead of the proper and politic time for such a move, Hoover argued that it was the only hope of keeping the government from falling and salvaging American prestige in England.

Lloyd was to put his plan of withdrawal from the Suez Canal before the House of Commons on Monday, December 3. On the previous Thursday, November 29, the same group of us met again to listen to Hoover with one newcomer, Reuben Robertson, the Deputy Secretary of Defense, joining the conference. Hoover told us that the American plan for increasing Britain's oil supply should be announced the next day, Friday, so that Lloyd and his fellow Conservatives would have time over the weekend to use this good news to rally support.

Radford was still uneasy about the effect that this premature gesture of friendship to England might have among the Arabs. Specifically, the Admiral was worried about the last remaining pipeline. Hoover said that our proposal for adding to the British oil supply had been explained to King Saud, whose Arabian oil flowed through the pipeline, and that Saud had no objections to the plan, provided British and French tankers were not used for its transportation. A few days before, the Russians had offered to give some of their oil to Western Europe, and Hoover pointed out that the Russian offer made the American plan seem less objectionable to the Arabs. But Radford was not impressed by these arguments. He reminded us that the only surviving pipeline ran through Syria on its way from Arabia to the Mediterranean and that Saud did not have as much influence in Syria as Nasser did. Humphrey turned to Radford and asked him point-blank if he thought the time for putting the plan into action had not yet arrived. Radford agreed that something had to be done for the British and the French but he thought there had not been sufficient consideration given to what might happen as a result of the proposed action. Radford suggested that somebody better be ready to tell him what was to be done if things did not turn out right.

The Admiral added that Russian interference in Egypt was holding up the British from moving their forces out of the canal zone, but Hoover felt that Nasser had not gone as far as the Russians wanted. "Nevertheless, the Russians are calling the tune in Egypt," Radford said.

Hoover told Radford that we were not going to be able to get rid of Nasser on that issue, and Radford agreed. He thought we were over a barrel, and more so since the Russians were getting oil from the Sauds and offering it to the British. Radford wanted to be sure that no one overlooked what might happen as a result of the proposed action.

With that Hoover agreed, but called Radford's attention to the fact that we had at least won one point—the British had agreed to get out of Suez.

Flemming asked if the United States could call for immediate United Nations action if the oil pipeline were blown up by the Syrians. Radford said that in such a case he was not sure that we could get United Nations action. That would be particularly true, Humphrey said, if the British and the French had not yet withdrawn from the canal.

Radford finally agreed with the rest of us on the need for announcing the oil reinforcement plan the next day, after he weighed the importance of Arab disapproval against the importance of alliances in Western Europe. Radford admitted that if the announcement was delayed any longer we would be in worse trouble with NATO. Besides, Radford reasoned, if we waited until Tuesday until Lloyd announced that Britain was going to comply with the United Nations resolution we would not get any credit in Europe.

I asked for a summary of the questions we would have to face in the Middle East after the oil plan was put into effect. Radford replied that we faced the possible loss of Tapline and very likely riots by Nasser's sympathizers around the central oil installations in Arabia. Iranian oil would not be enough, he added.

Humphrey pointed out that we would be asked what made us change our mind about not waiting for British compliance with the UN order before coming to their rescue with additional oil. But if the British were going to act on Monday anyway, Humphrey said, the speculation could only last forty-eight hours. He wanted to know whether, if the Syrians blew up Tapline, the President could not call it aggression and resist it.

Hoover thought aggression would be hard to show because, as he expressed it, we could not prove either that it was Communist aggression or that it was actually the Syrians who blew up the pipeline.

Radford predicted that the Russians would claim that the British would never get out of Egypt when our oil pool plan went to work for them. Humphrey reminded Radford that the British would prove that statement a lie by announcing their withdrawal on Monday.

Flemming asked for a consensus on putting the plan out at noon on the following day and there was no dissent. Humphrey warned that the reporters would be looking for reasons why we did not wait for compliance. "If there are reports spread around that we have secret information that Lloyd is going to announce compliance, the backbenchers in the House of Commons may vote against the Conservatives for spite. We ought to agree on how we are going to handle public relations."

Flemming stated that the State Department would handle the points that Humphrey had raised and that his Office of Defense Mobilization would handle anything on the technical aspects of the oil pool and distribution plan.

After it was approved at the next morning's meeting of the National Security Council, the American plan to add 200,000 barrels of oil daily to the quota of 300,000 barrels then being shipped to Western Europe from the Gulf of Mexico and the South American ports was announced and had the desired effects. In Britain public opinion took a turn for the better and its Conservative Government remained in office. Somehow the small surviving pipeline in Syria stayed intact. The immediate crisis began to subside.

14　The Eisenhower Doctrine

The defeat of the attempt by Britain and France to settle the Suez Canal controversy by military force temporarily destroyed the prestige and political power of those two nations in the Middle East. The disappearance of Anglo-French influence from the Arab world created what Eisenhower described as a power vacuum in that strategic area. Unless the United States undertook to fill the vacuum and made clear to the world the intention to do so, the President said, the Soviets could be counted upon to move into the Middle East and we would find ourselves in an intolerable situation. When Dulles returned to his duties at the State Department after his operation, he and the President worked on a plan for protecting the security of the Middle East nations against Communist aggression which, like the Formosa Resolution, would have the added force of a Congressional endorsement behind it. This was the program that became known as the Eisenhower Doctrine.

In essence, the Eisenhower Doctrine offered to assist any independent Arab nation in the Middle East against open Communist aggression and authorized the President to use United States Armed Forces to safeguard such government from overt attack if the threatened government requested such protection. The President's proposal also offered a broad economic and military aid program involving $200 million in which any nation or group of nations requesting it could participate.

The President planned to present his Middle East proposal to the Republican leaders of Congress on the last day of the year of 1956 and to discuss it on New Year's Day with a bipartisan gathering

271

of Senate and House chieftains so that it would be given top priority in the January session at the Capitol. Much to the irritation of Senator Knowland, the broad outline of the plan stole its way out of the State Department and appeared in the newspapers before the meetings took place. The President explained at the bipartisan meeting that he was asking for authority from Congress to use military force to repel Communist aggression in the belief that if he was armed with such authority he would never have to use it. He assured the Republicans at his session with them that he had no intention of entering into local conflicts in the Middle East that did not involve Communist expansion. Eisenhower told Senator Saltonstall, for example, that an Egyptian attack on Israel, even with Communist-supplied arms, could not be considered Communist aggression unless it could be clearly proved that Egypt was under Red domination at the time. As Eisenhower and Dulles themselves admitted, the difficulty in any American attempt to stop the spread of Communism abroad was in trying to prove that an internal upheaval which posed as a nationalist struggle was really under the direction of Moscow. The Eisenhower Doctrine suffered from that weakness, but it seemed to be unavoidable. Urging the Congressmen to make the plan their first matter of business in the January session, the President said to them, "I just do not believe that we can leave a vacuum in the Middle East and prayerfully hope that Russia will stay out." To show how strongly he felt about this problem Eisenhower made a personal appearance on January 5 before Congress to deliver a special message on the Middle East proposal.

"Russia's rulers have long sought to dominate the Middle East," the President said in his message. "The reasons are not hard to find. They do not affect Russia's security, for no one plans to use the Middle East as a base for aggression against Russia. Never for a moment has the United States entertained such a thought. The Soviet Union has nothing whatsoever to fear from the United States in the Middle East, or elsewhere in the world, so long as its rulers do not themselves first resort to aggression. That statement I make solemnly and emphatically."

Eisenhower asked Congressional approval of authority for the President to use armed force in the Middle East "to secure and protect the territorial integrity and political independence of such nations requesting such aid against overt armed aggression from any nation controlled by International Communism." He also asked for funds to strengthen the economies of the Middle Eastern countries. ("Words alone are not enough.") The President concluded his speech with this thought:

"The occasion has come for us to manifest again our national unity in support of freedom and to show our deep respect for the rights and independence of every nation—however great, however small. We seek not violence, but peace. To this purpose we must now devote our energies, our determination, ourselves."

The Eisenhower Doctrine ran into rough going in the Senate after being passed in the House without any difficulty. As was the case with the Formosa Resolution, many Democratic and several Republican Senators felt that the President's request for Congressional support in the possible use of military force during an indefinite future emergency was merely an attempt to make Congress share the responsibility for a decision that belonged to him. Others argued that Eisenhower was asking for authority which the Constitution delegated to Congress. There was also the natural resentment of the supporters of Israel against courtship of the Arab nations, and a feeling among many Senators that a direct deal between the United States and the Arabs, without the participation of either the British and the French or the United Nations, might weaken our Western European alliances and the authority of the UN. Critics also pointed out that the Eisenhower Doctrine did nothing about such immediate Middle Eastern problems as the continued dispute between Egypt and Israel and the working out of a permanent agreement with Egypt over the use of the Suez Canal, which at that time was still blocked and unusable.

The anti-Dulles faction in the Senate wanted to know exactly how the President's $200 million for economic development and military aid was going to be spent. Dulles and Eisenhower planned to send James Richards, a former Chairman of the House Foreign Affairs Committee, and a conservative South Carolina Democrat, on a fact-finding and salesmanship mission to the various Middle Eastern countries to find out if the Arab governments were going to accept the Eisenhower proffers and how the economic and military aid funds could be best divided and used. But Richards could not leave on his sales trip until he had something to sell. He had to wait until he could offer the Arabs a program which had the official backing of Congress, thus adding greater assurance of support in future years. Obviously Eisenhower could not arrange any detailed program of expenditures until Richards brought back his report. Some of the Senators could not understand why Richards' journey and the spending plan had to follow their action on the resolution. "We are being asked to buy a pig in a poke," Senator Russell said to Dulles in the Senate hearing on the plan. "Why didn't you send Richards out there as soon as he was employed? Then his report would have been brought back by this time."

The argument riled Dulles.

"If we are going to have to pinpoint everything," the Secretary retorted, "if Congress is not willing to trust the President . . . we can't win this battle."

Senator Fulbright had a more comprehensive question. He wanted Dulles to produce for the Senate's information and guidance a complete review and rationale of the Middle East policy of the State Department, going back to 1953 when Dulles visited Egypt and, according to Fulbright, gave General Naguib "a silver-plated pistol."

During the next day's session at the hearing, Dulles did not help matters by replying to a question from Senator Wayne Morse with a clumsy remark. Morse wanted to know if it would not be better to bring Britain and France into the Eisenhower plan as partners in providing military protection against Communist aggression so that "American boys won't have to fight alone." Dulles tried to explain to Morse that in such an emergency it would be more advantageous to have British and French forces deployed in Western Europe rather than in the Middle East. But when he began to put that explanation into words, the Secretary came out with an unfortunate blunder: "If I were an American boy, as you term it, I'd rather not have a French and a British soldier beside me, one on my right and one on my left."

At his next meeting with the legislative leaders in the White House the following Tuesday, Eisenhower said that Dulles was feeling very much "down" because of the slip of his tongue.

"We read a good deal about these supposed blunders of Foster's," the President said. "The other day someone was talking to me about this and I pressed him to be more specific about it. Well, he said, for one thing Foster had been too abrupt in withdrawing us from the

Aswan Dam project. The facts are that Egypt turned down our proposal because of the condition we set. Then they got into negotiations with the Communists for arms and then came back to us wanting to go ahead on our original terms. At that point, we were not going to renew the original terms."

Joe Martin remarked that attacks such as the one that Dulles was then undergoing were part of the opposition's plan of criticizing one Cabinet member after another. Senator Bridges said that much of the fire against Dulles came from within the State Department itself. He reported that at a recent dinner, given by a State Department official and attended by Stewart Alsop and Senator Clark, the whole evening had been spent tearing Dulles apart.

The next day at his press conference, the President was asked if he still regarded Dulles as the greatest Secretary of State of modern times—as he had often said—in view of the difficulties that Dulles was having in the Senate with the Eisenhower Doctrine resolution. The President's attention was also called to recent charges from Democratic Senators that Dulles was to blame for jeopardizing our alliances with the British and the French during the Suez crisis.

Eisenhower stood firmly behind Dulles, as he always did, and emphasized again that every action taken by the Secretary of State in the Middle East negotiations had the personal approval of the President "from top to bottom."

"I think I once described before this group something of the life of Secretary Dulles," the President said to the Washington reporters. "His grandfather having been Secretary of State, he started at the age of six years old believing honestly in his heart that the greatest position in the world was that of Secretary of State, and honestly, I think he still believes it, and he should. . . . Now during those years he studied and acquired a wisdom and experience and knowledge that I think is possessed by no other man in the world. I am the last person to say that he and I have not made mistakes. We are human, and if we haven't made mistakes, then we have done nothing."

The President then turned to the arguments of Dulles' critics:

"They don't bring out any particular project. They just talk about great blundering and lack of leadership. I have seen no proposals, no constructive proposals, for what even should have been done with the benefit of hindsight. On the contrary, we just hear these generalized attacks, which I assure you are easy to make. But I have no reason whatsoever for changing my opinion of Secretary Dulles, as I expressed so often to you people."

Eventually, after two months of debate and strong opposition from isolationist and economy-minded Senators, the Eisenhower Doctrine was approved in the Senate by the decisive vote of seventy-two to nineteen. But by that time the President's effort to provide a long-range plan of protection against Soviet encroachment in the Middle East was overshadowed by a more urgent showdown in that part of the world, which forced the President to take a firm stand against most of the prominent leaders of both parties in Congress and against popular opinion in the United States. Eisenhower's unhesitating support of the United Nations position against Israel in the Gaza Strip and Gulf of Aqaba controversy in that winter of 1957 was one of the courageous decisions that he made as President.

When the British and the French surrendered to the United Nations demand for a withdrawal of their military forces from the Suez area in December, they did so unconditionally, in keeping with the basic UN principle that armed force cannot be used as a means of winning political objectives. But Israel, their ally in the invasion of Egyptian territory, wanted two conditions from Nasser before withdrawing her troops. This was, of course, exerting pressure at the point of a gun and Nasser was naturally supported by the United Nations when he refused to listen to Israel's demands under such circumstances.

The first condition that Israel demanded was United Nations police occupation of the Gaza Strip, the disputed twenty-five-mile section of Mediterranean coastal land that the Egyptians had occupied since the 1949 armistice between the two warring countries and the scene of many border raids. Israel also wanted Egypt's guarantee of free passage of shipping through the Tiran Strait, which connects the Gulf of Aqaba, where Israel's southern port of Elath is located, with the Red Sea and the Indian Ocean. This access to the sea from its southern border was a vital factor in Israel's economic plans, as important to that new nation as access to the Gulf of Mexico is to the United States. Israel was in the process of building an oil pipeline from the Gulf of Aqaba to the Mediterranean as a new route for petroleum that would by-pass the Suez Canal. However, the narrow Tiran Strait leading into the Gulf of Aqaba was controlled by Egyptian artillery batteries on the shore of the strait at Sharm el Sheikh, on the southern extremity of Egypt's Sinai Peninsula, but now occupied by the Israeli. Since 1951, the Egyptians had been preventing ships bound for Israel from passing through the waterway.

Israel sought help from the United States in gaining these two objectives in return for withdrawal of her troops. Dulles recognized the validity of both of the demands but he could not approve of the forceful method that Ben-Gurion was using to get them. If Israel withdrew her forces first with no conditions, in accordance with the United Nations order, and then bargained peacefully, Dulles would give the Israeli political help in gaining the concessions that they wanted from Nasser. Dulles outlined what he would do in Israel's behalf in an *aide-mémoire* that he gave to Ben-Gurion. The Secretary of State promised, in return for an unconditional withdrawal of Israeli forces, to ask the United Nations General Assembly to station an emergency police force on the Gaza Strip. In the Sharm el Sheikh–Tiran Strait situation, Dulles went further. He offered to send an American ship through the strait to establish the right of free passage to the Gulf of Aqaba. But Dulles made no firm guarantees in his *aide-mémoire* about what the United States would do if Nasser resisted both of these moves. Ben-Gurion wanted something stronger than Dulles' offer before he would withdraw from Egyptian territory. When the British and the French pulled out of Suez, the Israeli also drew back from the canal zone, but they remained in the Gaza Strip and along the Gulf of Aqaba and in the Sharm el Sheikh area.

While Dulles was negotiating with Israel, King Saud of Saudi Arabia was invited to Washington for a state visit and for talks with the President and the Secretary of State. As a friendly gesture to all the Arabian states, it was Dulles' recommendation to the President that Saud's visit would straighten out a lot of questions about the new Doctrine, which would greatly promote its acceptance by Saudi Arabia and other Middle East states. The news of Saud's trip to the United States angered Israel and made Ben-Gurion more determined than ever to hold out for a conditional withdrawal. The Arabian King had supported Nasser and had urged the destruction of Israel. When Nasser seized the Suez Canal, Saud had sent him ten million dollars as a token of encouragement. But the great wealth of the Arabian King came from the American-owned Arabian American Oil

Company combine, which paid annual royalties to Saud of around $300 million, the source of most of his income. So if a start were to be made somewhere in establishing friendlier relations with the Arabs, Saud was the logical leader to approach. The invitation to the King was resented in Congress and all over the country; Mayor Robert F. Wagner of New York refused to give the monarch an official welcome to the city.

"You don't promote the cause of peace only by talking to people with whom you agree," Eisenhower said in defense of his invitation to Saud. "You have got to meet face to face the people with whom you disagree at times to determine whether or not there is a way of working out the differences and reaching a better understanding. . . . I therefore deplore any discourtesy shown to a visitor who comes to us as a representative of a government or of a people, and whose purpose is to see whether he can assist in ameliorating any of these difficulties. This does not necessarily imply any approval of any internal actions in such countries."

At the time of Saud's visit, it was reported that the United States had extended another invitation to Tito, the nonconforming Communist leader of Yugoslavia, and this provoked even more of a storm. A group of Congressmen circulated a petition asking the President to cancel the reception to Tito, who obliged them by announcing in Belgrade that he had decided for various reasons, including "the atmosphere," to put off his visit to the United States.

Eisenhower told the Republican Congressional leaders after his talks with Saud that our principal aim in dealing with the King was to strengthen him as a counterpoise to Nasser in the Arab world. The President said he found two sensitive spots in his discussions with the King. Saud was afraid that the efforts by Dulles to help Israel neutralize the Gaza Strip and free the access to the Gulf of Aqaba might force Nasser to resort to war. He was also touchy about his country's lack of arms. The President could see that Saud was under pressure from his own people to obtain arms from some source and the Soviets had made frequent offers of weapons to him at lower prices than he could find in the West. Saud was afraid that he might have a revolt on his hands at home if he extended the lease on the fifty-million-dollar United States Air Force base at Dhahran in Saudi Arabia without an arms agreement with the Americans.

The Saudi entourage, in its ceremonial robes and hoods, was the strangest group of visitors I encountered in all of my years at the White House. When the King referred to his relationship with his people, he sounded like a ruler from medieval times. The President told us later that he enjoyed his conversation with King Saud. At one point, when Eisenhower turned the conversation to hunting, he discovered that Saud did his hunting only with falcons. The President delved back desperately into what little he remembered from historical novels about the ancient sportsmen who went into the field carrying hawks on their cadges. "I had to comb the Crusades for that one," he confided to us later with a grin.

Saud's visit to Washington was enough in itself to stir up resentment in Congress against the White House and the State Department. At the same time, a strong majority in the United Nations General Assembly, consisting of the twenty-seven nations in the Asian-African bloc and the Soviet Union republics and satellites, were preparing to call for economic sanctions against Israel to force her to make an unconditional withdrawal from the Egyptian territory she was occupying on the Gaza Strip and the occupied territory along the Gulf of Aqaba. Dulles had worked hard with Dag Hammarskjöld and with a Western group in the UN led by the Canadian foreign minister, Lester Pearson, to avoid such an impasse with Israel by getting Egypt to allow the Gaza Strip and Sharm el Sheikh to be occupied by United Nations police forces after the Israeli withdrew. Nasser refused to submit to any such conditions. Dulles likewise failed to get Ben-Gurion to compromise in return for the promises of future support outlined in the Dulles *aide-mémoire*. Now the United States had to make the hard choice whether or not to join the United Nations majority in imposing sanctions on Israel. Supporting Nasser on this issue would be unpopular both in Congress and throughout much of the nation, but all the legal arguments favored it. Besides, if the United States government opposed the sanctions, it would undo all of the progress Eisenhower had been making with the Sauds and push many Asian and African nations toward the handsome proposals which were being made by Russia.

Dulles and Lodge flew to Thomasville, Georgia, where Eisenhower was vacationing, and decided with the President that the White House had to make a stand against Congress and against Israel. This meant trouble in Washington. Not only were Lyndon Johnson and the Democratic policy committee in favor of giving Ben-Gurion the guarantees that he wanted, but Senator Knowland, the Republican leader in the Senate, was in complete agreement with Johnson. Knowland threatened to resign from his position as a U.S. delegate to the United Nations General Assembly if sanctions were imposed on Israel. He wanted to know why sanctions had not been voted against Russia for her defiance of the United Nations resolution condemning the use of armed force in Hungary.

The President cut short his vacation in Georgia and flew back to Washington to have it out with the leaders of both parties in Congress at a tense and strained meeting in the Cabinet Room at the White House on February 20. The meeting began early in the morning, at eight-thirty sharp. There were fewer pleasantries than usual as the leaders of Congress gathered in the Cabinet Room to await the President, who came in on the dot. Besides Dulles and Lodge, five of the White House staff besides myself, Persons, Hagerty, Goodpaster, Bryce Harlow and Arthur Minnich, were there, each in his own official capacity. The men in the room represented all shades of political opinion. There were the Democrats like Johnson, Fulbright, Carl Hayden and Mike Mansfield who were in philosophical tune with Eisenhower on foreign policy generally, but against him on this issue, either as a matter of personal conviction or because of the stand taken in the Democratic caucus. Beside them were the Democratic leaders in the House, Rayburn, John McCormack, Tom Morgan and Tom Gordon, who would be naturally reluctant to support a Republican President on such a hot controversial question. Heading the Republicans from the Senate was the resolutely incompatible Knowland, flanked by Bridges and Millikin, and Everett Dirksen, who had with considerable political gallantry come around to accept more and more of Eisenhower's views and solutions to major foreign problems. There were also the Republicans who were almost invariably at the President's side in the crucial decisions—Leverett Saltonstall, Charlie Halleck, Alex Smith, Alexander Wiley and John Vorys. Richard Nixon was at the meeting but the Vice President sat through the whole two and a half hours of serious, and sometimes heated, debate without joining in the argument. In clashes of Congressional opinion such as this one, Nixon's role as the presiding officer of the Senate gave him pause, as did his reluctance to become involved in a battle between Eisenhower and Knowland.

The President opened the meeting with a strong and explicit explanation of why he was in favor of putting pressure on Israel to comply with the United Nations demand for an unconditional withdrawal. Such compliance was needed for Israel's own good, he said, pointing out that Ben-Gurion's government would soon be in a dangerous financial crisis unless it obtained help from the Export-Import Bank, which would be possible only if peace were restored. Furthermore, the President went on, there could be no resumption of full-scale traffic in the Suez Canal and no end of the brawls between the Egyptians and the Israeli unless the excuses for Arab retaliation against Israel were completely removed.

Eisenhower warned the legislators that Russian influence among the Arabs would most certainly increase if the Israeli continued to resist the compliance order. Besides, there would be further interruptions in the supply of oil from the Middle East, with more disaster to the economy of Britain and the Western European nations.

"And then the whole thing might end up in a general war," the President said.

I could see that Dulles and Lodge were pleased with the President's forceful statement even though it was plain that the legislators were by no means convinced. Lyndon Johnson turned and looked at Senator Russell with a determined expression which seemed to say that he was not going to yield an inch. Knowland was wearing his classical toga of lofty defiance. Only Carl Hayden preserved his appearance of utter benignity, but then Uncle Carl had no other appearance. All of them were marking every word that Eisenhower had to say, some of them waiting with obvious impatience to voice their disagreement. We could see that the President was making a skillful and well-reasoned attempt to persuade the leaders to the course of action he had decided on.

Disarmingly, the President told the legislators that he was well aware of their opposition to sanctions against Israel and that he could understand their attitude. He reminded them that the United States had applied sanctions only three months earlier against the United Kingdom and France for exactly the same purpose when oil from the Gulf of Mexico and the Caribbean was withheld until these powers agreed to withdraw from Egypt. Then Eisenhower stated flatly that he did not know how to protect American interests in the Middle East except through the United Nations. If the United States failed to support the United Nations on the Israel issue, he declared, it would be a lethal blow to the principles of the world peace organization.

"Nobody likes to impose sanctions," the President concluded, "but how else can we induce Israel to withdraw to the line agreed on in the 1949 armistice? The Arabs refuse to discuss a permanent settlement until that move is made."

Eisenhower turned to Dulles for his comments, but before Dulles could speak Johnson interrupted to mention a letter that he had written to the Secretary of State protesting against sanctions on Israel. The letter had appeared in a New York newspaper and Johnson wanted to say that it had not reached the newspaper from his office. He added that he had not even discussed the subject matter of the letter with Senator Knowland, but he thought it significant that he and Knowland had both come to the same conclusion on the sanctions question.

"After all," Johnson said, "there are times when Congress has to express its own views."

"I certainly have no objection to that," the President said.

Johnson looked at the President for a moment with a wry smile and said, "Thank you."

Dulles was sure of himself, solid in his convictions, unshakable and firmly uncompromising as he faced the disagreeing Congressmen. He told them that if Israel were allowed to defy the withdrawal order any longer, the basic principle of the United Nations forbidding any individual nation from taking the law into its own hands would become ineffective and worthless. The Secretary pointed to the fact that Israel, along with Britain and France, had agreed to withdraw its troops from Egypt as soon as the United Nations emergency occupation force arrived in the Suez area. That had been more than three months ago. Britain and France had lived up to the agreement and had withdrawn at a considerable cost of prestige and loss of political power, Dulles argued, but Israel had refused to leave, even though he and Hammarskjöld had assured Ambassador Eban that Egypt would probably accept a neutral administration in the Gaza Strip and that the United States would exercise the right we considered ours to free passage to the international waters of Aqaba, and were prepared to join with others in their exercise of the same right. Either sanctions had to be imposed, Dulles said, or some forceful alternative had to be found.

In answer to a question from Senator Wiley, Dulles drove home another important point in the administration's support of sanctions: the rest of the world believed that on any crucial question such as this one Israel could control United States policy because of the strong favor it enjoyed in America. Therefore, Dulles said, the Arabs were watching us intently and, if we confirmed this belief, they would feel compelled to turn to Russia. "But this does not mean that we have to follow an anti-Israel policy," he added.

While this discussion was in progress, Knowland had been busily penciling some notes on a memo pad. He took the floor to offer a five-point counterproposal in the form of a United Nations resolution imposing economic, moral and diplomatic sanctions against any nation violating the charter provision against aggression. It then called for the Israeli forces in the Gaza and Gulf of Aqaba regions to be replaced by UN troops until either a United Nations settlement or an Egypt-Israel agreement could be reached. Knowland reminded the meeting that the present UN police force in Egypt was there with Nasser's consent and would have to be withdrawn if Nasser demanded it. He suggested that a neutral zone be established between Egypt and Israel. Knowland felt that his plan for imposing sanctions on any nation, large or small, that disobeyed a United Nations order would avoid the suspicion that Israel was being made the victim of a double-standard penalty system.

I waited to see how Dulles would handle Knowland's proposal. Dulles said nothing; he leaned back in his chair and let the others talk about it. In a meeting like this one, the Secretary of State never bothered to knock down a suggestion or an objection if he thought that it would be knocked down in the general discussion, and that was what happened to Knowland's idea. After it was talked over, Lodge read to the group a resolution similar to the one Knowland suggested, which had been put before the United Nations three weeks earlier only to expire in a long and inconclusive series of negotiations. Knowland finally capitulated and admitted that it did not seem feasible for the United States to vote against sanctions on Israel.

"How much support could be found for applying sanctions against Russia for its failure to comply with the UN resolution on Hungary?" Knowland asked Lodge.

"The UN will never vote for sanctions against either Russia or the United States," Lodge said, and that ended that line of thought.

Other Congressmen had other ideas and suggestions but the fact remained that a vote on sanctions in the United Nations was unavoidable and the United States had to take a position on it. Lodge reminded the legislators that since November, when Eisenhower opposed the use of force by the British, French and Israelis in Suez, there had been a steadily increasing respect for the United States among the Arab people. "Now they won't understand it if we abandon our position on the Israel withdrawal," Lodge said. "Unless the Israelis withdraw, the canal will not be reopened."

Knowland asked if we could postpone United Nations action on the sanctions for two weeks while further attempts at a settlement with Ben-Gurion were made. Lodge told him that if we asked for a postponement, it would appear as if we were opposing the sanctions.

The President, with the help of Joe Martin and John Vorys, attempted to get from the leaders a unified statement of Congressional support for the stand that the administration was taking on the necessity of an immediate withdrawal by Israel. Fulbright suggested a Congressional resolution asking for a withdrawal but Rayburn put the damper on that idea by saying that it would only cause a prolonged and fruitless debate in the House and the Senate. Eisenhower asked if the group at the meeting would agree to a statement similar to the resolution that Fulbright had suggested. Johnson said he had reservations about such a statement and Rayburn doubted that the bipartisan leaders could ever agree on the language in it. John McCormack announced flatly that he would not be a party to any statement from the people assembled in the Cabinet Room.

"But doesn't everybody here agree that Israel should withdraw?" Vorys asked.

"I am not sure all would agree unless it could be made certain that Israel would get justice after she withdraws," Fulbright said.

McCormack said that a withdrawal by Israel might only make negotiations with Nasser more difficult. Vorys said, "If Israel doesn't withdraw and if Egypt attacks Israel with Russian support, we'll be in a worse position in the Middle East than we are now."

Again Knowland, joined this time by Saltonstall, asked if the United Nations action against Israel could be postponed for a few weeks and again Lodge explained patiently why this could not be done.

It became obvious that the Congressional leaders were too conscious of the unpopularity of the stand that the President was being forced to take against Israel to be willing to share with him the responsibility for it. They were anxious to let Eisenhower have all of the credit for this declaration. Speaking for the Democrats, and for many of the Republicans as well, Senator Russell ended the discussion by saying that there was no hope for a unanimous agreement and that the President should simply shoulder the burden alone and make a statement to the people similar to the one he had made at the beginning of the meeting.

"I have been thinking about doing just that for the past ten days or so," Eisenhower said. "Here's what I thought I would say." He quickly listed the main points of a speech that he would give on the radio and television networks that same night.

"America has either one voice or none, and that voice is the voice of the President—whether everybody agrees with him or not," said Sam Rayburn, relieved to have the discussion over and done with at last. As the Senators and Representatives filed out of the Cabinet Room, Lyndon Johnson hastened to announce to the waiting reporters, "Our views have not been changed."

Eisenhower asked Dulles to work with Lodge on a draft of a speech and Jim Hagerty called the television and radio companies to arrange for time on the networks. After lunch Dulles came to the President's office, where Eisenhower compared what the Secretary had written with notes that he had made himself. Coming to a point in the text that seemed to him obscure or clumsily worded, he would quickly write in a sentence or two, read it over with pursed lips and say to Dulles, "Foster, don't you think this sounds a little better?" He had been unable to shake off a nagging cold before his vacation in Georgia had been interrupted and when he went on the air at nine o'clock that night, he began with an apology for his "very stubborn cough." He explained that he had met that morning with the leaders of Congress, who had advised him to lay his views of the Israel

problem before the American people. He did not say how much disagreement with his views there was among the Congressional leaders.

The President told his listeners that Israel's insistence on firm
guarantees as a condition to withdraw its invasion raised a basic question of principle:

"Should a nation which attacks and occupies foreign territory in
the face of United Nations disapproval be allowed to impose conditions on its own withdrawal? If we agree that armed attack can
properly achieve the purposes of the assailant, then I fear we will
have turned back the clock of international order. . . . If the United
Nations once admits that international disputes can be settled by
using force, then we will have destroyed the very foundation of the
organization, and our best hope of establishing a world order. That
would be a disaster for us all."

Eisenhower did not avoid the "double-standard" argument which
pointed to the United Nation's failure to punish Russia for its invasion
of Hungary, but he disapproved of the comparison. "It would indeed
be a sad day if the United States ever felt that it had to subject Israel
to the same type of moral pressure as is being applied to the Soviet
Union," he said. "There can, of course, be no equating of a nation
like Israel with that of the Soviet Union. The people of Israel, like
those of the United States, are imbued with a religious faith and a
sense of moral values. We are entitled to expect, and do expect, from
such peoples of the free world a contribution to world order which
unhappily we cannot expect from a nation controlled by atheistic
despots."

The President avoided the word "sanctions" in discussing his support of United Nations action against Israel, preferring the less technical and more understandable "pressure," but left no doubt about
his position if there was "no choice but to exert pressure on Israel
to comply with the withdrawal resolutions."

As soon as Eisenhower had finished the statement of his position,
things began to move. The next day before the Israeli legislature in
Jerusalem, Ben-Gurion said that his government would make further
efforts to reach an understanding with the United States. The day
after that in the United Nations General Assembly the resolution
asking for a denial of military, economic and financial assistance to
Israel was introduced by Lebanon with the support of Iraq, the

Sudan, Pakistan, Afghanistan and Indonesia. Lodge delayed taking a final U.S. position on the resolution, pending further talks between Dulles and the Israeli. Nine days after the President's broadcast and before a vote on the sanctions resolution was taken, Golda Meir, the Israeli Foreign Minister, announced to the General Assembly that her government was "now in a position to announce its plans for a full and complete withdrawal." There were some further delays and harsh words on both sides but gradually the specter of sanctions faded away.

Eisenhower's troubles in the Middle East did not end when the Israeli troops pulled back from the Gaza Strip and Sharm el Sheikh. A few weeks later the President was in Bermuda for a meeting with Harold Macmillan, the new British Prime Minister, to patch up the few remaining differences between their governments. Guy Mollet, the Premier of France, had been in Washington at the end of February on a similar fence-mending mission. In both conversations, the future of the Suez Canal and Russia's designs on the Arab nations were major topics of discussion.

During his second term in office, Eisenhower tried to work in closer harmony with the Democratic-controlled Congress by holding bipartisan meetings with the legislative leaders more frequently than he did during his first four years in the White House. After he returned from Bermuda, the President invited the spokesmen from both parties on the Hill to listen to a report on the conference with Macmillan.

The President and Dulles both remarked on the feeling of frankness and mutual trust that had prevailed at the Bermuda meeting. To some extent, Dulles attributed the understanding relationship between the President and the Prime Minister to their friendship during World War II, when Macmillan had served as Eisenhower's political adviser in North Africa. Both men carefully avoided any discussion of the differences of opinion that had led to the break between their governments five months earlier. Macmillan has said since then that he thinks history will someday show that Britain was right in invading Suez. But having been badly burned economically by the closing of the canal, the British were in no mood to antagonize Nasser further, and the conversations had turned to getting the canal into operation again with a look at some alternatives. A pipeline through Turkey was then in the planning stage and huge tankers to carry oil around Africa's Cape of Good Hope were being constructed, but, as Dulles explained in answer to a question from John McCormack, the pipeline and the ships would not be in operation for several years. Even then Britain would not be completely free from reliance on the canal. As it turned out, after long and enervating negotiations with Nasser, the canal users had to agree to Egypt's terms because the British could not afford to insist on anything else.

Eisenhower agreed at Bermuda to supply missile bases in the United Kingdom with American atomic IRBMs. This would give Britain retaliatory power to deter such threats as Moscow had used during the Suez debacle. It would also give the United States a strategic wall of defense in the British Isles and incidentally relieve some 2,300 American troops for duty elsewhere. Dulles assured the legislative leaders that the atomic warheads for these missiles would be kept under our control. He added that no secret agreements of any kind had been made with the British at Bermuda.

Senator Knowland wanted to know what the reaction of the other NATO governments would be to our missile deal with the British. Dulles admitted that there might be some difficulty in putting the arrangement into operation but we already had atomic weapons on the Continent and obviously Britain offered the best bases for intermediate-range missiles. Eisenhower added that it was much better for everybody concerned to have these weapons manned by the soldiers of the country in which the bases were located. Mike Mansfield asked about our fifteen-hundred-mile missile, which was then in the development stage. Donald Quarles, the Deputy Secretary of Defense, told Mansfield that the arrangement discussed at Bermuda hinged on that missile's successful development but that it was coming along well.

Dulles said that the British government still was far apart from the Americans on the issues of recognition of Red China and trade with that Communist country. The Secretary felt, however, that Macmillan had a better understanding of our attitude toward China when they had finished their discussion of the subject. When the meeting came to a close, there was the usual question about what sort of a statement should be issued to the press about the matters that had been under discussion. Sam Rayburn said that he was like President Calvin Coolidge in at least one respect: he had found out early in life that he never was obliged to explain anything that he had not said.

During the following year there were a series of explosive developments in Jordan, Syria and Lebanon, and all involved, directly or indirectly, the application of the Eisenhower Doctrine. Any one of these disturbances could have precipitated a general war if Eisenhower and Dulles had met them with a course of action either too reluctant or too meddlesome.

In Jordan a powerful faction of anti-Israel agitators and Communist sympathizers ran riot in Amman and forced the resignation of King Hussein's Premier. Only the week before, Eisenhower had been asked if the Middle East protective doctrine would apply if Jordan were attacked. The President had said that his doctrine would indeed authorize American military aid to that government if it were requested and if the aggression were Communistic. King Hussein issued such a call for help, declaring that Jordan's internal crisis was "the responsibility of international Communism and its followers."

Eisenhower and Dulles acted swiftly. From Augusta, where he was on a brief vacation, the President announced that he viewed the independence and integrity of Jordan as vital. The next day the Sixth Fleet was moved from the French Riviera to the eastern Mediterranean and the first application of the Eisenhower Doctrine was underway. With this assurance, the twenty-one-year-old King selected a loyal government and made it stand up.

Syria presented a different problem. Here was a nation that had turned away from the West and into the Soviet orbit long before the crisis at Suez. In the summer of 1957, the Syrians were staging wild anti-American demonstrations in Damascus and threatening their pro-Western neighbors in Turkey, Iraq and Lebanon. Obviously, the turmoil was Communist-inspired but, in contrast to the situation in Jordan, the Syrian government wanted nothing to do with any assistance from the West and there was therefore little that Eisenhower could do about it. This was an example of the weakness of the Eisenhower Doctrine, which the President had pointed out to the leaders in Congress.

The President told the Republican leaders of Congress on August 27 that he was determined to build up the military strength of the countries around Syria, even if such expenditures used up his entire Middle East emergency fund. He mentioned that King Saud had contended that the troublemakers in Syria were overambitious army officers rather than Communists. Saud had insisted that no true Arab could be a Communist, and Eisenhower was reminded that General de Gaulle once told him that no true Frenchman could be a Communist.

While we kept military aid moving into Jordan, Turkey and Iraq, the President told the Congressmen there was little else that we could do except to make sure that the Russians themselves did not take over Syria. Eisenhower said that Nasser felt that the Syrians were going too far in their antagonism of the West. "But we'll get no help from Nasser in Syria," the President said. "He's too interested in keeping the Egyptian-Syrian-Yemen alliance together."

And then throughout the fall and winter of 1957 and into the spring of 1958, Lebanon was torn by Communist-provoked dissension. Intelligence reports from Beirut were so disturbing in May that when Eisenhower was questioned about the situation in the Middle East at a press conference, he asked the reporters to excuse him from commenting on the subject. He explained that the tension and unrest were so great in Lebanon and the other Arab countries that anything at all that he said might be misinterpreted for propaganda purposes by the extremists. Later in the month in a meeting with the Congressional leaders, the President warned them that he might have to run the risk of war by intervening with military force in Lebanon without prior discussion in Congress. "In this case, if there has to be a public debate about the course of action, there would be no use in taking it at all," he said.

The President of Lebanon, Camille Chamoun, appealed for aid first to the United Nations Security Council and later to the Arab League, charging that Nasser was plotting to overthrow him and bring Lebanon into an alliance with Egypt and Syria in the United Arab Republic. Dag Hammarskjöld personally accompanied a United Nations observation team to Lebanon to conduct an investigation, but the UN observers formally reported that there was not enough evidence of the smuggling of Syrian arms and the massive Communist infiltration that Chamoun had reported. Thus Chamoun's position was further weakened. In an effort to halt the street fighting that was raging almost continuously in Beirut, Chamoun announced that he would retire from office at the conclusion of his term in September. It seemed that the West had met with another reversal in dealing with Nasser and in the attempt to get the United Arab Republic around to a negotiable position.

On July 14 two messages came to the White House from the Middle East almost simultaneously and sounded an alert for immediate action. The first message reported a revolt in Iraq that caught Washington and the rest of the Western world completely by surprise. In the early hours of the morning in Baghdad, insurgents had seized and shot King Faisal, one of the West's best friends in the Middle East, along with the Crown Prince and the Premier. An Iraqi Republic had been proclaimed and the end of the Baghdad Pact was loudly heralded in Cairo.

Shortly after Eisenhower received this shocking news, a second message came from Lebanon. Now convinced that he was next on Nasser's list, Chamoun formally requested the aid of American military forces in Beirut. At nine-forty-five that same morning, already clear in his mind about the course that the United States government must follow in the emergency, the President met with the National Security Council, and obtained approval of his plan. At two-thirty that afternoon the Congressional leaders of both parties came to the White House and the President and Dulles told them as much as they knew about what was going on in the Middle East, and what had to be done.

Giving the Congressional leaders a summary of recent Soviet political activities, Dulles said that it was time to bring a halt to the deterioration in our position in the Middle East, if the United States was going to salvage anything out of that part of the world. The President put before the Congressmen the decision which faced him and left no doubt in their minds how it was going to go. They had some difficulty in differentiating between the application of the Eisenhower Doctrine and interference in a purely internal civil uprising; some of them thought it about as logical to send troops to Iraq as to Lebanon. None of the leaders attempted to dissuade the President from the course he was planning to follow but they made it plain that they had little enthusiasm for his decision and no desire whatever to share in the responsibility for it. Once again, as it had been with the sanctions against Israel, the President was left to act on his own.

The Central Intelligence Agency and the military intelligence sources had given the President no forewarning of the sudden revolt in Iraq, and the Congressmen did not hesitate to point this out at the meeting. However, in such a small and isolated country as Iraq it was possible for such a plot to be kept within a handful of people whose followers did not know exactly what was in the wind until the wind began to blow. Eisenhower did not hold Allen Dulles accountable for the fact that he had no warning in advance of the uprising in Iraq.

The next morning Jim Hagerty announced that a battalion of U.S. Marines, supported by carrier planes of the Sixth Fleet, had landed at Beirut and was standing guard at the airport and at public buildings in the city. After the landing, the President prepared a message on film and tape, which was broadcast that day. "The mission of these forces," he said after explaining the events in Iraq and Lebanon that had led to his decision, "is to protect American lives—there are about 2,500 Americans in Lebanon—and by their presence to assist the government of Lebanon to preserve its territorial integrity and political independence." The next day, while the President was having further discussions of the Middle East situation with the Republican leaders of Congress, the meeting was interrupted so that he could be given a message signed jointly by the Shah of Iran and the Presidents of Pakistan and Turkey. The message hailed Eisenhower's action as a "bold and appropriate decision" which would "not only ensure the protection of the independence of Lebanon . . . but will at the same time strengthen the determined position of Iran, Pakistan and Turkey and also renew and increase the faith of the free world in the leadership of the United States for the defense of the free nations." The President was deeply pleased by the message, but, as he remarked to the Republican legislators at the time, he hoped that the Middle Eastern nations would not begin to think that American military aid under the Eisenhower Doctrine was the only kind of action that could be taken on their behalf.

At the Cabinet meeting on July 18, Dulles delivered a long discussion on the events in the Middle East in which he listed three disadvantages under which the Western powers labored in their relationship with the Arabs—the existence of Israel, which serves as a constant stimulant, or irritant, to Arab nationalism; the traditional anti-Western fanaticism of the Arabs, about which we can do little; the demagoguery of Nasser, which the Russians can exploit but which we cannot, in good conscience, employ to our advantage.

Dulles said that he and Eisenhower were under no illusions that they had solved any problems in sending the Marines to Lebanon; they were using military force only to prevent the dangerous situation in the Middle East from getting any worse, and to reassure many small nations that they could call on us in time of crisis. There can be no question that they achieved that purpose. The President and the Secretary of State came to believe later that the Russian government was astonished and taken aback by our display of strength and determination at Lebanon. There was a change in the tone of Khrushchev's letters to the President in subsequent months, a more conciliatory note and a stronger inclination to negotiate rather than to threaten.

Nevertheless, it was my own feeling at the time that sending the Marines to Lebanon, like sending the soldiers to Little Rock, was a frustrating and unhappy experience for Eisenhower. In both instances he was keenly sensitive to the critical repercussions that followed his decisions and he would have preferred to take any other honorable course if one had been open to him. Looking back on both decisions with the benefit of hindsight, he probably underestimated the effect of his action at Little Rock and overestimated the gravity of the Lebanon situation and the effects of his intervention in that Middle East brushfire. But in his efforts to contribute to the freedom of these small nations, Eisenhower succeeded in establishing a clearer identity for the United States as a friend and protector of the weak and the defenseless.

In the summary which he gave to the Cabinet on July 18, Dulles made one comment that applied not only to the troubles in Lebanon and Iraq in 1958 but also to the troubles in the Congo in 1961. The Secretary recalled that Stalin in 1924 predicted that the Communist victory over the West would come with the rising nationalism among the peoples of Asia and Africa.

15 Modern Republicanism

Eisenhower's performance in the final weeks of his 1956 re-election campaign went way beyond what any of us on his staff, the Republican National Committee or Congressional and state candidates anticipated. It surprised the Democrats and even the President himself. Everybody had expected Eisenhower to conduct the kind of high-level, dignified and mild campaign that old-school politicians look down upon. He accepted the nomination after two major illnesses only under the condition that he would not be obliged to undergo a hard-hitting schedule of barnstorming and whistle-stopping tours. He was determined to stand on his record and not get into political slug fests with the opposition. But by the end of September, Eisenhower was plunging angrily into the fight, accusing the Democrats of spreading "wicked nonsense." Only the Suez crisis kept him from throwing his resolutions overboard in the closing weeks before the election and getting into a free-swinging offensive.

The change in Eisenhower's attitude came about gradually. As late as the end of August, none of us around him could see it on the horizon. Early in September he showed an example of calm and dispassionate political morality rarely exhibited by a presidential candidate. At a press conference Adlai Stevenson was quoted as saying in a comment on reports of serious unemployment in Detroit that "all the news is good." Hagerty talked over this apparently verified blunder with me and we agreed that it ought to be called to the attention of any voters who might have missed it when it was first printed. Hagerty issued a statement criticizing the Democratic candidate for hailing unemployment as good news because it suited his political

294

purposes, and Eisenhower was promptly asked by the press what he thought of Hagerty's statement. The President defended Stevenson. He said that he was sure his opponent must have been misquoted.

I had an experience at the same time similar to Hagerty's. At a luncheon for party workers in Chicago, I agreed to answer questions from the floor and one of the questioners wanted to know what I thought of Dulles inviting Stevenson to attend a foreign policy conference as an observer and consultant, and what were his qualifications. I said that Dulles made his own decisions on such matters and I did not know what qualifications Stevenson had for such an assignment. This was played up in the newspapers as an attempt on my part to derogate Stevenson's qualifications as a consultant on foreign affairs. When I returned to Washington, I explained to Dulles that I had intended my reply to be simply factual; I did not in fact know what Stevenson's qualifications were. Dulles did not undertake to explain, but indicated that he was satisfied with my answer.

In planning to remain aloof from the fisticuffs of the battling parties, Eisenhower had not yet felt the effects of liberal dashes of adrenalin from the emotions that were to be well exercised during the campaign. The Democrats said things that made him mad and when his old adversary, Harry Truman, charged that the national finances were being endangered by "this bunch of racketeers in Washington," the President began to boil. His resistance to the constant pleas from Republican candidates and "good friends" weakened and he agreed to speaking engagements that he had refused to consider a few weeks earlier. Then Stevenson attacked Milton Eisenhower and the President's gloves came off. He could stand jibes at himself and his administration but when members of his family came into the line of fire, it was something else again. Stevenson said that Milton had been assuming responsibility for our relations with Argentina and that under his advice Perón had been appeased with loans that piled up balances of more than a hundred million dollars. The President came back at Stevenson sharply.

"They are very disturbed that the United States government gave Mr. Perón's government more than $100 million," he said. "It is true that the government loaned Mr. Perón's government $130 million, but it wasn't a Republican government. It was the Democratic government in 1950 and '51. From the time I came in until Perón went out,

the government did not sign one single loan agreement with Mr.
Perón."

The President also declared that his brother's principal accomplishments in Argentina, where he went on a mission at the request
of the State Department at the sacrifice of his own vacation time, was
to assist in the lifting of press censorship and the relieving of repres-
sion on political minority groups.

A few days later Eisenhower delivered his "wicked nonsense"
speech in Cleveland, accusing the Democrats of "distortions" that he
had declined to specify earlier. The "wicked nonsense" line delighted
Governor Dewey, who sent me a long and constructive memorandum
on campaign advice, which, he said, had come to him from a "real
expert." Dewey's expert advised, among other things, running against
Harry Truman again instead of Stevenson, "scaring hell out of the
voters about war, about income taxes, high prices and depression"
and putting a wallop into every speech. It was difficult to tell Eisenhower to slug an opponent because he was convinced that for him
slugging was both unnecessary and ineffective as a vote-winning device. But when the Democrats stirred his indignation he forgot that
theory and did some slugging just the same.

One Democratic argument that annoyed Eisenhower was the
shadowy charge that the administration was following a "tight money"
policy, an insinuation that few people knew anything about but which
impressed the vast ranks of borrowers. One day during the campaign
a reporter asked him about high interest rates and the exchange revealed that the newsman assumed the President had control of the
policies of the Federal Reserve Board. Eisenhower had to point out
to him that the Federal Reserve Board is an independent agency
removed from presidential authority and influence. As Eisenhower
often observed with some irritation, the President is held responsible
for everything. In the same press conference, incidentally, Eisenhower
expressed strong opposition to the constitutional amendment limiting
the President to two terms. "The United States ought to be able to
choose for its President anybody it wants, regardless of the number
of terms he has served," he said.

One of the problems of the 1952 campaign plagued us still in 1956;
no matter what Robert Montgomery, the President's television adviser, and the various lighting experts tried to do, the appearance of

the candidate on the television screen was never satisfactory. Eisenhower's ruddy and healthy glow too often came out as a ghostly gray. With the technical talent that was available, I could never understand this. It was often suggested that the President should use make-up but he drew back from powder and paint. "An old soldier doesn't feel very good under that sort of thing," he said.

As Eisenhower took the bit in his teeth and assumed a schedule of personal appearances that we had not dared to suggest to him six months earlier, we noticed that he seemed to get once again a therapeutic lift from the crowds and excitement, and that seemed to reinforce his physical stamina. I began to be concerned about the increasing load that he was taking on, but his doctor, General Snyder, said to me, "Let him get tired. It'll do him good." Eisenhower had a favorite campaign joke that year that he used again and again, the one about the man in the street who told the Republican worker that he was going to vote for Stevenson because "I voted for him four years ago and everything has been wonderful ever since."

At a gathering of Republican leaders in Gettysburg, the President made a special effort to express his satisfaction in having Nixon as his running mate on the ticket. The aura of preconvention uncertainty about Nixon had not quite been dispelled. The Democrats were displaying placards that said, "You can still dump Nixon." Eisenhower talked at length to the party heads and workers about the unusual experience that Nixon had gained in the first term by being included in every important meeting of the administration and by his goodwill tours abroad. The President had been puzzled by the massed attacks made on Nixon by the Democrats and at one meeting in the White House with the Vice President and the Republican leaders from Congress he had brought the question up for discussion. The Congressmen suggested several reasons why Nixon had been selected as a target. They felt that the ultra-New Dealers among the Democrats regarded Nixon as a symbol of the conservative opposition that had placed on them the uncomfortable "soft on Communism" label. They also believed that the Democrats resented the wedges that had been driven between moderates and radicals of their party by Nixon's attacks.

Nixon asked the President and the Congressmen not to be concerned about him. He said that if he could continue to divide the

Democratic moderates and left-wingers he would be willing to endure the consequences. He added that the conservative Democrats took little stock in the charges of irresponsible extremism that were leveled against him. Many Democrats, Nixon said, were privately bitter about the lax handling of security affairs in Washington before 1953.

On election night, Eisenhower was more pleased by taking Texas again and adding Louisiana to the Southern states he had carried than he was by any of the other victories in his national landslide. As the returns came in, Eisenhower joined his friends and staff in a suite at a Washington hotel. As the results became conclusive, I found him in an adjoining room discussing with Nixon what he should say in his talk to the television and radio audiences later in the night. "You know, I think I'll talk about Modern Republicanism," he said.

My mind went back to the previous June when the President was in Walter Reed Hospital, recovering from his ileitis operation, and I had brought him a copy of Arthur Larson's book, *A Republican Looks at His Party*. The book was a discussion of the role of the Republican party in the modern age, and ran closely with Eisenhower's brand of politics, with its increased emphasis on Lincolnian service to the people and international responsibility, in contrast to the older Republican traditionalism. When I read it, I marked some paragraphs that seemed to me to be almost identically the same as observations I had heard from the President. I told him in the hospital that I thought he might be particularly interested in Larson's descriptions of contemporary Republicanism. From day to day, as I visited Eisenhower I noticed that his bookmark was moving steadily through the pages and one day he mentioned to me that he thought Larson had done well in his conception of the modern party and its beliefs. In August, Larson, who was then Under Secretary of Labor, appeared on television on *Meet the Press*. He was asked if the New Republicanism, about which he had written "so enthusiastically," reflected his notion of Eisenhower's political philosophy or if it was based on the President's own ideas. Larson said the book was based on the President's ideas. The next day at his press conference the President was asked how he felt about Larson's statement. Eisenhower said that although he might not agree with every word in Larson's treatise, "he expressed my philosophy of government as well as I have seen it in a book of that size."

But it was not until election night that "Modern Republicanism" was formally used by Eisenhower himself as a description of what he thought the party should stand for in response to the needs of contemporary America—a moderate government, with a sound fiscal policy, but with more willingness than the Republican administrations of the past to serve the needs of the people in common welfare where they cannot serve themselves and to take a position of responsibility in preserving peace and tranquillity abroad. "I think that Modern Republicanism has now proved itself," the President said on television and radio when he was re-elected, "and America has approved of Modern Republicanism. As we look ahead, let us remember that a political party deserves the approbation of America only as it represents the ideals, the aspirations and the hopes of Americans."

Eisenhower did not intend to label his progressive followers as Modern Republicans in an attempt to divide his party, but to a considerable extent his use of the new and liberal-sounding brand did just that. There were a great many conservative Republicans who did not want to be Modern Republicans and they said so. During the battle in Congress over Eisenhower's proposed $72 billion budget in 1957, his highest up to that time, the increased expenditures were blamed on Modern Republicanism. It was pointed out then to the President that the new label was being applied to the big budget, big spending and no tax reduction. Eisenhower replied with annoyance that Modern Republicanism had nothing to do with budgets. "Modern Republicanism, as I have said time and again, is to follow the Lincoln dictum of what government is for, and then to do it within the concept of competitive economy, sound fiscal arrangements and a sound dollar." The Lincoln dictum that Eisenhower referred to is a favorite of his, which he has quoted often:

The legitimate object of government, is to do for a community of people whatever they need to have done, but cannot do *at all,* or cannot *so well do,* for themselves—in their separate, and individual capacities.

In all that the people can individually do as well for themselves, government ought not to interfere.

As the publicizer of Modern Republicanism, Larson became a marked man. Some time after the election, Larson left the Department of Labor to succeed Theodore Streibert as director of the United States Information Agency. As soon as he was appointed to his new position, he found himself in trouble with the old-fashioned Republicans and Democrats in Congress over his agency's appropriations, which were chopped from $144 million to $105 million. Eisenhower did not need to be told that Modern Republicanism as well as economy was behind the attack on Larson's budget.

As his first term came to a close, Eisenhower could look back on four years crowded with study, discussion and decisions on such a wide variety of problems that even a quick and cursory review of only the more notable ones raises the question of how he found the time to handle half of them. Along with bigger and most urgent foreign and domestic issues—Russia, China, Korea, Indo-China, the Middle East, Hungary, the budget, taxes, economic programs, agriculture, defense, civil rights—the President was confronted daily with such things as water power, atomic energy, natural gas, highways, the Saint Lawrence Seaway, the mix-up over the distribution of Salk vaccine, tideland oil rights, the TVA and the Dixon-Yates imbroglio, amendments to the Taft-Hartley labor act, strikes, aid to schools, foreign trade and tariffs, the Oppenheimer case and other cases of internal security, health insurance, public housing, the Post Office, civil aviation, Mutual Security and Civil Service regulations. This superficial run-down does not take into account such other time-consuming duties as meetings with the press, members of Congress and visiting heads of state and foreign diplomats, not to mention conferences on party politics, patronage and the preparation of speeches, and the constant efforts to fill vacancies in important government jobs.

Keeping abreast of this work load required a steady round of thoughtful, deliberate daily decisions and yet Eisenhower was often criticized as an indecisive President. It would be more accurate to say that sometimes he did not make a decision, or take a public stand on an issue, when it was not necessary for him to do so, which is not at all the same as being indecisive. Having enough decisions, and hard ones, to make as it was, he was not eager to take on more when he was not required to declare himself. This was in keeping with the advice he often gave others never to miss an opportunity "to keep your mouth shut."

A good example of a controversial issue on which Eisenhower did not take a stand because he never had to do so was the debated labor

The Assistant to the President at his desk in the White House, June, 1956.

(N. Y. TIMES)

On most weekdays, Sherman Adams called a staff conference for 8:30 A.M. (l. to r.) J. W. Barba, assistant counsel; Bernard Shanley (front), appointments secretary; Kevin McCann (rear), speech writer; Commodore Edward Beach, naval aide; Homer Gruenther, staff assistant; Earle Chesney, staff assistant; Harold Stassen, special assistant on disarmament; Fred Seaton, department liaison (later Sec. of Interior); James P. Hagerty, press secretary; I. Jack Martin, Congressional liaison; Gerald P. Morgan, special counsel; Bryce N. Harlow, administrative assistant; Col. Robert L. Schulz, military aide; Col. Andrew J. Goodpaster, staff secretary; Gabrial Hauge, economic consultant; Maj. Gen. Persons, deputy assistant to the President. <small>(N. Y. TIMES)</small>

Key men of the White House staff: James Hagerty, Gerald Morgan, Maj. Gen. Wilton B. Persons and Bernard Shanley, in Persons' office.　(N. Y. TIMES)

At top of the President's official family: John Foster Dulles, George Humphrey, Vice-Pres. Nixon and Sherman Adams.　(N. Y. TIMES)

In summer of 1955 the author, seen here with Gen. Alfred M. Gruenther, Supreme Allied Commander, visited the NATO installations in Europe.

In July, 1955, the Big Four met at Geneva. Seated in the Garden of the Palace of Nations (l. to r.), Soviet Premier Nikolai Bulganin, Pres. Eisenhower, Edgar Faure of France and Prime Minister Anthony Eden of Great Britain.

Mr. Adams getting a report from Dr. Paul Dudley White in Denver, Oct., 1955, after the President's heart attack (UPI); and (below) the President returns to Gettysburg to recuperate; (l. to r.) the author, Rowland Hughes, President Eisenhower, Gettysburg Postmaster Oyler and Sinclair Weeks. (WIDE WORLD)

The President signs the 1956 farm bill as Sherman Adams and Gerald Morgan look on.

In Jan., 1956, Prime Minister Anthony Eden and Selwyn Lloyd, British Foreign Secretary, came to Washington for a series of talks on international affairs.

(UPI)

"Hey, Sherm.... What Team Are You Playing On?"

Cartoon by Jim Berryman in the Washington *Evening Star.*

"Maybe You'd Better Start Out With **A Funny Story**"

Cartoon by Herblock in the Washington *Post.*

A recent photograph of the author and Robert Frost at Pres. Dickey's home at Dartmouth, Hanover, N. H.

In Sept., 1957, Ark. Gov. Orval Faubus arrived at the U.S. Naval Base, Newport, for a meeting with the President.

question of the "right to work," whether an employee in a union-organized shop should be required to belong to the union, whether he wanted to or not. Senator Barry Goldwater and other conservatives tried to get the President to come out against compulsory union membership because they felt that it was a denial of the worker's freedom. Eisenhower listened to them with intent interest, but he also listened to James Mitchell, his Secretary of Labor, who held a contrary opinion. In 1954, when opponents of compulsory union membership were defending the section of the Taft-Hartley Law which permitted the states to prohibit union security provisions by so-called right-to-work laws, Mitchell came out strongly in a speech before a CIO convention in Los Angeles against the jurisdiction of the states in this field. Jerry Persons came to me in the White House, shaking his head sadly, saying that Mitchell would be under fire from Goldwater and many other Republicans in Congress who were belligerently on the other side of the fence. The next day the President was asked at his press conference if he agreed with Mitchell's thinking. Eisenhower said that Mitchell was not speaking for the administration. He pointed out that Cabinet members had the privilege of expressing their own opinions, especially when the official policy is under discussion and had not been decided. As I have said, Eisenhower never officially met the issue of compulsory union membership because he did not have to meet it. If he had, I think he would have been inclined to leave the question of jurisdiction to the states, with the power of decision.

The whole abstract question of whether a President has the responsibility to take a stand on a public issue when he has no strong or definite opinion on it one way or another was something that greatly interested Eisenhower at that time. He brought it up in a Cabinet meeting late in 1953, when Mitchell read a proposed message to Congress on amendments to the Taft-Hartley Law. The businessmen in the Cabinet were in favor of restrictive labor legislation and so were most of the Republican leaders in Congress. Mitchell and other people in the administration wanted no basic changes in the Taft-Hartley Law. The President had no pronounced convictions on the matter. He asked the Cabinet to consider what the extent of his responsibility was. Where he had no strong feelings about the merits of a program, did he have to inject himself into the argument? The question was never definitely answered and is worth further reflection by students interested in the scope of presidential responsibility.

On the other hand there were many questions on which Eisenhower had decided opinions that he did not express publicly simply because he was cautious about rushing into a public argument without a good reason. Sometimes he remained cautious even when he had a good reason to speak out. Without his sense of restraint, some of the comparatively tranquil pages in the history of the United States during the Eisenhower years might have been written in blood and turmoil. The needs of the time seemed to call for a President of deliberation, one who even seemed to hesitate occasionally, as against a leader with equal qualities of statesmanship who was a man of impulse.

Eisenhower regarded Mitchell as one of his most capable Cabinet members. Not long after Mitchell replaced Martin Durkin in the fall of 1953, the President said to me when I was talking with him about a minor conflict between the Labor and Commerce departments, "I have picked my last Secretary of Labor." Eisenhower originally selected Durkin, the head of the American Federation of Labor's plumbers union, in the hope that with one of its own men at the helm of the Labor Department organized labor would go to him instead of to the White House in seeking government help in its problems. The President felt that the White House had gotten too deeply and unnecessarily involved in labor-management disputes during the Truman administration and he wanted to break that precedent. But we soon found out that the CIO union leaders refused to deal with Durkin mainly because he belonged to the AFL, to which he would eventually return to use the knowledge and prestige he had gained to the disadvantage of the CIO. A Secretary of Labor who was unacceptable to Walter Reuther and such other CIO chiefs as David J. McDonald of the United Steelworkers could hardly function as the administration's intermediary in all labor matters as Eisenhower wanted his Labor Secretary to be. This was one reason why Durkin did not last long in the Cabinet; as a Truman Democrat, he was also basically opposed to the Eisenhower philosophy of government.

Mitchell agreed with the President that labor officials should be discouraged from carrying their grievances to the side doors of the White House as Truman had encouraged them to do. With cool logic, the Secretary established a hands-off policy for the President in the strike against the Louisville and Nashville Railroad. Even after the processes of the Railway Labor Act became exhausted and there were apparently no further legal means of reaching a settlement, Mitchell kept the President from intervening, despite pressure from several state governors and members of Congress. Eisenhower left it up to the disputants to settle their own argument, making it plain to them that any government help or suggestions for reaching a settlement would come from the federal officials involved in the case but not from the White House. When both labor and management faced up to the fact that the strike was not going to be settled by the President, the bargaining took on a new significance and disputes were soon resolved. In the first six years that he was in office, Eisenhower invoked the injunctive process only six times, half as often as Truman had done. If this was a less spectacular method of handling national emergencies than Truman's personal diplomacy, it made the arbitration machinery provided by law more effective. Mitchell gave the President credit for settling the Southern Bell Telephone strike in 1955 by a comment he made at a press conference on May 4 of that year. When he was asked what he was going to do about the strike, Eisenhower simply pointed out that mediation and conciliation service was available and said that "the law does not intend that the executive department as such shall intervene." The warring factions took the hint and made peace.

Mitchell walked into a difficult situation when he took over the Labor Department: Sinclair Weeks, the Secretary of Commerce, felt that he had a responsibility to protect the interests of business and industrial management in the formation of the administration's labor policies. After Durkin resigned, the American Federation of Labor charged that the Department of Commerce was calling the plays in labor-management matters. There had been, in fact, a constant conflict between Weeks and Durkin on the preparation of the administration's recommendations on proposed amendments to the Taft-Hartley Act. Senator Taft himself told me at one point that he was afraid the White House might send him two sets of proposals, one from Durkin and another from Weeks.

Mitchell did not expect to become the voice of organized labor in the government but he had no intention of letting the impression get around that his legislative recommendations were being unduly influenced by the Department of Commerce, no matter how erroneous such an impression might have been. He came to me in October, 1954, after he had been in the Cabinet for almost a year, with a list of instances where he thought the Commerce Department had given strong indications of trying to dominate the decisions in labor-management policy. One of these was a Commerce proposal for bringing labor unions under the jurisdiction of the Sherman Anti-Trust Act, a moot question on which the administration had not taken an official position but which organized labor naturally opposed.

These differences between Mitchell and Weeks could have easily erupted into newspaper headlines if it had not been for the patience and mature good sense of both men. I spent many hours with both Secretaries sitting across the table from each other while they ironed out their differences themselves and came to an agreement on practically every issue between them. As the Secretary of Labor in a Cabinet that included such businessmen as Humphrey, Weeks and Wilson, Mitchell was blessed with a rare intuition that enabled him to sense exactly how far he could go in holding to an independent opinion on a public labor-management issue without materially disassociating himself from the administration's policy. When he did leave the Eisenhower policy line, he did so openly after consultation with the White House, but always was careful to avoid positions that were associated with union extremists.

Although he seemed hesitant at times, there were other times when Eisenhower would make an unshakable decision in the face of strong political pressure and the urging of close friends. The President was personally in favor of the bill to amend the Natural Gas Act when it came before him early in 1956. The amendment relaxed the mandatory price control which the government exercised over gas at the wellhead, which the President believed discouraged exploration, restricted production and thus worked against the best interests of consumers. The legislation was backed by the Republicans, by the oil and gas companies and by many of Eisenhower's friends in his native state of Texas, many of whom owned large interests in underground resources.

And then, early in February when the bill was about to be passed, Senator Francis Case of South Dakota rose in the Senate to announce that a lawyer representing an oil company had contributed twenty-five hundred-dollar bills to the Senator's forthcoming campaign fund, and although he had intended to vote for the bill, he announced he would now vote against it.

When the bill passed, Eisenhower had already made up his mind to veto it, and no amount of persuasion could change it. Senator Knowland, supported by Senator Bridges and the Republican leader in the House, Charlie Halleck, argued with the President that such a veto, in the face of the undisputed merits of the bill and the long preparation that had gone into it, would cast a reflection on every member of Congress who had voted for it. The Republican leaders also contended that presidential disapproval would play into the hands of the left-wingers, who wanted regulation regardless. They also insisted that it would be impossible to get another such gas bill through Congress for a long time to come.

Eisenhower refused to budge. He said that he had already heard too much about his party being controlled by big business and that he refused to leave his administration open to the charge that the oil industry could get a bill approved in Washington by throwing money around. He vetoed the bill. "My great friends in the oil industry— and it is filled with them—have sent me messages that were not full of satisfaction and applause," he remarked later. "But they have accepted it as an honest act," he added.

On a somewhat similar issue, the claim of the states of Texas and Louisiana to submerged tideland oil deposits, the President took another militant stand that brought him as close to being at odds with Attorney General Herbert Brownell as those two men ever came during their close association together. Long before he became President, Eisenhower had become interested in the tidelands oil dispute and made a study of its historical origin, which he discussed at a Cabinet meeting in 1953. He said that when Texas was being admitted to the Union, the state had offered to cede its rights to the offshore lands to the federal government if the government would assume responsibility for the state's public debt. The offer was rejected. This convinced Eisenhower that the federal government had no legal right to the tideland oil as President Truman had claimed. During the 1953 campaign, Eisenhower promised to support Congressional action on behalf of the states and he carried on the fight after he was elected, although Senator Millikin and other Republican leaders in Congress strongly advised him to stay out of the controversy.

Examining the problem from a detached Justice Department viewpoint, Brownell conscientiously disagreed with the President and took the Justice Department's traditional position that these offshore resources belonged to all the people, and not just to the people of Texas. Brownell was willing to go so far as to permit the states to take out oil from the tidelands but he did not believe that they rightfully had title to the deposits. The President came out publicly against this view, pointing again to the facts surrounding the admission of his native Texas to the Union.

"I believe I can read English," Eisenhower said with some heat, "and after I formed my conviction, I have never found anything to change it."

To the President's satisfaction, a tidelands oil bill in favor of the states was finally passed after a filibuster, although the measure left unanswered the two big questions about the location of historic boundaries and the administration of federal oil ownership beyond those boundaries on the continental shelf. Eisenhower said in a statement when he signed the bill, "Recognizing the states' claim to these lands is in keeping with the basic principles of honesty and fair play."

The only woman who served in Eisenhower's Cabinet, Oveta Culp Hobby, did an excellent job in organizing the new Department of Health, Education and Welfare, but after the department was launched Mrs. Hobby ran into rough going. Although a brilliant administrator, she had little luck with a legislative program that was progressive and ably presented. Her first important new legislative proposal included a health insurance plan, calling for a federal reinsurance corporation that would provide the backing and encouragement for private plans to offer low-cost hospitalization and physician services. Largely because the American Medical Association regarded the plan as a step toward socialized medicine and the conservatives in Congress saw it as the beginning of another great spending program, Mrs. Hobby's program never got off the ground. Then came her troubles with the distribution of the Salk polio vaccine.

The President believed the principle of sharing responsibility between the federal and state governments together with private agencies should apply to this new program, and Mrs. Hobby worked out a plan to divide the distribution responsibility between the various state health departments, the National Foundation for Infantile Paralysis and the drug manufacturing companies. There was uncertainty and confusion behind the scenes because the requests for the vaccine from all over the country engulfed the administrators before their distribution plans could be efficiently arranged. On the day the President presented a citation to Dr. Salk officially acknowledging the success of his vaccine, Mrs. Hobby summoned the drug distributors to a meeting to work out an arrangement. While Mrs. Hobby told the Cabinet later that this had been a completely satisfactory meeting, it had to be a closed-door affair. There were trade secrets and the possibility of antitrust aspects that could not be aired publicly, she explained.

As the newspapers were quick to point out, however, the statement from Mrs. Hobby's office about what went on at the meeting took longer to prepare than the all-day meeting itself. The reporters made much of Mrs. Hobby's later protest before a Congressional committee that "no one could have foreseen the public demand" for the vaccine. As a matter of fact, few medical authorities anticipated the widespread and eager public acceptance of the vaccine. Usually there is a reluctant resistance to any new preventive medicine put out for wholesale public vaccination, but as Mrs. Hobby and the President soon learned when the hullabaloo about the confusion surrounding the distribution unexpectedly came down around our ears, there was little public resistance to the polio vaccine.

It took several months to get the mix-up straightened out. The President felt that the states should come forward with their own plans for distribution and control. This delayed somewhat public understanding of his determination that no child would be denied the vaccine because of inability to pay for it. When he found that the states were going to wait for the federal government to do the whole job, he quickly told Mrs. Hobby that the federal government would pay for the three inoculations of every poor child in the nation if necessary, even if he had to take the money out of the President's national emergency fund. Eisenhower finally became so concerned about the possibility of the public becoming panicky or of the distribution getting into black market operations that he told the Republican leaders in Congress that he was ready to have the government take over the responsibility for financing and distribution while the vaccine continued in short supply. Mrs. Hobby pleaded with him to give the states a chance to co-operate.

At no time did the federal government take over the Salk vaccine program, although there were many critics who felt that it should have done so. It was pointed out that there was no confusion about the distribution in Canada, where the entire plan was under government supervision.

In all of the tension and anguish of the Salk crisis, there was never a serious difference of opinion between Mrs. Hobby and the President that changed his high opinion of her ability as an administrator. The troubles in the introduction of the polio vaccine program were largely due to differences between the various medical factions involved, that were far beyond Mrs. Hobby's control. For example, at one point the Public Health authorities advised a halt in vaccinations to await an examination of children who had received the vaccine while at the same time Dr. Scheele, the Surgeon General, was saying that no interruption in the vaccinations was necessary. Such conflicting statements left the country a little mystified. When Mrs. Hobby resigned as Secretary of Health, Education and Welfare in July, her resignation had no connection with the Salk vaccine controversy. She had explained to the President several months earlier that the illness of her husband in Texas would require her to give up her work in Washington. Before she left, the President praised her performance as a Cabinet member and said that she had demonstrated that properly trained women were just as competent as men in carrying out heavy executive duties in government.

As an example of how times quickly change, a year after the public clamor for polio vaccine, the President was obliged to make an urgent public appeal to people who had not been immunized to shake off their apathy and come forward for vaccination. Marion Folsom, who had succeeded Mrs. Hobby, was able to report then that even where only one or two doses had been administered the incidence of paralytic polio had declined 75 per cent.

In that spring of 1955, at the same time that she was embroiled in the Salk vaccine controversy, Mrs. Hobby encountered another trying experience when she tried to launch in Congress a program providing federal aid to the states for school construction. Eisen-hower's administration was severely criticized by such Democrats as Adlai Stevenson for not relieving the shortage of classrooms that was harassing the country during its explosive population growth. The President himself was deeply concerned with the problem; he often said that he viewed education as a security need as vital as military preparedness, and he was acutely conscious of the strides that the Russians were making in science with their accelerated educational system. But any move to push a federal school aid bill through Congress was complicated then as now by the perennial question of whether such aid should be extended to Church-sponsored parochial schools and by the arguments over whether the racially segregated schools of the South were entitled to federal funds. There was also the fear that federal aid might lead to federal control of the curriculum. Public education in the United States has always been regarded as a state and local responsibility, and local opinion about the needs and requirements of schools varies so much in different sections of the country that any kind of national plan meets with widely conflicting reactions.

Mrs. Hobby's Health, Education and Welfare Department worked intensively for many months with Samuel Brownell, the Federal Commissioner of Education and the Attorney General's brother, on a school aid program that was presented to the President and the Cabinet on January 14, 1955. It called for the federal government to give limited financial help to a state school authority, a public corporate device for the financing of school construction through public bond issues and other borrowing plans without burdening the state government or the school districts with the direct responsibility for the debt structure. Such an authority system had already been established successfully in Pennsylvania. Under the Hobby-Brownell plan, the federal government would purchase bonds from these state authorities when they were unable to sell them on the public market at reasonable interest rates. The long-term cost of the program to the federal government would have been low, only around $15 million. To get the financing of new school buildings started, $100 million would have been advanced to the state authorities, but this money would have been returned over a three-year period.

Humphrey did not care for some features of the financing plan.

He felt that it might lead to charges that the federal government was competing against private financial interests in the public securities market, and he suspected that the debt limitations could be by-passed. The President gave the plan warm support but he questioned whether it would provide real relief to the national school shortage, and he wanted to make sure that the state governments would share equal responsibility with the federal government. Nixon and others in the Cabinet backed the program because they felt that it was urgent for the President and the administration to become identified with some effective school construction plan.

The program was brought up for discussions at Cabinet meetings and Congressional leadership meetings all that spring. Samuel Mc-Connell, the ranking Republican on the House Education and Labor committee, called it the best school bill ever devised. But McConnell was from Pennsylvania, where the authority idea had caught on. Congressmen from other parts of the country were more dubious. The parochial school aid question got into the argument and slowed up the bill's progress. In May Mrs. Hobby reported that she did not even expect the bill to be reported out of committee in the Senate. It was caught in a shower of Democratic counter-proposals that called for bigger and more direct federal handouts for education, which included one bill from Senator Lister Hill of Alabama which provided for $500 million in direct grants over a two-year period.

The President directed Howard Pyle, his deputy assistant in charge of inter-governmental relations, to organize a public relations campaign in an attempt to draw public attention and support to the administration's proposal. He asked Cabinet members to awaken interest in the Hobby-Brownell bill among their friends outside of Washington. But, as he noted in a legislative leaders' meeting at the end of the year, a program for school aid such as this one, that lacked the glamour of huge federal expenditures, could gain no ground in Congress. Mrs. Hobby probably summed it up well in one White House discussion about the bill when she said that it seemed as if the Democrats were determined to keep Eisenhower from getting any credit for good work in the areas of social progress and human welfare.

The Eisenhower administration never did solve the problem of classroom shortages. There was virtually not a single responsible educator in the country who came forward to defend the school authority idea sponsored by Mrs. Hobby and Samuel Brownell and warmly endorsed by the President in 1955. So an entirely different approach had to be taken in 1956. This time the administration proposed the direct purchase of local school district bonds that were unable to find any other market. In addition Eisenhower backed a direct grant program to school districts which met a test of need. But the Republicans and conservative Democrats were reluctant about spending the $200 million the plan would have cost; the educators damned it with faint praise and the bill went down to defeat in the House by a handful of votes.

Eisenhower finally broke new ground in Federal assistance to education when he signed into law on September 2, 1958, the National Defense Education Act. National urgencies in education had taken on a new and quite different aspect with the launching of the Russian Sputnik and the discovery of how woefully deficient we were in the production of advanced scholars in science and technology. Although Congress turned down Eisenhower's request for a limited number of incentive scholarships, it did give him most of the program he asked for in his special message of January 27, 1958. The national security now required the federal government to play an emergency role, the President told the Congress, specifically coming to the rescue in a broad variety of programs designed to improve the quality and quantity of education in science and mathematics, promote better teaching, discover and encourage individual talent and further more competent teaching of foreign languages.

This program turned its back on the more fundamental problem of classroom deficiencies, which had to give way to more temporary emergencies. Whatever would have to be done about the shortage of classrooms Eisenhower left to his successor.

One of Eisenhower's most frustrating experiences in his first term as President was the controversy over the Dixon-Yates contract with the government to build a privately owned electric power plant at West Memphis, Arkansas, to supply power to the city of Memphis and the Atomic Energy Commission. The negotiations with Dixon-Yates were seized upon by the Democrats in the Senate in 1954 and ballyhooed for political propaganda as a sinister plot between the administration and big business. The Democrats charged that the purpose of the Dixon-Yates negotiations was to award to private interests power business that rightfully belonged to the New Deal's publicly owned Tennessee Valley Authority. The Democratic National Chairman, Stephen A. Mitchell, and Senator Wayne Morse went so far as to point out that one of the directors of the Southern Company, a partner in the undertaking, was Eisenhower's close friend, Bobby Jones, the former golf champion. Morse said something in the Senate about the golf stick becoming the power yardstick.

The President was not trying to take business away from the colossal TVA but he did feel, as a lot of other people did, that the TVA was big enough already and he was opposed to further expansion of the huge government-owned power empire into new territory where it would enjoy a publicly subsidized rate-making advantage over tax-paying private power companies. Eisenhower said that he looked upon the expansion of the TVA as a form of "creeping socialism." He was deeply concerned about the growth of this federal power monopoly at the expense of the taxpayers of New England and the Middle West, whose industries were moving into the South because of the attraction of the TVA's cheaper power rates. But as much as he was opposed to its expansion, he always was careful to point out every time the subject of TVA came up that he was not out to cripple it or turn it over to private interests.

When the President was going over the budget in 1954, Director Joseph Dodge called his attention to a TVA request for funds to build a new steam-generating plant at Fulton, Missouri, near Memphis, which, in addition to meeting new demands within the region, would reach out into new territory never before serviced by the TVA. Eisenhower and Dodge went over the figures and called in Lewis Strauss, Chairman of the Atomic Energy Commission. The proposed plant was to supply power to Memphis and to replace elsewhere in the TVA system a large block of power that the TVA was feeding to the AEC plant at Paducah, Kentucky. The President, Dodge and Strauss agreed that there should be no further expansion of the TVA with public money; if the city of Memphis needed more power it could build its own plant or buy from a private utility company, and the AEC could also use privately produced electricity, as it was doing in the Ohio River valley. The President also decided to charge the TVA an adequate rate of interest on the public investment in its power facilities. This new policy, along with the administration's opposition to new TVA steam-generating plants, started the rumbling in Congress that Eisenhower was out to cripple the TVA.

When the TVA directors learned that Strauss was considering private power sources, they requested him to relieve the strain that was being put on their facilities by the AEC plant at Paducah, now that their plan for the Fulton plant was being discarded. In the spring of 1954, the Atomic Energy Commission and the Bureau of the Budget entered into negotiations with Edgar H. Dixon's Middle South Utilities to build the plant at West Memphis for the dual purpose of replacing in the TVA system there the power being consumed by the AEC in Kentucky and supplying electricity to Memphis. Dixon was to share the financial burden of the hundred-million-dollar project with the Southern Company, whose chairman was E. A. Yates. Hence the Dixon-Yates tag that was put on the contract.

Before the negotiations were completed, Dodge bowed out as Director of the Budget, and was replaced on April 15 by his assistant, Rowland Hughes. Earlier, Dodge had felt the need of a consultant thoroughly familiar with the financial and technical details of such an undertaking as the Dixon-Yates contract and selected Adolph Wenzell, a retired vice president and director of the First Boston Corporation, an investment banking firm. In February, Wenzell told Dodge and Hughes that the First Boston Corporation was planning to participate in the financing of the Dixon-Yates plant if a contract were actually negotiated and asked them if his status as a consultant to the Bureau of the Budget would stand in the way of the First Boston Corporation's interest in the venture.

It did not occur to Dodge or Hughes then that Wenzell in his capacity as an adviser and former member of the Boston banking firm might have been advising Dixon and Yates at the same time that he was advising the government. Furthermore, as far as the Bureau of the Budget was concerned, Wenzell was not a key figure in its decisions on the Dixon-Yates contract, although he did take part in some of the conferences on certain financial aspects of the agreement.

The President was well aware of the political trouble that he was facing in calling a halt to the invasion of new territory by the TVA and he went over the Dixon-Yates proposition carefully with the Republican leaders in Congress before he announced his intention to accept the Dixon-Yates proposal to build the West Memphis plant. He looked around the table in the Cabinet Room and asked for dissenting opinions but there were none. As he expected, a storm broke on the Democratic side of Congress and, as it grew worse during the rest of 1954 and into 1955, the President became all the more angrily determined to fight it to a finish. At a Republican leadership meeting in May, he said that he would veto any attempt by the Democrats to build the steam-generating plants for the TVA that he had disapproved. "It's time to stop being bulldozed!" he exclaimed.

The President was subjected to such an unrelenting barrage of insinuating questions about the Dixon-Yates transaction that in August, 1954, he asked Hughes and Strauss to prepare for release to the press a complete chronology of the government's role in the negotiations. Unfortunately, one item of information was left out of the chronology by Hughes and this omission became a main bone of contention when the Democrats discovered it later. Hughes made no mention of the fact that Adolph Wenzell had served as a financial consultant in the Bureau of the Budget when the Dixon-Yates contract first came under consideration.

In October, the Democrats switched their line of attack from charges that Eisenhower was wrecking the TVA to a question of ethics in the negotiation of the contract. This placed Lewis Strauss, whose AEC was representing the government in the Dixon-Yates transaction, on a political spot and the President came strongly to Strauss's defense. "I can't think of any man in government whom I trust more as to his integrity, his common sense and his business acumen than Lewis Strauss," Eisenhower declared. But the conservative and often uncompromising Strauss had enemies among the Democrats in Congress. Late in January, 1955, the joint Congressional Committee on Atomic Energy, raising doubts about the actions of some of the subsidiaries involved, advised a cancellation of the contract. The President noted that the vote on this resolution was strictly along party lines.

Then, in February, the Democratic Senator from Alabama, Lister Hill, came up with what appeared to be the dual role of Adolph Wenzell and the unhappy omission of Wenzell from the chronology released the previous August. When Hill asked Hughes about Wenzell, the Budget Director said that the banker had been a government consultant but he did not volunteer any information to the Senator about Wenzell's connection through the First Boston Corporation to the Dixon-Yates group. Hughes told Hill he had omitted Wenzell from the chronology to avoid possible political controversy over a matter that was not really significant in the contract negotiations.

Hill made a speech in the Senate, saying that Wenzell had apparently participated in government conferences on the contract at the same time that he was arranging financing of the Dixon-Yates partnership by the First Boston Corporation. The Senator also charged Hughes with covering up Wenzell's dual role. When Eisenhower wanted to know about the substance of Hill's charges, Hughes unfortunately neglected to tell the President the full facts of the extent to which Wenzell was involved in the Dixon-Yates transaction. Consequently, the President was left with the impression that Wenzell had nothing to do with the actual arrangement of the Dixon-Yates contract. He said at a press conference, "Mr. Wenzell was never called in or asked a single thing about the Dixon-Yates contract. . . . He was brought in as a technical adviser and nothing else, and before this contract was ever even proposed." Later in the same press conference, he indicated some haziness about Wenzell's role when he admitted there might have been "an overlap of a week or two" when Wenzell could have been advising the Budget Bureau on some aspects of the Dixon-Yates contract. Immediately after the press conference the President found out, of course, to his great irritation that his information was neither wholly accurate nor quite complete. Hagerty then issued an amplifying statement, which said that from January 14 to April 3 Wenzell had in fact been an adviser to the Budget Bureau on certain technical details of the contract.

Greatly to my surprise, I was accused by the Democrats of interceding with the hearings in Congress in order to hold back certain information pertinent to the case. On Saturday, June 11, 1955, I received a call from Hughes, who asked me if I could arrange a postponement of the Security and Exchange Commission hearings that were scheduled to open the following Monday concerning the financing plans of the Mississippi Valley Generating Company, the newly formed Dixon-Yates subsidiary. Hughes explained that the Budget Bureau needed the advice of attorneys who would not be available before the hearings were scheduled to open on the following Monday. Hughes had questions about the propriety of submitting certain evidence at the hearings and about the appearance of witnesses. I called Sinclair Armstrong, the SEC Chairman, and relayed Hughes's request to him. After consulting with members of the commission, Armstrong called me back to tell me that the request was granted.

Senator Kefauver pointed out later that on that Monday a vote was scheduled to be taken in the House of Representatives on an appropriation for the transmission line between the Dixon-Yates plant and the TVA facilities. He claimed that Wenzell would have been one of the witnesses at the SEC hearing on the same day and that I requested the postponement of the hearing in order to delay Wenzell's testimony about the Dixon-Yates financing until after the House vote. Such a motive never entered my head when I called Armstrong and, to the best of my knowledge, Hughes and the other administration officials involved had no thought of the House vote on the transmission line appropriation when they asked for the postponement of the SEC hearing.

The Dixon-Yates battle never came to an ultimate showdown because the city of Memphis decided to build a power plant of its own. From the President's viewpoint, this was preferable to a privately owned plant financed by the federal government and on July 11 he ordered the Dixon-Yates contract canceled. Dixon and Yates immediately sought to recover $3,534,788 which they had spent on the project. When the Atomic Energy Commission decided that no damages were due because Wenzell's role had been improper, Dixon and Yates brought suit, and the case dragged through the courts until 1961, when the Supreme Court decided in the government's favor.

Wenzell was an unfortunate victim of a political vendetta. He never had an influential voice in any of the important decisions that were made by the Bureau of the Budget on the Dixon-Yates contract. His presence, as a competent consultant in a minor advisory capacity at a few conferences about the technicalities of the negotiations, was distorted and exaggerated by the Democrats far beyond its actual importance. Wenzell never attempted to conceal from Dodge and Hughes his Boston firm's financial connection with the Dixon-Yates group, as he certainly might have done if there had been anything sinister about it. Furthermore, there was nothing improper about the Dixon-Yates contract itself or the reasons for it. From the point of view of the government and the taxpayers, it was a good contract under the circumstances, carefully scrutinized by the Atomic Energy Commission, the Department of Justice, the Federal Power Commission and the General Accounting Office. It was an improvement over previous contracts with private concerns; it placed a ceiling on the amount of construction costs which could be absorbed in power rates; it fixed a limit on operating costs which could be carried to rates—it even placed a ceiling on the earnings of the plant.

Eisenhower's only motive in sponsoring the privately owned power plant was to check further growth of the TVA, which he regarded as a product of the "whole-hog" theory of the previous Democratic administrations—the idea that the federal government must undertake great resource development projects alone, freezing out the energy and initiative of local government and local people engaged in private enterprise. "This whole-hog mentality," he said during his 1952 campaign, "leans toward the creation of a more extensive and stifling monopoly than this country has ever seen. The present [Truman] administration's answer to further resource development is the Valley Authority, a supergovernment blueprinted in Washington, D.C., and manned from there. You don't need more supergovernment." Having been elected on such views and intentions, Eisenhower was trying to carry them out.

After the open-skies inspection plan that Eisenhower presented to the Russians at Geneva was finally thrown down by the Soviet government early in 1956, the President and his willing and eager assistant in charge of disarmament proposals, Harold Stassen, reached down to pick up the pieces and start over again. Eisenhower never gave up on disarmament, and the energetic Stassen, carrying maps, charts and voluminous technical research, stayed close at his side. Sometimes the President found Stassen way ahead of him. To the members of the Cabinet, accustomed to long and futile discussions of the subject, disarmament was something as theoretical and abstract as calculus. To Dulles it was a problem that never seemed to get out of the laboratory where it had been ever since he had become familiar with it in the Wilson administration—often experimented with but a workable and acceptable formula for applying it never discovered. But to Eisenhower and Stassen, disarmament was a real and urgent necessity of today, the only means of gaining peace and security.

The President spent long hours of discussion in search of ideas to break the disarmament deadlock with Russia. In 1956 he exchanged letters on disarmament with Bulganin, who was then Chairman of the Soviet Union's governing council and the spokesman for Nikita Khrushchev, the head of the Russian Communist party. In more recent years, the talkative Khrushchev realized that he did not need a spokesman. Eisenhower looked on the correspondence as a basis for promoting mutual confidence that would set the stage for definite talks and proposals. A letter from the Soviet leader on January 23 proposed a twenty-year treaty of friendship between the United States and Russia. Eisenhower replied that the two countries were already bound in such a pact by the United Nations Charter. The President wrote to Bulganin: "I wonder whether again going through a treaty-making procedure, and this time on a bilateral basis only, might indeed work against the cause of peace by creating the illusion that a stroke of the pen had achieved a result which in fact can be obtained only by a change of spirit." Discussions of disarmament between the Americans and the Russians always came back to the two proposals that were exchanged at the 1955 Geneva summit conference, Eisenhower's open-skies and mutual aerial inspection, with the Soviets opposing this idea and hammering away at reductions in the levels of armed forces, especially our military bases in Europe. Eisenhower and Dulles were wary of Russian proposals for limitations on standing forces and military budgets as too easy to evade. What should be controlled, they maintained, was weapons, not men, because fire power or nuclear strength could be more accurately checked by inspections.

Yet the President never lost heart. He kept telling Dulles and the military chiefs, who were skeptical about the chances of working out any kind of an inspection agreement with the Soviets, that we must not stand still. He spent hours with Dulles and Stassen on the questions of diplomatic approaches and with Strauss and the military leaders on technicalities, insisting on concrete proposals. It was Stassen's duty, as the President's disarmament co-ordinator, to bring the State Department, the Defense Department, the Atomic Energy Commission and other government agencies that were concerned into areas of agreement. When they reached an impasse, as they did often, the President himself would call them together and get them moving ahead again.

Dulles patiently did his best to work with Stassen, but the Secretary was skeptical of people who got off by themselves where he could not keep tabs on what they were doing in fields that affected policies for which he was responsible. Dulles recognized Stassen's capabilities, but he knew Stassen was an eager beaver who would follow his own diplomatic channels and might undertake negotiations on his own with the Russians in an effort to reach an agreement. In 1957, when this happened, Dulles came to the conclusion that Stassen's efforts were so disconcerting to our friends in Europe that they had to stop.

Before attending the meeting of the United Nations Disarmament Subcommittee in London in March, 1956, Stassen came up with some concrete policy positions on which proposals to the Soviets could be based. These he put before the President and Dulles, with recommendations for positive and aggressive action. Stassen had worked with a special study and research group for a year on the report. One of the most appealing arguments for disarmament in the document was Stassen's picture of the benefits to the American people from a disarmament program that would bring an end to the tremendous expense of building modern weapons and maintaining a nuclear defense arsenal. A third of these savings could go to balance the budget and reduce taxes, Stassen suggested, and another third to new schools and hospitals, highways and other national needs, with the rest devoted to strengthening the economic programs in the undeveloped nations.

The report from Stassen's study group pointed out, among other things, that no international disarmament plan acceptable to us could assume anything but bad faith on the part of the Soviet Union and Communist China. The study held that it would be impossible to assume that one nation could obtain certain and positively accurate knowledge of the extent of nuclear production and resources in another nation, nor could it be assumed that control of another country's nuclear production would ever be possible. Any agreement would have to be supported by positive proof that the participating nations were complying with the agreement. No reliance could be placed on a world government, in Stassen's view.

Stassen said that estimates of Russian nuclear attack capability varied widely, but at that time (the study was based on 1955 estimates) it was generally agreed that a decisive surprise attack could be launched by the Soviets by 1965, plus or minus a few years. The Stassen studies indicated that the United States would have the striking power in 1960 that the Russians would have in 1965, along with the ability to make a strong retaliatory attack. Some experts estimated that other nations would soon match the capability of the United States and Russia and that mutual deterrent power would act as a powerful restraining factor.

The international disarmament plan that Stassen recommended in his report was based on mutual inspections of all kinds of weapons, chemical and bacteriological as well as nuclear and conventional. Rigid economic and diplomatic sanctions would be applied as punishment to any government that failed to open itself to complete disclosure or refused to discontinue weapon-testing. Stassen admitted that even the most efficient disarmament plan could only serve as a protection against an annihilating surprise attack. Because there was no way of knowing the exact present size of Soviet weapon stockpiles, the Russians could continue nuclear production, claiming that the new products had been made earlier before the agreement went into effect. And even if nuclear weapons were abolished, there was no sure way of halting Russian or Chinese aggression.

Stassen argued in conclusion that the United States must move ahead forcefully to reach some basis for a disarmament agreement because the development of intercontinental missiles and thermonuclear weapons was making the danger of a devastating attack more urgent as each day passed. He called for a direct approach to the Soviet leaders, clearing away the underbrush of old, mistaken assumptions and stressing the need for safeguarding mutual survival. It turned out that Stassen was to get the opportunity for such a face-to-face meeting with Khrushchev much sooner than he expected, and in his usual confident and unhesitating manner, he made the most of it.

While he was in London as the United States representative at the United Nations disarmament conference, which opened on March 18, 1956, Stassen and his wife were invited to a Soviet reception for Khrushchev and Bulganin given by Ambassador Malik at Claridge's. There was such a throng milling about Khrushchev and Bulganin that Stassen did not try to get near enough to have any personal conversation with them. Just as he was on the point of leaving the reception, Gromyko came to him for an exchange of greetings and learned that the Stassens had not yet had a chance to talk with Khrushchev and Bulganin. He then asked the Stassens to follow him into an adjoining room and summoned Bulganin, who, in turn, called Khrushchev away from the crowd outside. The talkative and exuberant Khrushchev began immediately to discuss disarmament with Stassen. The conversation went on until Stassen, conscious that he was monopolizing the guest of honor's time at the reception, said apologetically that he did not wish to impose on him. Khrushchev waved the remark aside, saying that such opportunities for getting together with an American government official did not come to him often, and went on talking.

Khrushchev told Stassen that he was unable to understand the American insistence on aerial photographic inspections. He said that only the Russians' respect for Eisenhower, the author of the open-skies proposal, had kept them from rejecting it completely. Zhukov was against aerial inspections, Khrushchev said, implying that the opinion of the Soviet military leader who had been Eisenhower's wartime friend should carry some weight in the White House. Russia did not want any pictures of anybody else's country, he added, and he was unable to see why the United States wanted photographs of the Soviet Union.

Stassen patiently went over the reasons why we had decided that aerial observations were the most efficient means of carrying out an effective inspection system in such vast countries as Russia and Communist China. Ground inspection could not keep up in a jet age. The United States always wants to know everything, Khrushchev argued, going on at length about the mania of the imperialists for peeking into other people's bedrooms and gardens. "You treat the Soviet Union like a rich uncle treats a pauper nephew," he said and cited what he called our interference in the internal affairs of Guatemala as an example of our improper meddling in the private business of neighbors.

Khrushchev found out that Stassen was not one to be easily browbeaten. When Stassen got wound up, even such an adept interrupter as Khrushchev could do nothing but listen. Stassen said that the aerial inspection plan, like all disarmament agreement proposals, would be worthless unless Russia had some confidence in the good intentions of the United States, and that there could never be peace between the two countries as long as there were suspicion and friction on either side. He told Khrushchev that he was shocked by the Russian leader's castigation of the Americans and by his total misconception of the American attitude toward Russia. The United States respected Russia and recognized it as a great nation, even though its economic, social and political systems were opposed to ours. As proof of that recognition the American President had participated with the Soviet Union heads in the Geneva conference. Didn't Khrushchev appreciate the significance of Eisenhower's willingness to attend that summit meeting?

Khrushchev conceded that point but suggested that perhaps Eisenhower had gone to Geneva out of personal curiosity. Maybe the President had merely wanted to see what kind of men were running the Soviet Union, Khrushchev said; maybe he wanted to form an opinion of their characteristics and their ability at the conference table. Wasn't Eisenhower criticized in the United States for going to Geneva?

Such criticism by the political opposition was a part of America's freedom of speech that Khrushchev might have some difficulty understanding because it was at variance with the Russian system, Stassen replied. It was our way of doing things and we believed in it and it had made our nation strong and successful. Stassen reminded the Soviet leaders that the President had replied to such criticism by declaring that he was trying to avoid a war that would damage both America and Russia and the whole world.

Khrushchev agreed with this sentiment. He said that there were only a few madmen in the United States and in Russia who disagreed with it.

Bulganin and Khrushchev both expressed doubt that the United States had serious intentions of going through with a disarmament agreement. They mentioned the latest letter received by Bulganin from Eisenhower, in which the President repeated his disapproval of the Soviet offer of an agreement based on the reduction of troops rather than on a limitation of weapons. They said that they regarded the letter as an effort by the President to avoid their earlier offer of a treaty of friendship.

Khrushchev referred to various incidents which he claimed were evidence of American unfriendliness, among them a refusal of entry for a group of Russian cooks who wanted to look at kitchens in the United States. "Now cooks are only armed with knives, forks and spoons and they could do the United States no harm," he said. He also mentioned a party of agricultural experts whom he wanted to send to America to inspect some seed corn he had bought from an American dealer who had come to see him. But by the time we had agreed to admit two inspectors he had decided that he could get along without the corn.

Bulganin entered the conversation to say that the Soviet Union, after thirty years of strong growth, was no longer afraid of anybody and, as an example of that self-confidence, he mentioned that a visa to visit Russia would now be given to any American who wanted it. Stassen observed that this was quite a departure from past Soviet policy and Khrushchev readily agreed with him, calling the open door to tourists a major change in his government's policy. Khrushchev recalled a conversation that he had with Stassen in 1947 in which he had predicted that the United States was about to suffer a great economic depression and Stassen had disagreed with him. "You were right," Khrushchev said, "but I do not agree that your system can correctly be called a people's capitalism."

Khrushchev told Stassen as the conversation drew to a close that he did not think the time was yet ripe for disarmament. But Russia would wait peacefully until that time came, he added. The United States could also wait, Stassen said, but during the waiting period other nations would inevitably develop nuclear capability and increase the danger to peace.

"That might be true," Khrushchev said. "But what can be done about it?"

Stassen insisted that a start toward disarmament had to be made by the United States and Russia now, with no further waiting. Khrushchev repeated stubbornly that the Soviets would not agree to the open-skies plan. Would the United States match Russia in reducing its armed forces by a million men and reducing arms in proportion, he asked. Stassen came back to aerial inspection and Khrushchev impatiently told him that no aerial inspection would be necessary if the Americans would agree to the reduction in force levels.

"Without inspection, how can we quiet the suspicions that will arise?" Stassen asked. "Suppose we agree to reduce the forces and then the generals in the Soviet Army charge that the United States is not making the reductions. Wouldn't that cause great trouble?"

"I'll take care of our generals," Khrushchev said. "If they don't agree to our political decisions, they will be changed."

Khrushchev said that the United States could make a start toward disarmament by reducing its troops in Germany. "The Soviet Union would be ready to act with you," he said. Stassen said that it would be difficult to make such a reduction unless East and West Germany were reunited under a government of the German people's own choosing. Khrushchev replied that Russia was ready to reduce its forces without considering the German question. Stassen suggested that a test strip of territory be used for a trial of aerial inspection but Khrushchev was not interested, unless the Americans were willing to agree to a reduction in forces. The discussion ended with Khrushchev asking Stassen to carry on further disarmament talks directly with the Russians through Andrei Gromyko, instead of through the United Nations disarmament subcommittee. Khrushchev said that he did not care for the procedure of the subcommittee; it seemed to him to consist mainly of hair-splitting in order to avoid decisions. Stassen, believing in the direct approach himself, agreed to Khrushchev's suggestion.

At the London conference that spring the Russians echoed what Khrushchev said to Stassen at Claridge's; they proposed cutting the armed forces of the United States, China and the Soviet Union down to 1.5 million men each and those of Britain and France to 650,000 each, but they refused to consider aerial inspection. Stassen placed several American proposals before the subcommittee, including one for a demonstration test of aerial inspection procedure over thirty thousand square miles of United States and Russian territory. Eisenhower remarked, "The Russians apparently continue to put down as the most important thing that there be an agreement of some kind before there is any system of determining whether either of us is living up to the agreement." That May the Soviets announced that they were planning to reduce their armed forces by 1.2 million men within the following year, but they refused to say how many men would be left in their forces after the reduction was made.

Khrushchev had boasted during the conference that Russia would soon have missiles with H-bomb warheads. When Eisenhower was asked to comment on Khrushchev's statement, he let it be known obliquely that the United States was also doing things with H-bombs. "We know how expensive these things are when you put them on airplanes," he said. After the London conference, Bulganin and Eisenhower exchanged two more letters on disarmament and in his second one, which arrived in Washington ironically when the Soviet Army was invading Hungary in November, Bulganin struck a rather surprising new note of hope. He said that Russia was prepared to consider using aerial photography to the east and west of a line separating NATO forces in Europe and those participating in the Warsaw Pact. The Soviets were still unwilling to test aerial inspection in Russia itself, but for them to express any interest at all in the American-sponsored plan for a reciprocal surveillance from the sky was something of a concession.

The arms question entered into the presidential election campaign that fall when Adlai Stevenson promised that if he were elected one of his first moves would be to seek an agreement with the Soviets ending further H-bomb tests because of the fall-out of Strontium-90, the radioactive ingredient that Stevenson referred to as causing bone cancer, sterility and various other diseases. Stevenson said, however, that he was not opposed to tests with smaller nuclear weapons.

Hagerty and I agreed that the scare headlines that Stevenson was getting called for some action by Eisenhower in straightening out the facts for the millions of people who were deeply troubled by the ominous reports. The President asked the Atomic Energy Commission and other agencies to submit to him every fact in their possession on the effects of Strontium-90 fall-out from thermonuclear tests. He found that in the opinion of the National Academy of Sciences the elements received by the average person from such ex-

posure at the prevailing rate of testing was only a small fraction of
the amount of the same material that he would absorb in his normal
lifetime from natural sources and medical X-rays. Eisenhower also
pointed out that the danger from fall-out could not be avoided just
by limiting the size of the bombs, as Stevenson had seemed to suggest. "Fission is the basic phenomenon of the smaller weapons," he
said. "The idea that we can 'stop sending this dangerous material
into the air' by concentrating upon small fission weapons is based
upon apparent unawareness of the facts."

The President urged Stassen to keep on searching aggressively for
a new way to break the disarmament deadlock at the next United
Nations Disarmament Subcommittee meeting in London in 1957.
Stassen prepared for presentation in London a long list of proposals.
When these ideas were ready to be discussed, the President went
over them in a meeting attended by Dulles, Stassen, Wilson, Radford
and William Jackson. Stassen wanted to conduct exploratory talks
with the British and needed an agreement about the subjects for negotiation. Dulles wanted to try an agreement that would test the intentions of the Soviets. Radford was wary of any agreement to reduce
our strength that would be based on the good faith of the Soviets.
Strauss talked about the difficulty of detecting underground blasts
and of devising a reliable inspection system. Nobody completely
agreed with anybody else. His patience exhausted, the President interrupted the game of musical chairs. "Something has got to be done,"
he declared. "We cannot just drift along or give up. This is a question
of survival and we must put our minds at it until we can find some
way of making progress. Now that's all there is to it." The discussion
began again until it reached the point where the President said to
Stassen, "Now take these things we've discussed to Lewis Strauss and
the Defense people and get up a paper on which they can agree." As
everybody arose to leave the room, Stassen collected his notes and
went back to work again. That was how it went with disarmament
talks most of the time.

But the 1957 five-power disarmament conference that opened in
London in March of that year proved to be a notable exception to
the general rule. Stassen worked intensively with the representatives
of the Soviet Union, Britain, Canada and France through a series of
negotiations that lasted for six months in an atmosphere of remark-

able harmony and mutual determination. Even Dulles, who was usually skeptical of disarmament efforts, became deeply impressed by the progress that was made. Reviewing the conference later, the Secretary said, "I believe more progress toward disarmament has been made at these talks than has ever been made before in the long history of efforts toward disarmament."

During the first few months of the meeting the Russian representative, Valerian Zorin, showed a willingness to co-operate with the Western powers that excited a real hope for peace. There was much speculation in Washington about what was causing the big change in the Soviet attitude. Eisenhower, fighting a battle in Congress over the high defense costs in his budget, said that he thought that perhaps the Russians, like the Americans, were feeling the painful economic strain of the expensive arms race. On the questions of the banning of nuclear tests, conventional weapons disarmament, reductions in troop levels and the arrangements about an international control system, Zorin bargained seriously and realistically. Then in April, the Russian negotiator went back to Moscow for consultations and returned with a proposal to open the skies of Eastern Europe, a part of western Russia and Siberia in exchange for the right to survey the United States west of the Mississippi, Alaska and most of Western Europe. As one observer said, the Soviets were asking a large *quid* for a small *quo,* but the door to reciprocal aerial inspection was finally open.

The excited and optimistic Stassen hurried to Washington to discuss the Soviet proposal and possible counteroffers to it with the President and the Cabinet, the National Security Council and leaders of Congress. "More honest and hard work is being done than has been our experience in the past," Eisenhower said happily. Then complications developed in Moscow and among the NATO governments in Western Europe.

The Soviets balked at attempts to widen the aerial inspection zones they had proposed. Recalling Khrushchev's invitation to him in the talk at Claridge's to deal directly with the Russians, Stassen took a gamble. Throwing the prescribed conventional approaches to the winds, he went to work on the Russians himself. Instead of working through the subcommittee, he began to carry on his own negotiations with the Soviets and this stirred up anger and suspicion among the

British, French and Canadians. Stassen felt it was the only way to get something done; he reasoned that if he could move Zorin by private persuasion he could always patch up later the resentment that he was causing among our Western Allies.

Dulles came to the White House, thoroughly exasperated with what Stassen was doing in London. I never saw the Secretary more upset and I could see then that Stassen's service in his present role was already dated as far as Dulles was concerned. The Russians were taking charge of Stassen, Dulles declared, and they were using him to drive a wedge between the United States and the Western European powers. The turn that the negotiations in London was taking was causing trouble for Konrad Adenauer, the Chancellor of West Germany and a strong supporter of the United States and NATO. The political opposition fighting Adenauer in West Germany's election campaign, the Social Democrat party, was in favor of seeking unification of Germany through a direct deal with the Soviet Union instead of bargaining as a member of NATO with the backing of the United States, Britain and France, as Adenauer advocated. The Social Democrats were now pointing out to Adenauer's embarrassment that the United States was itself negotiating directly with the Soviets on disarmament while Germany's unification was still unsettled.

Stassen was called to Washington again for more consultations and Adenauer made a hurried trip from Bonn to the White House. Dulles issued a sharp statement which said of the London conference, "This is not a bilateral negotiation. . . . We are not going to throw into discord the views of our allies just in order to make speed with the Soviet Union." Stassen's impromptu experiment might have been hailed with praise if it had succeeded, but it had only upset Dulles and the Western European governments without winning any lasting co-operation from the Russians.

Dulles himself went to London to put the negotiations back on the original track. The Western powers drew up a comprehensive disarmament plan which agreed to the demands that the Russians had made for reductions in armed forces and a two-year ban on nuclear tests, but with the condition that the ban should be lifted after two years if either side failed to halt the production of nuclear weapons for military purposes. To safeguard against a surprise attack, the plan provided for aerial inspection. This plan, presented by the

United States, Britain, France and Canada, was also approved officially by all of the other NATO governments through their London embassies and in its final form represented an agreement of sixteen nations.

The earlier friendly attitude of the Russian representative at the conference began to change during the summer sessions. In August, Zorin complained about the slowness of the proceedings and objected to the Western argument that it was necessary to obtain approval from each of the nations located in the proposed European inspection zone before opening their skies to reconnaissance planes. On August 27, two days before the Western plan was formally presented, Zorin stunned the conference by suddenly slamming the door against all further negotiations with a violent ninety-minute attack against the West, charging "the aggressive North Atlantic bloc" with playing "a double game" and claiming that the United States in sponsoring the aerial inspection plan was only seeking intelligence data "in preparations for aggression." Only Stassen remained undaunted. He flew to Washington and assured the disappointed President that the East and the West were still close to a first-step agreement, but few people believed anything further would come out of the conference.

When the disarmament negotiations collapsed, Stassen had few supporters in the administration outside of the President, who always admired his boundless energy and his abundant supply of new ideas. With the recollection of other projects that had gone astray, Stassen's proposals now seemed doubtful and unstable to many people around the President. But everybody, including Dulles, had to admit that it was Stassen who had brought the United States and Russia closer to an understanding on many issues than they ever were before or since, no matter how naïve or undiplomatic his methods may have been.

"Now it is quite true that we did not reach at this point agreement with the Soviets," Dulles said after the London conference. "But the fact of the matter is that at least sixteen nations, representing a very large segment of military power in the world, came to agreement, at least among themselves, on highly significant proposals covering the entire range of armament from the aspect of trying to prevent the misuse for war purposes of the upper space down to the question of conventional armaments and dealing with various aspects of the nuclear weapon problem. If you will compare what was accomplished now, as between what you might call the present allies, essentially the members of NATO, with the result that attended the League of Nations disarmament talks at Geneva after the First World War, you will see that the achievement now is really quite monumental in comparison with the total inability at that time for the then allies to come to agreement among themselves. . . . I feel confident that over the span of years the measure of agreement which was arrived at at London will prove significant and will advance the cause of limitation of armament."

Dulles tried to keep the spark of hope alive by obtaining an endorsement of the Western disarmament plan by the United Nations General Assembly on November 14, 1957, by a vote of fifty-six to nine, in an attempt to reactivate the subcommittee. But the Soviets refused to make another try at negotiations.

Eisenhower said his last official word as President on disarmament in his farewell address on January 17, 1961: "Disarmament, with mutual honor and confidence, is a continuing imperative. Together we must learn how to compose differences, not with arms, but with intellect and decent purpose. Because this need is so sharp and apparent I confess I lay down my official responsibilities in this field with a definite sense of disappointment."

16 Little Rock

Because the United States Supreme Court announced its historic decision against racial segregation in the public schools on May 17, 1954, when Eisenhower was in office as President, it has been widely assumed that the Eisenhower administration was responsible for this highly controversial civil rights action. In the South, Eisenhower himself has been denounced as the author of the school desegregation law and in the North he has been praised for it. The President's identification with the Court's decision was strengthened, of course, in 1957 when he was forced by the duty of his office to order the paratroopers of the 101st Airborne Division to move into Little Rock to support the federal law.

Actually, Eisenhower had nothing to do with the Supreme Court's decision. The legal action to bring the issue of segregation in the schools before the Court was started before Eisenhower became President. As a matter of formal and customary procedure, Brownell in his capacity as Attorney General submitted argument that segregated schools were prohibited by the Fourteenth Amendment, and while this position was in agreement with the President's views, he was not personally involved with the decision in any way. The decision came to him, as it did to most people, as somewhat of a surprise, and Eisenhower was careful not to comment on the wisdom of the Court in reaching its conclusions.

Eisenhower himself took a moderate view and was convinced in his own mind that progress toward school integration had to be made with considerable deliberation. But in general principle he thought the Supreme Court decision was correct and personally he had no quarrel with it. As he remarked later when the trouble broke out in Little Rock, he was strongly aware that many people were emotionally opposed to the decision. "You cannot change the hearts of people by law," he said. One day at a Cabinet meeting the President mentioned a discussion he had on one occasion with Senator Harry Byrd of Virginia on the question of how to approach the desegregation process. Although Byrd held to the "separate but equal" doctrine that had prevailed in the South since the passage of the Fourteenth Amendment, he believed with the President that, when school integration came, as it inevitably would, the process should begin with the most advanced classrooms at the college and university level, working down gradually over a period of years through the high school and finally to the elementary grades.

A remote connection which Eisenhower had with the Supreme Court decision was his appointment of the Chief Justice, Earl Warren, who read the decision and was given wide credit for the fact that the decision was a unanimous one. When Warren was being considered for the position, along with a few other outstanding possible candidates, after the death of Chief Justice Fred M. Vinson in 1953, I was astonished to read in a Southern California newspaper a report that was headlined, "Top Ike Aide Stops Warren High Court Bid." The story said that I was blocking Warren's appointment because Eisenhower was not politically obligated to the California Governor. It would have been impossible to dream up a more complete fabrication. In selecting a Chief Justice, the President studied a list of names that he had asked Brownell to prepare. In consultation with Brownell, Eisenhower went over each name with great care. Although I was asked my opinion about the decision I did not participate in the discussion when it was finally made, and certainly had no objections to the choice. Dulles' name was on the list but he made it plain that his only ambition was to be Secretary of State.

The President said later that a persuasive factor in making him decide in favor of Warren was the Governor's relatively young age and good health. "If you can call a man of approximately my age relatively young," he added. Also under consideration were several highly regarded members of the federal and state judiciaries but Eisenhower felt that they were too advanced in years to fill Vinson's place in Washington. Warren was the only political officeholder on the President's list. Eisenhower admired his reputation for integrity and honesty and his middle-of-the-road philosophy and liked him personally, having become well acquainted with him during the 1952 campaign.

Long before the Supreme Court decision made racial equality the hotly debated national issue that it was in later years, Eisenhower was working quietly but steadily to break down barriers against the Negro in the armed services, in government employment and in the Southern-influenced District of Columbia. In 1952, when I was recommending people for key positions in the incoming administration, he made a point of insisting that he wanted qualified Negroes to be considered. Eisenhower told me then that he disagreed with his Southern friends who contended that Negroes were primarily seeking social equality; he believed that the Negro was more anxious for economic equality— an equal chance for a job and a good education, equal justice before the law and an equal right to vote.

Under Eisenhower's direction, Lois Lippman, who served on our secretarial staff during the campaign, became the first Negro to work in the White House office and Frederic Morrow was the first Negro ever to be appointed an administrative officer in the staff of the President. While Eisenhower was President, a Negro sat in at Cabinet meetings for the first time in history when J. Ernest Wilkins, the Assistant Secretary of Labor, represented his department when Secretary Mitchell was absent from Washington. There were many other such firsts in the administration's breaking of the color line: Scovel Richardson, Chairman of the Parole Board, later appointed as a federal judge; Archibald Carey, Chairman of the President's Employment Policy Committee and an Alternate Delegate to the United Nations; Cora M. Brown, associate general counsel in the Post Office Department, and many others.

During the 1952 campaign, Eisenhower said that he was in favor of eliminating "every vestige of segregation in the District of Columbia." Up until 1953, Washington had the prejudices and many of the discriminations of a Southern city. When the President appointed Samuel Spencer as the President of the Board of Commissioners of the District of Columbia, he had an understanding with Spencer about steps that should be taken in the capital for racial equality. Spencer, a capable and co-operative commissioner, was able to report soon afterward to the White House that hotels and restaurants were changing their policy against admitting Negroes. The moving picture theaters voluntarily followed suit. Discrimination was abolished in capital Housing Authority projects and the District government issued a regulation against discriminatory employment practices by its contractors. On November 25, 1953, the District reached an important milestone by adopting a policy of nondiscrimination in personnel activities throughout its departments and agencies.

However, "one swallow does not make a summer," as Eisenhower often used to point out. As anybody who has lived and worked in Washington well knows, the adoption of official regulations does not make equality. Eisenhower attended a Lincoln Day Box Supper at the Uline Arena in February, 1954. The choir from Howard University that was to sing on the program came to the front door of the arena through a mix-up in signals. When the singers were asked to enter at a rear door, they refused to do so and went back to their campus. The President knew nothing of the incident until he was asked about it at his press conference the following Wednesday, and had to turn inquiringly to Jim Hagerty.

"I am told by Mr. Hagerty that the bus driver was instructed to go around to the door by which I entered, and he refused to go around to that place," Eisenhower said. "And I hope there is no connection between those two facts." That broke the press conference up in laughter.

Then the President added seriously that if the choir had been treated rudely because of its color, he would be the first to apologize.

When the Supreme Court's decision was announced, the President promptly summoned the commissioners of the District of Columbia to the White House and told them that he hoped that the capital city would take the lead in desegregating its schools as an example to the rest of the nation. The following September a policy of nonsegregation went into effect in the Washington schools without any disturbances.

Meanwhile, the administration was making big strides in removing segregation from the armed services and from federal employment practices. Because of Eisenhower's determination to make progress in these areas of discrimination, where the previous administration had accomplished little, we gave one member of the White House staff, Maxwell Rabb, who later served as Secretary to the Cabinet, the special duty of acting as trouble shooter on what we called minority problems. Whether he was dealing with Representative Adam Clayton Powell, the Harlem Congressman, who was a vigilant champion of Negro rights, or with a Southern-born personnel director about discriminatory practices, Rabb had a way of taking the listener into his confidence and getting him to share the problem at hand with a sympathetic understanding. After a talk with Rabb, the Texas-born Robert Anderson, who was then Secretary of the Navy, promptly abolished segregation in mess halls and lavatories and racially designated drinking fountains in the Navy yards at Charleston and Norfolk. In a comparatively short time, a program for complete desegregation in the armed forces was under way, doing away with racial quotas and Negro units, and discrimination in housing, schools, hospitals, transportation and recreation at all Army, Navy and Air Force bases and installations. By 1955, this program was in full effect.

In his 1956 State of the Union message, Eisenhower took a bolder step than many of his close counselors deemed advisable when he asked Congress to establish a Civil Rights Commission to examine charges "that in some localities Negro citizens are being deprived of their right to vote and are likewise being subjected to unwarranted economic pressures." The first draft of this proposed civil rights legislation also sought to make lynching a federal offense and to eliminate the poll tax as a prerequisite to voting. This was, of course, asking for trouble from the Southern Democrats in Congress.

Behind the request for such laws was national pressure being put upon the Department of Justice to intervene in cases such as the Emmett Till killing, where state and local justice meted out to the Negro seemed rather different than white man's justice. Till, a fourteen-year-old Negro boy from Chicago, was visiting relatives in Mississippi when he made the error of whistling at the twenty-one-year-old white wife of a country storekeeper. Four days later he was seized and taken away from his uncle's cabin and three days after that his body was found and identified, weighted and sunk in the Tallahatchie River. The storekeeper and his half-brother were tried and found not guilty because "the body was too decomposed to be positively identified." The Till killing was followed by two more racial-hatred-inspired murders.

When the President's message was discussed at a Cabinet meeting before it was sent to Congress, Brownell remarked that the proposal for a Civil Rights Commission would be inflammatory because it would be interpreted in the South, quite correctly, as a federal action against the white citizens' councils. These were being organized in many localities to bring economic pressure on anybody who favored compliance with the Supreme Court decision on desegregation in the public schools. The Southern states were already talking then about abolishing public education rather than submit to the Court's ruling. Brownell said that this was far and away the greatest issue in the social field faced by the nation in a long time. Max Rabb, who was present, said that he disagreed with Brownell. "This is not just the biggest issue in the social field," Rabb said. "It is the biggest issue of any kind in the United States today."

The politically realistic Nixon observed that no matter how big and important the issue was he doubted that the Democratic-controlled Congress would ever let a civil rights bill get out of committee. Nixon was almost right; it took many long delays and postponements before the administration's proposal was allowed to come up for a vote in the House.

On March 9, 1956, J. Edgar Hoover came to a Cabinet meeting to discuss recent investigations by the FBI on conditions surrounding civil rights in the South. He said that racial tension had been steadily mounting since the decision of the Supreme Court. He reported finding organized economic pressure groups dedicated to keeping Negro children out of white schools. Hoover said, however, that there were fewer lynchings.

At the same meeting, Brownell presented a newly revised version of the original civil rights proposal. The provision for making lynching a federal offense was dropped as unnecessarily inflammatory in the light of Hoover's report. Along with the request for a bipartisan Civil Rights Commission, the legislation asked for three laws: an extension of the law protecting the right to vote in primary elections, giving the Justice Department the choice of taking civil as well as criminal action against violators; a broadened civil rights law giving the department more choices in determining violations; a law establishing within the Justice Department a special Civil Rights Division headed by an Assistant Attorney General.

Eisenhower talked about his responsibility for enforcing the Supreme Court's decision, which, he pointed out, had already made desegregated schools a matter of constitutional law, even though the Court had allowed compliance to be carried out at a "deliberate" pace. The President said he had hoped that the decision would be followed by constructive action but instead there had been statements of defiance from the South.

There were objections from the Cabinet to Brownell's proposals for legislative action. Stassen did not think any of Brownell's recommendations had a chance of being passed by Congress. Benson suggested waiting a few years until the Republicans gained control of the Senate and the House. The Georgia-born Marion Folsom, whose Health, Education and Welfare Department's programs would be affected by the racial issues, felt that, in asking for anything more than the Civil Rights Commission, Brownell was attempting to point to the conclusions that he wanted the commission to reach. I said that the whole package would be accepted by Congress only if careful planning were given to the timing and the manner of approach used in its presentation, and the President then asked Brownell to bring the program back to the Cabinet again for more discussion before he sent it to the Hill.

Two weeks later Brownell placed the program before the Cabinet for another review. He admitted that there was considerable doubt about two of his proposals, the one giving the Justice Department authority to take civil as well as criminal action against violators of the right-to-vote law and the one broadening the civil rights law to give the Justice Department greater discretion in handling violations.

Wilson said that the racial issue was hot enough without adding more fuel to it. Folsom was still opposed to everything except the creation of the commission. If you want a commission to pass judgment on civil rights cases, he argued, why anticipate their recommendations by asking Congress for laws in the very field which the commission is to investigate and make recommendations?

Dulles said that he was strongly convinced that laws which departed from the established customs of the people were impractical. Perhaps he was thinking of the repealed Eighteenth Amendment. Eisenhower mentioned that after a recent talk with Billy Graham he had come to the conclusion that, as a result of recent tensions, some of the hard-won advances in recent years toward better race relations had actually been lost. Wilson sided with Folsom in arguing that Brownell's controversial civil rights proposals should be left to the Civil Rights Commission, when and if created. But Arthur Flemming and Mitchell backed Brownell in contending that the statement in the President's State of the Union message had promised a strong civil rights program and that a proposal for a Civil Rights Commission would be inadequate. Faced by this rift of opinion in the Cabinet, Eisenhower asked the Attorney General to hold up the program until they had discussed it together.

Meanwhile a dispute broke out between the federal courts and the University of Alabama that stirred up new trouble in the South over the school segregation issue. A young Negro graduate student, Autherine Juanita Lucy, was barred from admission to the university because of her color. The local Federal District Court, backed by the Federal Court of Appeals, ordered the university to admit her and she began to attend classes. After a series of student demonstrations on the campus, Miss Lucy was suspended by the university authorities for her own safety. She then brought two legal actions against the university's trustees in an effort to gain reinstatement, one of them a contempt citation for deliberately permitting the mob demonstration. This so incensed the trustees that they summarily expelled her for her "unfounded charges of misconduct" against them.

When Eisenhower was asked if the Department of Justice would investigate the happenings at the University of Alabama, he made it clear that he had no intention of interfering in the affairs of a sovereign state unless it was absolutely necessary for him to do so. "I certainly hope that we could avoid any interference as long as the state, from the Governor on down, will do its best to straighten it out," the President said.

When Brownell finally sent a letter to Congress on April 9 requesting civil rights legislation, his earlier proposals had been considerably toned down. He asked now for the bipartisan Civil Rights Commission which would have the power to subpoena witnesses in investigations concerning interference in voting or the use of economic pressure because of race, color or creed; a Civil Rights Division in the Department of Justice; authority for the department to initiate a petition to prevent any individual from being deprived of his civil rights; federal prosecution of any person charged with intimidating a voter in a federal election; access to the federal courts for anybody with a civil rights complaint; federal authority to bring civil suits against conspirators attempting to repress anybody's civil rights.

Eisenhower told the Republican legislative leaders on April 17 that he had gone over these proposals very carefully and that he did not see how they could be more moderate or less provocative. He said that Brownell had been under considerable pressure from his own staff to make the program more drastic. The President was well aware of blasts against the program in Southern newspapers but he said that the newspaper editors "seemed to want to shout whenever they hear the words 'civil rights' without even reading what was in the proposals." On the other hand, the President added, the extremists on the Negro side of the question did not seem to understand that although federal troops could be sent into the South to enforce desegregation laws, soldiers cannot force the state authorities to keep the schools from closing their doors against white and Negro children alike. If the South turns to private school education, Eisenhower warned the Republican Congressmen, the Negroes in those states will have no educational opportunity at all.

The issue grew still warmer as the Republican party endorsed the Supreme Court's decision in its 1956 campaign platform. Eisenhower emphasized and re-emphasized on many occasions during the months after the convention that as President he had no choice but to uphold the decision. "The Constitution is as the Supreme Court interprets it, and I must conform to that and do my very best to see that it is carried out in this country," he said.

At the end of the year, Congress had still failed to pass the civil rights legislation Brownell had requested, and at the leadership meetings in December and January he renewed his efforts. But in the spring of 1957 there were only more reports of foot-dragging and delays. Knowland said in March that the Democrats had let it be known that if the Republicans insisted on pushing the civil rights proposal, they might have considerable trouble moving other legislation that the administration wanted.

The President received an appeal that winter from the Reverend Martin Luther King to come into the South and make a public speech on the moral issues surrounding the desegregation question. I showed

the invitation to Brownell and we both agreed that such an expedition
could not possibly bring any constructive results. I wrote a reply to
the Negro clergyman, declining his invitation, and when the President
was asked about the reply at a press conference, he said, "I have expressed myself so often wherever I have been about this thing that I
don't know what good another speech will do right now."

Late in March I received a letter from Adam Clayton Powell, who
said that the President's decline of the King invitation had been widely
criticized by Negroes. Powell suggested that Eisenhower make a
public reply to a letter that the Congressman enclosed, pointing out
the "immediate and continuing need" for outspoken discussions of the
relationships between races, religions and sections of the country.
Eisenhower did not reply to Powell's letter publicly, but an alternative to the speech that Dr. King had requested, an expression from
the administration of support for desegregation, was arranged at a
meeting between Dr. King, Nixon, Senator Ives and Secretary of Labor
Mitchell.

Then the civil rights program that Brownell had sent to Congress
ran into an unexpected complication. One of the proposals gave the
federal courts the authority to use a contempt action in enforcing an
order against interference with the right to vote. An amendment was
proposed in Congress interposing a jury trial between the court and
the enforcement of its order. The Attorney General quickly recognized
the jury trial amendment for what it was: a shield for the offender
against a summary action which was traditionally a part of the constitutional process. He urged the amendment's defeat. Representative
Keating of New York predicted that at least twenty-five Republicans
in the House would vote against the bill altogether and that others
would vote for the jury trial amendment because they would not
understand what it involved. But when the House finally got around
to voting, the bill was passed by two to one after the jury trial amendment went down in a narrow defeat.

Nobody needed a divining rod to detect the fight that was brewing
in the Senate. The administration expected a filibuster and other
evasive tactics but the Democrats surprised us by launching a head-on
attack on the merits of the bill itself. Senator Richard Russell of
Georgia declared on the Senate floor that the bill was an attempt by
the admininstration to force "a commingling of white and Negro

children in the state-supported schools of the South." He charged that the real purpose of the legislation was "to punish the South."

Eisenhower denied the next day at a press conference that he had any intention of punishing the South and described the civil rights bill as mainly an action against interference with voting rather than a "cunning device to integrate the races," as Senator Russell had expressed it. The next question came fast and went to details that the President was uncertain about: Would he be satisfied with a bill restricted solely to protecting the right to vote, with no provisions relating to integration in the public schools? Eisenhower put off answering that one. "In reading over parts of the bill this morning, I found certain phrases I didn't completely understand," he said. "Before saying more on this subject, I want to talk with the Attorney General and see what they do mean." The President's air of doubt and hesitation surprised some of his supporters in Congress, who were making an all-out effort to get the bill passed.

At the July 9 meeting of the Republican leaders in the White House, Senator Dirksen explained that Russell's sharp objections grew out of his argument that the bill was a "forcing act," drawn to enable the use of federal military forces to destroy separation of the races in the South. Brownell said that the President already had enough authority to use armed forces to enforce federal laws. In this bill, the Attorney General said, the administration was not seeking the use of force but only peaceful procedures. Eisenhower affirmed this by explaining that the administration only wanted to keep federal court orders from being flouted. All of the Republican Senators in the leadership group felt that compromises and modifications would be necessary. Knowland said that if everything in the bill was struck out, the Southerners still would not like it.

The President made another reply at his July 17 press conference that proponents of the bill were disappointed about. Some of them thought they felt the rug being pulled from under their feet. Eisenhower was asked if the Attorney General should be permitted on his own motion to bring suits to enforce school integration in the South. Not without a request from local authorities, the President said. A reporter pointed out that Part III of the bill, the section giving the Department of Justice authority to initiate a petition on behalf of any individual being deprived of his civil rights, allowed the Attorney

General to make such a move on his own. "If you try to go too far too fast . . . you are making a mistake," Eisenhower said, but he was uncertain whether an action should begin only when a state or local official requested it.

This uncertainty in the administration about some of the technicalities in the bill divided the supporters of civil rights legislation in Congress and played into the hands of the Southern Senators, as they intended. Eisenhower spent most of the meeting with Republican leaders on July 30 asking questions about legal technicalities of the jury trial amendment and getting some of the legal interpretations of various other provisions in the bill unsnarled. Facing another press conference the next day, he had no intention of being caught off base again. "Let's remember that we have to make all this clear because there are more nonlawyers than there are lawyers in the country," he said. The President said that the matters under discussion reminded him of the story about the bright young law school graduate in Mississippi who twice failed the local bar examinations. His father went to the examining board and asked to see the test questions. After one quick look at the questions, he exclaimed, "For goodness' sake, you gave him the Negro examination!"

The next day the President told the reporters that the jury trial amendment was at odds with thirty-six different laws already on the books that specifically rule out jury trials in contempt cases. "I support the bill as it stands and I hope it will soon be passed," he said. But the Senate ignored the President's plea and in the early morning of August 2 adopted the jury trial amendment by a vote of fifty-one to forty-two. The President and Brownell were bitterly disappointed. They felt that this amendment made the rest of the bill ineffective. Later, on the morning of the vote, after the silent prayer at the opening of the Cabinet meeting, the President said that this was one of the most serious political defeats he had suffered in four years.

For a few weeks that August it seemed as if the President's Civil Rights Act of 1957 was going down the drain. With the jury trial amendment and other changes, the bill had lost its teeth and William Rogers, the Deputy Attorney General, described what had been done to it in the Senate as the most irresponsible action he had seen in all of his experience in Washington. Rogers said that putting such a law into effect would be like handing a policeman a gun without bullets. The

President received many letters from prominent Negroes, Ralph Bunche among them, urging him not to have anything to do with any sham bill. But Eisenhower did not want to veto a civil rights bill. Although unacceptable as passed by the Senate, he hoped some compromise could be found that would save it from being killed in conference committee and still leave it with enough meaning so that he could conscientiously sign it. It would be the first legislation in eighty-two years to strengthen the constitutional rights of the Negro citizen. On the other hand, the President understood that if he vetoed the bill, no matter how weak, it would be taken as a defeat of civil rights legislation and a broken Republican promise. The Democrats would see to that.

"I cannot understand how eighteen Southern Senators can bamboozle the entire Senate," Eisenhower said with disgust at a Republican leadership meeting.

It turned out that reaching a compromise on the bill was much easier than Eisenhower and his spokesmen in Congress had expected. The Northern Democrats and pseudo-liberal Republicans who had joined in chopping up the proposal when it came to the Senate soon backtracked when they saw their handiwork threatened by a presidential veto. The major areas of difference were narrowed and the jury trial amendment was changed so that a jury could be used only in cases involving voting rights and even then only when the judge himself decided upon a jury trial. And so, after two years of hard work, the President and the Attorney General finally had something to show for their labor. The bill the President signed into law fell short of what they had hoped to have, but it made progress in the right direction and, on the whole, was acceptable to them.

Before I had time to draw a relaxed breath, however, I found myself unexpectedly involved in a battle resulting from the Supreme Court's decision that proved to be one of the most dramatic episodes in my political life.

When Little Rock came into the news as the scene of a disturbance over plans to desegregate its schools, I could not help recalling Eisenhower's appearance in that capital city of Arkansas on September 3, 1952, during his first presidential campaign. The arrangements had been made with the usual precautions that we followed in the South, with the rally being staged outdoors where the segregation question could not mess things up. In his talk, Eisenhower deplored the meddling of the government in affairs where it did not belong. The recent attempt of the Truman administration to get into the steel business had not been successful, he reminded his listeners.

"Thank goodness for a Supreme Court!" Eisenhower exclaimed and the people of Little Rock cheered and applauded. Old observers said it was the warmest welcome any candidate ever got in Little Rock.

Exactly five years later to the day, September 3, 1957, in defiance of the decision of that same Supreme Court, the Governor of Arkansas, Orval Faubus, stationed troops from the state's National Guard around Little Rock's Central High School. They were put there, the Governor explained, solely to preserve order. But their orders also were to prevent Negro students from entering the school to attend classes.

The trouble in Little Rock came about when the city's school board tried to put into effect a plan for the gradual desegregation of the Little Rock schools that it had drawn up in compliance with the Supreme Court's decision and an order of the District Court. The Supreme Court in Washington had directed in 1955 that school authorities should file with the local Federal District Courts such plans for proceeding with desegregation with "all deliberate speed." The Little Rock plan called for Negroes to be admitted to previously segregated senior high schools by 1957, to junior high schools in 1960 and to elementary schools in 1963. The plan was approved by the Federal District Court of Arkansas in 1956. The National Association for the Advancement of Colored People filed a suit of protest against the plan, arguing that it took too many years to accomplish desegregation, but the Circuit Court of Appeals disallowed the NAACP suit and told the Little Rock school board to go ahead with its carefully timed schedule.

The school board was preparing to admit a group of seventeen Negro students, selected for scholastic ability and social adaptability, in the previously all-white Central High when the Little Rock schools opened after the summer vacation on September 3. A group of indignant white mothers filed a petition in the state's Chancery Court to halt the school board's plan. Governor Faubus himself testified at a hearing on the petition on August 29 that integration of the high school would cause mob violence and bloodshed. The state court granted an injunction against the school board.

Then the school board took its troubles to a key figure in the Little Rock controversy, Federal Judge Ronald N. Davies. Judge Davies of Fargo, North Dakota, was temporarily assigned to the Arkansas District to fill a vacancy on the federal bench there. He promptly disagreed with the Governor, set aside the order of the state court and forbade anyone to interfere with the school board in carrying out its desegregation plan. On the opening day of school, however, Faubus called out the National Guard, ostensibly "to prevent racial violence," but effectively putting a block against carrying out Judge Davies' order. They were there to enforce neither segregation nor desegregation, the Governor explained. Judge Davies told the school board he would take the Governor's word at face value. Then he issued an order to the board to proceed with the plan of integration. When the Negro students approached the school the next morning, September 4, they were stopped and prevented from entering by the soldiers. The Governor thus put himself in open defiance of the supreme law of the land. In flaunting an order of the federal judge he had taken on a tough adversary, who had the Attorney General and the President of the United States behind him.

On that same day, the Wednesday after Labor Day, the President, with Mrs. Eisenhower, left Washington and went to the naval base at Newport, seeking a few weeks of rest and peace after the long struggle with Congress over the big budget and the civil rights bill. He liked the golf course at the Newport Country Club, close to the cool and pleasant commandant's residence where he was staying. He was looking forward to entertaining a few friends whom he could beat when his game was right. But now he had Governor Orval Faubus on his hands.

Soon after he arrived in Newport, the President received a telegram from Faubus, complaining that he was being investigated by the federal authorities, that he had been told of plans to take him "into custody, by force," that the telephone lines to his executive mansion were being tapped. Eisenhower learned from Brownell that Judge Davies had requested a survey in Little Rock by the Justice Department to see if there was any substance for the Governor's warning that integration of the high school would cause an outburst of violence in the city. Judge Davies doubted that the feeling against having Negroes in Central High was as explosive as the Governor was making it out to be, and the Mayor of Little Rock, Woodrow W. Mann, agreed with the Judge that the Governor's interference was unwarranted. As Eisenhower wired back to Faubus, there was no plot to take the Governor into custody and his telephone lines had not been tapped.

Faubus had asked the President for an assurance of "understanding and co-operation." Eisenhower said in his reply from Newport, "The only assurance I can give you is that the Federal Constitution will be upheld by me by every legal means at my command."

For reasons that were never clear to us in Washington or to the President in Newport, the Little Rock school board at that point proved to be a weak reed. The board backed down and asked Judge Davies to put aside his order for the immediate integration of the high school "until calmness may be restored." But the judge was not to be influenced by the sudden faintheartedness of the school board any more than he had been by the dire forebodings of the Governor. He refused to allow any further delay in carrying out his order. "In an organized society there can be nothing but ultimate confusion and chaos if court decrees are flaunted, whatever the pretext," he said in a statement, which also called the board's plea "anemic." The judge pointed out that there was no indication that there would be interracial violence in Little Rock.

The President, now apprised by the Attorney General that responsibility for his own action was becoming more imminent, flew back to Washington on Saturday for a conference with Brownell, where they agreed on positions the federal government would take in what appeared to be a worsening impasse. Eisenhower, as he did when a soldier, wanted to give Faubus every opportunity to make an orderly retreat by no longer defying the order of the Court. But, the President insisted, even though he would explore every alternative to the use of force, there could be no compromise or capitulation by the administration on this issue.

On the following Monday, Judge Davies asked the Attorney General to enter the case and on the same day I found myself entering it, too. I received a telephone call from Brooks Hays, the representative in Congress from the Fifth District of Arkansas where Little Rock was located. Hays and I had been close friends ever since I had served with him in the House of Representatives in 1945. Quiet, soft-spoken and modest, he was a rare person and an even rarer type of politician because he never seemed to be influenced by personal or selfish motives. At a meeting or in a casual discussion, you always felt better for having Hays around. He was now calling me on the telephone from Little Rock to offer his services as an intermediary in an effort to bring the Governor into compliance with the law and to an agreement with the President. While I was talking with Hays, I realized the extent of the personal sacrifice that he might be making in offering himself as peacemaker in the Little Rock crisis. A Democrat, facing a campaign for re-election to Congress again in 1958 in a district where feeling against the administration was running high because of the segregation issue, he had everything to lose in trying to get Faubus to accept the Supreme Court decision. It would have been the politic thing for Hays to ignore the fight between the Governor and the federal government; there was no reason for him to get messed up in it. Other members of the Arkansas delegation in Congress were giving the conflict a wide berth. But Hays was a man of deep convictions, and he was hurt and disturbed by the disrespect for the Constitution being shown before the nation in his state and district. He felt a moral obligation to do something about it, even if it meant political suicide. I still think that Hays showed one of the greatest exhibitions of sheer courage in modern political history when he walked into the line of fire at Little Rock.

Hays asked me if I thought Eisenhower would agree to a personal talk with Faubus if the Governor requested it. I said that I thought such a meeting could be arranged, under one important condition: Faubus would have to indicate beforehand his willingness to comply with the federal law and the Supreme Court decision. Eisenhower would hardly take kindly to a personal conference with a state governor who was standing in open defiance of the Constitution.

However, the Little Rock situation was now a matter in which the Attorney General was principally concerned rather than the White House staff and I pointed out to Hays that Brownell would have to be consulted. The Attorney General, in his official capacity as chief law enforcement officer, might now find himself in the position of having to force the Arkansas Governor's compliance with the order of the District Court. Faubus had just been served with a summons to appear before Judge Davies on September 20 to explain why he was still obstructing the order by preventing the Negro students from attending Central High School. I could see that Brownell might have little enthusiasm about a meeting between the President and an official who had a summons from a federal court to appear and explain why he was in open defiance of its order. But knowing the President's usual reaction to such a request I told Hays to go ahead and see how Faubus would react to his proposal.

While I was waiting to hear from Hays, I asked the President how he would feel about the value of a talk with Faubus if the Governor requested it. Without a moment of hesitation, Eisenhower said that he would be in favor of it, under the proviso I had expected him to mention—that the Governor not come to the meeting in his present mood of defiance.

Hays telephoned me from Little Rock and said that Faubus wanted to see Eisenhower. "What would be a convenient time for the President?" Hays asked.

I explained to Hays that before we could get down to setting a time and date for the meeting, I would have to know what Faubus was going to say in his request for the conference. I was certain that the Justice Department would be opposed to the President seeing Faubus until the Governor discontinued his obstruction of the federal court order and removed the National Guard troops from Central High School. Obviously, this was something that Faubus was in no position to do at the present time. But I knew that there would be no chance of getting a meeting for him with the President unless he first gave us some kind of a statement indicating that he had at least an intention of observing the federal law.

I made this clear to Hays and the patient and willing Congressman began a series of difficult negotiations with Faubus in an attempt to get such a statement of good intentions out of the Governor. It was hard going for Hays. At one meeting, Faubus would be co-operative but later in the same day, after conferring with advisers, he would become uncertain and evasive. Finally Hays read to me on the telephone a message that Faubus would send to the President. It mentioned that he had accepted the federal summons and that "it is certainly my intention to comply with the order that has been issued by the District Court. May I confer with you on this matter at your earliest convenience?"

That seemed good enough to me, so I told Hays that if Faubus sent the telegram to the President at Newport he would receive a prompt and favorable reply. Later, Hays called me to say that there would be some minor word changes, but the purport of the telegram would be as we had discussed it.

The telegram arrived on Wednesday afternoon when Eisenhower was starting a round of golf at the Newport Country Club. Jim Hagerty brought the wire to him as he was holing out on the first green. They sat down together in a golf cart that the President had used most of the time since his heart attack. Eisenhower studied the telegram and together they worded a reply that Hagerty took back to the naval base. Then the President walked on to the second tee and drove off.

I found out later that the message which Eisenhower received from Faubus was not the same as the one that Hays had read to me on the telephone. Instead of declaring his intention of complying with the order of the court, Faubus wired the President that "it is certainly my desire to comply with the order that has been issued by the District Court in this case, consistent with my responsibilities under the Constitution of the United States and that of Arkansas." It seemed to me that a desire was quite different from an intention.

When Hays called me again to make arrangements for his trip to Newport with Faubus, I asked him what had happened to the wording of the message that we had agreed on over the telephone. Hays said that he had done his best but apparently the Governor's advisers had dissuaded him from any more direct statement.

The President had given Faubus a choice of two dates and he selected Saturday, September 14, at nine o'clock in the morning. Hays and the Governor were flying to Providence and staying in a hotel there on Friday night and I arranged for a helicopter to pick them up on Saturday morning and bring them to Newport. Earlier that same Saturday morning Brownell, Gerald Morgan, the President's Special Counsel, and I flew from Washington to the naval station at Quonset, Rhode Island, and there we changed to a helicopter that landed us on the lawn in front of Eisenhower's summer White House office at the headquarters building of the Newport Naval

Base on Coasters Island in Narragansett Bay. Brownell was doubtful about whether any good results would come from the meeting with Faubus. He and the President had discussed the meeting on the telephone at some length. The President reasoned that the Governor must be coming to Newport to find some means of working out with the federal government a compliance with the court order, without surrendering his own prerogatives and losing too much prestige. But Brownell did not think it would be that simple, and it turned out the Attorney General was right.

We went upstairs in the headquarters building to the President's offices on the second floor, where we found Eisenhower in a bright and good-humored mood, as he usually was before tackling an important and difficult job. We talked over with him the procedure that we would follow during the meeting. The President had a fairly large outer office, where Mrs. Whitman and Tom Stephens had their desks, with enough space for a conference of six or eight people. Beyond this larger room was the President's own personal office, only big enough for his desk and chairs for two or three visitors. The President wanted first to talk alone with Faubus in the small office. They would then come outside to join Brownell, Morgan, Hays and myself in the larger room for a general discussion of the situation.

While Brownell and Morgan waited upstairs, Hagerty and I went out on the lawn to watch the helicopter coming in from Providence. A group of alert reporters and news cameramen gathered around us. This meeting was, of course, the big story of the day. When the helicopter landed, Hays and I exchanged warm greetings. He introduced me to the Governor and I introduced both of them to Hagerty and after a brief pause for pictures we walked up the gravel path to the base headquarters.

Eisenhower with his two legal advisers was waiting for Faubus in the outer office, where there were a few minutes of cordial and pleasant talk about the Governor's trip from Little Rock and the historic location of the naval base. I had never met Faubus before. He was a quiet-mannered but forceful and determined man but my first impression of him was that he would not be unreasonable or difficult to deal with.

The President took the Governor into the small office and closed the door behind him, and the rest of us sat down in the outer room to discuss the statement that would be issued after the meeting. Eisenhower mentioned later that Faubus seemed confused about the course he should take, as if he were torn between the alternatives which confronted him. His compliance with the federal law and his duties as Governor of Arkansas as he saw them were in conflict. Perhaps in the back of his mind he hoped to convince Eisenhower that Arkansas was not yet ready for integrated schools, even to the point of persuading the President to join with him in asking the federal court to reconsider its order and delay the desegregation process. He talked about some ugly plans that were afoot in Arkansas if integration were to be forced upon the schools of Little Rock, which he did not believe he, nor any other authority in the state, would be able to cope with. Eisenhower did his best to convince the Governor that if he joined forces with the federal authorities in a moderate but firm show of law and order the crisis would fade into a routine that the people of Arkansas could live with. The President said that he was well aware that the Supreme Court's order was cutting into the established customs and traditions in such communities as Little Rock but that gradual progress in desegregation had to be made.

Eisenhower and Faubus talked together for twenty minutes and then they rejoined us in the larger outside office for a general discussion. Brownell gave a clear and precise review of the chain of events that had led to this meeting of the President and the Governor. Despite his almost self-effacing manner, Brownell was a man of great tenacity and persistent purpose who could not be shaken when his mind was firmly made up, as it was on the Little Rock issue. He laid down the federal government's position to Faubus in plain language: the desegregation law did not need to be liked or approved, but it had to be obeyed. While Brownell talked and while the President went through a summary, Faubus listened intently in inscrutable silence. He did say at one point that he understood the reason for the law and recognized its validity but beyond that he was noncommittal. When the meeting ended, Faubus merely said that he would go back to Providence and talk again with Hays, who would call me before he issued any statement.

We expected Faubus to state that he would comply with the law but none of us could figure out whether or not he would withdraw the National Guard troops from Central High School. As he left to go back to Providence with the Governor, Hays agreed to call me to let us know what Faubus was going to say, and I knew he would do his best to make the statement satisfactory to the President. Eisenhower wished the Governor luck and said that he hoped that the situation in Little Rock would work out all right.

As soon as the two Arkansas travelers took off for Providence, Brownell and I worked with Hagerty on a statement for the President. The Governor of Arkansas, we wrote, had stated his intention to respect the decisions of the United States District Court and to give his full co-operation in carrying out his responsibilities in respect to those decisions.

Meanwhile, in Providence, Hays was having more trouble with Faubus. After we had waited for two hours, Hays called to tell me that the Governor was still pondering and asked me what we thought he should say. I told him that we wanted Faubus to say that he would comply with the law and withdraw the National Guard troops from the high school. Hays said he would call me back and we sat down to wait again. Hays had my sympathy. I could imagine what he was going through in trying to persuade the stubborn Faubus to make a straightforward and unequivocal declaration that school integration was the law of the land and the Governor would obey it.

Finally, Hays called me once more and after a long and baffling conversation, with frequent pauses while he turned away from the telephone to try to reason with Faubus, we arrived at what seemed to be as satisfactory a statement as we were going to get. It was far short of what we wanted. Faubus was repeating virtually what he had said in his telegram to Eisenhower requesting the meeting: "I have assured the President of my desire to co-operate with him in carrying out the duties resting upon both of us under the Federal Constitution. In addition, I must harmonize my actions under the Constitution of Arkansas with the requirements of the Constitution of the United States." After considerable persuasion, the Governor added a sentence which said, "The Supreme Court decision of 1954 which voted integration . . . is the law of the land and must be obeyed." He also expressed a hope that the complexities of the integration problem would be "patiently understood" by the federal authorities.

In other words, Faubus made no definite or significant departure from his position before he came to Newport and we were not sure that anything had been accomplished at the meeting. The President was hopeful and somewhat optimistic. Brownell was quietly skeptical. The Attorney General was convinced from the start that Faubus would use every means he could contrive to thwart the order of the Court. After the meeting his opinion had not changed. It was apparent that Brownell's reservations about the advisability of the meeting were well taken. It is difficult to see anything of value that came from the meeting, but I felt that under the circumstances the President had to let Faubus come and talk with him.

That Saturday in Providence, when Faubus issued his statement, he was asked by a reporter if the National Guard troops would still be on duty at Central High when school opened the following Monday morning. He said, "That problem I will have to take care of when I return to Little Rock." The troops remained at the school all of the next week. On Friday, the Governor appeared for his hearing before Judge Davies. His attorneys argued that the Governor was carrying out his duty under the Arkansas Constitution to prevent violence when he barred the Negro students from entering the school and that such a performance of duty was not open to question by the federal court. But Judge Davies promptly ordered the Governor to stop obstructing the attendance of the Negro students by the use of the National Guard or otherwise. The Governor announced on a television and radio broadcast that he would comply with the judge's order and withdraw the guardsmen but that he would seek, by every legal means, to vitiate the order.

The next Monday morning when the troops were withdrawn and the school was opened to the Negro students for the first time, an angry crowd of around five hundred men and women gathered at Central High, held back by barricades thrown up by the city and state police. Yelling threats against the Negro students, the mob rushed on two Negro newspaper reporters, and while the unlucky reporters were being knocked down and beaten, nine Negro youngsters arrived on the scene in two cars and managed to get into the school building unnoticed through a side door. When the crowd learned that the Negro students had entered the school, it broke over the barricades and fought the police and state troopers in an attempt to enter the building. Fearing for the safety of the Negro children the authorities took them home. Integrated classes had lasted a little over three hours.

That same afternoon the President was on his way to the Newport Country Club when an urgent call from Brownell caused him to turn back. As soon as he learned the details of what had happened at Little Rock he issued a statement which was blunt and vigorous. "The federal law and orders of a United States District Court . . . cannot be flouted with impunity by any individual or any mob of extremists," he said. "I will use the full power of the United States including whatever force may be necessary to prevent any obstruction of the law and to carry out the orders of the Federal Court." Eisenhower followed up his statement with a proclamation setting forth the traditional authority and responsibiltiy of the President, reaching back to 1795, to use troops to enforce the federal law. In solemn form the President then did "command all persons engaged in such obstruction to cease and desist therefrom and to disperse forthwith."

But this had little effect in Little Rock. The violence which Faubus had predicted continued. This was his justification for his stand against Judge Davies' order. It was the sort of mob violence which Judge Davies and Mayor Woodrow Mann of Little Rock, both of whom had discounted the Governor's prophecies, had not expected. After the demonstration at the school, Mayor Mann contended that the crowd had been stirred into a fighting mood by imported "professional agitators" and continued to insist that resentment against desegregation in Little Rock was not so strong as the riot indicated. There was support for the Mayor's argument. Arkansas was not the Deep South. In other parts of the state several communities had integrated their schools earlier without incident. Little Rock itself did not have some of the discriminatory practices of most Southern cities; there was no color line in the public transportation facilities, for example. But whether the disorder at Central High was skillfully contrived or not, the mob was still at the school the next day and the Negro students were too frightened to run the risk of trying to attend classes. That meant that the President had to take action.

Deeply troubled, Eisenhower talked with the Army Chief of Staff, General Maxwell D. Taylor, and later with Secretary of Defense Wilson as soon as he returned from Louisiana that evening. Shortly after noon the following day the President signed an Executive Order authorizing Wilson to use "such of the armed forces of the United States as he may deem necessary" to remove the obstructions. Within two hours Wilson and Taylor had acted; the Arkansas guard was taken into federal service and the first group of five hundred soldiers of the 101st Airborne Division arrived at Little Rock that afternoon and another five hundred that same evening.

Back in Newport, the President went to work with Hagerty on the text of a message that he would deliver on television and radio that night. The President flew to Washington to make the address from the White House, partly because of the broadcasting facilities that were available there but mostly because he felt that it would not be appropriate to deliver such a serious and important message from a vacation headquarters. In announcing that he was now forced by the continued demonstrations against the Negro students to order Army troops to the high school, he said solemnly, "The very basis of our individual rights and freedoms rests upon the certainty that the President and the executive branch of government will support and insure the carrying out of the decisions of the federal courts, even, when necessary, with all the means at the President's command. Unless the President did so, anarchy would result."

Thus the President was finally forced to do what he had said in July would never be "a wise thing to do in this country." For Eisenhower had repeatedly stated that he could not imagine any set of circumstances that would ever induce him to send federal troops into any area to enforce the orders of a federal court. Those circumstances had nevertheless occurred, and the President performed a constitutional duty which was the most repugnant to him of all his acts in his eight years at the White House.

The next morning the nine remaining volunteers from the original seventeen Negro students slated to enter Central High were driven to school in a U.S. Army station wagon, escorted by armed paratroopers in a convoy of jeeps. They had no trouble entering the school. Around the building, the soldiers encountered some verbal abuse and a few physical scuffles. One man who refused to obey an order to move was pricked slightly by the point of a bayonet. The next day on a national television network Faubus spoke about "the warm red blood of patriotic American citizens staining the cold, naked, unsheathed knives" during the "military occupation" of Arkansas.

Earlier the President had been criticized for a lack of force in dealing with the Little Rock situation. Now that he was using every force at his command he was royally chastised for his action. Eisenhower was especially disheartened by a charge from Senator Russell of Georgia which seemed to him to be something far beyond political criticism. Russell accused the President of "applying tactics that must have been copied from the manual issued to the officers of Hitler's storm troopers." The President sent Russell an indignant telegram:

> The Arkansas National Guard could have handled the situation with ease had it been instructed to do so. As a matter of fact, had the integration of Central High School been permitted to take place without the intervention of the National Guard, there is little doubt that the process would have gone along quite as smoothly and quietly as it has in other Arkansas communities. When a State, by seeking to frustrate the orders of a Federal court, encourages mobs of extremists to flout the orders of a Federal court, and when a State refuses to utilize its police powers to protect against mobs persons who are peaceably exercising their right under the Constitution as defined in such court orders, the oath of office of the President requires that he take action to give that protection. Failure to act in such a case would be tantamount to acquiescence in anarchy and the dissolution of the union. I must say that I completely fail to comprehend your comparison of our troops to Hitler's storm troopers. In one case military power was used to further the ambitions and purposes of a ruthless dictator; in the other to preserve the institutions of free government.

With the Army's paratroopers on daily duty at Central High, the situation in Little Rock settled into an impasse that the Governor and the other local and state authorities made no attempt to relieve. The possibility of removing the federal military force was considered by the Southern Governors Conference at its annual meeting in Georgia. Governor Luther Hodges of North Carolina was asked to sound me out about arranging a meeting between the President and a committee consisting of Hodges and three other governors, Collins of Florida, Clement of Tennessee and McKeldin of Maryland. Eisenhower asked me to tell Hodges that he would be glad to discuss with the four governors not only the Little Rock situation but the whole general question of how the Southern states proposed to meet the Supreme Court's order to integrate the schools. The governors had no desire to multiply their troubles. Hodges told me that he had been specifically instructed by the Southern Governors Conference to limit the conversation with the President to a discussion of the withdrawal of the troops from Central High School.

Eisenhower could sympathize with their reluctance and agreed to the limitation. The President met the four governors in his West Wing office with Hagerty, Howard Pyle and myself attending. Brownell told the President it would be better if he himself did not participate. Knowing full well how the Deep South felt about the Justice Department's role in the Little Rock controversy, he thought the talk would go better without him. So he sat by himself in my office, available for consultation with the President and the staff when needed. The problem boiled down to drafting a declaration of peaceful intentions for Faubus to send to the President so that the troops could be removed. After talking with Eisenhower, the governors adjourned to the windowless reception and conference room across the corridor from the President's office familiarly known as the Fish Room because there had been bowls of goldfish kept there during previous administrations. We left the governors to draft a message themselves for Faubus to send. When they had finished, Brownell agreed that it would sufficiently indicate the good intentions of the Arkansas Governor, and Eisenhower approved it.

Then the four governors reached Faubus on the telephone and discussed the statement with him. They found themselves in the same hard tussle that Brooks Hays had suffered through in the hotel room in Providence after the Newport meeting. After they had gone through much of the same kind of a performance, including a series of telephone calls, long waits, word changes and revisions, with Hagerty, Pyle and myself being called in for conference after conference, there was at long last an agreement on a sentence which we were told that Faubus would use. It read: "I now declare that I will assume full responsibility for the maintenance of law and order and that the orders of the Federal Court will not be obstructed."

Eisenhower joined with the governors in a statement in which he said that he had been informed that the Governor of Arkansas had authorized the Governors of North Carolina, Tennessee, Maryland and Florida to state that he was prepared to assume full responsibility for maintaining law and order in Little Rock and would not obstruct the orders of the federal court. Accordingly, the President was to announce, the Secretary of Defense had been directed to withdraw the federal troops from Little Rock and to return the Arkansas National

Guard to the Governor of that state.

This peace pact had to await the formal release of the message from Faubus in Little Rock. It was a long wait. The governors left the Fish Room and went to get themselves a snack and soon came back in the evening to resume their vigil. At last the text of Faubus' statement came from Arkansas. When the governors saw it, they were stunned. Faubus had changed the wording of the key sentence in the approved message and it now had an entirely different meaning.

Instead of "I now declare that I will assume full responsibility for the maintenance of law and order and that the orders of the Federal Court will not be obstructed," the text he had given out in Little Rock said, "I now declare that upon withdrawal of federal troops I will again assume full responsibility, in co-operation with local authorities, for the maintenance of law and order and the orders of the Federal Court will not be obstructed by me." The addition of the two words "by me" that Faubus had slipped on to the end of the statement changed the whole meaning; now he was not taking responsibility for continued defiance of the court order in Little Rock by anybody except himself. The declaration was worthless from Eisenhower's standpoint. It promised no compliance.

The "by me" floored all of us. The governors, all of whom had acted in complete good faith, were nonplused. I was once again badly disappointed. Only Brownell, as at Newport, was not surprised; he had expected nothing better from Faubus all along. I had to locate the President, who was that evening attending a private farewell dinner for Charlie Wilson, who was retiring from the Cabinet, and explain to him that the mission of the Southern governors had ended in failure. Eisenhower prepared with Hagerty and me another statement which was issued that night:

The statement issued this evening by the Governor of Arkansas does not constitute in my opinion the assurance that he intends to use his full powers as Governor to prevent the obstruction of the orders of the United States District Court. Under the circumstances, the President of the United States has no recourse at the present time except to maintain Federal surveillance of the situation.

The last chapters of the Little Rock story are not yet written. Peace was maintained forcibly in the school but there was no way of knowing how bitter the feeling may have been in the homes of the

Central High students. As Eisenhower said at the time about the Supreme Court's decision, it takes a long time to bring moderation, decency and education to bear on a subject that so deeply stirs the human emotions.

The courageous Brooks Hays was defeated by a segregationist opponent when he ran for re-election to Congress from his Little Rock district in 1958. But Hays did not remain in the ranks of the unemployed for long. President Eisenhower appointed him as a member of the Board of Directors of the Tennessee Valley Authority and in 1961 President Kennedy made him the Assistant Secretary of State in charge of the State Department's relations with Congress, a position for which he is admirably qualified. There was never a more respected man on Capitol Hill.

17   More Budget Battles

Eisenhower's New Republicanism received a rough baptism of fire in 1957 in the bitter battle of the budget, which that year listed expenditures of more than seventy billion dollars for the first time during his administration. This unprecedented high in spending plans for the fiscal year of 1958, almost $72 billion, a rise of nearly three billion dollars, caused a flurry across the country and made the Republican conservatives and moderates alike wonder if the progressive spirit of their modern party that the President had talked about after his re-election in November might not be turning toward the philosophy of the New Deal.

Concern that Eisenhower might be wavering in his determination to keep down the costs of government was deepened by what appeared to be a rift in fiscal policy within the President's own official family. George Humphrey was preparing to leave the Cabinet at that time to return to his steel business, where he was urgently needed, but delayed his departure for several months at the President's request in order to help Eisenhower get over the budget hump. In December, 1956, when the size of the new budget became fairly well fixed, Humphrey wrote a letter to the President warning against weakening the soundness of the dollar and stressing the need of getting stability re-established in the cost of living. Pointing out the difficult task facing the President, Humphrey said, "If we fail to put our house in order so that we are able to make an honest tax cut, I believe we will so shake the confidence of the great mass of thinking Americans that we will lose more in private spending than we can possibly gain in Federal spending."

360

This letter was the forerunner of the public criticism that the Secretary appeared to have of the 1958 budget but which Humphrey intended as fortification for the President in resisting expected increases by the Congress.

Behind the budget trouble was the increasing cost of running the government, brought on by inflation, the pressure to raise federal salaries and the Defense Department's urgently necessary but terrifically expensive arms race against Russia. The pressures on the government for public spending are framed around programs that Congress creates and a President can do nothing spectacular to curtail their costs. He can try to slow down the rate of spending, stop recommending new public responsibilities, and, in certain instances, actually withhold appropriated funds from the stream of expenditures. But laws are laws and once they are on the books, retrenchment is like paddling upstream against a swift current.

In the early months of 1957, the economy was in a delicate condition and the recession that began later that year was already faintly visible ahead as Eisenhower was wondering where the income was coming from to pay the bills. A $72 billion budget had to have an expanding economy to stand on if the President was going to avoid deficit spending in a period of peacetime prosperity, a reversal of the "solvent purpose" that he had preached since his first campaign in 1952. At best, if the revenues could continue to keep abreast of the mounting government costs, it would still be a tight squeeze.

What Eisenhower could do, and did do, was to provide what George Humphrey called an air of confidence, a show of reassurance that reduced the fear of recession much more than it did the fear of inflation and further depreciation of the currency. Humphrey was doubtful that the President and the government could do much anyway except to provide what Humphrey thought was the only real contribution—inspiring confidence in the financial soundness of the economic system.

Nevertheless Eisenhower and his economic advisers, Hauge and Burns, and later Raymond Saulnier, who replaced Burns as the Chairman of the Council of Economic Advisers in 1957, did not give up in their attempts to find remedies that the government could apply. Late in 1955 Burns and his staff came up with a plan for assisting chronically depressed localities, such as Lawrence, Massachusetts, where the community had been impoverished by the southward-moving textile industry. The proposal called for an area development agency within the Commerce Department to provide capital improvement loans in co-ordination with municipal and state development organizations. The businessmen in the Cabinet were unenthusiastic about such new loan programs but the President favored the idea. When the proposal went to Congress, Senator Paul Douglas of Illinois, then a proponent of a bill for outright grants for public works, loaded it with subsidies and other provisions that Eisenhower and his more conservative associates would not accept.

The question of reviving some of the economic controls that Eisenhower had boldly demolished in 1953 came up from time to time in Cabinet meetings. The businessmen turned their backs on such suggestions usually but they had some trouble refuting Burns on January 16, 1956, when he argued for consumer credit controls on a stand-by basis as a hedge against inflation. Humphrey insisted that such a request for a stand-by check on consumer credit, to be used when needed, would shake public confidence. The administration's deep dislike of any kind of controls prevailed in the end and Eisenhower went no further than to call to the attention of Congress the need for considering the subject of consumer credit and the effects of mass installment buying. He did not ask for any discretionary authority to exercise or to delegate emergency controls.

The subject of tax reduction came up periodically for thorough consideration in Cabinet and Congressional leadership meetings. I remember at one Cabinet meeting during a discussion of the tax structure, Sinclair Weeks asked Humphrey what would happen if there was a drop in corporate earnings, on which the Treasury was so dependent. Humphrey said with great feeling that the country was in a terrible fiscal situation. The United States, the Secretary pointed out, was more dependent than any country in the world on income taxes when it should be relying on the far safer basis of taxes on gross earnings. When Dr. Burns talked about an estimated surplus of three billion dollars for fiscal 1957, Humphrey warned that Congress would say the administration had been hiding a nest egg so that a tax cut could be made later on in an election year. With a straight face, Dulles looked Humphrey directly in the eye and said, "Have we such a nest egg, George?"

Eisenhower did not warm up to arguments for tax cuts when they were plainly motivated by political reasons. He felt the need of debt reduction just as great and chided the Cabinet for their talk about tax cuts when the prospective surplus could easily melt away like "snow in summer," as Rowland Hughes had warned.

In the late spring and early summer of 1956, when there was a definite slowdown in economic growth, there was increasing talk in the Cabinet meetings of a possible tax cut as a stimulant to business. But the rising defense and agriculture costs discouraged such a reduction. In one meeting in July, Humphrey noted that between 20 and 25 per cent of the gross national income was being drained off in taxes, threatening the accumulation of capital necessary to provide an employment base for the growing labor force. He pointed to the growing abuse of the tax laws in the seeking of loopholes for social and entertainment expenses that were disguised as business investments, cautioning that if the American people lost their confidence in the tax laws, the government would find itself in an impossible situation, similar to that of the French government. He said that he was sure that the people would soon demand tax relief that could be given only through a reduction in government expenses. "If we're going to keep on starting expensive new programs," Humphrey said, "we're going to have to terminate some of the old ones."

In the fall the worry about a recession began to die down but up until December there was continued discussion about how to improve upon prosperity, without any very clear indication whether stimulants or sedatives were needed. Burns wanted the Federal Reserve Board to ease some of the anti-inflationary restraints that had been placed on credit in order to open some "safety doors" for small business, including some direct lending, but Humphrey did not think this would have much of any effect on the situation. The President felt that federal building programs should move slowly, so that they could be used when there was a slack in the economy. In December, when the new budget was being prepared, Eisenhower asked Raymond Saulnier, who had by then succeeded Burns, to stress the need of holding down every item of federal expenditure. At the same meeting, Randolph Burgess, the Under Secretary of the Treasury, saw no prospects in 1957 or 1958 for a surplus sufficient to allow any tax cut. We were again near the temporary debt limit of $278 billion and the limit was about to revert shortly to the regular figure of $275 billion. Eisenhower had little desire to face Harry Byrd, the stern guardian of the Senate Finance Committee, whose approval the administration had to get in order to obtain Congressional authorization for another temporary rise in the debt limit.

The new burgeoning budget of almost $72 billion shared the agenda with the Middle East problems when the Republican leaders came to the White House for a discussion with the President on the last day of 1956. Percival Brundage, the Director of the Bureau of the Budget, began the discussion by admitting that the budget was on a rising trend again after being reduced in 1953, 1954 and 1955. Most of the increase in this budget for the fiscal year ending in 1958, which was to give Eisenhower his toughest fight, was due to the cost of the Defense Department, specifically to missile development. Eisenhower said that some of the military chiefs and the service Secretaries would agree that their budgets were properly balanced and adequate, but, the President added with a wince, these same men would tell the Congressional appropriations committees that they could use another billion or two. "They don't know much about fighting inflation," Eisenhower said. "This country can choke itself to death piling up military expenditures just as surely as it can defeat itself by not spending enough for protection."

Brundage also warned that the new government pay raises could trigger inflation. Senator Knowland told the President bluntly that the pay raises would be passed by Congress whether the administration wanted them or not and that it would take a presidential veto to stop them. Eisenhower shook his head with an air of discouragement and said that there had been remarkable stability in the cost of living since the last pay increases. He added that if people did not understand that freedom was conditioned on self-discipline they would end up with a different form of government. But almost in his next breath, while discussing recommendations for military pay raises from Ralph Cordiner's study group, the President found himself admitting that something had to be done about the loss of able young personnel from the armed forces because of insufficient financial inducement.

It was at this meeting on the day before New Year's Day that Humphrey began to voice the displeasure with the new budget that he later expressed more vividly in his widely publicized letter to Eisenhower. He pointed out that the projected increase in revenues from taxes to an estimated $74 billion was predicated upon a consistent growth of the national economy that could hardly be expected to last forever. Senator Styles Bridges remarked that the Democrats in Congress could be counted upon to increase the agencies' appropriations to still bigger figures with the agency heads helping their effort and leaving the Republican Congressmen out on a limb. That stirred up the President. If anything like that happened, he said, "I want to know about it."

The next day, New Year's Day of 1957, the President discussed the budget with both Democratic and Republican leaders in a special bipartisan meeting. Although the campaign had been fought with some bitterness the previous fall, the President was extending the olive branch in a friendly mood that day in a hope for better relations with the Democratic-controlled Congress during the coming year.

"The Constitution assumes that the executive and the Congress will get along together," Eisenhower said quietly. "I give you my heartfelt assurance that I will always do my best to get along with the Congress to further the matters we have been discussing together today. In the consideration of these subjects no question of partisanship will move me one inch.

"I am convinced we must do everything possible to keep down federal expenditures," he said. "If you come to the point where you think higher expenditures have to be made, let's confer together before your decision is finally made. You are as welcome in this office as anybody. This Congress is under Democratic control and you, as the leaders, have the right and indeed the duty to call upon me whenever you see the need, just as I have the duty to call your attention to a need that I see. And I assure you that if anyone in this administration violates this mutual understanding he will hear promptly from me."

The President wished the Democratic leaders a happy New Year. "This is said with the fact in mind that we belong to different parties," he added, laughing, "and, of course, I belong to the better one."

Sam Rayburn said, "Mr. President, all of us hope you feel as well as you look."

This friendly mood between the White House and the Democrats in Congress disappeared two weeks later when the budget was submitted. The President's apprehension that the opposition would increase the figures in the budget turned out to be groundless; the opposite occurred. There was a prairie fire of public opinion that the federal government was about to spend too much of the people's money and the conservatives of both parties took advantage of the prevailing sentiment to cut programs left and right.

When the Cabinet met a week before, George Humphrey read a letter he had prepared and wanted to know what the Cabinet thought about his sending it to the President. Eisenhower had no objections, but Dulles called it too critical and Budget Director Brundage was sure it would be interpreted as a rift within the administration. Humphrey said he wanted to handle it so that it would best serve to improve public relations. The President agreed with Humphrey that publicizing the Secretary's stern warning would help discourage Congress from increasing expenditures even more.

When this letter was published it was held up gleefully as evidence that even Eisenhower's own Secretary of the Treasury felt that his administration was too extravagant. The Humphrey letter did in fact include one paragraph that seemed to support such a contention:

Long hours of painstaking and conscientious work have gone into the preparation of the budget for fiscal year 1957-58 by all Departments of the Government. They all should be commended for the effort they have made. But it is not enough. The overall net results are not sufficient. Only the most drastic action will suffice.

This sounded to the country as though the Secretary of the Treasury was indeed criticizing the budget of the administration. What added fuel to the fire was Humphrey's off-the-cuff remarks to the reporters that the budget was too high, and that if federal spending did not come down we could look forward to a depression that would curl your hair.

Humphrey included in the letter an expression of hope that Congress might find ways and means of suggesting proper cuts in the proposed spending. Eisenhower little suspected when he approved the release of the letter that within a few weeks Congress would be accepting Humphrey's invitation with a vengeance and that instead of fighting further increases in his budget he would be trying to stop the Congress from using the meat ax on it.

At a press conference after the Humphrey letter was made public,

Eisenhower took pains to explain that Humphrey's remarks were made in connection with his letter, and when he predicted a "hair-curling" depression he was talking about the results of a long-term continuation of spending at the present rate. Of Humphrey's letter, the President said, "I not only went over every word of it, I edited it, and it expresses my convictions very thoroughly."

Eisenhower was questioned about the Secretary's request for Congressional assistance in reducing the appropriations. He went even further than Humphrey; if Congress can cut the budget, he said, "it is their duty to do it." In the New England vernacular, that gummed up the sapworks. Eisenhower had meant only to encourage the usual parings in the budget that Congressional committees customarily make but it sounded as if he hoped Congress would make the deep and substantial cuts that he and the administrative heads of the government soon found themselves opposing. It sounded, in other words, as if the President were passing the responsibility to Congress.

The reporters moved in fast with further questions. They pointed out that when Eisenhower went into office he had said that he hoped to bring down federal expenditures to $60 billion a year or less. Now he was asking to spend $72 billion. Did this represent a basic change in his philosophy of government? Why the increases in domestic spending?

Eisenhower said the reasons for the $72 billion budget were plain enough—pay increases for an increased number of people on the government payroll, three million in the armed services and two and a half million in civil service; the long-neglected guided missile program, the B-52 jet bombers, the early warning system and a great variety of new weapons. As for new expenditures in domestic programs, "As long as the American people demand, and in my opinion, deserve, the kind of services that this budget provides, we have got to spend this kind of money." But the implication behind the reporters' questions was obvious and it came out into the open at later press conferences that spring; didn't the bigger domestic spending reflect Eisenhower's growing deflection from the traditional conservatism of the Republican party? He warmly denied it, emphasizing that his Lincolnian conception of the obligation of the government to do for the people what they could not do for themselves was limited by Modern Republicanism's respect for a sound fiscal policy and a competitive economy. Modern Republicanism, he repeated, was not the cause of the big budget.

There was talk at the Cabinet meetings early that year of applying an arbitrary cut in expenditures to all departments of the government such as the one that Eisenhower had ordered in 1955 to achieve that year's balanced budget. But Eisenhower himself pointed out that increases in salaries, interest rates and the need for modernizing weapons would make such an economy move impractical in 1957. Dulles called attention to the increase in government services made necessary by the increase in population, and the increased cost of American obligations abroad. There was discussion of an arbitrary order from the President that would direct each department to withhold 5 per cent of its allotted budgetary funds until that money was released by the President. But that procedure would have run into snags, it was agreed, and the idea was dropped.

Although the administration was having difficulty finding ways to cut expenses, its critics on Capitol Hill were not hampered by such inhibitions. By March, the hounds were in full bay. Almost the whole of Eisenhower's meeting with the Republican leaders from Congress on the sixth of that month was devoted to a discussion of what position to take about the clamor of the Democrats and the conservative Republicans for deep budget reductions. It was clear that the foreign programs would be the main targets, especially Mutual Security. John Taber, the ranking Republican on the House Appropriations Committee, said there would be trouble over State and Health, Education and Welfare requests because those two departments had nowhere near the number of employees they had indicated as a basis for their previous year's budgetary estimates. Taber was also distressed by the high maintenance and operations costs in the Defense budget. "Those commanders out in the posts are not riding herd on them closely enough," Taber said. "The Budget has got to be cut and it would be a good thing for the Republicans to help cut it where it can be cut properly." One of the leaders mentioned to Eisenhower that despite all the outcry from the Democrats about the administration's extravagance, Lyndon Johnson was looking for an extra $1.8 million for some Coast Guard cutters that he wanted for some reason or other, apparently to safeguard Texan shrimp fishermen in the Gulf of Mexico. Senator Dirksen remarked correctly that $65 billion in the budget was marked for expenses that could not be cut, defense costs, interest on the public debt and other statutory obligations.

The President told about the fight he had been going through with the Defense Department budget. During the period when the figures were being prepared, he had sought reductions but found himself licked before he started, he said, because of the department's prior authorizations. He mentioned that later that same day he was meeting with Defense officials to discuss their present spending, which was running over the current budget. "And that is exactly what will happen again next year with these so-called firm estimates that we are putting together with so much work and sweat in this 1958 budget," the President said. "This will continue to happen as long as the department has to carry out every program ordained by Congress, whether it is practical and essential or not."

Humphrey complained that the members of Congress were seeking money for their own pet personal projects while cutting expenses indiscriminately everywhere else. He described one committee hearing where he argued against the efforts of two Republicans to spend a large amount of money for Coast Guard planes while his Treasury Department budget was being reduced without anyone specifying exactly where the reduction was to be made.

"The administration has worked hard on this budget," Humphrey said to the Republican legislative leaders. "Up to now, the talk in Congress about cutting it has been concerned with things that are peanuts. Congress ought to be talking about cutting programs, not bits and pieces of programs. It is the constitutional duty of the President to send up a budget to Congress showing the things that should be done in the coming year and how much they will cost. It is then the constitutional duty of Congress to review that budget and to take action on it. The executive branch cannot spend unless Congress authorizes the expenditures and appropriates the money. If you are going to make any real progress, you have got to re-examine these programs and find out first what the Republicans in Congress are willing to cut out and then get busy and see if Congress is willing to eliminate them. Of course foreign aid will be hit because cutting those expenditures will not affect the constituents of anybody in Congress, but remember this—by spending money in foreign aid we can save even more money in other fields, notably in the armed forces that we have to keep overseas. I'm not against the Mutual Security Program. Percy Brundage and I know of eight or ten programs where certain specific items can be cut. Now you can consult the leaders and see if they have the nerve and the votes to make such cuts and if they do, the administration will accept them."

Joe Martin suggested that Humphrey should draw up a list of reducible budget items that the leaders could go over at their next meeting. Humphrey came back to the subject of percentage reductions. He thought it would be practicable for Congress to grant the President the authority to make a 5 per cent reduction in any budget item, leaving the President the discretion to apply this saving where he thought it could be best made. The Postmaster General had already had such a privilege in his department for a long time. Then, Humphrey explained, Congress would not have to specify where the reduction should be made. Any other across-the-board cutting method made no sense, Humphrey said, because such indiscriminate reductions made some programs impossible to carry through. Senator Bridges told the Secretary that this was an old issue in Congress and that it had never won approval because Congress feared that in giving the President such authority it would give him the arbitrary power to scuttle certain programs that the legislators wanted.

As the meeting came to a close the Republican leaders told the President and Humphrey that their invitation to Congress to cut the budget had caused some confusion on Capitol Hill about who was supposed to be leading whom. If the administration was committed to this $71.8 billion budget, Senator Saltonstall asked, how did the White House plan to support its figures and also encourage Congress to cut them at one and the same time? Humphrey replied that the administration had never claimed that the present figures in the budget could not be changed if Congress would agree to eliminate certain programs which were there because Congress wanted them there. Saltonstall said that this attitude seemed to indicate that the President was putting the onus of leadership on Congress. Humphrey reminded the Senator again that Congress had a constitutional duty to change the budget as it saw fit and there that particular discussion came to a dead end.

But a few days later the House of Representatives in an impudent mood passed a resolution asking the President to tell Congress how to cut his budget. In the Senate, Lyndon Johnson also made a public plea for guidance in reducing government expenditures. Several of us on the White House staff and in the Cabinet urged Eisenhower to come back at the House with a letter telling the Congressmen exactly how they could economize. We knew that the President could give the Democrats on the Hill plenty of specific suggestions for saving money that they would not want to hear. We were joined by the Republican Congressional leaders, who were becoming increasingly annoyed by the way that the Democrats were stealing the traditional role of champions of thrift and fiscal conservatism that had always been occupied by the GOP in Washington. The President agreed that some attention should be called to the fact that many of the expensive programs in the budget had been enacted when the government was under Democratic administration. Senator Bridges reminded Eisenhower of a remark once made by Sam Rayburn to the effect that Carl Hayden, the benign Democrat on the Senate Appropriations Committee who was a proponent of public works and reclamation projects, had smiled more billions through Congress than anybody else in history.

Eisenhower himself was deeply concerned by the way the Democrats were piling up expenditures in the Defense program. He told the Republican leaders that he wanted them to oppose any new spending plan that the opposition introduced, recalling the billion-dollar addition that the Democrats had tacked onto the Defense budget the year before. Repeating his familiar theme, he said, with finality, "There is no defense for any country that busts its own economy."

The President sent his letter to the House on April 18. It reminded the Congressmen that his administration had removed a quarter of a million employees from the federal payroll, made a $7.4 billion tax cut in 1954 and produced three balanced budgets in a row. He wrote that all federal expenditures could not be controlled by the budget planners; pensions, public assistance and interest on the public debt accounted for $17.6 billion of the 1958 budget. None of these expenses could be reduced, the President reminded the Congressmen, "unless and until Congress revises or repeals the governing laws."

The President's letter emphasized that 63 per cent of the budget, some $45 billion, was marked for protection of the country and that the Defense Department was pressing for more dollars for missiles, technological research and electronic equipment. He wrote: "I most solemnly advise the House that in these times a cut of any appreciable consequence in current expenditures for national security and related programs would endanger our country and the peace of the world."

The remaining expenditures in the budget, around nine billion dollars, covered a limited area of government expenses for civil functions, housing programs, public health and public works where any multibillion-dollar cut would seriously cripple essential services. But, the President added, there were many other places in the budget where Congress could make sizable savings. Firing from both barrels, he proceeded to name them:

Adjust postal rates and wipe out the Post Office's deficit. Change government interest rates to encourage private capital to participate in federal loan programs. Charge the users of public facilities, such as airports. Require the states to participate in disaster assistance programs. Throw out river and harbor projects not soundly approved by U.S. engineers and require more local funds in such public works. Follow up on money-saving legislation recommended by the Hoover Commission, such as the Accrued Accounting Act. Sell or return to the states and to county or local town governments surplus federal land not essential for future uses. Project the costs of unbudgeted programs so that Congress can see how much new programs are going to cost. Give the President veto power over specific items in appropriation bills, a power that many states give their governors.

The President promised that prompt approval of these recommendations would give much relief to the budgetary situation but his letter brought little reaction in Congress. As he well knew, every one of these ideas had been presented to the House and Senate at one time or another and all of them had been found politically unpalatable. They were sound recommendations but the Democrats claimed they were delaying and diversionary; Senator Bridges and the Republican conservatives said they were too mild.

Previous budget-cutting by Congress caught up with the legislators in April and caused them considerable embarrassment. Earlier, Postmaster General Arthur Summerfield had come to the House Appropriations Committee with a request for funds to tide the Post Office through the current fiscal year. In 1956, Congress had pared down the Post Office's budget to less than it would need to get its operations through fiscal year 1957. Summerfield had warned the legislators that he would be running out of funds in the fourth quarter of the fiscal year but his warning was ignored. The Post Office had asked for $41 million to get it through the year but the House Appropriations Committee refused to give Summerfield more than $17 million. The Congressmen figured that somehow he would be able to make ends meet. Summerfield informed the committee that unless the rest of the $41 million was handed over the nation's mail service on Saturdays would be stopped. On Saturday, April 13, the mail was not delivered.

Clarence Cannon, the House Appropriations Chairman, called Summerfield's threat a hoax. He found out that the Postmaster General was not bluffing. Summerfield placed his predicament before the President. He could not operate the Post Office without funds and he had no legal right to spend money at a rate faster than it had been appropriated by Congress, so he had no choice but to curtail the postal service. There would be a national howl, to be sure, but the situation had been explained to Congress and Congress had done nothing. Eisenhower told him if there was no alternative to do what was necessary but be sure the leaders in Congress were notified.

When the mail stopped, Cannon's committee immediately authorized another seventeen million dollars, which was still not enough to meet the Post Office's costs. Then, a little frantically, the committee pushed through a bill for what Summerfield had originally requested, indignantly blaming the Postmaster General for not anticipating the emergency.

Eisenhower took some satisfaction in the outcome of the situation that Cannon and his committee had gotten themselves into. He told reporters that Summerfield had acted with "my complete approval." And so Congress learned that although the mail couriers could withstand the elements in the completion of their daily rounds they were not immune to financial exhaustion.

The President took his budget problem to the people in a nationwide television and radio address on May 14. The question was, he said, how big the budget should be and it reminded him of the time that Abraham Lincoln was asked by a man who was criticizing the length of Lincoln's legs, "How long should a man's legs be?" Lincoln looked down at his long and lanky legs and replied, "They ought to be long enough to reach the ground." And so it was with the budget,

Eisenhower said; it had to be big enough to allow for the cost of the essentials that were needed for the country's security and its necessary services. Point by point, the President went over these essentials and concluded with words that he had used many times before: "I can see no immediate relaxation of international tensions to provide the basis now for substantial reductions in these programs for preserving and waging peace. In fact, the gains we have already made impel us to press forward with no letup."

Eisenhower's battle with Congress over the budget made it clear to the Washington observers that the President was getting more support from the liberal Republicans, such as Senators Case of New Jersey, Javits of New York, Cooper of Kentucky and Bush of Connecticut, than he was from the conservative Republican leadership. Eisenhower was asked if he was planning to work with the liberal wing of his party in Congress in getting his future legislation passed rather than through the Republican leadership. This question of working with a rump leadership had come up before, but the President and his staff were aware of the chaos it could create. A newsman remarked to Eisenhower a few days after his televised speech on the budget that many Republicans in Congress "think you have grown less conservative, and moved somewhat to the left." "If anything, I think I have grown more conservative," the President replied. "Always I have said I believed in sound fiscal policies, preserving the value of the dollar in the interests of us all, particularly in the interests of the men and women who must live on pensions and government bonds and all that sort of thing in their old age." But the needs of people today are different than those of 1860, he added, and the government could not shut its eyes to the modern responsibilities of leadership. It was in this press conference discussion that Eisenhower's attention was called to a statement made by his brother Edgar, who complained that the President was being swayed by the liberal influence of Milton Eisenhower and Sherman Adams. The President grinned and said, "Edgar has been criticizing me since I was five years old."

The specific area in this 1957 budget war where the basic philosophic difference between the President and the conservative Republican leadership was brought out sharply was in the battle for Mutual Security funds. Time did nothing to ease this annual struggle for the President. Whether Congress was in a thrifty mood or on a spending spree, Eisenhower had to make a personal fight every year for the Mutual Security appropriations that he considered necessary for the maintenance of world peace. For the fiscal year 1957, he asked for $4.8 billions for Mutual Security and ended up with $3.8 billions. That year Senator Knowland and other Republican leaders were incensed as usual by proposals to send financial aid to Yugoslavia and India. Knowland referred again, as he always did in those debates, to Tito's declaration that nothing would ever separate Yugoslavia and Russia and he argued that both Tito and Nehru seemed to be bent on persuading other countries to desert their alliances with the United States.

The President argued himself hoarse trying to explain the need for assisting neutral countries that were not allied to the United States in defensive military agreements. He tried to point out that the neutralism of such nations as Yugoslavia and India did not always work to the disadvantage of the free world by any means, and, therefore, we should not be too demanding about the attitudes of such nations. Nothing was to be gained if you turned your back on them, he contended. Dulles joined with the President in stressing the strategic value of economic and military assistance to a socialist country like Yugoslavia, which could serve as an independent buffer between Russia and the NATO governments and which could conceivably detach satellite nations behind the Iron Curtain from the influence of Moscow.

In theory, the Mutual Security idea was unassailable. It enabled us to keep up a defensive shield against Communist expansion in foreign countries unable to provide their own protection and it maintained this defense at a far lower cost than we would have had to pay to station our own armed forces in those parts of the world. These treaty arrangements also permitted us to maintain U.S. military bases in overseas locations where, as Admiral Radford put it, an American plane could make ten missions to an enemy target in the time required for one trip to the same destination from a base in the United States.

In the areas where most of the Mutual Security funds were being spent—Korea, Formosa, Southeast Asia, Turkey and Pakistan—the results were generally successful but there was also just enough failure to keep the supporters of the plan on the defensive. Continued growth of Communist influence in Indo-China, the division of Vietnam and the unabated hostility of Red China, coming after the loss of North Korea, raised doubts in Congress about the wisdom of our investments in the Far East. Some of the Congressmen who were willing to approve the military aid aspect of the Mutual Security plan were doubtful about the value of its economic and technical assistance programs.

Eisenhower and Dulles were deeply convinced that the so-called uncommitted countries, as well as those that were definitely on our side, had to be shown that friendship with the United States could bring them something better than guns and jeeps. But too many legislators in Washington could not understand that, for us, world leadership carried with it the responsibility to help the underdeveloped nations fight poverty and disease if for no other reason than to maintain our own place in the ideological competition.

This was the great dilemma that faced Eisenhower during those years when the President seemed to deny his own conservatism in his urgent appeals to the Congress for funds to carry on the essentials of the Mutual Security Program. With these struggles fairly fresh in mind, there is no reason to support the assumption that even as persuasive a protagonist as Eisenhower could have induced Congress to come forward with a long-range economic development program that would have deterred the Communists in their plans to hack away at Laos until they had created another situation like Korea and Vietnam.

In most of the years of his presidency, Eisenhower was not able to induce Congress to appropriate funds to cover the bare bones of a program that always seemed more concerned with putting out fires than it did with a soundly planned project to get the countries involved onto their economic feet. The situation that confronted Southeast Asia, especially countries like Laos and South Vietnam, could not be handled with any Marshall Plan approach, which applied with such spectacular success to the industrialized areas of Western Europe. Here there was little or nothing on which to build, and the administration quite naturally had to turn first to a variety of quick-acting, expensive remedies that corrected little except the crises of the moment.

Assuming the Congress had been in the mood for investments in the new horizons, which it definitely was not, there was not then nor is there now any clear and soundly conceived economic program that is yet ready and acceptable to replace the need for the huge sums that have to be spent to maintain even the *status quo*.

As to the tenuous contention that we made a bad guess in the political support we gave to the government of Laos at the time of and subsequent to its acquiring independence, it can fairly be said that no Southeast Asian government could have offered *per se* any guarantees of stability in the unsettled state of affairs then existing. So it became a matter of judgment in arriving, not simply at the decisions in the Laos developments, but at those that involved other countries in that troubled region. The Western position was too often only a toehold which we were obliged to maintain as best we could. To imply that the judgment was poor in one instance is to say that in every country where freedom's shield has held firm the decisions, or the gamble if you prefer, have had happier results. Perhaps it is truer in this region than in most other parts of the world where we have had to face tough political decisions that what has worked has been right; what has failed at least has had the benefit of the best judgment of which we were capable under all the circumstances and with all the facts available to us at the time.

After swallowing the one-billion-dollar cut that Congress made in his Mutual Security Program in fiscal 1957, Eisenhower came right back to ask Congress for $4.4 billion for the next year, hoping to replenish some of the funds that had just been pared from the program. This time he was supported by a report from a citizens' committee, headed by Benjamin Fairless, the former chairman and president of the United States Steel Corporation, which had made a thorough survey of the Mutual Security Program. The report by the Fairless committee strongly declared that the economic development of foreign countries uncommitted to the Soviets was in the long run as important to the security of the free world as the military protection we had undertaken to support.

The Fairless report pointed out one obvious flaw in the Mutual Security plan that Eisenhower and Dulles were trying to correct. This was the Congressional restriction against giving a foreign nation economic aid for more than one year at a time, which made it impossible for a borrowing country to make a long-range economic

development plan based on a continuing program of American financial help. As a part of the new program that he proposed to Congress
in 1957, Eisenhower asked for a Development Loan Fund that would
finance foreign economic development over a period of several
years, which Congress later provided by suitable legislation.

On May 9, before he sent to Congress a special message on his
Mutual Security Program, the President discussed it in detail at a
meeting in the White House with the legislative leaders from both
parties. "I would rather see anything else in the budget cut than these
programs," he told the leaders, referring to the military and economic
expenditures of the Mutual Security plan, to which he added the
United States Information Agency program and the State Department's foreign operations to make "one vital parcel which we must
not neglect." He stressed the fact that the budget as a whole could
never be reduced to any significant extent until the threat to world
peace was lessened. "All of us are too realistic to believe we are going
to make any spectacular reductions in the farm program, the veterans'
program or any other such benefits," he said. "Great savings can be
made only in defense expenditures." The change in the tense foreign
situation that could make such savings possible, he argued, will never
come as a result of a continued armament build-up. "We can't just sit
and wait for something to happen to eliminate the threat," he insisted.
"Nor can we persuade people just from the pulpit."

The President also announced that because the Defense Department was able to reduce the cost of the military items in the Mutual
Security Program he was cutting the $4.4 billion he had asked for
in January to $3.86 billion.

That same day, the President made an appeal to the public on
radio and television in a desperate effort to save the Mutual Security
Program from being virtually crippled in Congress. He declared that
the need for such spending and loaning of money for economic development and military assistance abroad was far greater than the
need for lower taxes, bigger dams, deeper harbors, higher pensions
or better housing at home. Hitting hard on the importance of long-
range economic aid which would be provided by the Development
Loan Fund program, he declared that Communist exploitation of
poverty was as great a danger to free nations overseas as the menace
of military weapons. "We do not seek to buy friends," he said. "We

do not seek to make satellites. We seek to help other peoples to become strong and stay free."

The President carried the battle for Mutual Security to Capitol Hill and fought it every step of the way. He brought key figures from Congress to the oval room study at the White House for urgent personal talks after office hours. Eric Johnston was enlisted to stage a public demonstration in behalf of the Mutual Security effort which was attended by notables from all walks of life. Knowing the President's intense concern for the program, the Democrats attempted during that summer's uproar over the proposed civil rights legislation to use a threat to cut Mutual Security expenditures as a blackjack to force through certain changes in the administration's civil rights stand. Eisenhower called in the Republican leaders and told them that as much as he wanted the Mutual Security funds, he would not allow the issue to be shuffled around in any kind of parliamentary trade.

But in the all-out fight by Congress against the $72 billion budget, Mutual Security was doomed for a slashing no matter how hard the President fought for it. It was plain that something had to go, and here was an expense that the Congressmen could hack at without antagonizing the voters back home in the way that a cut in agricultural spending or proposed federal pay raises would have done.

The argument about what could be cut from the domestic programs without causing national distress was never conclusively answered in all of Eisenhower's years in the White House. Harry Byrd, the soundest of the fiscal conservatives in Congress, said that five billion dollars could be taken out of the civilian and nondefense expenditures in the big 1957 budget but nobody could show exactly how this could be done. As the President had already told the Congress, it was beyond him, with $45 billion committed to national defense, how anybody could take any such sum as Byrd had suggested out of the remaining $26 billion that paid for such items as the farm program, veterans' pensions and the interest on the public debt, as well as the entire costs of actually running the government.

The failure of Senator Knowland and other Republican leaders in Congress to give the President any substantial backing on the Mutual Security issue caused some political commentators to suggest that Knowland should resign as the Republican minority leader in the Senate. It seemed strange, after all, for the chief spokesman of the President's party in Congress to disagree with one of the principal features of the President's policy. "The organization of the political parties within the Senate is a matter for Senate decision," Eisenhower said.

But wouldn't the President punish the Republicans who refused to go along with his program, the reporters asked him. Eisenhower said he wasn't going to punish anybody. He did feel, however, that when a political party agrees on a platform, it should remain true to it and unless conditions change, it should stick to it through thick and thin. A reporter asked if the President would support in the Congressional elections of 1958 those Republicans who "didn't do anything for him" with the same enthusiasm as he would feel for those who had helped him. "I hope I am never accused of being so namby-pamby that I don't have degrees of enthusiasm about people who stand for me and who stand against me," Eisenhower said. "I most earnestly believe that the Congress and the White House should be occupied and controlled by the same party, for the reason that you can then fix responsibility. . . . When it comes down to who I am for enthusiastically and who I am for because he is a Republican, there is a very wide difference."

In August, Eisenhower, with great reluctance and bitter disappointment, had to accept Congress' decision to limit Mutual Security to a maximum $3.4 billion. Then Congress chopped still another $600 million off that reduced figure and in September he signed an appropriation bill that called for only $2.8 billion. It was a serious and disturbing personal defeat for him, but the next January he was in there fighting for Mutual Security again.

And when Congress was finished with the over-all budget for the fiscal year of 1958, it was cut by four billion dollars. But what happened later recalled Robert Burns's observation about the best-laid schemes of mice and men. Before the fiscal year of 1958 came to a close Congress had not only restored the four billion dollars but had added another $4.5 billion to the spending authority, originally requested by the President. The feast-or-famine cycle was once again reversed, this time turned around by the 1957-58 recession, or as some of us called it, "the side-slip in the economy." The politicians were then running in the other direction, trying to provide unemployment relief and stimulants to put business back on the upgrade.

18 Fight to Free Foreign Trade

June, 1958, was a disturbing and unhappy time for Eisenhower and all of us at the White House. Dick and Pat Nixon had just returned from their trip to South America, where they had been jeered, spat upon and, finally, in Venezuela, almost seriously injured by an angry mob that attacked the car in which they were riding. Why were the Vice President of the United States and his wife publicly abused and ridiculed in these countries where our prestige had once been so high? If the wild demonstrations against the Nixons had been aroused by Communist agitators, as it was reported, why were the Reds so successful in stirring up such an open and defiant anti-American resentment? The answers were not hard to find.

It was something deeper than political ideology. The underprivileged people in economically undeveloped countries, not only in Latin America but in Africa, Asia and many parts of Europe, were not so much interested in the nature of the conflicts between Communism and Western Democracy. Their struggle was against neither, but with poverty, malnutrition, disease and illiteracy and their principal interest in Russia and the United States was to find out which of those two great powers would give them the help and encouragement that they needed. The modern world with its miracles of communication was bringing them an understanding of privileges and advantages they had always been denied, and they now began to reach for them. This was especially true of the new and insecure nations that were emerging in Africa and Southeast Asia from what had been the colonial empires of Britain, France, Belgium and the Netherlands.

Eisenhower had always accepted the responsibility of the United

381

States to assist the undeveloped countries to get onto their economic feet, both as an indirect weapon against Communist aggression and as one firm foundation for building the peace. The four or five billion dollars a year that the United States government was spending in the whole Mutual Security effort Eisenhower regarded as only a temporary expedient. It could not go on forever, and besides, it would not in itself build any permanent structure for peace. It would have to be replaced by some other economic plan that would give these countries the opportunity to build up their own trade and commerce and thus earn their own living.

This meant that the United States in its own self-interest would have to take the lead itself in freeing up world markets, and that would have to include our own. Even though such policy could not avoid some economic dislocations here at home, we could no longer expect to sell our products wherever we wished in the markets of the world and maintain a wall against the foreign manufacturer who wanted to compete in our domestic market. Moreover, the urgent diplomatic pressures we brought on our allies not to trade with the Iron Curtain countries in strategically important commodities did not make much sense when we shut out these products from our own markets. Many of them either had to find a Western market somewhere or look to the East. This protective wall of tariffs and quotas had to be lowered. As the pungent George Humphrey expressed it one day at a Cabinet meeting, the honeymoon was over. A businessman himself, with no relish for competition from abroad, Humphrey nevertheless agreed with Eisenhower that if Communism was to be checked and peace established the foreign nations must be given a viable position in the market place. "We've had it good but now things have got to change," Humphrey said. "We've been making the automobiles and the farm machinery and everything else and selling them all over the world. Now we have to help other countries to make them and they will want to sell them here."

Naturally, this was an economic fact of life that most American industrialists and businessmen and the conservative politicians in Congress did not want to hear. Organized labor did not care for it either. There was still another strong argument for lowering the protectionist barriers against the import of foreign goods into the United States that Lewis Douglas had pointed out in a letter to

Eisenhower in 1953: as the world's biggest creditor, America could no longer keep foreign products out of its own country without facing discrimination against American products abroad. Douglas' letter made a distinct impression on the President and shortly after he received it he began to talk with Hauge and me about how the administration should go about liberalizing the government's trade policies.

The President needed first a study by a commission or citizens' committee which would bring in recommendations for a new foreign trade program and support it when Eisenhower sent it to Congress. Secretary of Commerce Sinclair Weeks and I agreed that the commission's recommendations would carry more weight, especially among the Republican leadership in Congress, if we could find an important American industrialist to head it up. The conservatives in Congress would be more inclined to listen to a businessman, whereas they would pay little attention to the views of an economist from a college campus who had never met a payroll, bargained with a labor union or sold products on a competitive market. Weeks suggested Clarence Randall, the recently retired chairman of the Inland Steel Company. It was an inspired recommendation. Randall's position as a capitalist was unassailable; he had been the steel industry's spokesman when President Truman had tried to take over the steel companies during the strike in 1952. He was also a brilliantly intelligent man who had traveled widely around the world and shared Eisenhower's convictions about the need for free trade as a peace weapon. He had remarkable ability in an argument to explain a complex proposition with clear simplicity and to stick to a position with calm control, a necessary quality in an encounter with Congressmen. And, most important of all, he was willing to take the job.

Among the commission of seventeen outstanding members which studied every aspect of foreign trade policy were several men whose views on the question of tariffs and other protective barriers were diametrically opposed to those of the President, Lewis Douglas and Randall himself. This minority of conservatives had in it the ranking Republican members of Congress, Senator Millikin and Representatives Simpson of Pennsylvania and Reed of New York, as well as David McDonald, the president of the United Steelworkers, who wanted the government to provide financial aid to workers and com-

munities that might be affected by foreign trade competition. Mc-
Donald's idea was rejected by the seventeen-man commission by a
vote of sixteen to one. In the middle of January, 1954, Randall told
me that he was ready to present the commission's findings to the
President. I made an appointment for him to see Eisenhower on
January 21. The President listened to Randall intently and agreed with
his conclusions completely, as did Gabriel Hauge, who kept in close
touch with Randall and his work in the White House. Two days
later the report was made public and shortly thereafter Randall was
appointed as the President's special consultant on foreign economic
policy. On February 26, he gave the Cabinet a full analysis of his
commission's report, the result of four months of intensive research.
The commission made a trip to Paris, for example, where it listened
in four days to twenty-eight leaders of the European diplomatic corps
and representatives of international organizations, each interview
lasting for forty-five minutes.

The commission's report supported Eisenhower's view that financial aid offered no lasting solution of the economic problems of
foreign countries. What was needed, the report said, was private
business investments abroad, which should be encouraged by a reduction of the tax on income from such overseas ventures. Randall's
group recommended a three-year extension of the Trade Agreements
Act (the reciprocal trade treaties) and authority for the President
to negotiate new multilateral agreements in which he would have
the option of reducing tariff rates by 5 per cent per year for three years.
Another recommendation in the report that was to stir up later controversy in Congress advocated a resumption of peaceful trade between the East and the West. Randall held that trade was the best
device for penetrating the Iron Curtain. Furthermore, the report said,
"We must not ask nations to become our friends and allies and at
the same time impose upon them a limitation that reduces their
standard of living." There was a strong faction in Congress at that
time, led by Senator McCarthy of Wisconsin, that wanted to stop
Britain and our other allies from trade with Red China, Russia and
other Communist countries. Randall wanted no wavering on the part
of anybody in the administration on the position that his commission
and the President were taking in favor of a freer foreign trade policy.
"I recommend," he said, "that *prima facie* the report become the

policy of the administration and that it not be deviated from, except for strong cause."

The State Department, conscious of the need to strengthen our ties with many strategically situated countries, wanted to go further than the commission in freeing our foreign trade policy. Dulles was anxious to give special treatment to Japan, an important ally that was largely dependent on foreign markets; if we lost the friendship of Japan, Dulles and Eisenhower often said, the Pacific would become a Communist lake. The report proposed to give the President the authority under certain conditions to exempt foreign bidders from the provisions of the Buy American Act, a law passed during the 1933 depression which required the federal government procurement agencies to give a preference to domestic suppliers. This preference was 5 per cent at the time, but in recent years had been 25 per cent, a differential added to the foreign bid in computing the price on which the award was made. Brownell did not think it practical to reduce the differential, and Eisenhower agreed with him.

Before sending the new program to Congress, Eisenhower and Randall went over it carefully with the Republican legislative leaders. Senator Millikin and Representatives Simpson and Reed, the Republican leaders on the Randall Commission who were in disagreement with practically the entire report, wrote out and submitted their minority views. Millikin was opposed to tariff reductions and to the granting of authority to the President for simplifying rate structures and definitions. All three of the dissenting Republicans were against investment guarantees, the proposed modification of the Buy American law and the relaxation of East-West trade restrictions and changes in the minerals policy.

Randall assured the Congressional leaders at the meeting that the program did not advocate any radical across-the-board tariff reductions and that the peril points and escape clauses would not be disturbed. Senator Knowland, always a defender of American business against the threat of foreign competition, resented the fact that the Randall report had been approved as the administration's program before it was placed for consideration before the Republican leaders. He reminded Randall rather sharply that these meetings were supposed to be for advance discussion and consultation, not merely to announce a previously resolved and already entrenched position. Knowland told Randall that he was sure that the changes in the Buy American Act would not pass as written; he pointed out that some manufacturing plants in the United States had been closed recently because the government had been buying generators from foreign companies. Eisenhower agreed that there were two sides to this problem and suggested certain exceptions should be made for three reasons: a threat to national security, severe unemployment and unfair competition with small business, and that was the way the recommendation went into the foreign trade message.

No amount of persuasion could convince Reed that a relaxation of East-West trade restrictions would not be giving valuable aid to the Russians. Gabriel Hauge suggested a statement saying that the new foreign trade program would not weaken the Battle Act, which prevented the sending of strategic materials to Communist nations either directly or through our allies, enforced by the withdrawal of our assistance under the Mutual Security or other foreign programs. But Millikin would not let the matter rest there. He did not intend to make life any easier for the Soviet warmongers, he announced. The President tried to explain patiently to the Senator that the United States could not live alone in the world. Neither could it keep our allies such as Britain and France from resuming their traditional trade with other countries so they would not have to depend upon us.

Milliken argued that the foreign trade legislation would cause greater trouble in Congress than any program proposed by the administration up to that point. He insisted that we ought to be eliminating restrictions against United States trade abroad instead of agreeing to new reciprocal trade treaties as the Democrats had been doing for twenty years. He doubted that the program would bring any demonstrable net advantage to the nation and he predicted that it would cause a rift in the Republican party and in public sentiment as a whole.

But Eisenhower was not to be swayed by such objections. His foreign trade message to Congress on March 30, 1954, embodied virtually verbatim all of the recommendations of the Randall report. The President declared that the United States must take the initiative in removing man-made barriers to mutual trade and "to make it clear to the rest of the world that we expect them to follow our lead." He repeated in his message what Lewis Douglas had written in his memorable letter in 1953: "If we fail in our trade policy, we may fail in all. Our domestic employment, our standard of living, our security and the solidarity of the free world—all are involved."

Yet the President could not get out of Congress at that time any more than a bare one-year extension of the Reciprocal Trade Act. Even in the executive department, progress toward getting administrative action was faulty, sometimes even recessive. Dulles was a stern watchdog, who often kept the courses of action from wandering away from the President's policy. One day in a Cabinet meeting late in July, Dulles listened intently to an involved discussion of technicalities concerning a proposal from Arthur Flemming, the Director of the Office of Defense Mobilization, for the appointment of a presidential committee to work out recommendations for the protection and development of such domestic strategic resources as oil and other energy supplies. Dulles moved in fast, pointing out that there was a strong implication that the appointment of such a committee at that time might be considered a restrictive measure that foreshadowed "import quotas, higher tariffs and similar actions that fly in the face of the administration's declared policies." This would cause a panic in South America, he warned, and coming on the heels of Eisenhower's recent and reluctant decision to raise the tariff against Swiss watches, it would seem to indicate to foreign nations that the administration was leaning toward a protectionist trend in trade policy. "It is next to impossible to conduct foreign policy on the basis of declared principles when so many actions point to an entire contradiction of that policy," Dulles complained with some anger.

The increase in the tariff on Swiss watches had been imposed by Eisenhower ostensibly to give needed protection to the American watch industry but it was actually a political compromise forced upon the President to avoid driving all of the protectionists in Congress into the trenches to fight his entire trade program. Dulles had seen the necessity for the decision and recognized that in the give and take of legislative maneuvering such concessions had to be made. But he still regarded the trade restriction against Swiss watches as a serious blow to the credibility of our trade policy intentions throughout the free world. The watch decision invoked the "escape clause" provision that had been used in trade agreement treaties since 1943 and finally written into law by Congress in 1951 in a deal by the Democrats to win conservative support for their reciprocal trade bill. In effect, it allowed separate tariff action to be taken against specific items, the imports of which were found by the President to be causing serious injury to domestic production. There had been a similar attempt to put a higher duty on imported brier pipes but Eisenhower had rejected it. In fact, out of forty-five escape clause cases that had been heard by the Tariff Commission, only thirteen had been referred to the President and of these there were five cases where the tariff had been raised and five where the plea was rejected. The other three cases were deferred. One day at a Cabinet meeting a case on British bicycles was being discussed. Robert Cutler protested, quite out of order, "The British make a damn sight better bicycle than we do. Leave them alone." Eisenhower said to Cutler, "You already have your British bicycle, so you shouldn't be worrying about the tariff."

Hauge was the White House staff officer who handled the cases sent to the President for a decision. He described in detail at one Cabinet meeting in 1954 the policy that was followed by Eisenhower, which he called "a doctrine of clear showing of necessity." The President would be flooded by escape clause applications from domestic manufacturers if he relaxed his standards, Hauge said, and if he went to the other extreme Congress might act adversely on trade legislation. Humphrey pointed out in the discussion that 1954 was really the first year of a competitive world economy, citing as an example the increased importation of Belgian steel. Dulles quickly reminded Humphrey that damage had been done to American exports because of the restriction that the government had placed on foreign imports.

At the same meeting Dulles discussed at length one of his favorite topics, the urgent need for stimulating the economy of Japan, a country that direly needed freedom to trade not only with the United States but with the Communist countries, particularly Red China. Eisenhower felt that such Japanese commerce behind the Iron Curtain would hurt Russia rather than help the Soviets because it would turn Peiping away from Moscow and create a friction between the Communist countries. Dulles pointed out that Japan was the only highly industrialized nation in the Far East and it could not find enough markets to support itself in the United States and other Western countries. This was again reminiscent of Stalin's prediction that the capitalistic system in the world would begin to fall to pieces when the products of Germany and Japan failed to find Western markets. In the world's balance of power, Dulles said, the economic security of Japan was vital to the military security of the United States.

The criticism from Dulles that the administration was moving one way in announced foreign trade policy and the opposite way in practice received such wide circulation in Washington that the President had to reaffirm his position at a press conference. "I have heard people say that I have backed away, or abandoned, the plan that was developed through the Randall Commission, which I sent to Congress with a strong endorsing message," he said. "Nothing can be further from the truth." To get better results, he brought the highly respected Joe Dodge, his first budget director, back into the government service as his special assistant to co-ordinate foreign economic policy.

At the end of the year, there were some clashes at the leadership meetings again between Randall and Knowland when Randall announced the administration's determination to keep on pushing for a liberal program. There was prolonged controversy about the Buy American differential when it was presented to Congress again in 1955. At one meeting on that issue which lasted all day, I was handed the assignment of explaining the administration's position. The President wanted as a final draft an order that would give the head of the federal agency making the purchase an option on two ways of determining the differential; either 6 per cent of the price including duty and costs incurred in the United States after arrival or 10 per cent of the price, not including duty and costs. Knowland wanted to know where the pressure for such a proposal had come from. He said that he was under pressure from his constituents to make a change in precisely the opposite direction. All that he heard, he said, was complaints about unfair foreign competition in doing business with the federal government. American manufacturers, Knowland reported, were always reminding him of the taxes, social security fees and labor costs that a manufacturer in a foreign country did not have to pay.

One foreign trade problem that has always defied a workable and acceptable solution is the disposal of surplus agricultural commodities in the world market. Whenever the subject came up, Dulles had a nervous tremor. We could find no domestic use for the billions of dollars' worth of farm commodities in government warehouses and storage bins, but to dump them on foreign markets would have raised havoc with some of the best friends we had in the world. No solution has yet been found for this surplus puzzle, but in 1954 the administration at least tried a new and bold approach. It was clear that an able administrator was needed whose sole duty would be to search for every possible avenue that might lead to getting rid of these huge inventories that hung over the domestic market and added infinitely to the complicated farm problem all over the nation. Benson and the Commodity Credit Corporation officials were burdened with too many domestic concerns to give much attention to the possibilities of foreign disposal. After discussions with the President, Dulles and Benson, I succeeded in bringing in Clarence Francis as a special consultant on surplus commodity disposal. Francis wasted no time in putting together an interagency committee and it proceeded to get something done. One of the results was the Agricultural Trade and Development Act, better known as PL 480, which was designed to expand foreign markets for our agricultural goods. Its principal feature was an authorization for selling surplus commodities abroad in exchange for local currencies, which, not being convertible, had to be spent within the country itself.

PL 480 naturally caused some trouble for Dulles. Canada and Australia and other foreign countries that exported agricultural products protested what appeared to be a threat to their markets. These countries discreetly let it be known that they were in no position to compete with the United States giveaway programs, and we had to be very careful that their markets were not disrupted, as the President had promised.

But a year later, when Francis took stock, he found that he had programmed the disposal of $500 million worth of surplus commodities. In 1955, it was over $100 million in actual disposals and in 1956 $350 million. In the next four years $1.5 billion worth of goods went overseas. Within two years Francis and his co-operators pushed 330 million pounds of surplus butter onto the market and an inventory of 570 million pounds of dried milk almost completely disappeared. But Francis could not keep up with the ingenuity of the American farmer. Grain inventories continued to grow. Wheat skyrocketed to nearly a billion bushels; corn pushed on up over a billion bushels; barley and grain sorghums slid up, and so it went. And there was always Dulles, keeping careful watch over any trespass on the traditional markets of our friends. Francis found it hard going.

In the White House, we searched continually for alternate plans. It seemed grievously wrong for such great quantities of food grains to be deteriorating in government warehouses when there was so much hunger elsewhere in the world. It always seemed to me that a "no-country" committee under United Nations auspices could render a great service in distributing food surpluses in areas of the world where they were urgently needed. Crops that could not be sold could be given away without a tag of identification to reveal the donor, thus eliminating suspicion that the distribution was being made for political propaganda or other questionable motives. Dulles said it wouldn't work. An anonymous giveaway of American goods would not set well with Congress, he felt, and the loss of American control over the distribution might raise the question of whether we were giving food to enemy countries. However, I was not convinced by Dulles' argument and I still think such a plan should be tried under appropriate safeguards.

The President favored bartering food for such scarce minerals as manganese. On January 15, 1954, Secretary of Commerce Weeks in his capacity as chairman of the consultive committee that considered matters of trade with Communist countries brought before the Cabinet a request for a license to export surplus butter to Russia. William Rand, who was filling in at the meeting for Stassen, suggested that the butter could be traded for manganese or some other strategic material and that idea appealed to Eisenhower. He reverted to it often in later meetings. But nothing much came of the idea. The Russian bid for our butter also led nowhere. Jim Hagerty pointed out that American housewives would hardly approve of the idea of butter being sold to Russia at prices less than families had to pay for it in the United States. In the end the proposal was defeated because of the effect that it would have in such countries as the Netherlands, where exported butter was a vital source of income. An effort by Francis to market twenty million pounds of surplus butter overseas on a bid basis was rejected for the same reason. Francis, by this time a little frustrated, asked how his committee could get anywhere except through such transactions as this. "The family of nations," Eisenhower replied, should not have to suffer for the mistakes of the United States government in allowing the accumulation of food surpluses.

The most delicate area of our whole foreign economic operation was the one that covered East-West trade. We maintained an absolute embargo on all trade with the Chinese Communists and a "selective" one against the Soviet Union. This was not the policy followed by our allies. The United States tried to use the withholding of Mutual Security and other funds as a weapon to restrict trade behind the Iron Curtain by the NATO governments and Japan. Eisenhower and Dulles were under constant pressure from Britain and other allies who wanted to resume their traditional trade in the Far East and Eastern Europe. After the Korean War, restrictions against Russia were substantially reduced but those against China were still held tightly. There were reports in Washington in 1955 that the administration had given Britain the green light on trade with Red China and this stirred up the conservatives in Congress. The McClellan committee started to look into foreign trade policies. Eisenhower mentioned at the time that a publicized investigation of trade between the NATO governments and Russia and China could lead to serious problems for our allies. If the desperate economic straits of some of the Western countries became known, the Soviets could take advantage of the situation by either refusing to trade or by exacting more rigorous terms.

Senator Saltonstall remarked to Eisenhower at one leadership meeting that the proposed Senate investigation was being urged by people who held three points of view: those who were against Communism, those who opposed helping foreign allies with their problems and those who saw in such an investigation an opportunity for making political capital. "Why did you bother mentioning the first two?" Eisenhower asked. Eventually the British went ahead on their own in trading with China, which did not help the President in his battles with the conservatives in Congress over Mutual Security funds.

In January, 1955, the President renewed his plea for his foreign trade program, which was essentially the same as the one he presented in 1954. He also asked for the United States to become a member of the Organization for Trade Co-operation, better known as OTC, explaining to Congress that failure to assume membership in this operating organization would be taken throughout the free world as a lack of interest on our part in the expansion of world trade. In turn, the President argued, this could lead to foreign restrictions against exports from the United States, strike a severe blow against our military alliances abroad and turn some neutral countries toward the Communists. But in spite of the strong case that the President made for joining OTC, Congress did nothing about it and the year closed with no progress except an extension of the Trade Agreements Act.

Eisenhower continued his battle for OTC membership all through 1956 and into 1957. We then made an earnest effort to gain public support for the President's foreign trade program, which would replace the Trade Agreements Act, due to expire on June 30, 1958. Harold Boeschenstein, a member of the Department of Commerce's Business Advisory Council and a man with a fine understanding of the need for more liberal trade policies, was asked by the President to campaign for his program among the leaders of the business and industrial community throughout the country. At the same time Sinclair Weeks, who had become a devoted champion of the crusade, worked for the cause within the government. Over the years the biggest obstacle to an enlightened trade policy had been the disenchantment of the nation's businessmen with the State Department's attempt to lower the tariffs. Eisenhower and Dulles hoped that the identification of such well-known business figures as Boeschenstein and Weeks with their foreign trade proposal would do much to counteract popular resistance, and it did. The President also made a special effort to bring his trade problem closer to the business community, and, on November 25, 1957, established the Trade Policy Committee, a Cabinet-level group, with Weeks as its chairman. This move was designed to bring the views of business people closer to trade agreement decisions.

The efforts of Boeschenstein and his associates, notably Henry Kearns, the Assistant Secretary of Commerce for international affairs, came to a grand climax in a Washington Conference on International Trade Policy which was staged with impressive fanfare in the capital late in March, 1958. The conference ended with a dinner where Eisenhower was the speaker, stating once more in the strongest terms the vital importance of world trade.

"We cannot find safety in economic isolation at a time when the world is shrinking," the President declared that night. "For us to cower behind new trade walls of our own building would be to abandon a great destiny to those less blind to events and tides now surging in the affairs of men."

Congress listened and granted four more years of reciprocal trade agreements. It was not all that Eisenhower wanted but it was something that gave him at least a measure of satisfaction. When he signed the bill on August 20, 1958, he gave the legislators a moderate pat on the back. The free nations of the world could at least be assured of some continuity in the trade policy of the United States, he said with a sigh of relief.

But as Eisenhower often expressed it, you could never say never in setting down a policy of government; there always seemed to come a time when a rule that you believed in with faith and complete trust had to be broken. On March 10, 1959, the President had to go against the principles that he had fought for in his foreign trade policy and impose quota restrictions on foreign crude oil and its derivatives being imported into certain parts of the United States.

To disturb the best-laid plan, there always seemed to be the unpredictable human factor. In this case it was the men who headed two large oil-importing companies that refused to join in voluntary restraints and to heed the warnings of the government of what would happen if they failed to do so. Oil was coming into the United States from foreign fields at such a rate that the American oil-producing centers were being forced into desperate straits. In February, 1958, the President said at one meeting in the White House that oil production in Texas was down to nine days a month. Incentive for exploration was gone. A year later, the situation had gotten so much worse that the President could put off his difficult line of action no longer. The imposing of import quotas on oil was primarily an economic decision brought on by an economic emergency, but the action of the President was based upon security considerations, in accordance with the law. Congress had specifically delegated to the President the power to impose restrictions on the imports of oil if he found they threatened the national security. When the President asked Leo Hoegh, the Director of Civil and Defense Mobilization, to make a finding whether the situation did actually threaten the security of the country, the President's action quickly followed Hoegh's affirmative answer.

Although Eisenhower did not reach all his foreign trade goals, he followed a consistent policy of trade expansion, fought off the protectionists and worked hard to meet the competition of the Communist economic offensive. He and Dulles saw the change in the nature of the world struggle, from the emphasis on the arms race and the open threat of war, to the stealthy economic offensives of the cold war. Eisenhower called the economic threat the more dangerous, but many of the weapons he wanted to use against it the Congress would not give him. The difficulties he had in getting approval of his trade policies took away any glimmering hope he might have had to embark on any new and bold foreign economic policy to prove to the world, as C. D. Jackson expressed it, "the true magic of our system and its potency in new and imaginative terms."

Most people in the United States still do not understand the significance of what Eisenhower was trying to do in pushing back the barriers of world trade. A businessman in the Midwest who feels the competition of a Japanese electronics company naturally does not relate that problem to the protection of freedom in the Pacific and the defense of our own shores. The limited support that Eisenhower's foreign economic policy received from Congress and the American people raises grave questions, the same questions that were asked when the angry crowds tried to assault the Nixons in Caracas: Are we what we would like to appear to be in other parts of the world? We cannot continue to convince the hungry and the impoverished of our good intentions when we maintain the old barriers and while the Congress shows increasing reluctance to commit the Government to anything more than stop-gap economic assistance. We cannot have it both ways. We cannot follow the old protectionist paths and expect to win economically healthy friends to our side of the great decision. In building for our own future security, it is these questions that will have to be faced with more realism than we have given them so far.

19   The Arms Race

Certainly a most remarkable service for a famous general who had spent forty years in the Army was Eisenhower's conscientious and relentless effort during the cold war with Russia to keep America from draining its economy by plunging into a frantic build-up of military strength. It could have been his greatest service. In his first State of the Union message in 1953, Eisenhower said, "Our problem is to achieve adequate military strength within the limits of an endurable strain on our economy. To amass military power without regard to our economic capacity would be to defend ourselves against one kind of disaster by inviting another." And in his farewell address in 1961 he warned against an immense military establishment that would lead to the domination of the government by "a permanent armament industry of vast proportions."

If the military leaders expected to enjoy unlimited spending privileges with a free hand to build a defense establishment based on their own conceptions because they had a West Point graduate in the White House, they soon found themselves doomed to disappointment. When the five-star general resigned his commission and as President became the civilian Commander in Chief of the armed services he turned out to be much less sympathetic to the grandiose schemes and ambitious plans of the Pentagon than his predecessors had been. In fact, Eisenhower's personal experience as a professional soldier and as the wartime commander of the greatest expeditionary force that the world has ever seen made him, if anything, harder to deal with when fear-inspired pressures came from Congress to spend another billion for a jet bomber program or a new missile project. He always refused to be stampeded. He had his own definite ideas about what was needed for national defense and during his long career he had heard too many fearsome warnings from military experts to be easily moved by them. "If I had listened to all of the advice I got during those years, advice that reflected deeply felt but, let us say, narrow fears, there would never have been a plan for crossing the Channel," Eisenhower once said. "Indeed, I don't think we would have crossed the Atlantic Ocean."

Much to the impatience of the uniformed generals and admirals in the Pentagon and the military-minded members of Congress, Eisenhower insisted upon looking at every big defense spending proposal in the light of what effect it would have on the economic strength of the country. He repeated over and over again, as he did in his budget message in 1954, his deep conviction that economic strength cannot be sacrificed for military strength. To keep military power within reasonable bounds, he was dedicated to the belief that the control of the Defense Department should be held in fact as well as in theory by civilians rather than by the Joint Chiefs of Staff. He also made a determined effort as President to bring a real unity rather than a nominal one into the organization of the Defense Department simply because he was convinced that a war in the nuclear age could not be won with separate campaigns on land, on the sea and in the air but only with the closest co-ordination and unity of effort. When he attempted to put this belief to work by changing the organizational structure of the Pentagon he was quickly in trouble with the three services, the Army, the Navy and the Air Force, all of which wanted to preserve their traditional identity and autonomy. When Eisenhower went into office in 1953, all of the civilians on his staff expected him to have little trouble in carrying out his defense policies. We felt the American people had voted for him with a thorough knowledge of his military background and in the belief that they could place complete reliance on his judgment about the needs of national security during the increasing tension of the cold war. In this area of government, at least, it seemed as though there could be little opposition to his decisions. But in his attempt to bring unification to the armed forces and to keep military spending within safe limits, Eisenhower had to fight as hard as he did for Mutual Security, freer foreign trade and disarmament. He clashed frequently with such military leaders as the late General Hoyt Vandenberg, General Matthew Ridgway and General James Gavin and with those champions in Congress of bigger and bigger defense budgets, Senators Stuart Symington, Henry Jackson and Lyndon Johnson.

When Eisenhower began a comprehensive review of our whole defense strategy in 1953 and ordered some fundamental changes centered around the use of nuclear weapons as the principal deterrent rather than conventional forces, his troubles with the separate services began. As this plan commenced to emerge, it was dubbed "The New Look." When he took office Eisenhower was irritated to find that the Defense Department under the Truman administration had been trying to prepare the armed forces for a confusing and heavily expensive variety of strategy plans to meet various kinds of wars. There was no clear-cut policy about whether or not nuclear weapons would be used in an outbreak of hostilities with Russia, for example. This meant that budget allowances were still being made for enough Army ground troops and Naval sea forces to fight a nonnuclear world war, the theory being that atomic weapons might be excluded in such a general conflict unless the Soviets began the use of them first. At the same time, the Air Force was preparing for a nuclear war. There were also plans for short wars, for police actions like the Korean War, for peripheral wars, for infantry war, for air wars and for completely destructive atomic attacks. As the nonmilitary minded but sensible George Humphrey remarked after his first look at the Defense budget, the military planners seemed to be following six plans of strategy simultaneously, two for each branch of the services.

Eisenhower cleared away some of this underbrush by ordering the Pentagon to assume that if we got into war it would be fought with nuclear weapons. This decision instantly diminished the importance of ground troops, to the chagrin of the Army, and of large aircraft carriers, to the discomfort of the Navy, and it gave a priority in budgetary funds to the Air Force, to the intense anguish of both the Army and the Navy. The basic defense strategy, advocated by Dulles, was the build-up of a strong deterrent force of atomic and thermonuclear striking power, which in those days before the development of long-range missiles could be delivered only by bombers under the Strategic Air Command. But this decision did not necessarily mean that the President intended to go hog-wild in spending money on the

Air Force either. During his first few months in the White House, he made a cut of five billion dollars in the Air Force budget, provoking an outburst from General Vandenberg and charges in Congress that the administration was more interested in budget balancing than in defending the nation. The cut was made by the President, as he explained at the time to the Republican Congressional leaders, because the Air Force was ordering and obtaining new planes for its expanding wings before it had the personnel to fly them or the bases to land them and that meant that it was asking for appropriations far ahead of its requirements.

The New Look, with its planning predicated on nuclear retaliation, logically led to an order from Eisenhower to reduce the number of Army ground troops. He reasoned that after a large atomic attack any massive deployment of ground forces would be impossible; decisive damage would already be done by one side or the other before troops could be moved into a vital area. "If you want to be coldly logical about it," he said at one meeting in the White House when the proposed reductions in force levels were being discussed, "the money being spent for ground forces could be used to better advantage on new highways to facilitate the evacuation of large cities in case of an enemy attack." The global strategy worked out by Admiral Radford, the Chairman of the Joint Chiefs of Staff, and Dulles also called for the increasing use of indigenous troops in overseas areas such as Asia and the Middle East and it discouraged widespread deployment of American forces abroad.

The President outlined these views in a letter to Secretary of Defense Wilson on January 5, 1955, in which he asked for a reduction in the armed forces during the following year, bringing the level down from 3.2 million to around 2.85 million. This proposal was strongly opposed by General Matthew Ridgway, then the Army Chief of Staff, and it started a rumbling in Congress, where it was already being charged that we were rapidly losing our superiority over Russia, if indeed we were not already beginning to fall behind. Ridgway was called to testify before a Congressional committee and he warned that the cuts in the forces would "jeopardize" national security. A few months later Ridgway retired and wrote his memoirs, charging that Eisenhower's restrictions on military spending were based not so much on concern for the economy of the country as on "political considerations." That hurt Eisenhower, especially since he felt that his efforts to keep military spending in check was causing him far more political trouble in Congress than it was winning him or the Republican party any new popularity. The controversy between Eisenhower and Ridgway had personal overtones to it. Ridgway had been the President's successor in the command of NATO forces and Eisenhower's comments about Ridgway's service in that assignment had been less than glowing. Ridgway also claimed that Wilson had ordered "a directed verdict" by the Joint Chiefs of Staff on the troop reduction proposal and had ruled against any disagreement with the President's stand.

In a leadership meeting the following June, Senator Saltonstall reported that legislation calling for an increase in the armed forces seemed to be making some headway in Congress and suggested to the President that it might be more discreet to give in to the measure rather than to take a licking. Eisenhower was indignant. "I am getting a little tired of having to defend myself against the charge of being out to wreck the Army," he said.

"You mean you want to put up a fight?" Saltonstall asked him.

"Indeed I do," the President said. "There are much better uses for that money. What's the need of increasing the Army by 150,000 men at the cost of $450 million in this age of modern warfare? Where would they be stationed? What we need is a good reserve program."

The reserve program that he was referring to had been introduced in Congress a few months earlier. Eisenhower thoroughly believed in the principle of universal military training as the only way that every able-bodied man in the United States could learn the means of self-survival for himself. But he knew that Congress would not approve it, so he had sent Congress a more moderate program. In May, Leslie Arends, the Republican whip in the House, told Eisenhower that many Congressmen were against the proposal because the Pentagon had not tried to make the existing reserve program work. What they wanted, Arends reported, was a universal military training program!

"I'll tell you one thing," the President said to Arends. "If they don't make a real effort to make this program succeed, there will be the damnedest fight at this end of Pennsylvania Avenue that you ever saw."

Eventually, the President stopped the attempt to increase the size of the armed forces and won his reserve program battle. But in 1956 after Trevor Gardner resigned as the Assistant Secretary of the Air Force in charge of research and development in a battle with Wilson over missile projects, the whole question of whether the United States was lagging behind Russia in armaments broke out again in Congress. This time such potent Air Force leaders as Nathan Twining and Curtis LeMay testified that the Americans were trailing the Soviets in plane production.

Gardner had come into the Air Force early in the administration as an assistant to Secretary Harold Talbott and had been responsible for the reactivation of long-range missile research in 1953 by a committee of scientists under Dr. John von Neumann, later a member of the Atomic Energy Commission and a mathematician who had played an important role in the development of thermonuclear energy. It was said at the time that the dispute between Gardner and Wilson was concerned with budget funds for missile research, but Gardner later told a House appropriations subcommittee that he had no complaint about money. Actually the argument was concerned with crash programs for missile development; the administration was not moving as fast as Gardner felt it should go. Everybody who left the Defense Department after a battle with Wilson seemed to write a magazine article about the fight later. In his article, which was published in *Look,* Gardner said that "short-sighted limitations" had held back missile programs. He also claimed that the Soviets were surpassing our Air Force in quality as well as in quantity.

This was a presidential election year, of course, and the Democrats did not hesitate to capitalize on Gardner's charges. A Senate armed services subcommittee, whose chairman was Senator Symington, began an inquiry into United States military air strength as it compared with that of the Soviets. Symington and Senator Henry Jackson kept up a running barrage of accusations that we were seriously behind the Russians in missiles. Coming from the Democrats, such talk rankled all of us at the White House because it was well known that during an economy wave in 1948 the Truman administration had dropped all missile research work completely.

Reuben Robertson, then the Deputy Secretary of Defense, mentioned this to Eisenhower one day during a discussion of Symington's charges. The President said that he remembered that low ebb in the defense effort well because at that time, while he was serving as President of Columbia University, he had been asked to attend Defense Department meetings as a consultant. When he learned that the defense program was going to be drastically cut he asked to be relieved of his consultant's duties because he did not want to be identified with any such reductions. As I later mentioned in a 1958 speech that got me into hot water with the Democrats, it was not until 1952, just before Truman went out of office, that his administration spent as much as one million dollars a year on missile research and development. In 1956, when Eisenhower was under fire from Symington, we were spending a billion dollars a year on missiles and a large amount of money on rockets. Robertson and Donald Quarles, the Air Force Secretary, reminded Eisenhower at that time that a total of 25,000 people, 10,000 of them scientists, were working then on the missile program at the rate of 50,000 overtime hours a week. And yet, as a reporter mentioned to the President in a press conference that April, the Democrats were saying that the administration was not making a maximum effort.

Eisenhower admitted frankly that we were behind in certain fields of missile development. "There are only so many scientists and there are only so many facilities," he said. "You get to the point where mere expenditure of money in a field like this does no good. We are about at our limit."

Eisenhower pointed out that any effective missile war must be completely destructive, and added that we had the means of delivering these bombs in such a way that they could not be effectively intercepted. As to the missile program, the President insisted that we were then doing "everything that science and brains and resources can do to keep our position in a proper posture."

Eisenhower's troubles with the military leaders and their spokesmen in Congress reached their summit in April, 1958, when he made a determined attempt to bring some real unification to the Defense Department. Wilson was lucky enough to escape that battle, having retired by then as Secretary to be replaced by Neil H. McElroy, the president of the Procter and Gamble Company. In his stormy term as Secretary of Defense, Wilson had leaned upon Eisenhower with his intimate knowledge of the defense establishment and its personalities a little more than the President wanted anybody in his Cabinet to lean upon him. Wilson wanted an hour a week alone with Eisenhower to discuss routine problems, many of which the President thought Wilson should solve by himself. Wilson's reliance upon Eisenhower was entirely natural but resulted in the President getting somewhat impatient with having to listen to departmental difficulties that he thought had not been sufficiently shaken down. Eisenhower wanted policies sharpened up with enough study and discussion so that he did not have to go through the preliminaries himself. Wilson complained later that he did not see the President often enough to obtain necessary guidance but the President did not have any such concern.

Eisenhower was always well aware of the criticism that was directed at him for not being fully informed and for avoiding many of the controversies of his administration. But he brushed off such comments impatiently, ascribing them to a lack of understanding of the delegation of authority that he regarded as the essential of his staff system. As he once told me, he felt that he had refined the staff system and had made it work and he believed that the results he had gotten from it over the years proved its worth beyond that of any pattern of executive operation that he knew.

Unification had gone through its baptismal stage at the Pentagon in 1947, but with all the bloodshed the outcome had been indecisive. At that first skirmish, the results amounted to little more than the establishment of a new Cabinet post called the Secretary of Defense, an office clothed with few powers. Two years later some more progress was made; the Secretaries of the Army, the Navy and the Air Force lost a little of their autonomy and their right to sit at the Cabinet and National Security Council meetings unless they were invited by the President or designated by the Secretary of Defense. But the three branches of the armed services remained competitive and independent.

In 1953, when Eisenhower became President, he asked Congress for and, after considerable debate, received more power and staff facilities for the Secretary of Defense. At the same time new additional assistant secretaries were added, and the responsibility for the management of the staff of the Joint Chiefs was given to the Chairman, Admiral Arthur Radford. In the first overhauling in 1947, Radford, like most Navy officers, had been opposed to unification. But in the long discussions about military strategy aboard the U.S.S. *Helena* in the Pacific late in 1952, during Eisenhower's trip to Korea, Radford admitted to the President-elect that he had been wrong in 1947 in his disapproval of a unified command; he had come to share Eisenhower's belief that nuclear weapons and the need for close co-ordination of land, sea and air forces in a nuclear war called for a removal of the old barriers between the services.

It soon became apparent that the progress that Eisenhower had made toward unification in 1953 did not go far enough. When nuclear weapons began to be used by ground force artillery and Navy submarines as well as by Air Force jet bombers, the traditional rivalries became more intense and indefensible. Then each service developed its own missile program, competing between themselves for research funds and scientific talent. Eisenhower decided that the real key to the unification problem was in the Defense Department's budget. Congress approved and appropriated money that was designated specifically for the use of each of the services. The Army, the Navy and the Air Force could deal separately with the House and Senate committees in trying to outdo each other in seeking funds for competing and duplicating programs including their individual pet projects, with a complete disregard for the Defense Department's central policy goals. In 1955, after General Twining and General LeMay testified before the Symington subcommittee that the Soviet Union was surpassing the United States in air power, Congress gave the Air Force an additional $900 million for B-52 jet bombers that it did not need. Wilson, supported by the President, refused to spend the money but Symington and other members of Congress tried to force the Secretary of Defense to use it. There was no better example for the reason for the budgetary approach to unification than this skirmish over Air Force appropriations. In order to be sure the three services did not go to Congress again with an expenditure program beyond the limitations he wanted observed, Eisenhower summoned Wilson and a few other civilian defense chiefs only to be told that the services had already been setting up their own goals. "Put every single person on the spot to justify every single nickel," he told Wilson. "When they talk about their 'requirements,' let Wilson approve the use of the word. I have listened to the term all my life. Next year the demagogues will all be gone and everybody will be looking to save money. You people never seem to learn whom you are supposed to be protecting. Not the generals," he exploded, "but the American people." Looking Wilson straight in the eye, he said, "You have got to be willing to be the most unpopular man in the government."

Eisenhower wanted to change the method of providing funds for the armed forces so that the Secretary of Defense would request and receive all of the department's money with the authority to use it within the services as he saw fit. This would stop the Army, the Navy and the Air Force, not to mention the Marines, from going over the Secretary of Defense's head to grind their own axes in Congress and it would eliminate much of the rivalry between them. Eisenhower also wanted to broaden and deepen the authority of the Secretary of Defense in many other ways, especially by removing the Secretaries and the Chiefs of the three services from the chain of operational command and limiting their function to administrative duties. The President also favored putting all research and development projects under the Secretary of Defense. In other words, Eisenhower was anxious to invest as much authority as possible in the civilian head of the armed forces, the Presidential appointee who was a member of the Cabinet and the National Security Council, in order to provide a check against too much power in military hands. This centralized authority would provide a faster and more efficient system of unified operations.

In order to provide the Secretary of Defense with the closest access to top military knowledge and experience, Eisenhower's reorganization plan called for the Joint Chiefs to act only under the authority of the Secretary of Defense, giving him the professional assistance needed for the strategic planning and operational direction of the unified commands. Eisenhower privately favored the idea of organizing a group of the most skilled and talented officers from all of the service branches, regardless of seniority and rank, to serve as an advisory council that would work with the Secretary and the Chairman of the Joint Chiefs on all the problems and decisions of the armed forces. But the President did not push the idea for such an advisory group too hard because he knew that it would be seized upon in Congress as a plot to turn the Defense Department over to a general staff of the Prussian type of military elite. Such a charge had been made against Eisenhower when he first proposed a reorganization of the Pentagon in 1953, and it was to come up again. Actually, of course, the domination of defense policy by a small group of military men was just the thing that Eisenhower was trying to avoid; his only thought in organizing such an advisory council was to comb the services for the best possible talent and make its advice available at the top of the chain of unified command where it could do the most good.

Eisenhower worked hard on the reorganization plan himself after the groundwork was planned by Charles A. Coolidge, who acted as a special adviser to the Secretary of Defense on the project. There were also recommendations from a task force of the second Hoover Commission, headed by Charles R. Hook, and from an informal advisory committee assembled by Secretary McElroy, consisting of Radford, Robert Lovett, Nelson Rockefeller, William Foster, and Generals Omar N. Bradley, Alfred Gruenther and Nathan Twining. Eisenhower mentioned the plan first in his 1958 State of the Union Message and then sent it to Congress on April 3 with a strong call for action that pulled no punches. Modern warfare has outmoded the traditional organization of our military services, he said, and obsolete concepts of divided and opposing compartments of command within the competitive branches of the military forces are denying the nation an effective defense. The President referred in his message to service rivalries that "find expression in Congressional and press activities which become particularly conspicuous in struggles over new weapons, funds and publicity. It is just such rivalries, I am convinced, that America wants stopped."

The plan for unification provided for defense appropriations to be made only to the Secretary of Defense, with full and flexible authority for him to administer the funds. It changed the offices of the three Secretaries of the armed services into administrative agencies, removing the Secretaries and their Chiefs of Staff from the operational chain of command and giving commanding officers in the theaters of operations full unified command over land, sea and air forces within their areas. The plan also enlarged the authority of the Secretary of Defense and called for the establishment of a Director of Defense Research and Engineering to supervise all military and naval research functions. "There will be plenty of political heat on this question," Eisenhower said to us as he gave the proposal a last look before sending it to the Hill. And he was quite right.

As all of us expected, the biggest bone of contention was Eisenhower's proposal to take away from Congress the prerogative of distributing budgeted funds among each of the three branches of the armed services. At a meeting of the President with the Republican leaders two days before the reorganization plan was submitted, Knowland reminded Eisenhower that Congress would not give up this privilege lightly. The President reminded Knowland in turn that Congress should not overlook the present cost of duplications among the services.

In the background, there were many past and present controversies and old scars of disagreement that were not directly related to the unification plan but they nevertheless added uneasiness and apprehension about the Eisenhower proposals. The origin of these doubts ranged from vague, "inside dope" stories that Russian military superiority was being hidden from the President to wild rumors about the contents of the hushed-up Gaither Report; from incidents surrounding the resignation of Lieutenant General James M. Gavin to the explosive Girard case.

General Gavin, a wartime paratroop commander and one of the most publicized figures in the military service, announced that he was resigning his position as head of the Army's research and development projects in January at the same time that the President announced his plan to reorganize the Defense Department. Gavin was asked to testify before Lyndon Johnson's Defense Preparedness Subcommittee. He said that he was leaving the service because he had been told that his chances of promotion had been jeopardized by his disagreement with Eisenhower's military policies. Coming from such a respected officer as Gavin, these comments generated considerable heat in Congress.

The disagreement in policy between Eisenhower and Radford on one hand and Gavin and Ridgway's successor as Army Chief of Staff, Maxwell D. Taylor, on the other was mainly concerned with the question of whether the Army should be developing strong ground force units for combat in limited warfare, such as was fought in Korea. Gavin and Taylor held that there was a likely possibility of future conflicts needing highly mobile task force strength with ground troops equipped with tactical nuclear weapons of relatively small yield. This added up to expensive equipment—tanks, trucks, weapons carriers, helicopters—and a larger and more costly level of standing forces. George Humphrey was correctly reported at that time to be standing guard over the public purse and opposing many of these expensive programs on the ground that their proponents failed to make a convincing case for them. Eisenhower invited Humphrey to the meetings of the National Security Council to express his opinion as freely as though he were a member. In coming to many crucial decisions the President wanted the principal points of view out on the table whether they agreed with his position or not. The decisions about manpower levels and strategic planning were Eisenhower's and not Humphrey's. It was the President who made the decision against maintaining elaborate plans for fighting limited wars with ground troops because he did not believe any sizable war in the future would be fought without the use of massive nuclear weapons on both sides. Therefore, he argued, high troop levels were an unnecessary expense.

Gavin also favored bigger expenditures on the space program. After he retired from the service, he wrote magazine articles and a book on his complaints against the New Look military policy, as did General Taylor. Eisenhower did not conceal the irritation that Gavin's action caused him. He told Senator Saltonstall at a leadership meeting that he did not know of Gavin's plan for retirement until he read it in the newspapers. He seemed to be puzzled by the reasons for it. Gavin had told the Johnson subcommittee that the Defense Department needed, among other things, a more centralized authority and Eisenhower pointed out that this was the main aim of his reorganization plan. Besides, the President said, he understood that Gavin had a very good chance of becoming a four-star general within a year, at the age of fifty-three, which was most unusual in peacetime.

The Girard case seemed to the President and to many of us in the White House to be a much more significant and important international incident than it was regarded by the press and the public. It aroused a strong indignation among members of Congress, especially Senator Knowland, and seemed to me to stir up a resentment against the administration's military policy that did not make the path of Eisenhower's bill for unification any easier.

One of the policies of the Defense Department that Eisenhower strongly supported against considerable opposition was the so-called Status of Forces treaty, which gave foreign governments jurisdiction in cases of legal action against American service men or women for offenses committed overseas, unless the offense occurred in the line of the defendant's military duty. When Eisenhower was in command of the NATO forces in Europe in 1951, he had been instrumental in drawing up the terms of the treaty. On January 30, 1957, an American soldier in Japan, Specialist Third Class William S. Girard of Ottawa, Illinois, fired an empty shell from a mortar weapon at a group of Japanese women who were searching for brass casings on a firing range at Somagahara, seventy-five miles north of Tokyo. One of the women was killed. A commission investigating the incident decided that Girard was not on official duty at the time and he was turned over to the Japanese authorities for prosecution.

A storm broke out in Congress. In the Senate, Knowland and Bridges argued passionately for the right of the United States to hold jurisdiction over its soldiers in foreign countries and, in the House, Representative Frank Bow of Ohio introduced a resolution asking our withdrawal from all Status of Forces treaties with those nations where our troops were stationed. Eisenhower looked into the case and admitted that in Girard's particular circumstances the decision to give jurisdiction to the Japanese courts seemed to have been a mistake. Girard had not fired the fatal shot in the line of duty; he had been playfully experimenting with a makeshift weapon and a charge of gunpowder that had not been issued to him by his commanding officer. But he was on duty at the firing range that day and the incident had occurred on government property, where the Japanese woman was trespassing. Nevertheless, whether the procedure had been right or wrong, this was only one case and Eisenhower saw no reason because of one mistake to force the United States government to break its promises to other countries around the world and to withdraw from all Status of Forces treaties. There had been fourteen thousand other cases in Japan where Americans had voluntarily conceded jurisdiction to Japanese courts and all had been tried with eminent fairness. Eisenhower felt that he had no choice but to fight against the Bow Amendment.

Knowland was equally determined to fight for what he considered the basic rights of American service men stationed overseas. In an argument over the Bow Amendment and the Girard case at a meeting in the White House on July 9, the Senator pulled off his gloves and staged the most angry scene I had seen in the Cabinet Room since Senator Taft had exploded over the budget deficit back in 1953. Joe Martin, the Republican leader in the House, reported that the Democrats were pushing the Bow Amendment to embarrass the Republicans and that if it came up alone, rather than as a rider on another bill, it could probably not be beaten. The President was astonished to hear this, because the Democrats in previous years had introduced the same international treaties that the Bow Amendment aimed to break. Knowland asked Eisenhower to issue an Executive Order assuring an American trial for any American soldier accused of a crime on a military post or on military duty in a foreign country. He said that he thought this assurance had been made in 1951 when legislation permitting Status of Forces treaty arrangements had been first under consideration. Robert Dechert, attending the meeting in his capacity as the Defense Department's general counsel, explained to Knowland that such an order against waivers of jurisdiction would only cause foreign governments to clamp down on the many (97 per cent) waivers that they were now making in our favor.

That was when Knowland blew his top. Pounding his fist on the table, he shouted, "A young man drafted in peacetime, sent overseas against his will, assigned to a duty—by God, I don't think he ought to be turned over for trial! He's wearing the uniform of our country. I wouldn't want *my* son to be treated that way! We're being derelict toward them."

In a studiously quiet manner, Dechert pointed out that the Japanese authorities had agreed, before Girard was turned over to them, that if he was convicted, he would receive a very light sentence. Dechert also reminded the Senator that the Bow Amendment was broad enough to demand a breaking of any treaty that provided for a possibility of the United States waiving jurisdiction. He told Knowland that there had been no commitment made at the time that the legislation on Status of Forces arrangements was adopted, implying that the United States would not yield jurisdiction in every case where there was a question of whether the offense had been committed on a military post or during military duty. Eisenhower firmly announced that he would neither yield nor compromise on the Bow Amendment dispute.

The Republican leaders reluctantly agreed to do what they could to stall action on the amendment and the President arranged an exchange of letters with Martin to make known his strong objections. If Knowland was steamed up by the issue, it was obvious that Eisenhower was steamed up, too. At the following week's meeting with the leadership from Congress, he warned that passage of the Bow Amendment could mean that many foreign powers might refuse to allow American service men into their countries on an extraterritorial basis, exempt from their own laws. "If the Republicans in Congress desert me on this issue," he said, "I'll be more disappointed than I have been about anything that has happened to me since I've been in office."

The President was explicit in his letter to Martin:

In my judgment, the passage of any such legislation by the Congress would gravely threaten our security, alienate our friends, and give aid and comfort to those who want to destroy our way of life. No longer does anyone suggest that we can safely withdraw behind the boundaries of fortress America. Yet this could be the ultimate effect of enacting this resolution. I can think of no recent legislative proposal which would so threaten the essential security of the United States.

That settled the Bow Amendment. Knowland could have no complaint about how Girard was handled by the Japanese court. He was found guilty, sentenced to three years and immediately the sentence was suspended. It was, the Japanese said, a childish whim and it involved no malice. But the dispute that it had excited back in Washington left a few scars that were still unhealed when Eisenhower's defense reorganization bill came up before Congress a year later.

None of us on the White House staff paid much attention to the reports in Washington that the clashes of opinion between Eisenhower and the military leaders on questions of defense spending and the magnitude of the Russian threat were due to a lack of information about Soviet armed strength on the President's part. The intelligence that the President was receiving about Russian military capability could not always be precisely accurate. After all, the Russian strength was not completely visible and many of the estimates of it that we received from intelligence sources were based on leaks, defections, boasts, official news releases from the Soviet government and hearsay. If a Russian missile or rocket fizzled and collapsed on the launching pad, the failure was kept a secret. Only their impressive accomplishments were announced to the world. As Dulles liked to say, there were certain advantages in running a dictatorship. But our own failures at Cape Canaveral and our disputes at Congressional hearings about our lag in the arms race and in weapon technology and development were spread across the front pages of the newspapers for the Russians and everybody else to see.

The evaluation of all intelligence data was the responsibility of the National Security Council, to which was reported all strategically important information coming into the United States. The discussions of policy based on these evaluations always brought out the differing points of view, which the President listened to faithfully, taking charge of the discussions himself. Eisenhower took this responsibility more seriously than almost any other duty of his office. Although accused of being poorly informed without thoroughly digesting conflicting points of view, it was impossible to refute such criticism because the deliberations of the Council had to be bound by secrecy.

These evaluations and the policies that resulted were based on no snap judgment. The preparation for each weekly meeting and the staff work was intensive and thorough, bringing out the differing points of view in addition to the consensus recommendation. Eisenhower never missed a Security Council meeting except when he was ill or absent from Washington. It would have been impossible for him to sit through so many of these detailed and exhaustive discussions and to remain poorly informed about the military capability of any other nation in the world.

In addition to the close attention he gave to the work of the National Security Council, Eisenhower ordinarily had from six to ten hours a week of private conversation about world affairs with Dulles, which was enough in itself to keep him well informed. Besides, there were daily conversations about highly confidential matters with heads of state, foreign diplomats and government officials, and daily intelligence briefings every morning in his office as soon as he arrived to begin his work. The insight and the penetration that he showed in his questions and comments at the National Security Council and Cabinet meetings convinced all of us who worked with him that he always had a knowledge of current world happenings as accurate and up to date as anybody with his multitudinous duties could acquire. Eisenhower's critics often overlooked the fact that the President already had the education of a lifetime in world problems that he had observed firsthand in every country where he had been stationed as an officer in the Army. These had been more than military experiences; many of them had called for political wisdom and great diplomatic skill, and above all an understanding of the people with whom he had to deal.

And yet the armchair strategists continued to harp in newspaper articles that the President did not really know what was going on, especially in Russia. I remember one day Eisenhower receiving a letter from a friend telling him that Joseph and Stewart Alsop had made what seemed to him a sensible estimate of how Russia's military strength surpassed that of the United States. The President saw red. He called in his secretary, Mrs. Whitman, and grimly dictated an answer. After a lifetime of study in military matters, he told his friend, he now realized that in this atomic age a war could no longer be won because it would bring destruction to both sides. Therefore, he reasoned, comparative military strength is no longer a vital issue— economic and spiritual strength is just as important. Then he reminded his friend that he had access in the government to information from experts, technicians, consultants and various other advisers who knew more about Russia and its military strength than the Alsops did.

The speculation in Congress about the contents of the mysterious Gaither Report had its effect on the progress of Eisenhower's proposals for defense unification. In the spring of 1957, the President asked a group of able private citizens under the chairmanship of the late H. Rowan Gaither, Jr., then chairman of the board of the Ford Foundation, to make an evaluation of the state of defense readiness with the co-operation and guidance of the National Security Council. The report which the Gaither committee submitted in the following November contained several extraordinary findings and recommendations, some of which, within somewhat loose limits of accuracy, eventually found their way into the newspapers. The Democratic leadership in the Senate asked the President to make the report public, but the President decided, for several reasons, not to do so.

Eisenhower decided that publication of the Gaither study could serve no useful purpose. It contained figures of estimated American casualties from a surprise attack by the Soviets upon the United States that were hypothetical but still deeply shocking. The President reasoned that public knowledge of these speculative conclusions, based on assumptions that could be challenged, would do the nation much more harm than good. The report included a recommendation for a nationwide nuclear bomb shelter construction program. Eisenhower felt that the public and Congress were not yet ready to accept the tremendous financial sacrifice that such a gigantic building project would require.

The President's refusal to divulge any part of the Gaither Report started rumors in Washington that the administration was unwilling to face the realities of the security situation. There were also stories that the President and his associates had been shaken at last out of their "complacency." Such reports were purely figments of reportorial imagination. Because of the respected competency of the Gaither committee's membership, its reasoning and recommendations received sober consideration. But the judgments of the report were balanced against opinions and evaluations from other equally qualified people who held somewhat differing views.

President Eisenhower's Special Message on Defense Department Reorganization was somewhat overshadowed by another important special message which was sent to Congress one day earlier, April 2, 1958. The priority given to the presentation of this message was not merely a matter of chance; it was highly significant and it showed which of these two problems was carrying the greater national interest that spring. The April 2 message asked for the creation of a new National Aeronautics and Space Administration. The space age had dawned in the previous October when the Soviet Union proudly announced the successful launching of Sputnik, the first man-made earth-circling space satellite. Ever since that time the American people and Congress had been wondering what the President was going to do about it.

This question was put to Eisenhower at a press conference a few days after the Russian accomplishment stirred the world. The President's reply gave his listeners some idea of the difficulties of space exploration. He recalled that in the spring of 1955 the United States had decided to attempt the launching of a satellite sometime between June, 1957, and December, 1958, in connection with the observance of the International Geophysical Year. The purpose, "as it was told to me," the President said, was solely for scientific information and the sum requested and approved was $22 million. Then instrumentation was added to the plan and the cost went up to $66 million. " 'This seems logical,' we said, so we did it," Eisenhower added. Then the scientists found that they needed observation stations and that sent the cost to $110 million "with the notice that they might have to go up even still more."

The high costs of missile development and space rocketry had greatly hampered research in those fields until Sputnik I came along. Then Congress, with the national pride at stake, could not spend money fast enough in its eagerness to beat the Soviets to the moon. Until that time nobody in Washington had really given much consideration to the possible importance of an invasion of space as psychological propaganda or even as a scientific achievement. There were too many other critical urgencies. But when Sputnik was launched, the same Congressmen who had been cutting funds for scientific research a few years earlier came to the President begging him to make a strong statement that would restore the people's trust and confidence. Eisenhower said he preferred to play down the whole thing. I was asked what I thought about it and I made a widely quoted remark about the administration not being intent on attaining a high score in any outer-space basketball game. I was only trying to reflect the President's desire for calm poise but I had to admit on reflection that my observation seemed to be an overemphasis of the de-emphasis.

Although Eisenhower maintained an official air of serenity, he was privately as concerned as everybody else in the country by the jump ahead that the Russians had made in scientific enterprise and he began to carry on a series of earnest discussions with a group of fifteen outstanding scientists connected with the Office of Defense Mobilization's science advisory committee, then headed by Dr. I. I. Rabi. With great enthusiasm and determination the President wanted the scientists to tell him where scientific research belonged in the structure of the federal government, how the output of our colleges and universities was to be increased and how we were going to meet the competition during the next ten years. As a result of these preliminary studies, the President decided to create a new position on his own staff, Special Assistant to the President for Science and Technology, and he was fortunate enough to persuade Dr. James R. Killian, the president of the Massachusetts Institute of Technology, to take the job. He also enlarged the ODM's science advisory committee and reconstituted it as the President's Science Advisory Committee.

Killian went hard to work. Early in 1958 he was able to report to the Cabinet that a great increase in scientific co-operation had been arranged with our allies in the NATO alliance and that basic research was being stepped up through transfers of Defense Department funds to the National Science Foundation. The three services got into a healthy competition to put rockets into space, hardly in keeping with the spirit of the President's new unification plan, but at that time every effort needed to be encouraged. On the last day of January a proto-type satellite, tiny but well instrumented, was pushed into space from Cape Canaveral by an Army Jupiter-C rocket engine. This U.S. Explorer hardly held a candle to Sputnik but it relieved some of the national frustration and showed that the Americans were capable of accepting the Soviet invitation to join them in space.

The subject of a federal space organization then began to take on shape and substance. At a meeting with the Republican leaders on February 4, the President said that for the present at least the rocket projects would remain in the Defense Department. The mechanics of space rocket launching were similar to those of military long-range missiles and keeping the work in the hands of the armed services would avoid a costly duplication of effort. Dr. Killian was doubtful about this arrangement, and Vice President Nixon supported his view that our position before the world would be more acceptable if the nonmilitary aspects of space research and exploration were conducted by an agency that had no connection with the military. The President reminded them that the government was in no position to pour un-limited funds into expensive scientific projects that promised nothing of value to the nation's security. He remarked that he would rather have one good Redstone nuclear-armed missile than a rocket that could hit the moon, for we had no enemies on the moon. Eisenhower also recalled that a few years back he had "bled his eyes out" begging the legislative leaders for an atomic-power peace ship, a completely worth-while project that Congress had refused to approve.

Knowland wanted to know if a rocket capable of reaching the moon could not be hurried along for its psychological value. "If we are anywhere near it, we ought to push it," the Senator said, after protesting that the world-wide impact of Sputnik had almost nullified the value of the American Mutual Security Program. Eisenhower replied abruptly that he was not going to be pushed into an all-out effort in every one of these glamour performances without any idea of their eventual cost. Besides, he wanted to know first what government agency was going to co-ordinate and sponsor such an ambitious project as an attempted lunar probe. He, of all people, would not be a party to setting up another competition between the Army, the Navy and the Air Force.

That brought Nixon again to his earlier argument in favor of a nonmilitary space agency. He said that he felt that the Defense Department would downgrade any project that did not contribute to weapon advancement. Eisenhower repeated again that the Defense Department already had the necessary hardware and that he saw no reason to pay for duplicating it. "I don't rule out that eventually there might be a Department of Space," the President said, "but for the present I want to go on record as not being at all interested in volunteering to be the first man to land on the moon."

The President stayed firmly on his charted course and the historic message that he sent to Congress on April 2 requesting America's first space agency specified that peaceful scientific exploration of outer space would be powered by Defense Department missiles. However, the National Aviation and Space Agency would be independent and financed by funds directly appropriated to it.

"Recent developments in long-range rockets for military purposes have for the first time provided man with new machinery so powerful that it can put satellites into orbit and eventually provide the means for space exploration," the President's message began. "In fact, it is now within the means of any technologically advanced nation to embark upon practicable programs for exploring outer space."

During a preview of plans for the new agency, Senator Knowland asked Dr. Killian for reassurance that space projects might not become secondary in priority because so many of the scientists from the National Advisory Council on Aeronautics who worked on the military missiles would be involved in the agency. Killian said that he thought the main problem would be overenthusiasm for space exploration, if anything. The act setting up the agency went through Congress easily and the organization began to function under the burden of too great expectations. Dr. Killian had to stress more than once during Cabinet meetings when he was pressed eagerly for news about the infant agency that the Russians, with their achievements in rocket thrust development, were two years ahead of us in space technology. But the catching-up process began to increase its momentum and miracles began to incubate. When the spectacular photographs taken in outer space were shown in 1960, the United States could hold up its scientific chin again.

Eisenhower had no such eager co-operation from Congress when he presented his plan for the unification of the Defense Department. One of the most influential figures on the Hill in all matters concerning Defense Department legislation was Carl Vinson of Georgia, the Democratic Chairman of the House Armed Services Committee, popularly known as Uncle Carl. Despite heroic efforts by the White House staff to line up support for the President's proposal, Uncle Carl remained stolidly opposed to a few principal provisions that were the heart of the plan. Only a few days after his message went to Congress, a reporter told the President that some very powerful Senators and Representatives were against his suggestions. Eisenhower threw out a warm challenge: "I don't care how strong they are or how numerous they are. . . . It just happens I have a little bit more experience in military organization and the directing of unified forces than anyone on the active list."

Unfortunately for the President, his Secretary of Defense, Neil McElroy, did not appear to share Eisenhower's spirited dedication to the reorganization plan when he appeared to testify on it before the House committee. In sending his recommendations to Congress, the President had drafted most of the wording of the bill himself. This was a rare procedure. Usually the President left the drafting of a bill to the ranking member of his party on the appropriate committee to work out with the department head concerned. This time, because Eisenhower had drafted himself, almost word for word, the legislation that he wanted enacted it was assumed in the House that he was taking an unshakable no-compromise stand on it. But McElroy gave the committee the impression that the administration would be willing to make concessions. He was unable to give the inquiring Congressmen any specific examples of the "outmoded concepts" that Eisenhower had cited as the main reason for the need of unification. He indicated that the terms of the bill were in some respects broader than was necessary, but the President was in some degree responsible for McElroy's comment since he had said that he did not regard the exact language of the bill as necessarily sacrosanct. This weakened the President's case somewhat and gave Uncle Carl Vinson the opening to drive in objections to some of the key provisions.

After McElroy left the door open, the President jumped up fast to close it but the room was already filled with snow. McElroy admitted to Uncle Carl's committee that the Secretary of Defense did not actually need the sweeping powers to assign and transfer that the bill conferred upon him. The President reversed the Secretary and came back strongly to assert that any retreat from this position of demand for supervisory control would make unified strategy impossible. Eisenhower sent word to Congress that no concessions would be made because they had already been made before the bill was submitted. What they were considering were the bare essentials, he declared.

While he was pondering over the fate of his proposal, Eisenhower remembered that he had often urged other people to bring pressure on Congress in behalf of their important projects. He decided to do the same thing himself. He wrote a letter which he sent to various friends in the business world and in the professions in different parts of the country, asking them to send messages to Congress in support of the reorganization bill and to get their friends, bosses and fellow workers to do likewise. "I guess I must have sent out around 450 letters," Eisenhower told me later, "and I found out that it brought a flood of messages to Congress."

The provisions in the framework of the bill that Uncle Carl found objectionable included the one that removed the service Secretaries from the operational chain of command. The President wrote to Vinson that he did not want this changed and furthermore the Secretaries and the Joint Chiefs should be stopped from their practice of by-passing the Secretary of Defense and taking their grievances directly to Congress. Eisenhower also complained that another change being made in the bill would allow one member of the Joint Chiefs of Staff to hamstring proposed defense improvements for several months at a time, to endorse stand-patism and to evade civilian authority. A third elimination that Vinson favored would have allowed the Joint Chiefs, in Eisenhower's opinion, to promote disunity and interservice rivalries.

The President found himself involved in a hot argument at the meeting with the Republican leaders on June 24 about defense policies and his reorganization bill. That day Senator Saltonstall brought him word that there was a movement afoot in Congress to raise the force levels, and to build more submarines and a nuclear-powered aircraft carrier, with an increase of one billion dollars in the defense budget. With an air of resignation, Eisenhower confessed that his efforts since 1953 to modernize the armed forces seemed to be futile. "Now they want a nuclear carrier, enormously expensive, and useless in a big war," he said. "Congress seems to be going on the theory that we have to have all of everything everywhere all the time."

Saltonstall unwittingly put his foot into a hornets' nest by remarking casually that the reserves, the National Guard and the Marines all had great popular appeal.

"Why?" the President said. "Why? I ask you, why? The Marines are a great fighting force but in the last war they were no better than the Rangers or the paratroopers. Probably they had better publicity. I made the two largest amphibious landings in history without a single Marine. You listen to people talk about the Marines and you have difficulty understanding how these two great landings could ever have been accomplished. Every service is pleading for more manpower and that is why I want more authority for the Secretary. One man then can make the decisions. But now everybody on the Hill is being an expert."

Senator Knowland said that it was obvious that the President was not going to get everything that he was asking for in the reorganization bill. Eisenhower said that he was deeply concerned about the first two of the three points on which he was in disagreement with Vinson. Even in those first two points he might be agreeable to a change in language, he added. He said that he was so agreeable that he had gone as far as accepting an amendment that John McCormack had proposed, despite the fact that McCormack himself was confused about its meaning and surprised when it had been adopted.

"If this bill is unsatisfactory, I will have to veto it," the President said unhappily. "For eleven long years I have been fighting for what I believe and I can live with what I have if necessary. After all, the Commander in Chief has the power which is in the Constitution to make assignments. Otherwise he is not the Commander in Chief. This I have never questioned, except perhaps in one instance, when

Truman removed a very eminent man. I have never been rough with a service Chief of Staff, with the possible exception of one man whom I told, when he served out his time, that his usefulness was over."

It turned out that Eisenhower's bill was passed by Congress without the three provisions that he had argued for and lost. He signed it on August 6, observing that it was a major advance toward real unification, even though there was still much to be done in bringing centralized control to the armed forces. His effort to reorganize the defense establishment was one of the brightest episodes of his public career because it was the dedicated and selfless work of a professional soldier to strengthen civilian control over the military.

While Eisenhower waged his struggle, he was spattered at every turn by criticism that was often so snide and petty that it became ridiculous. One day in the summer of 1958, Senator Bridges came to the White House to report that Senator Symington had made a speech about "surrender studies" that were supposed to have been made in the Pentagon, an alleged plan of procedure for the United States to follow if the country was defeated by a surprise nuclear attack. Bridges wanted Eisenhower to refute the charge that there were such documents in the Defense Department's files.

Eisenhower's reaction was explosive. "Surrender plans?" he said. "I may be the last person left alive but there won't be any surrender in the next two and a half years, you can be sure of that! If there was as much as a semblance of anything like surrender studies being considered around here, the Pentagon would get the most thorough shaking up in its history! Why would a Senator put anything like that into the Congressional Record?"

The President paused and shook his head.

"Well," he said, "I'd better not get a stroke over a thing like that."

20   An Evening at the White House

I have saved a few of the letters I received while I was the Assistant to the President. One of them is from an elderly parishioner of St. John's Church in Washington, known as the Church of the Presidents, where I attended services on Sunday. On one occasion I was asked to read one of the lessons at St. John's and afterward this older gentleman, who always carried an umbrella to church, even on bright and sunny Sundays, sent me the following note:

It was my privilege at yesterday's Sunday morning service to hear you so expertly read the first lesson at St. John's Church. From my seat in the front pew, I could follow your reading, and must hereby express my appreciation for your enunciation which conveyed the Scriptural meaning to me perfectly, so perfectly that I am certain that you would have made a great reader and cleric and a far better Pastor than an official administrator in government affairs. It is truly regrettable that you are a statesman with a vast salary instead of a decent clergyman with a modestly earned stipend in the place of my friendly enemy, Dr. Eldridge, for his preaching has proved as useless as your statesmanship.

The folder of letters that I brought home from Washington also includes a pleasant note that I received in February, 1956, from a prominent Democrat whom I had never met, Jesse Jones, the Texan head of the Reconstruction Finance Corporation during Franklin D. Roosevelt's administration, who designed and presented to the White House the coffin-shaped table in the Cabinet Room. I might have been very much surprised by Jones's letter if I had known about a previous one that he had sent to President Eisenhower early in 1954:

422

DEAR MR. PRESIDENT:

I have thought for some time that you should find another place for Governor Adams and replace him with a Western man who has a better understanding of the delicate position he occupies in making decisions for you.

With all good wishes,

Sincerely yours,

JESSE JONES

The letter that I got from Jones two years after he wrote about me to the President, however, went like this:

DEAR GOVERNOR ADAMS:

While a good many years ago I had a summer home at North Conway, I do not recall having ever met you, but wish to congratulate you most heartily for the great help you are to the President.

Cordially and sincerely yours,

JESSE H. JONES

I also have a note written to me on my birthday in 1955 by Robert Cutler, who was Eisenhower's first presidential assistant for national security affairs, in which Cutler says that I remind him of a cold-boiled Bostonian named Bob Homans, a descendant of John Adams who was epitomized after his death as a man with a soul of granite through which ran fine flaws of humanity. And there is a message sent to me at a time when things were going badly for me. It was from my friend, Lady Astor, a brisk woman with a snap in her eyes, and it contained counsel from her Bible: "Be not afraid nor dismayed by reason of this great multitude for the battle is not yours but God's."

I hoped that Bobby Cutler was joking when he accused me of having a few flaws of humanity in a granite heart, but there were many people in Washington who would have been quick to endorse such a description of me. One day when Leonard Hall was trying to persuade me to attend a meeting of the Republican National Committee, he said to me, "You know, a lot of those people think you have horns." From my first month in the White House, I was conscious of this feeling but there was not much that I could do to correct it because the nature of my work made me avoid the limelight and my working hours left me little time for social life. I was too busy to think about establishing myself as a sparkling personality. The only article that I ever wrote for publication while I was on Eisenhower's staff was one about music for the *New York Times*. Bill Lawrence, one of the Washington correspondents for the *Times,* came to me one day in 1957 asking if he could write up an interview with me about my interest in music. I told him that it might turn out better if I wrote it myself and, much to my surprise, the short article that I wrote appeared on the front page of a special records and music section of the Sunday *Times,* entitled "Music Eases a White House Task." That made me out quite a writer, I thought.

One of my most treasured possessions is a letter from Mrs. Edward MacDowell, the widow of the famous American composer, written after her ninety-eighth birthday. Last year I had the honor to vote for Edward MacDowell's admission to the Hall of Fame; his compositions will always live in the hearts of music lovers. Mrs. MacDowell wrote: "I remember so well the last time I saw you. I can see my shabby sitting room and you and your wife calling." She well knew when she wrote this that I knew she was almost totally blind.

I also appeared a few times on television, in the interests of the Republican party and the administration, notably on "Meet the Press" on the Sunday before the 1956 presidential election, a delicate spot to be in at such a time, but I was overwhelmed later when the President called me to tell me that he had watched my cross-examination at the White House and he thought it was great. Lawrence E. Spivak, the impresario of that news panel interview show, wrote me the next day an invitation to come back to "Meet the Press" at some less tense occasion when we could spend the whole half-hour in sweetness and light. That time has not yet arrived and I suppose it never will.

My interest in music led me into some extracurricular attempts to improve the cultural facilities of the nation's capital, where, rather astonishingly, there is no center for the staging of opera and the other performing arts such as there is in all of the capital cities of Europe. When legislation was passed in September, 1958, providing land for such a project with the condition that the building must be constructed with private funds, I made up a list of suggestions for the President to consider appointing to a board of citizen trustees whose first duty would be to raise the building funds. Although Washington is still without the performing arts center it sorely needs, I know this project will sometime succeed.

It was one of my more pleasant duties to entertain the wandering minstrels who came to visit the White House, always with the hope of performing for the President. Among the choral groups were two beautifully trained choirs from small colleges in Gabriel Hauge's land of Minnesota, to which the President listened as graciously as he did to the glee club from my own Dartmouth. I entertained many top-ranking musicians at lunch at the White House, among them Artur Rubenstein, the concert pianist with whom I developed a strong personal friendship; Isaac Stern, the violinist; Charles Munch, conductor of the Boston Symphony Orchestra, over the years perhaps the world's greatest such musical organization, and Leonard Bernstein, the conductor of the New York Philharmonic, who visited us just after his *West Side Story* opened in Washington before becoming a great success on Broadway. One of my last musical reunions in the White House was with Werner Janssen and Howard Mitchell, both nationally known conductors. Janssen's *Oh, Doctor!* was the best musical show ever written by an undergraduate at Dartmouth.

I arranged another luncheon at the White House in the early days of the Eisenhower administration for Robert Frost, who "said" a few of his poems to the President's staff. On a later trip to Washington, Frost spoke to me about Ezra Pound, the eccentric poet who had been sentenced to a federal prison for preaching Nazi propaganda in Europe during World War II. He had later been transferred to a mental institution under penal confinement. Frost had no sympathy for Pound's views but as a fellow poet he was appealing for leniency because of his mental irresponsibility. Subsequently, Frost talked with the Justice Department officials and Pound was later released and went to Italy to spend his remaining days.

Five years later, on February 27, 1958, Frost came back to the White House again to be a guest at one of the President's stag dinners. When he went into office, Eisenhower discussed with his staff the idea of having small and exclusively male dinner parties at the White House for groups of fifteen to twenty men from all walks of life, just for the purpose of having a pleasant and informal conversation about anything that happened to come into their minds. His original thought of mixing important business and professional men with workers and smaller business people at these gatherings did not work out quite as he had intended. In the strange and impressive atmosphere of the White House, with the President of the United States himself sitting at the table with them, the lesser-known guests became awe-stricken and found it difficult to join freely in the conversation, especially when the president of a great corporation was in the room, ready to fill every pause in the conversation with his theories and anecdotes. So the people in the lower-income brackets appeared less frequently, although the officials of their labor unions sometimes came. John L. Lewis attended one of the early stag dinners and the President remarked afterward at a Cabinet meeting that John L. had been the life of the party.

If you were invited to attend what the President called "one of my small stag dinners," you received a note on monogrammed ("DDE") stationery, addressed to you by your first name if the President happened to know you that well. Here is one such letter which is in my file of Washington souvenirs:

I wonder if it would be convenient for you to come to an informal stag dinner on the evening of Tuesday, May twenty-eighth. I hope to gather together a small group, and I should like very much for you to attend if it is possible for you to do so.

Because of the informality of the occasion, I suggest that we meet at the White House about seven fifteen, have a reasonably early dinner, and devote the evening to a general chat. While I am hopeful that you can attend, I realize that you may already have engagements which would interfere. If so, I assure you of my complete understanding.

I shall probably wear a dinner jacket, but a business suit will be entirely appropriate.

With warm regard,

Sincerely,

DE

If you were not a member of the government and therefore lacked ready access to the President's secretary, you would send a note of acceptance and a week or so later, to jog your memory if it should be so derelict, you might receive a short note:

I am delighted to know that you will be able to attend the small stag dinner I am having on Monday evening. This is just to remind you that the time is 7:15; business suit. With warm regard,

Sincerely,

DE

At the appointed hour you presented yourself to the White House doorkeeper, who ushered you into the hands of the Secret Service men, who, in turn, either recognized you or checked your identity and showed you to the second-floor study, the oval room that Presidents in the early days used as their office. There the President greeted you and introduced you to the small assembly of guests. Looking around the room, your attention was attracted to cases containing memorabilia, such as jeweled swords, decorations and a letter from the Queen of England. On the wall you noticed perhaps two small paintings, one of an elderly man and the other of a woman in homey dress, which you guessed to be likenesses of the President's father and mother. Just to be sure, you asked him about the paintings and he confirmed your conclusion; they were posthumous portraits of his parents. He thought the likeness of his mother was quite good but that the one of his father was less lifelike and rather impressionistic.

As a waiter offered you a choice of a beverage, you counted seventeen other guests, divided into conversational groups of threes and fours. You joined in a pleasant exchange with one of the groups, and, in about three-quarters of an hour, the President suggested going to the state dining room for dinner and he led the way, perhaps with somebody like General Al Gruenther or Cardinal Spellman beside him. The single oval table in the dining room was decorated with a few flowers but without the elegant display that always accompanied the larger and formal state dinners. The President liked to place beside each guest's plate as a souvenir of the occasion a small black-handled jack-knife (with the blades closed so that the ties of friendship should not be cut) and a lucky penny (to counteract giving something that was sharp). The President himself arranged the seating plan for the dinner with his secretary, Mrs. Whitman, a day ahead of the appointed time, and the conversation was always spirited and jolly at the table and almost never lagged. Eisenhower was a superb dinner partner; he made his guests feel at ease and listened to them attentively and drew them out. The dinner usually had five courses with two or three excellent wines. Toward the end of the meal the conversation became more general and the President often brought to the attention of the whole group at that time a single topic that interested him and on which he wanted to seek everybody's opinion. Then the party adjourned to an adjoining sitting room for coffee, a cordial and cigars and an interesting discussion.

These evenings were never devoted to abstract discussions nor was the conversation ever highly intellectual. It was often concerned with public issues of the moment without becoming too serious and there was plenty of warm and entertaining storytelling without any loud hilarity. The time went by quickly and the President, who became as absorbed in the discussions as any of his guests, invariably kept them well entertained until eleven or after. He did not want any of his government associates who were present to take the initiative in bringing these evenings to a close. He alone decided when it was time to retire.

On the day that Robert Frost was to attend the President's stag dinner, he came to lunch with me at the White House staff mess hall. Frost was an old friend of mine and his visits to Washington were always happy occasions for me. The white-haired New England poet had many admirers in the White House during the Eisenhower administration from the President on down, and I am certain that he would have been the poet laureate of the United States at that time if our government had followed the British practice of awarding such an official title. I assembled some of Frost's admirers on the staff at the luncheon table—Mrs. Whitman, Attorney General Rogers, Hauge, Larson, Merriam, Morrow and Robert Rogers, who had orchestrated the President's 1953 prayer. The poet was then a month away from his eighty-third birthday and he said, with a twinkle in his eye, "There may not be much time left, you know."

The group that night was more of a family party than it usually was; it included the President's brother, Dr. Milton Eisenhower, and his son, Major John Eisenhower, who had a rich and memorable experience during his assignment in the White House for the last two years of his father's presidency. When Frost and I came into the oval room study, we greeted a fellow New Englander, Charles Coolidge, the brilliant, mild-mannered citizen of Boston who had the good sense to go back to Boston and resume his life there after he performed an admirable service for the administration in planning the reorganization of the Defense Department. We also saw Richard Amberg, publisher of the St. Louis *Globe-Democrat* and a dependable supporter of the administration, and Douglas Black, the president of Doubleday and Company, publishers of Eisenhower's best-selling war memoirs, *Crusade in*

Europe. I remembered one poster that was displayed during the 1952 campaign to embarrass Eisenhower, questioning the tax treatment of the income from his book, which was allowed as a capital gain. This was consistent with the tax laws at that time and did not give Eisenhower any special privilege. He once told me, when we were discussing tax treatment, that the changes in the code of the Internal Revenue Department after he took office had the effect of reducing his income by some forty thousand dollars under that of President Truman, although they were both paid the same salary.

There were usually a few captains of industry at the White House stag dinners, partly because the President had many friends in their ranks and also because he valued their opinions on the economic problems that were always facing him. On this particular night the chairman of the board of du Pont, Walter S. Carpenter, Jr., sat beside the host at dinner and Samuel Daroff, a Philadelphia manufacturer, Roy W. Johnson, vice president of General Electric, and Harlow Curtice, president of General Motors, were also at the table. Curtice and his rival, Henry Ford II, both visited the White House occasionally, being Republicans and Eisenhower supporters, but they never came to see the President at the same time. The rift between their two huge industrial organizations contributed to the unfortunate division of the Republicans in Michigan and helped maintain the dominance of the Democrats in that state's politics.

The rest of the party that Frost attended at the White House that evening included a banker, two Army generals, the Secretary of Defense and the administrator of the Mutual Security Program, James H. Smith, Jr., who had served previously as the Assistant Secretary of the Navy for Air. The banker was Charles S. Garland from the Baltimore firm of Alexander Brown and Son, whom old-time tennis fans would remember as the partner of R. Norris Williams in the doubles team that won the Wimbledon tournament in 1920. Garland was also the chairman of the board of trustees of Johns Hopkins University, of which Milton Eisenhower was president. The Army generals were Walter Bedell Smith, Eisenhower's chief of staff during World War II, and later director of the Central Intelligence Agency and Under Secretary of State, and Garrison Davidson, the West Point football coach of past years, at that time the superintendent of the Military Academy. General Davidson's wife was a sister of General Alfred Gruenther, another close friend of the Eisenhowers. Also at the table, and adding considerable distinction to the gathering, was Dr. James Killian, Jr., on leave from the presidency of M.I.T. to serve as the President's special adviser on science and technology. Needless to say, it was a highly memorable evening for Frost and the poet's presence made it a highly memorable evening for all of the rest of us.

I attended a few, but by no means all, of these stag dinners at the White House and they remain with me as the real pearls of my Washington recollections. My wife and I also went to several of the President's elaborately formal state dinners for visiting heads of state and other dignitaries. Eisenhower was rather hesitant about inviting his staff associates to these elegant and rather stiff affairs for fear that they would feel forced to accept the invitation as an official duty rather than from a genuine interest in the event. The last thing that Eisenhower wanted was to have somebody reluctantly sacrificing his personal time after office hours out of a feeling of obligation to please the Boss. He assumed that most people shared his own preference for a relaxed get-together with a few friends to a night of gala formality. He often urged us to feel free to decline his invitations to state dinners if they interfered with something else that we had planned to do. In the evenings when he had no official engagements or on weekends, the President liked to spend his time with some of his old friends whose faces were often seen at the White House or at Gettysburg—Bill Robinson, the entertaining George Allen, Cliff Roberts, Pete Jones, Bob Woodruff, Al Gruenther, Slats Slater, Freeman Gosden ("Amos" of the famous radio comedy team of Amos 'n Andy), Sig Larmon. Aksel Nielsen, Eisenhower's great friend in Colorado, was another face which the President was always glad to see wherever and whatever the occasion. This circle of friends purposely stayed out of the political spotlight and seldom appeared with Eisenhower at conventions and on campaign trips. But most of them were fellow members of the Augusta National Golf Club and would be there at some time during his golf holidays. He had a warm affection for Bobby Jones and they often met together at Augusta.

Eisenhower had many personal friends among the Democrats and this was one reason why he was reluctant to have his staff make extreme political attacks on the opposition party. One of the President's bridge partners was the late Chief Justice Fred M. Vinson, a Democratic Congressman before he was appointed by President Truman to the Supreme Court. Bernard Baruch was an enthusiastic Eisenhower supporter and the President listened to his views attentively.

I watched with interest the development of the friendship between Eisenhower and President Herbert Hoover. Hoover's work with his commission that was studying the organization of the executive branch of the government brought him into frequent contact with Eisenhower and the two men got along well together, although they differed on some principles. Hoover was vigorously opposed to Eisenhower's more liberal support of such public water resource projects as the Glen Canyon development on the Colorado River, for example. But the President admired the monumental work of the Hoover Commission as a whole and warmly applauded its recommendations for improving the efficiency of government operations, such as the suggested changes in the Budget and Accounting Act. The tribute that Eisenhower paid to Hoover at the conclusion of the commission's work gave the former President deep satisfaction. I met with Hoover often to discuss suggestions that he had for me to pass on to Eisenhower about government problems and twice my wife came with me to have dinner with him at his apartment. The three of us enjoyed these meetings and we became very friendly. In 1957 Hoover invited me to be his guest at the encampment of the Bohemian Club in California, which he described as "the greatest men's party on earth," and Eisenhower warned me that I would always regret it if I did not accept the invitation. But I never was able to find the time to go.

For the same reason, my heavy work schedule, I never enjoyed a busy social life in Washington. I had to decline many attractive invitations to dinners and receptions because my working day started at an early hour and I happen to be one of those people who cannot get along without a proper quota of sleep. It was this reticence that was partly responsible for my reputation in the capital as a frosty Yankee and other less complimentary figures of speech. Many of my invitations came from foreign embassies. When Menshikov came to Washington as the Soviet Ambassador he made a special effort to build up a friendship with me, obviously in the hope of reaching Eisenhower through me instead of through the customary diplomatic channels where he would have been confronted by the firmly disapproving Dulles.

As a matter of fact, Menshikov asked me in one talk that he had with me at the White House to arrange an appointment for him with the President without Dulles being present. Whenever I had a conversation with the Russian envoy, I always reported it to Dulles and the President, and whenever Menshikov attempted an end-run around the State Department, Dulles saw to it that he gained no yardage. One time I received word that Menshikov wanted me to come to the Russian Embassy for dinner, although I never received the invitation in writing. I asked the State Department to discuss the invitation with the Ambassador. He said that he was unable to recall it. Now and then State Department and other staff personnel not attached to the White House would spend a social evening with Soviet Embassy officials, always with the prior knowledge and approval of the State Department. The talk of the Russians always came back to the same familiar theme: if Dulles changed his belligerent attitude and if the United States vacated its overseas military bases and assumed a more compromising attitude, peaceful relations between the two powers would automatically follow. Although there was no disposition among Eisenhower's associates to fraternize with the Russians, now suddenly so friendly, Dulles always was apprehensive that the curiosity of someone in the administration might get the better of his sense of propriety.

My wife and I did manage to spend several delightful evenings, however, at the other embassies, usually at dinners that were given in honor of somebody in the government or in the foreign service who was either arriving in Washington or departing on an overseas assignment. At one tremendous reception at the British Embassy, I encountered a lady whose name I did not remember and I said to her, "It *is* nice to see you again." She said to me, "And do you know who I am? Or do I have to introduce myself to you for the third time?"

I was also momentarily taken aback one evening at the Belgian Embassy at a dinner given by the Ambassador, Baron Silvercruys, and the Baroness, for the Douglas MacArthur IIs, who were going to Japan where MacArthur was to serve as the American Ambassador. I was rather startled at the end of the dinner to find that each of the men at the table was being called upon to make some remarks appropriate to the occasion. I listened to the others, who, one by one, paid high praise and fine compliments to the MacArthurs. I wondered what on earth I could say when my turn came because I had never enjoyed a close personal association with the MacArthurs.

As I found myself being summoned to my feet, I suddenly recalled a story about something that had happened during the war on a railroad up in Vermont. Perhaps I could make this do. This line had a train that came down from Montreal, crossed a corner of Vermont and, after making its way through New Hampshire, eventually arrived at Boston if no unforeseen casualty intervened. On one such trip during the war, the conductor found himself short a brakeman. Although this was not so serious in Canada, when the train reached the Vermont boundary the conductor had to do something about it. So he recruited a young Frenchman in a village at the Canadian border for that duty, dressed him up in a blue coat with brass buttons and instructed him in the procedure of announcing the names of the stations at each stop. "I'll call out the stop at the front of the train," the conductor told him. "You listen to me and then you say the same thing from where you're standing at the back end of the train. Now let's go."

The young Frenchman, rather unfamiliar with the English language, had no serious trouble during the early part of the journey. He listened carefully to the conductor when the train pulled into Swanton, the first station, and he shouted, "Swann Tone! Swann Tone!" At Essex Junction, he called, "Essex Junkshone!" Then the train made its way into Montpelier Junction. The conductor at the front car announced briskly, "Montpelier Junction. Montpelier Junction. Change for Barre City and Montpelier, points on the St. Johnsbury and Lake Champlain Railroad and points on the Montpelier and Wells River Railroad." This was too much for the French boy. He turned to his passengers and shouted, "De same on dis end!" I waved my hand at the previous speakers around the table in the Belgian Embassy who had said so many nice things about the MacArthurs and I said to them, "The same on this end."

Looking back on the years that I spent with Eisenhower I think that the most memorable and eventful one was the campaign year of 1952 when I worked for primary votes in the snow of New Hampshire, toured the country on the same errand in other primaries, ran the floor work at the convention in Chicago, traveled again with him throughout the nation—thirty thousand miles by air and twenty thousand miles by train—and then sat back to watch the election returns. The later years in the White House may have been more important but they lacked the tremendous satisfaction of that first campaign.

A few days after he was inaugurated as President, Eisenhower wrote to a friend: "It is not given to any of us to foresee the future or what events, big and little, will come about to defeat the best-laid plans and the loftiest purposes."

The same could have been said at this end.

21 I Leave Washington

Congressmen and officials of the executive branch of the government in Washington are always receiving letters and telephone calls from constituents and acquaintances and friends back home who are either trying to get information and guidance or making complaints and seeking action about business transactions or personal affairs with various federal government departments and regulatory agencies. It may be a dispute about some contract or an attempt to get a Navy commission for somebody's nephew or something to do with the proposed location of a new airport or an effort to schedule a football game between a Southern college and the Air Force Academy. Usually there is not much that can be done except to pass along the request to the department or agency concerned, hoping for a reasonably prompt reply, and then to send back to the anxious constituent or friend the official comment that you have obtained from the department or agency, favorable, unfavorable or noncommittal as the case may be.

As bothersome and annoying as such requests can seem at times, every member of Congress and most other federal officials feel it a duty to pay courteous attention to them. I acquired that habit when I was serving as a Congressman in the House of Representatives, regarding the handling of petitions and questions from people in my New Hampshire district as part of my routine work as their representative in Washington. When I went to the White House I continued to feel a responsibility to give courteous attention to the inquiries of private citizens who sought information and legitimate help in matters dealing with their government. It was no longer the same duty it

435

had been in Congress, but the President himself repeatedly emphasized that every reasonable inquiry directed to his office should have a prompt and polite reply. This meant in many cases calling department and agency heads to find out what action was being taken on the matter in question. Being well aware that such calls could be misinterpreted by a sensitive department administrator as criticism of his work, or as interference or pressure from the White House, I asked the President's staff members to leave the responsibility for making these calls to me. I was afraid that a staff member might express an opinion or make a recommendation that would rebound and cause trouble. If such risks had to be taken, I wanted to be the one to take them. "Let me make the mistakes," I told the staff. As I look back, I was not sufficiently aware of the added importance that I might be giving to these inquiries by handling them myself. A call or inquiry from the Assistant to the President was much more liable to cause suspicion of interference than a call from a less prominent White House staff executive, but I was not alert to the fact at the time. If I had been, I might have saved myself later embarrassment.

One of the many letters that we received at the White House questioning decisions by Federal regulatory agencies was one written to me in 1953 by Murray Chotiner, complaining about a Civil Aeronautics Board ruling against a small non-scheduled carrier, North American Airlines, that Chotiner represented in a legal capacity. I knew nothing of the case and I had no personal interest in it, but Chotiner complained that the small carriers were being discriminated against and said that the White House ought to inquire into the situation. I did not hesitate to ask the Board about its policy and for a statement in the case that I might use in replying to Chotiner. I had known him as Nixon's campaign manager in the 1952 campaign, and felt that his request was a reasonable one and deserved a courteous reply. The Board prepared for me an explanation of its decision against the airline, which I sent back to Chotiner. I did not give the Board any opinion of my own on the case, for I had none, and I did not attempt to change the Board's decision in any way. The reply that I sent to Chotiner was what the Board recommended be said to him, and I therefore assumed that whatever I told him was entirely within the Board's own rules of procedure and propriety. Chotiner's client did not benefit from my inquiry since the previous decision remained unchanged.

Accordingly I was surprised to read in the newspapers in February, 1958, that the House Committee on Legislative Oversight had unearthed my letters to Chotiner as an apparent attempt by the White House to influence the decision of the Civil Aeronautics Board in the North American Airlines case. A request from my office to the Board for a reply to Chotiner's complaint about the decision was made to appear to be a deliberate use of pressure on the agency.

I found myself faced with the same charge in two other unrelated cases during the summer of 1958. One of them arose from a bitter complaint that I received from Allen S. Grew, an official of Raylaine Worsteds, Inc., a textile firm in Manchester, New Hampshire, about the treatment his company had received from the Defense Department in closing out a textiles contract. I turned Grew's complaint over to Colonel Robert Schulz, the President's military aide who acted as a liaison officer between the White House and the Pentagon, suggesting that he ask the Defense Department to prepare a suitable reply to the manufacturer. The replies prepared by the Department to this and other letters were brought to me by the aide and I incorporated them into letters to Grew, following substantially the same language as that in the replies suggested to me by the Pentagon officials. The Defense Department made no change in its decision and the Manchester concern received no help or relief. In fact, the company later went out of business, partly as a result of losses it suffered from the contract and the settlement the Department made in closing it.

However, the complaint from the manufacturer was forwarded in due time through channels to the Armed Services Board of Contract Appeals, where one of its members, in his own handwriting, attached a memorandum saying that the "intrusion" of the White House in the case was "highly unethical." This notation was brought to the attention of the House Armed Services Committee, which ordered a subcommittee to look into all the facts surrounding the termination of the contract. The chairman of the subcommittee asked me to testify at a closed-door hearing. After consulting with Gerald Morgan, the President's special counsel, I sent a letter to the chairman telling him that the only information that I had about the Manchester manufacturer's case was contained in several letters that I had received from him over a period of years. I said that I had turned them over to the military liaison aide at the White House, asking him to forward them to the proper officials at the Pentagon and to request that drafts of suggested replies be prepared. When these drafts were received from the Defense Department they were sent by me over my signature to the manufacturer with only minor editorial changes. "In no instance," I wrote to the subcommittee chairman, "did I send any of the incoming letters to, nor have any communication with, the Armed Services Board of Contract Appeals or any member thereof."

Inasmuch as this was all I knew about the case, I told the subcommittee that I could not see that any useful purpose would be served by my appearing at its closed hearing. The subcommittee decided that there was no evidence to support the contention that I had interfered in the Defense Department's handling of the case.

Although it had nothing to do with my declining to testify in this particular case, there was, as a matter of fact, a legal restriction against a Congressional investigative committee questioning a member of the President's staff about White House correspondence, telephone conversations and conference discussions. This question had come up during the Army-McCarthy hearings in 1954 when Senator McCarthy wanted to call me as a witness during those hearings to testify about my role in the preparation of the Army's complaint on the Cohn-Schine affair. The Attorney General decided after careful consideration that the records of my conversations and correspondence in the case were privileged information of the executive branch of the government that could not be disclosed to the Congressional branch. Brownell based his decision on an opinion written by the late Justice Robert Jackson of the Supreme Court when Jackson was the Attorney General. Jackson held that the executive branch cannot be required to make public its confidential records. Actually, I was never invited to appear at the Army-McCarthy hearings but if I had received an invitation I would have declined it on Brownell's advice. I did decline on the same grounds an invitation to appear before Senator Kefauver's committee in 1955 to testify concerning my request for a postponement of the SEC hearing on the Dixon-Yates contract, mentioned in an earlier chapter. I felt in that instance that my connection with the Dixon-Yates negotiations was so slight

that I could not have given the Kefauver committee any information
pertinent to the inquiry that it did not already possess.

The other case during that summer of 1958, in which I was
charged with bringing pressure on federal regulatory agencies, was
the House Committee on Legislative Oversight's investigation of
Bernard Goldfine's dealings with the Federal Trade Commission and
the Securities and Exchange Commission. In this instance, I not
only waived my privilege of not appearing before a Congressional
investigating committee; I requested the appearance myself without
being invited to testify and willingly gave the committee an opportunity to question me in any way that it wanted to do. I had a strong
reason for taking a different stand on appearing at this inquiry than
the one I had taken in the Army-McCarthy, Dixon-Yates and Defense Department contract hearings.

Although it seemed at times during the Goldfine hearings as if
I was on trial as much as Goldfine, the main purpose of the investigation was to uncover the extent of the Boston textile manufacturer's
evasion of government regulations in his irregular business dealings.
But the House committee's interest in Goldfine's affairs stemmed
originally from a suspicion that he received preferential treatment
from regulatory agencies because of his friendship with me. It
became plain that, in its investigation of Goldfine, the Congressional
committee intended to cast reflections on my personal conduct in
my position in the White House. Under the circumstances it seemed
to me that the usual restrictions against testimony by a White House
staff member did not apply. Although there were some objections
among my associates to my appearing voluntarily before the committee, they were removed when I made it clear that I was determined
to put myself before the committee for questioning because I felt a
personal responsibility to make a public disclosure of every bit of
information that I knew about the Goldfine case.

That information did not amount to much. Goldfine and I had
been personal friends for many years before I came to Washington
to work as the Assistant to the President but I knew little or nothing
about the details of his business dealings. I did not learn of his tax
arrears until some of the facts began to unravel as a result of the
hearings by the Legislative Oversight Committee; nor did I know
anything about his troubles with his East Boston Company's financial

operations. Our friendship began eighteen years ago when I was
Speaker of the House of Representatives in New Hampshire. We
were introduced by a fellow legislator, Norris Cotton, now a member
of the United States Senate. Cotton had described Goldfine as a
reliable textile manufacturer whose operations in Lebanon, where
Cotton lived, were an important economic asset to that region of
our state. Most of the large New England textile mills, once com-
prising the largest industry in that part of the country, were either
closing down or moving to the South in search of cheaper labor
and low-cost power. Goldfine was the exception, an apparently
sound businessman with a good reputation in the trade who was
determined to make a success of his business in the Lebanon area,
where his operations were sorely needed. He treated his employees
well, paid good wages and stayed out of labor trouble. I was not the
only New England governor who admired Goldfine's courage and re-
sourcefulness in holding fast while other textile men were moving out.

Goldfine also manufactured textiles in Northfield, Vermont, and
at Plymouth, Massachusetts, and had a small plant in Maine. He
once held a good-will meeting in Montpelier, Vermont, for the purpose of bringing together the managers of his companies and his
employee and union representatives. The governors of Vermont,
Massachusetts and Maine, besides myself, joined in that meeting.

Along with my official interest as Governor of New Hampshire
in Goldfine's effort to keep the textile industry alive in my state
grew a friendship between our families. Goldfine was a man with
a lot of good fun in him and we enjoyed his company. My wife and
I spent pleasant weekends with him and Mrs. Goldfine in Plymouth.
I became attached to his son, Solly. I kept track of his progress in
school and tried to help him when he got into scholastic difficulties.
I attended his wedding in Chicago and saw him often in New
Hampshire and in New York and Boston.

The House committee, in its investigation of Goldfine's affairs,
made much of the gifts we had received from him and some hotel
bills he had paid while entertaining us as his guests. This was not a
one-sided exchange and it covered a period of twelve years. We gave
the Goldfines presents and entertained them, too. The hotel accommodations that we occasionally occupied at the Sheraton Plaza in Boston
were maintained, as Goldfine explained it to me, for the convenience

of his friends and business associates. From time to time, he sent me gifts of clothing made from the products of his mills, including several suits and the vicuña coat that had wide publicity at the time of the committee hearings. Many of the prominent men in public life in New England at that time received such coats and I was one of them. He sent us a few blankets which were made at his mill in Northfield. In a similar spirit, I gave him a watch I bought in Europe in 1955 and later a small alarm watch like one of mine he admired, and Mrs. Adams gave the Goldfines one of her paintings. I never had any feeling that there were any strings attached to the gifts on either side. As for his business affairs, I never had any interest in them beyond the desire to see them continue to serve as an economic asset to the people who were dependent on these industries.

Early in 1954, Goldfine received a complaint from the Federal Trade Commission about a minor infraction by one of his companies of the government's grade labeling regulations. He asked me to find out for him some additional information about the reasons for the complaint. I asked the chairman to send me a brief memorandum that I could pass along to Goldfine in answer to his inquiry. That closed the matter as far as I was concerned.

Later at the House committee hearings, the counsel for the trade commission said that the memorandum sent to me contained information that I should not have divulged to Goldfine. But when I received the memorandum I was not asked to place any restrictions on its use. If the information in it was in any way confidential, that fact was not disclosed to me. At no time in my communications with the chairman of the Federal Trade Commission did I ask any favors or special consideration for Goldfine. I only asked for factual information about the labeling ruling.

A year later Goldfine asked me to arrange an appointment for him with the chairman of the Federal Trade Commission for the purpose of discussing another matter concerning wool labeling regulations. That was all he asked from me; he said nothing to me about the problem that he wanted to discuss with the chairman of the commission and I did not talk about it with anybody at the commission's office. Nor did I ask anybody to do anything or to refrain from doing anything about the matter. Goldfine obtained no preferential treatment from the commission. A cease and desist order was issued against his company because of improper labeling. I did not learn of the order until after it was issued.

My connection with Goldfine's trouble with the Securities and Exchange Commission was more remote and impersonal. In fact, this inquiry was not made by me at all. In 1956 Goldfine complained to me about treatment that he was getting from the SEC because of his failure to file with the commission reports on the financing operations of the East Boston Company, his realty firm. I asked Gerald Morgan, the President's special counsel, to find out from the SEC what the complaint was all about. Morgan did this without disclosing who had requested the information, so as far as I knew my name was not even used in connection with the case. The SEC only told Morgan that it was having trouble trying to get Goldfine to file the required financial report. I did not bother to pass on to Goldfine what Morgan reported to me because Morgan had found out nothing that Goldfine did not already know. Again, in this instance, neither Morgan nor myself made any effort to influence the SEC's action against Goldfine one way or the other.

In the late spring of 1958, when the Legislative Oversight Committee investigated the difficulties between Goldfine and the two government regulatory agencies, its examiners came across the hotel bills which covered hospitality Goldfine had extended to me over several years. When this information was made public by the committee in June during its hearings, I found myself in a political hotbed. I was on a brief fishing trip at the time at Parmachenee Lake in Maine, the same resort where I had taken the President in 1955, when Jerry Persons reached me on the telephone from Washington and told me about the disclosure which the committee had made that day. I quickly returned to Washington to face a situation which I knew would turn out to be a merciless inquisition.

The committee, like Congress itself, was controlled by the Democrats and that happened to be a time when the Democrats were especially anxious for my scalp. It was a Congressional election year. Only a few months before in Minneapolis, at the beginning of the Republican campaign, I had opened up on the Democrats with a hardhitting political speech which the opposition angrily assailed. I had listened for five years to the criticism of the Republican leadership that the White House was being too fraternal with the Democrats and I made up my mind to give them for once a speech which they could not find fault with. I asked Bryce Harlow, one of the most adept men in political semantics I ever knew, to help me.

I was loudly (and not quite inaccurately) accused of "taking the low road" while the President was keeping his campaign oratory on a high and dignified level. I had rubbed rather deliberately some old sores, recalling the military catastrophe of Pearl Harbor and the scientific catastrophe of losing our atomic secrets, and the policies that had lost China to the Reds and led to the Communist invasion of Korea and the war which I described as one "they couldn't end."

I knew, of course, that this speech was a radical departure from the President's own policy of avoiding extremely partisan outbursts, and so I talked it over with him before I left Washington. He said he understood such speeches were part of every political campaign but no one should expect him to get into that kind of a political attack. As I expected, he had to come to my defense later when he was asked about my remarks, explaining that some things had to be done in a way that he himself would not do them. I found myself warmly applauded, for a time at least, by the right-wing Republicans in Congress, the closest I ever came to being acceptable to the Old Guard. But I was never forgiven by the Democrats. That was in January and now in June the Democrats had me in a position where one of their investigative committees could level exaggerated charges to square accounts with me for attacking their party.

It was obvious that I would only be making myself an open target by appearing before the committee but I felt that in good conscience I should present myself in order to explain exactly what had happened and to make it clear that I had nothing to hide. I went to Eisenhower and told him of my decision. When I told him how I felt he agreed with me, expressed his sympathy and wished me luck. I wrote a letter to the chairman of the Legislative Oversight Committee, explaining fully the requests for information that I had made for Goldfine and my honest belief that I had done nothing improper in making such inquiries, and then stated my willingness to testify before the committee.

I made my appearance at the committee's hearings on the morning of June 17, taking Morgan with me as an adviser. I was also accompanied by my wife. I first explained to the committee in a prepared statement the difficulties and the sensitive misunderstandings that I encountered in my duties as Assistant to the President in trying to handle the great variety of requests for information and help on matters concerning various government departments and agencies that come to the White House daily from members of Congress, federal officials and private citizens. I pointed out that in considering such requests the President's staff tried conscientiously to differentiate between "requests that are proper and requests that are improper." I said that as far as I was concerned Goldfine's requests for information on rulings of the FTC and the SEC and his request for the arrangement of an appointment with the Trade Commission's chairman were given no more special consideration than any of the other such requests that we received from private individuals. If I had made mistakes in giving official attention to his requests, I said, the mistakes were those of judgment, not of intent.

As I look back now on that whole unhappy episode, these mistakes in judgment are plain enough. I never intended to seek special favors for Goldfine nor did I ask anybody to do anything for him. But I did not stop to consider that in making a personal call or an inquiry concerning a matter in which he was involved I might be giving the officials in the federal agency the erroneous impression that I had a personal interest in their ruling or decision on the case. Sometimes I did not take the time to consider that simply the origin of the call gave it such an implication. This was a blind spot of which I was not sufficiently aware, but those were busy days for me and I was continually working under intense pressure. I often acted on the spur of the moment when more reflection would have suggested a wiser course to follow.

In the statement which I gave to the House committee when I appeared at the hearing I mentioned another consideration which seemed to go to the heart of the matter. "Of course, a telephone call or a letter or a person-to-person statement when made by a White House staff member to an individual in an agency of the government receives prompt attention," I said. "But I would not wish to place myself in the position of insulting either the intelligence or the integrity of these officials by implying that they might allow themselves to be influenced in their decisions by such a telephone call, letter or statement."

While such a statement was well reasoned, the fact remains that no expression of interest, no matter how innocent or slight, is ever completely disregarded when it comes from the desk where I sat.

After giving the committee the full factual details of my relationship with the matters under investigation, I answered all of the questions that were asked of me. Most of the questions were unfriendly. I repeated again under examination by the committee's counsel that the inquiries I had made were routine and proper. The House Caucus Room at the Capitol where the hearing was held was jammed with spectators and with reporters and news commentators who were hanging attentively on every word that I said. Then, in answer to one question, I said that I might have acted with a little more prudence. This observation was not by any means a slip of the tongue. I said it deliberately; I had been imprudent and I was ready to admit it. As soon as I said it, I could see right away that I had given the reporters what they needed to make a sensational story. Everything else that I had said at the hearing became relatively unimportant to them.

I left the hearing with the feeling that the end of my service in the White House was in sight. I told Morgan to give Eisenhower a full report on what had been said at the hearing and I went back to my work, keeping a business luncheon appointment that I had made a few days earlier, but during the luncheon and all during the afternoon I wondered how the President would handle the embarrassing questions about me that would be put to him at the next morning's press conference.

Quite often, when the President was confronted with a controversial news development that required his comment, he would prepare a statement and present it to the correspondents at his news conference. Then he would close the matter from further discussion by announcing that he had nothing more to say on that subject. This was how he handled his comment on my testimony before the House Legislative Oversight Committee. Before his meeting with the press that morning he called me into his office, where he was talking over likely news questions with Jim Hagerty. He told me that he had written a statement about how he felt toward me and he proceeded to read it aloud. This was what he said:

Anyone who knows Sherman Adams has never had any doubt of his personal integrity and honesty; no one has believed that he could be bought. But there is a feeling or belief that he was not sufficiently alert in making certain that the gifts, of which he was the recipient, could not be so misinterpreted as to be considered as attempts to influence his official actions. To that extent he has been, as he stated yesterday, imprudent.

Eisenhower then went on to say, after voicing his belief in the truth of the testimony I had given the day before:

I personally like Governor Adams. I admire his abilities. I respect him because of his personal and official integrity. I need him. Admitting the lack of that careful prudence in this incident that the Governor yesterday referred to, I believe with my whole heart that he is an invaluable public servant, doing a difficult job efficiently, honestly and tirelessly.

When the President finished reading his statement to me, he stopped and looked at me for a moment and then asked me what I thought of it. I was unable to say anything. I felt that he had probably gone farther in expressing his confidence in me than I might have gone if our positions had been reversed. But I was too deeply moved to speak to him. He said that he would make the statement at the beginning of the press conference and he seemed quite certain that it would end, once and for all time, the speculation about whether I would remain at my position in the White House. Although it was natural for me to hope that Eisenhower was right in his assumption that his forceful statement would stop the clamor, I had strong misgivings that the problem was not going to be solved that easily.

As I suspected, the President's defense of me did not quiet the criticism, and the demands for my resignation grew louder as the summer months passed by. Most of the uproar against me came from the conservative Republicans, who had been blaming me for policies of the administration that they did not like ever since Eisenhower had gone into office. Here was an opportunity for them to remove me from the President's staff and they intended to take advantage of it. I kicked myself for having given it to them. Meanwhile, Goldfine was becoming more deeply enmeshed in widely headlined troubles with the Congressional investigators over his tangled business affairs. Although I was in no way involved in these disclosures, my name was linked with his in the newspaper stories that were written about him and I worried about the embarrassment that

I was bringing upon the President. But I tried to stick it out in my job because I knew that Eisenhower did not want me to resign.

In September I took a few days off to go on a fishing trip to the Miramichi River in New Brunswick with my wife and Alice and Jerry Persons. I departed from Washington with some misgivings; I could not leave my worry behind me and I knew that in my absence there would be a rising pressure of action against me from the Republican party leaders, who were then arguing that my presence in the White House would be a liability in the approaching elections. Soon after we reached the Miramichi country, the Republicans lost the election in Maine and the party leaders and political columnists were quick to award me a share of the credit for the defeat. I was pursued by the Canadian press, who wanted to find out if I was going to resign. Then I was reached on the telephone by Gerry Morgan, who said that he thought I ought to come back to Washington because Nixon and Meade Alcorn, the Chairman of the Republican National Committee, wanted to talk with me. So I went.

When I arrived in Washington, the President was away from the White House at his vacation quarters in Newport. He had been told by Alcorn that some of the large contributors to the Republican campaign fund in past years were reluctant to support the party financially in that fall's campaign unless I resigned. Disturbed by this report, Eisenhower asked Nixon and Alcorn to talk with me about it. But the President did not ask me to resign and neither did Alcorn or the Vice President. That decision was left to me.

As soon as I reached Washington, I saw Alcorn and he told me about his discussion with the President. I got in touch with Gerry Morgan, who knew nothing about the conversation between Eisenhower and Alcorn, and I asked Morgan to go to Newport the next day and discuss my situation freely with the President. I told Morgan that I would talk with him when he came back to Washington about what the President had to say to him and that on the basis of his report I would make a decision. Morgan came to me from Newport with a confirmation of what Alcorn had told me: the President was troubled by the feeling against me among the influential supporters of the Republican party but the decision on whether or not I ought to remain on the White House staff was still being left entirely up to me. It did not take me long then to make the decision. I felt that any presidential appointee whose presence in the administration becomes an embarrassment to the President for any reason whatsoever has no choice but to submit his resignation. I would have done so long before then if Eisenhower had not been so firmly opposed to my leaving his staff.

My wife felt that I should not resign without making a public statement on television about the reasons for my decision and several friends whose opinion I respected agreed with her. I called in an old friend and fellow Dartmouth alumnus, Charles F. Moore, Jr., a vice president of the Ford Motor Company, and he and Morgan helped me to prepare such a statement. Accompanied by Andy Goodpaster, I then flew to Newport to show what I had written to Eisenhower. Jim Hagerty, surrounded by a throng of newsmen, was on hand to greet us when we climbed out of the Navy helicopter on the familiar lawn in front of the base headquarters building. The President was waiting for me in the same small office upstairs where he had talked with Governor Faubus the year before.

I quietly handed to the President the draft of my statement and he sat down behind his desk to read it. It came as no surprise to him. I had told Hagerty the day before that I was preparing a statement on the reasons for my resignation that I would bring to the President for his approval. He paused at one point to lean back and laugh at one line that I had written, an observation that inasmuch as everyone else in the country had had his say about this episode it now seemed to be the time for me to have mine. When Eisenhower finished looking at my statement and gave it an emphatic nod of approval, he picked up a letter which he said that he and Hagerty had been going over and he read it to me:

NEWPORT, RHODE ISLAND
September 22, 1958

DEAR SHERMAN:

I deeply deplore the circumstances that have decided you to resign as The Assistant to the President.

Your selfless and tireless devotion to the work of the White House and to me personally has been universally recognized. In discharging the responsibilities of your vitally important post, with no hope of reward other than your own satisfaction in knowing that you have served your country well, your total dedication to the nation's welfare has been of the highest possible order.

Your performance has been brilliant; the public has been the beneficiary of your unselfish work. After our six years of intimate association you have, as you have had throughout, my complete trust, confidence and respect.

I accept your resignation with sadness. You will be sorely missed by your colleagues on the staff and by the departments and agencies of the government, with which you have worked so efficiently.

With warm regard and highest esteem,

As ever,

Dwight D. Eisenhower

When he had read the letter to me, the President looked up at me with a smile that seemed to reflect our years of friendship and close association and said, "Will this be all right?" I thanked him. There was nothing else that I could say. He said that he wanted nobody but me to make this decision and that under the circumstances he thought that I had acted wisely.

Hagerty joined us and we talked about the release of the news of my resignation. Eisenhower had written his letter to me on the assumption that it would be a reply to a letter of resignation that I would address to him but we decided that the President's letter could just as well serve as an acknowledgment of my public statement. I told Eisenhower that I wanted to deliver my statement on television when I returned to Washington. He asked Hagerty if the networks would make free time available to me and Hagerty said that they would if the President approved the request. When Eisenhower arranged with Hagerty for my television appearance, he got up from his desk and walked with me down the stairs and out of the building and across the lawn to the waiting helicopter. At the door of the plane, he held out his hand and gave me a word of encouragement, and I took my leave of the man in whose service I had bound myself back in August of 1952.

Hagerty came to Washington later in the day and saw to the preparations for my appearance on television from the studio at Broadcast House at six-forty-five that same evening. I asked my two closest friends on the White House staff, Jerry Persons and Gerry Morgan, to go to the studio with me. We had to shoulder our way through a crowd of excited and persistent newspaper reporters and cameramen. Being rather an old hand at appearing on television by this time, I submitted mechanically to the instructions of the technicians and to the application of a mild coating of make-up. The observers from the press wrote later that I was dignified and self-possessed. The reality of the situation had not yet taken possession of me.

I began my talk to the millions of people in the television audience with a reminder that there had been no responsible testimony of any attempt on my part to influence any officials in government agencies in their decisions. Nevertheless, I continued, I had been faced with a calculated and contrived attack that was intended to destroy me and to embarrass the President. I explained that I had not resigned earlier because I did not run away from adversity and because my resignation would have been misconstrued had it been submitted at the height of the controversy. I also pointed out that I had been extremely reluctant to leave the service of a great American who was giving himself so selflessly to the country.

I then mentioned the reasons that were now prompting my resignation: the feeling that my continued presence on the White House staff might hamper the progress of the President's programs and hurt the Republican party in the coming November elections. I announced that the President had agreed that morning in Newport to accept my resignation and that my decision to resign would not be subject to reconsideration.

"It is my steadfast belief," I said, "that the principles and programs for which Dwight Eisenhower stands serve the best interests of our country and, indeed, the people of the free world. They deserve to be strengthened through the support of every one of us. I believe that I can now best serve my President, and contribute to the support of his objectives, by the course that I have undertaken to follow. I am now about to retire after nearly six years from the position in which I have served with pride and which I have given my best efforts to hold with honor. Now, nearly twenty years of public service come to a close, but I can say that it has brought a depth of satisfaction that will always be with me."

That ended it. I went home alone, with the reporters and the cameramen still at my heels. I was serious about retiring from public service. I had been successively a town Representative and Speaker of the House in the New Hampshire legislature, a member of Congress in Washington, Governor and finally, for six years of the hardest pressure and under the most trying circumstances, the Assistant to the President. I had been shot at long enough and I wanted no more of it. That spring a physical examination at Walter Reed Hospital showed that I had what the heart specialists called a bundle branch block. I was told to slow up, but slowing up had been impossible in my job at the White House. I intended to do so now. I had received a number of attractive offers from industrial corporations but all of them would have required me to live outside of New England and our red house in the White Mountains looked pretty good to my wife and to me.

Shortly after I resigned the social secretary at the White House called me to tell me that the President was arranging a dinner in my honor, with square dancing afterward in the East Room. I had no heart at that time for square dancing. I declined and the President understood how I felt. He had planned to present to me at the dinner a huge sterling silver punch bowl. Instead he gave it to me privately one day in his office. On the bowl is inscribed:

> To Sherman Adams
> The Assistant to the President
> 1953-1958
> For Tireless Service to the Public
> Brilliant Performance of Every Duty
> and
> Unsurpassed Dedication to his Country
> From his devoted friend
> Dwight D. Eisenhower

Eisenhower was not given to gushing. He rarely paid anyone a compliment to his face. Occasionally he would take the time to write letters of personal appreciation, such as the one that I received from him at the end of each year that we worked together in the White House. At Christmastime in 1957, he paid me an exceptional compliment when he called me into his office and showed me a portrait he had painted of me. As he gave it to me he said a little apologetically, "I've made the whole thing a little too gray." I do not gush either. I wrote him a note of thanks which said, "I have a great many things to be thankful to you for. Already the painting you did of me is a family heirloom, and Rachel says I grow to look more like it every day."

22   Eisenhower Looks at His Years in Office

Today Eisenhower looks about the same as he did when I first met him in 1952 and his relaxed, sunny and cheerful disposition remains unchanged. Temperamentally, he was the ideal President. Although he had more than his share of discouragements that stirred him deeply and sometimes made him angry during his working hours, he had the happy faculty of being able to put them out of his mind when he left the office. After a hard day, he could sit down with friends in the evening and be as gay and as charming as ever. He had periods of depression, but he was always able to shake them off and snap back from a slump, as he did after his illnesses in 1955 and 1956.

I was astonished by Eisenhower's attitude when I visited him one afternoon in July, 1960, at his summer quarters in Newport. I had not seen him in three months. During that time he had gone through the U-2 uproar, the collapse of the Paris summit conference, Khrushchev's withdrawal of the invitation to visit Moscow and the last-minute cancellation of the trip he had planned to Japan. After such a series of disappointments, one coming quickly on top of another, I rather expected to find the President somewhat subdued, if not even a little bitter and disillusioned.

Not Eisenhower. When he greeted me that afternoon in the naval commander's pleasant residence at Fort Adams, he was as cheerful and buoyant as he ever was. He discussed the Japanese riots and his troubles with Khrushchev as calmly as if he were talking about something that had happened in Korea in 1953. He had a sort of who-
452

could-have-done-it-any-better attitude. Later, when Eisenhower left the room for a few minutes, one of his aides who was with us remarked to me that the President seemed far from weary or downhearted from the frustrating experiences that had crowded in upon his final year in office. On the contrary, his staff had noticed what they thought was a growing reluctance in the President to see his policies and programs pass along to a successor; so much so that some of those closest to him believed Eisenhower might have even considered running for a third term if there had been no constitutional prohibition against it.

That prompted me to ask Eisenhower when he rejoined us if he had thought about staying on in the White House for four more years. He shook his head and said, "Nothing like that!" but he grinned at me broadly, as if the subject might have crossed his mind. Like the aide, I got the impression that Eisenhower was leaving the presidency with some reluctance and that he would miss it. I know he was seriously concerned, as his second term of office entered the wane of its moon, about how his successor would continue the unfinished work to which he had devoted eight hard years. With his confident optimism, he might have sought re-election, if the Constitution had permitted it, so that he could have gone on with his work without interruption. Other outgoing Presidents must have felt the same reluctance to leave the task that never seemed to be completed. It is difficult for a conscientious man to turn over to somebody else a job to which he has dedicated himself and which he knows is not yet finished.

Eisenhower was a staunch supporter of Richard Nixon long before 1960, but he was disappointed by his party's failure to convert the younger independent voters who had voted for him in 1952 and 1956 into a lively Republican vanguard. He talked with Nixon constantly about this and kept after the Republican National Committee to pay more attention to the development of grass-roots organization. But Eisenhower's preaching and pleading for action never seemed to bring fruit. "What happened to all those fine young people with stars in their eyes who sailed balloons and rang doorbells for us in 1952?" he asked. Nor did Eisenhower hesitate to point to what he considered the principal reason for the lack of new young Republican blood. The younger liberals who made up a great part of the uncommitted electorate shied away from party affiliation with the archconservatives who seemed to continue to exert such influence in the party organization.

At Newport I mentioned that I had never heard him refer to John F. Kennedy. I wondered what he thought would become of his policies under Kennedy's leadership. He merely pointed out that Kennedy had not had the opportunity to observe world affairs from the close-range position behind the scenes that Nixon had occupied for the past eight years.

"You may remember that late in 1954 I went up to Boston to speak to a group of Catholic women," Eisenhower said to me. "Kennedy was very ill at the time. He was suffering from serious complications after a spinal operation. I mentioned in Boston that all of us were hoping for his early recovery. Soon after that I had a most complimentary letter from him. He went out of his way to tell me how much he approved of what I was doing, in the most complimentary terms imaginable." Eisenhower paused and shook his head. "Well," he added, "only the other day I noticed that he directed some extremely critical remarks at my administration. But that's politics, I suppose."

The talk I had that day in Newport with Eisenhower was a long and memorable one. He was looking back over his years in the presidency in a reflective mood and I had many things that I wanted to ask him. Naturally, I was curious about Khrushchev and I wondered what Eisenhower thought about the collapse of the Paris summit conference and the change that had come over the Russians after his talks with them in 1959 at Camp David, where Khrushchev had been quite friendly. I asked Eisenhower if he had noticed at Camp David any sign or hint of the hostility that broke out later in Paris.

"None at all," Eisenhower said. "At Camp David, they never showed the slightest intimation of any unfriendly intentions. As a matter of fact, when Khrushchev and I were alone together at Camp David he was very convivial with me, especially eager to be friendly. He kept belittling most of our differences and gave every indication of wanting to find ways to straighten them out through peaceful compromise."

Eisenhower became more serious. "That was when Khrushchev was alone with me," he said. "But when Menshikov and Gromyko were with us, Khrushchev acted differently. Then he became much more reserved and guarded in what he said and in his manner. When we talked about the various issues between us in front of Menshikov and Gromyko, Khrushchev kept reminding me that he would have to take up these matters with his government before making a decision on them. It seemed to me that he has much less confidence in himself than Stalin had, as a result, I think, of his feeling of his own insecurity in Russia."

Eisenhower feels that the disruption of the Paris conference and the cancellation of his invitation to Moscow were planned by Khrushchev some time before our U-2 reconnaissance plane was brought down in the Soviet Union. After all, the Russians knew when they were at Camp David that we were conducting high-altitude flights over their territory but they made no point of it at the time.

"The thing that evidently disturbed Khrushchev and made him change his mind about conferring with us in Paris was my visit to the Far East last winter, particularly my visit to India," Eisenhower said. "Remember that his own visit to India stirred up little enthusiasm. The fact is he had a rather cool reception. When he heard about the tremendous welcome I got in India, he felt he had to do something to make up for this important loss of prestige. There's no doubt that the people around him pressed him uncomfortably for some kind of counteraction. So he seized upon the U-2 incident to turn attention away from the deterioration of his own position."

At the time of the U-2 incident, some of Eisenhower's critics charged that the trouble it caused came from the President's policy of delegating too much of his authority. They assumed that the reconnaissance flight had conflicted with the Paris summit conference because it had been made without Eisenhower's personal knowledge and approval. I knew, of course, that this was a ridiculous assumption; I was familiar with the standard operating procedure of these high-altitude flights over foreign territories, because the U-2 program had started while I was working with Eisenhower in Washington, and I knew that none of these flights were made without the President's approval. I mentioned this to him.

"You're right," he said. "I made the decision, just as I have known about and personally approved every one of those flights. When they brought me the plan for this particular flight over Russia, I approved it as one among several within an intelligence policy already adopted. I had no thought of it having any possible bearing upon the summit meeting or on my forthcoming trip to Moscow. Except for unforeseen circumstances, it would not have had any. Even so, the whole story of that U-2 flight as we have it at the present time, may not be all that it appears."

"Foster Dulles' opposition to what he regarded as foredoomed summit conferences now takes on more aspects of wisdom," I said. "As far back as 1955, he discounted the value of your participation in such meetings."

"I have never built up promises of great results from summit meetings," Eisenhower said. "But I have always thought we should be ready and willing to look for any means of bringing about a better understanding, even to the point of my going anywhere in the world to try to accomplish it. Foster Dulles was a great man. You know, as much as he liked to run his own shop and do things his own way, he never made a major decision or took a definite line of action without consulting me. Foster had one great quality—somebody could disagree with him violently but he never bore any ill feeling after the argument was over. Do you remember that hot argument he had with Radford, the time he gave Radford a lecture in the strongest terms about what he thought Radford ought to keep in mind before coming to conclusions about the world situation?"

I remembered it very well. Dulles clashed so bitterly with Admiral Arthur W. Radford, then Chairman of the Joint Chiefs of Staff, over the atomic weapons program for South Korea that Eisenhower took Dulles to task privately after the meeting. Dulles had been fearful of the effect on India and other nations which had criticized what they called the belligerent attitude of the United States, and the Secretary thought Radford did not give enough consideration to the difficult problems which he had to face. "I told him I thought he had overstepped," Eisenhower recalled with a smile. "Foster agreed with me and said I was quite right. Afterward, when I mentioned this to Radford, he was surprised I had been upset by what Dulles had said. Radford took no exception whatever to Dulles' remarks. And of course Radford made his argument stick."

There was no need for me to ask Eisenhower about Japan; I knew the background of that problem only too well. After Eisenhower's invitation to Tokyo had been withdrawn, some second-guessers said the Communist-inspired riots and demonstrations over his planned visit could have been averted. There would have been no disturbances, they claimed, if Eisenhower had changed our mutual security arrangements with Japan several years ago. But even if the treaty arrangements had been modified earlier—assuming that we could have done so—there is no evidence that such modification would have prevented anti-American riots in 1960. Indeed, it is uncertain whether Japan, under such circumstances, might not have come under Communist domination and been lost to the West.

In trying to work out a security treaty with the Japanese, we were in a difficult dilemma. To keep Japan out of the Chinese Communist hands, we had to maintain mobile military strength in that country. These forces should have been Japanese and not American. But the Japanese Constitution included a provision negotiated by General Douglas MacArthur and our government after World War II forbidding the drafting of Japanese men for military service and the use of Japanese troops in offshore operations. Public sentiment in Japan strongly supported these antimilitary provisions. The Japanese people had had enough of war. But the provision made it difficult for Eisenhower and Dulles to work out any long-range, effective, anti-Communist alliance between Japan and her far-Pacific neighbors. In 1954, Eisenhower was studying ways and means of withdrawing American forces from Japan, for psychological as well as economic reasons, but to do so without substituting native troops for them might have meant a loss of Japan to the Communists. We could not afford to take that chance. Dulles that year made a full-scale report to the Cabinet on the critical role being played by Japan in the world balance and the necessity for keeping the Japanese out of Chinese Communist hands. He pointed out that Japan's surging industrial power would be of vital strategic value to the Chinese Communists and the Soviets. Dulles reminded the Cabinet that Stalin, in one of his last writings, had discounted the Communists' need to go to war in order to win world power. Stalin predicted that the problems of absorbing German and Japanese industrial power would shatter the economy of the Western capitalistic countries.

We had seen something of the problem Stalin was referring to in trying to make trade agreements with Japan. George Humphrey had pointed to what he called critical unemployment in the Pittsburgh area because of Japanese competition in the electrical instrument industry. Eisenhower asked him if it were not possible for American businessmen to make some sacrifices in such a situation in the interests of world peace.

"No," Humphrey said candidly. "The American businessman believes in getting as much as he can while the getting is good."

"Maybe that's the trouble with businessmen, George," Eisenhower said seriously.

Later, when Douglas MacArthur II went to Tokyo as our ambassador, the question of a new security treaty was reviewed again and MacArthur advised against it, urging us to leave well enough alone. We were still faced with the same impasse: a modification of the existing treaty was dangerous unless the Japanese were willing and capable of taking up a military role in the defense of the Pacific against Communism. At the same time, a provision in their Constitution which we had virtually prescribed forbade them such a role—and they had no desire for it anyway. That was why the overhauling of the treaty was delayed until 1959 and why the riots over its ratification by the Diet were being staged in 1960 at the same time that Eisenhower was scheduled to visit Tokyo. There had been no earlier indication that such a comparatively small gang of Communist dissidents could cause the Japanese government so much trouble and embarrassment.

I asked Eisenhower if he ever regretted running for President in 1952 and 1956 and if he had gotten real personal satisfaction out of his eight years in office.

"I believe I made the right decision when I decided to run in 1952 and I have never regretted it," he said. "The thing that really set me to thinking seriously about trying for the presidential nomination was the primary in Minnesota. I received a big vote before that in New Hampshire, but there I was a candidate with my name on the ballot. You saw to that. In Minnesota, they had to write my name in. Some people just wrote 'Ike,' and others spelled Eisenhower all kinds of different ways. Yet I almost took the election away from the leading Republican candidate on the ballot—who was it?—oh, yes, Stassen. With such expressions of support coming to me from all over the country I felt there was really the public demand that my friends had been trying to impress upon me. So I had to change my mind. In 1956 it was a different situation. The Republican leaders came to me and said there was nobody else in the party who could be sure of winning popular approval. They told me, virtually, that I had to become a candidate again if I wanted to see my policies continued. After I reached the conviction within myself that I was physically able to go through with it, there wasn't anything else I could do. I had been hoping that the Republicans would develop a stable of young, able candidates and that maybe one of them could be my successor. That seems to have been a failure. In 1956 there was nobody who said that I ought not to run again."

"Except Milton," I said, referring to his brother, Dr. Milton S. Eisenhower.

"Except Milton, and my son. The rest of you were all solidly convinced that I had to run again. After the election in 1956, when I found out that the Republicans had lost the Congress, I first had some doubts whether I should have run."

"I remember you once told me that the Constitution ought to be changed to provide some guarantee that the party of the President would control the majority of Congress," I said.

"It is the only way one party can be held strictly accountable for the acts of the government."

"I do not remember that you ever decided how this might be accomplished."

"Well, I think for one thing that the House ought to be elected with the President every four years," Eisenhower said. "In this way, the party that elected the President would be likely to win the majority of the House, at least. However, this was not true in 1956."

We talked about the Republican party and Eisenhower's unhappiness with its more conservative leaders. He recalled how he had been sought by Truman and the Democrats for their presidential candidate in 1952.

"When I declared myself a Republican in 1952," he said, "I did so upon the representation of some of my friends in whom I had the greatest confidence. I believe the more enlightened principles of the Republicans were closer to my own beliefs than those of the other party. But I could have been a conservative Democrat."

I remarked that the term "liberal," as it is used in politics, seems to have become associated with a belief in our international responsibilities as contrasted to the old belief in isolationism. I said this made no sense to me.

"None," Eisenhower agreed. "The term 'liberal' properly applies to principles of domestic government, such as the question of how much federal aid we should give to education and public housing, for example. Taft was more of a liberal than I was when you consider the education and housing legislation he sponsored. He was for strong federal participation in those fields and I was, and still am, philosophically opposed to it. I mentioned this to Taft once. He said to me, 'It is sometimes better to go along with the times.'"

When I was working with Eisenhower as his assistant in the White House, we had talked often about how the assorted array of constitutional duties assigned to the President made the office too much for one man to handle. I brought this up again at Newport to see if he still felt the same way. "Under present circumstances, with the world in the situation it is today, yes," he said. "The President must have authority to delegate more work and responsibilities to others." Eisenhower believes that the stature and authority of the President's immediate assistants must be raised so that they can free him of routine government management and give him time to concentrate on the bigger problems of world peace and disarmament, national security and domestic welfare.

Eisenhower had talked with me about a First Secretary long before Nelson Rockefeller's proposal for such a presidential assistant in foreign affairs. "I went over the idea many times with Foster Dulles," Eisenhower reminded me in Newport, "and Foster came to agree with it." Dulles was skeptical about such a foreign affairs executive at first. He insisted that nothing should come between the Secretary of State and the President.

Dulles first felt that he did not want operational responsibility and was content to let Stassen's Foreign Operations Administration have independent status. But the arrangement did not work too well, and Dulles found himself in another dilemma. He wanted tight control over the formulation of policy but this was difficult, particularly with a man of Stassen's dynamic disposition running the operations. So he persuaded the President to move the agency back into the State Department.

The type of First Secretary that Eisenhower had in mind would have top responsibility for co-ordinating and directing the nonmilitary offshore agencies, including the Mutual Security programs, the Information Agency and also the duty of attending to the heavy schedule of ceremonial functions with foreign heads of state which now take up so much of the presidential time.

Eisenhower favors a presidential assistant who could direct the fiscal and business management of the government, particularly the details of the budget that now require so much of the President's attention. There is also a crying need in the White House for somebody with enough rank and prestige to take over signing a great many of the various papers and documents that now call for the President's own name in his own handwriting—the countless minor commissions, military promotions, citations, messages, letters of congratulation and commemoration, and so on, including letters to some good citizens in Rhode Island or Wisconsin who happen to be observing their hundredth birthdays that week. Still the chances of getting public acceptance of such changes seem a little remote. There is really no acceptable substitute for the signature of the President of the United States.

In his last years in office, Eisenhower had two big objectives: a more favorable atmosphere for disarmament and peace abroad, and a reduction of federal government expenses and a balanced budget at home. His policies had been good for the domestic economy, and he said so. He began his presidency in a period of deficits and a mounting public debt. He left it with a current surplus and a balanced budget. His inability to reduce the debt was a comment on the country's economic situation. In any downward adjustment of the economy sufficient to increase unemployment, government programs to counteract the downturn quickly take precedence over budget-balancing and the result is likely to eat up any reductions that have previously been made by the administration in the public debt. Thus, debt reduction will in the future be conditioned on relatively full employment.

"The country has had great prosperity," Eisenhower said when I asked him if his years in office had given him satisfaction.

"Except, possibly, for the minor turndowns in 1954 and 1958," I said.

"But those were by no means severe," he said. "We kept to what we have called a middle-of-the-road course, away from the extremes favored by the reactionary conservatives of our own party and away from the vast spending schemes of the irresponsible elements of the Democratic party. This is the course that any administration must follow if its policies are to meet the needs of the times."

In seeking his other objective, a favorable climate for international peace and disarmament, Eisenhower had made a bold gamble to which many people were opposed when he invited Khrushchev to visit the United States. This gamble seemed to be about to pay off handsomely; out of Khrushchev's visit and the talks at Camp David came Soviet promises of a solution of East-West differences. Khrushchev made much of the achievements that could be reached at Paris and during Eisenhower's visit to Moscow. Then came the crushing disappointment of the Russian turnabout. In spite of its failure to bring new light and hope to the solution of the Russian riddle of intransigent hostility, Eisenhower had followed a consistent course as well as his conscience. He had long ago dedicated himself to keep constantly probing for a peaceful solution and never to give up.

When Eisenhower became President I believed that he was the greatest influence for peace in the world, and I believe it today. The conviction is deep in my mind that if Eisenhower could have been assigned the world peace mission with the complete support of the government and people of the United States he could have found better answers. But as he had pointed out to me long before, there is no substitute in our system for the influence and prestige of the presidential office and no other commission can command the same attention and respect.

With that statement no American can differ. Yet it meant that a great statesman and diplomat, perhaps the world's greatest, had to compromise his talents with the demands of many less important, even trivial, problems that someone else could have disposed of just as well. Eisenhower knew himself well enough to understand where his greatest strength was and what he could accomplish with it. His conception of the presidency showed this. "My job here, as I see it, is not to create friction, not to accentuate differences, but to bring people together so we can actually achieve progress," he said soon after he took office. This was not just his role in his own country; it was his mission in the world.

For his efforts, Eisenhower was attacked abroad and criticized at home. But he never gave up. "I feel pretty good when I'm attacked from both sides," he said. "It makes me more certain I'm on the right track."

The goal to which Eisenhower gave his finest efforts has yet to be reached. But his years as President saw the tide turn away from conventional war to a cold and relentless conflict that will continue to engage the best of the wit and wisdom that we possess. And in this competition Dwight Eisenhower still has much to give. I am only one among millions who hope that he will have that opportunity.

Index

468